Interpreting Company
Reports and Accounts

Interpreting Company Reports and Accounts

EIGHTH EDITION

Geoffrey Holmes

Alan Sugden

Paul Gee

FT Prentice Hall
FINANCIAL TIMES

An imprint of **Pearson Education**
Harlow, England • London • New York • Boston • San Francisco • Toronto • Sydney • Singapore • Hong Kong
Tokyo • Seoul • Taipei • New Delhi • Cape Town • Madrid • Mexico City • Amsterdam • Munich • Paris • Milan

Pearson Education Limited
Edinburgh Gate
Harlow
Essex CM20 2JE

and Associated Companies throughout the world

Visit us on the World Wide Web at:
www.pearsoneduc.com

First published 1979
Eighth edition published by Pearson Education Limited 2002

ISBN: 0-273-65592-2 Paper
       0-273-65597-3 Cased

British Library Cataloguing-in-Publication Data
A catalogue record for this book is available from the British Library

Typeset in 11/12 pt Times by 35
Printed and bound by Ashford Colour Press Ltd., Gosport

BRIEF CONTENTS

PUBLISHER'S ACKNOWLEDGEMENTS

We are grateful to the Financial Times Limited for permission to reprint the following material:

Tomkins extract from the LEX Column, © *Financial Times*, 1 July, 2000.

Whilst every effort has been made to trace the owners of copyright material, in a few cases this has proved impossible and we take this opportunity to offer our apologies to any copyright holders whose rights we have unwittingly infringed.

CONTENTS

**THE BALANCE SHEET:
CAPITAL EMPLOYED**

**ASSETS:
FIXED ASSETS**

CURRENT ASSETS

CURRENT LIABILITIES

THE PROFIT AND LOSS ACCOUNT

Parent company profit and loss account. *Disclosures required by accounting standards. Disclosures required by the UKLA Listing Rules.* Purple Book requirements. *Effect of accounting policies on profitability.* Accounting policies. What is it reasonable to capitalise? Research and development. Finance costs. Starting-up costs. Changes of accounting policy. Changes of presentation. *Retirement benefits.* Types of pension scheme. Defined contribution schemes. Defined benefit schemes. What to look for. Problems faced by actuaries and pension funds. Disclosure of information. FRS 17 Retirement benefits. *Exceptional items.* Basic purpose of the profit and loss account. Is it extraordinary or exceptional? FRS 3 definition. 'Headline' or 'normalised' earnings. FRS 3 Reporting financial performance. Comparative figures. *Ratios.* Horizontal analysis. Vertical analysis. Operating ratios. Improving the return on capital employed. Massaging the figures. *Segmental reporting.* Accounting Standard. Analysis of profitability. Non-disclosure.

The consolidated balance sheet. Goodwill on consolidation arising prior to 1998. Goodwill on consolidation arising after 1998. The consolidated profit and loss account. Unrealised profits on stocks. Parent company's own balance sheet. Parent company's own profit and loss account. Accounting periods and dates. Further statutory requirements.

OTHER

PREFACE

The aim of this book

In the Preface to the first edition we wrote:
'Given a sound knowledge of the basic components of a balance sheet and profit and loss account, *anybody with a reasonably enquiring mind* can learn a great deal about a company by studying its report and accounts and by comparing it with other companies. We have written this book to provide the basic knowledge required . . .'

The aim remains the same, although there have been significant developments since the first edition was published in 1979.

Accounting Standards

The Accounting Standards Board (ASB), set up in 1990, replaced a Committee which was prone to compromise solutions and had no power to enforce the rules it made.

Under the chairmanship of Sir David Tweedie the ASB has, in the last ten years, introduced a complete new set of rules, Financial Reporting Standards (FRSs), which are listed in Appendix 1. These include the introduction of the cash flow statement, strict rules on accounting for goodwill, and an FRS on derivatives, whose use and the trouble caused by which have grown enormously. The ASB has also issued a Statement of principles for financial reporting.

International Accounting Standards

A new urgency has been injected by the European Commission announcement that companies within the EU would have to use International Accounting Standards (IASs) from 2005 in order to list on EU markets. In this edition we have, in a revised Chapter 30, *International accounting comparisons*, included a table showing the main differences between UK, US and IAS accounting practices.

The Cadbury Committee

The recommendations of the Cadbury Committee and subsequent committees have stimulated requirements for more and more disclosure, some of which have been met by what Sir David Tweedie calls 'boilerplating', the use of standard wording that provides no useful information, and tends to clutter up company reports.

Key points

Because of the sheer increase in the volume of information contained in annual reports and accounts we have, in this edition, expanded the inclusion of 'Key Points' to help the reader sort out the wheat from the chaff.

New co-author

I would like to welcome my new co-author, Paul Gee FCA, whose accounting expertise has already proved invaluable.

Alan Sugden

GEOFFREY HOLMES FCA
1926–2000

A tribute

When Geoffrey Holmes joined *Accountancy* magazine as assistant editor in 1961, it had a circulation of around 17,000 and was barely breaking even. After ten years he became editor and, when he retired in 1989, the circulation had more than quadrupled to around 73,000 and it was highly profitable.

Geoffrey achieved this in many ways. He had the ability to recruit good people, both staff and contributors, and to help them develop. As his successor, Brian O'Kane, put it: 'He helped people blossom'. Those who worked with him will remember how he offered encouragement, rather than giving orders, and how he brought out the best in people.

His style of management was always open and constructive. He didn't sit in his office waiting for problems to come to him; he would 'go walkabout', talking to staff, listening to their ideas and helping them solve their problems for themselves. He also looked after people who worked for him, not as a policy but instinctively; it was part of his nature.

While at *Accountancy* he became an evening lecturer at the City of London Polytechnic, teaching 'Interpreting Company Reports and Accounts', one of the four subjects in the Stock Exchange exams. This is where I, as a student, met him. Having passed our exams, several of us took the lecturers out to lunch as a 'thank you', never expecting to see them again.

Over lunch Geoffrey said 'I have been asked to write a book on interpreting company reports and accounts' and I, as an investment analyst, said 'Do you want any help?'

That was twenty-five years ago. Since then we produced seven editions, with sales of more than 100,000. That we stayed in partnership so long was due mostly to his patience, his kindness and his good humour.

A.S.

Chapter 1

COMPANY REPORTS AND ACCOUNTS – AN INTRODUCTION

The purpose of this book

This book is intended as a practical guide to the interpretation of reports and accounts. In it frequent reference is made to the legal, accounting and UK Listing Authority's requirements that accounts have to meet, but this is done in the context of what interesting information to look out for, rather than to show how a set of accounts should be prepared.

Useful guides to *compiling* accounts include:

- *Financial Statements for Public Companies*, by Arthur Andersen, published by ABG Professional Information (Institute of Chartered Accountants in England and Wales [ICAEW])
- *UK and International GAAP* – by Ernst & Young, published by Butterworths
- *GAAP 2002 – UK Financial Reporting and Accounting* by Deloitte & Touche, published by ABG Professional Information (ICAEW).

The report and accounts

The report and accounts, normally produced annually, is the principal way in which shareholders and others keep themselves informed on the activities, progress and future plans of a company. Its style and content vary somewhat in line with the directors' views on its use as a public relations vehicle. As is permitted by law, a growing number of larger companies, e.g. DIAGEO, produce an annual review and summary financial statement as an alternative to their annual report and accounts, and shareholders may choose which they receive. DIAGEO include an interesting note in their Review:

DIAGEO *Extract from 2000 Annual Review*

Summary financial statement

. . . A summary financial statement does not contain sufficient information to allow as full an understanding of the results and state of affairs of the company or group as is provided by the full annual accounts and reports. . . .

To keep employees informed, some companies distribute a summary of their report and accounts to all employees, or include extracts in their house newspaper. Some produce and distribute to shareholders and/or employees a separate 'company profile'. But others argue that any unnecessary disclosure is risky in case the information may be of use to competitors.

Nevertheless, there is a minimum of information that must be disclosed to comply with the law. For example, the annual report and accounts must by law contain four basic components:

1. a directors' report;
2. a profit and loss account;
3. a balance sheet; and
4. an auditors' report.

The form and content of accounts are also subject to Financial Reporting Standards, about which we will have more to say in Chapter 2, and which add to the list of required contents. For example, FRS 1 requires all companies (other than *small* companies) to include a cash flow statement.

In addition, when a company's shares are listed on the Stock Exchange, the report and accounts have to contain further information prescribed by The United Kingdom Listing Authority (UKLA).

For instance, companies listed on the Stock Exchange have to produce a half-yearly (or 'interim' report.

Details are to be found in UKLA's book *The Listing Rules*, known in the City as 'The Purple Book'. We say more about the Listing Rules in Chapter 4.

The directors' report

Under the Companies Acts, a directors' report must give a mass of information, some of which is obvious from the accounts anyway, some of which is of comparatively little interest either to shareholders or analysts, and appears to have been motivated by political considerations, e.g. contributions for political purposes, but some of which may be of vital interest and importance to anyone interpreting the accounts, e.g. the review of the year and likely future developments.

The directors' report must also state the names of the directors and provide details of their shareholdings; provide particulars of significant changes in fixed assets and provide information on important events which have occurred since the end of the year, called '*Post balance sheet events*'.

Most companies include a *Chairman's statement* while some include a *Chief Executive's review* as well. Companies are also encouraged to include an *Operating and Financial Review (OFR)*; see Chapter 25.

Example 1.1 A typical profit and loss account

Profit and loss account for the year ended 31 December 2000

	£000	£000
Turnover		7,200
Cost of sales		3,600
Gross profit		3,600
Distribution costs	1,100	
Administrative expenses	1,300	
		2,400
		1,200
Other operating income		95
Trading or operating profit		1,295
Interest receivable		20
		1,315
Interest payable		100
Pre-tax profit on ordinary activities		1,215
Taxation		415
Profit on ordinary activities after taxation		800
Dividends		560
Profits retained		240

The profit and loss account

The profit and loss account is a record of the activities of a company for a stated period of time. This period, which is called the accounting period, is normally a year. Example 1.1 shows a typical profit and loss account; the Terminology box below explains the main terms used.

TERMINOLOGY

Profit and loss account

The **profit and loss account** is a monetary record of the activities of a business during an accounting period, which is normally one year. A balance sheet is drawn up on the last day of the company's accounting period.

Turnover (also called sales) is money received, or to be received, by the business for goods or services sold during the year.

Expenses are costs incurred in producing those goods and services, normally divided into:

(i) **Cost of sales** i.e. the cost of the goods themselves, e.g.. raw materials and wages

Gross profit = Turnover − Cost of sales

(ii) **Distribution costs** i.e. the cost of getting the goods to the customer

(iii) **Administrative expenses** i.e. other expenses which cannot be or are not allocated to particular products, i.e. which do not form part of cost of sales, or appear under other headings.

Operating profit or **trading profit** = Turnover − Expenses (i.e. (i) to (iii) above).

Where expenses (i) to (iii) above exceed turnover, the difference is an **operating loss**.

(iv) **Other operating income** is income and expenses which fall outside (i) to (iii) above, e.g. property income of a trading company, or patent income.

(v) **Interest paid** on borrowed money (**interest received**) represents income from interest on money lent, e.g. deposits at the bank.

Pre-tax profit = Operating profit + (iv) +/− (v)

Dividends are distributions to shareholders, i.e. the company's owners, paid out of profits after tax.

Depreciation is an expense appearing as part of (i) to (iii) above, as appropriate.

The cost of each fixed asset is written off over its expected life. Using the most common method of depreciation, **the straight line method**:

$$\text{Depreciation for the year} = \frac{\text{Cost of asset} - \text{Residual value}}{\text{Expected useful life}}$$

Corresponding figures or 'comparatives' are those for the same item for the preceding accounting period.

Accounts are required to include the figures for two periods, normally those for the year being reported on and corresponding figures ('comparatives') for the preceding year. For simplicity, at this stage we show only figures for the year.

The balance sheet

The balance sheet is a statement of the assets and liabilities of a company at the close of business on a given day, i.e. on the balance sheet date. The balance sheet is always drawn up on the last day of the company's accounting period.

Example 1.2 shows a typical balance sheet; the Terminology box alongside explains the main terms used in balance sheets.

Example 1.2 A typical balance sheet

Balance sheet as at 31 December 2000

	£000	£000	£000
Fixed assets			
Freehold land and buildings		950	
Fixtures and fittings		175	
Motor vehicles		535	
			1,660
Current assets			
Stock (of goods)		500	
Debtors		1,040	
Cash		5	
		1,545	
Less: Current liabilities:			
Creditors due within 1 year:			
Trade creditors	300		
Taxation payable	415		
Dividends payable	560		
Overdraft	90		
		1,365	
Net current assets			180
Net assets			1,840
Capital and reserves			
Ordinary share capital			1,000
Reserves:			
Retained profits: b/f		600	
for the year		240	
			840
Ordinary shareholders' funds			1,840

TERMINOLOGY

Balance sheet

A **balance sheet** is a statement of the assets and liabilities and ownership interest of an enterprise at the close of business on the balance sheet date.

Assets are things which a business owns and on which a book value can be placed.

Book value is cost less accumulated depreciation or, if the asset has been revalued, it is the valuation figure less any subsequent depreciation.

Liabilities are amounts owed by a business.

Net assets = all assets − all liabilities.

Fixed assets are assets (like land and buildings, plant and machinery) not held for resale but for use by the business.

Current assets are cash and other assets that the company expects to turn into cash (e.g. stock).

Assets can also be described as **tangible**, from the Latin *tango*, I touch (e.g. motor vehicles, land and buildings) or **intangible** i.e. not susceptible to touch (e.g. patent rights and trademarks).

Current liabilities, which are usually described as '**Creditors due within 1 year**', are the liabilities that the company expects to have to meet within twelve months.

As illustrated in Example 1.2, the modern accounting practice is to show the current liabilities below the current assets and to deduct them from the current assets to produce **net current assets**.

The **members** (**shareholders**) of a company provide some or all of the finance in the form of **share capital** (that is, they subscribe for shares) in the expectation that the company will make profits, and pay dividends.

Ordinary shareholders' funds is made up of ordinary share capital and all accumulated reserves.

Financial statements is the term which covers the annual accounts as a whole, i.e. the profit and loss account, balance sheet, cash flow statement and statements forming part of the statutory accounts.

THE ACCOUNTS OF A NEWLY-FORMED COMPANY

(The remainder of this chapter provides an introduction to the balance sheet and profit and loss account for those who are not already familiar with them. Experienced readers may like to turn straight to Chapter 2.)

The *balance sheet* is a statement of the assets and liabilities of a company at the close of business on a given day, i.e. on the balance sheet date. The *profit and loss account* is a record of the activities of a company for a given period of time; this period, which is called the accounting period, is normally a year, and the balance sheet always has to be drawn up on the last day of the company's accounting period.

When a company is formed the *members* (shareholders) subscribe for shares. For example, let us suppose that a company is formed with a share capital of 300,000 ordinary shares with a nominal value of £1 each, and that all the shares are issued at *par* (are issued to members at their nominal value of £1 each). At the same time the directors of the company negotiate with their bank manager to allow the company to overdraw by up to £150,000, i.e. they obtain an overdraft facility of £150,000, although this figure does *not* appear in the accounts. The balance sheet will then look like Example 1.3.

Supposing the company then

1. buys a freehold shop for £200,000
2. fits it out for £75,000, and
3. stocks it with £200,000 worth of goods.

It also

4. buys a van for £10,000.

The shop, the fittings and the van are all paid for with cash, and so are half the goods, but

5. the other half of the goods is supplied on credit; i.e. the suppliers do not require immediate payment, so they become creditors of the company (*creditors* are people to whom the company owes money);
6. by this time most of the £300,000 capital has been spent, and there is an overdraft: £300,000 − 200,000 − 75,000 − 100,000 − 10,000 = −£85,000. Companies normally have a small amount of cash in hand, even if they have an overdraft. Here it is £5,000, making an overdraft of £90,000.

The balance sheet would then look like Example 1.4 (superior figures refer to items in the above list).

Fixed assets are assets held not for resale but for use by the business. *Current assets* are cash and other assets that the company expects to turn into cash (e.g. stock), and *current liabilities*, usually described as *Creditors: due within 1 year*, are all the liabilities that the company expects to have to meet within twelve months. In modern accounting practice the current liabilities are normally shown below the current assets, and the total of the current liabilities is deducted from the total of the current assets to give what is called *net current assets*.

Let us suppose that the company then trades for a year, during which time it

7. sells goods for £1,200,000 – their cost plus a profit margin, and
8. buys goods for £850,000 in addition to the initial purchase of £200,000 which is called the *opening stock* (except for the first year this is the stock on hand at the end of the previous year).
9. At the end of the year, on the last day of the company's accounting year, there is £250,000 of stock, valued at cost price, on hand. This is called the *closing stock*.
10. Wages and other expenses for the year amount to £280,000.
11. In addition, a provision is made for the wear and tear on fixed assets during the year. This is calculated so that the cost of each fixed asset is written off over its expected life. The provision is called *depreciation* and, using the most common method of depreciation, the 'straight line' method, is calculated as follows:

DEPRECIATION *Straight line method*

$$\frac{\text{Depreciation}}{\text{for the year}} = \frac{\text{Cost of asset}}{\text{Expected useful life}}$$

For our company the depreciation charge for the year would be worked out as follows:

Fixed asset	*Cost*	*Life*	*Annual depreciation* £
Building	125,000	50 years	2,500
Fittings	75,000	10 years	7,500
Motor van	10,000	5 years	2,000
Depreciation charge for the year[11]			12,000

Notice that depreciation is charged only on the cost of the building (here assumed to be £125,000) and not on the value of the land (assumed to be £75,000), because depreciation is provided only on assets with a finite useful life.

Example 1.5 shows how the profit and loss account for the first year's trading would be calculated, assuming Corporation Tax at 25%.

During the year, in addition to the overdraft facility, the company arranged

12. a 20-year loan of £100,000 secured on the freehold land and buildings – this is called a mortgage debenture because the lender of the money (the debenture holder) has first claim on the property if the company goes into liquidation.

In Example 1.5 the interest on both types of borrowings has, for simplicity, been included in

Example 1.3 The new company's balance sheet

Liabilities		**Assets**	
	£		£
Ordinary share capital	300,000	Cash	300,000

Example 1.4 The balance sheet after purchase of fixed assets and current assets

Liabilities		**Assets**	
	£		£
Ordinary share capital	300,000	*Fixed assets*	
		Freehold land and buildings	200,000[1]
		Fixtures and fittings	75,000[2]
		Motor vehicles	10,000[4]
Current liabilities		*Current assets*	
Creditors: due within 1 year	100,000[5]	Stock (of goods)	200,000[3]
Overdraft	90,000[6]	Cash	5,000[6]
	490,000		490,000

Example 1.5 The first year's profit and loss account

	£	£	£
Sales (or Turnover)			1,200,000[7]
less Cost of goods sold:			
Opening stocks	200,000[8]		
Purchases	+850,000[8]		
	1,050,000		
Closing stock	250,000[9]		
Cost of goods sold		800,000	
Wages and other expenses		280,000[10]	
Depreciation		12,000[11]	
			1,092,000
Profit before tax			108,000
Corporation Tax			27,000
Profit after tax			81,000
Dividends (the directors recommend a 10% dividend on the nominal value of the issued share capital)			30,000
Retained profits (to be ploughed back into the company)			51,000

'Wages and other expenses'. It would normally be shown separately.

Our final illustration (Example 1.6) shows the balance sheet at the end of the year drawn up in the modern way, with the assets less creditors above the capital and reserves, rather than assets on one side and liabilities on the other. Notice that:

13. debtors (customers owing money to the company) owed a total of £80,000;
14. trade creditors were £120,000 – so almost half the stock was being financed by suppliers;
15. fixed assets are shown at cost *less* depreciation to date;
16. the 10% dividend has not yet been paid;
17. net current assets = current assets – current liabilities, i.e. £355,000 – 177,000 = £178,000;
18. *ordinary shareholders' funds* = ordinary share capital issued plus reserves.

Example 1.6 The balance sheet after the first year's trading

	£	£
Fixed assets[15]		
Freehold land and buildings		197,500[11]
Fixtures and fittings		67,500[11]
Motor vehicles		8,000[11]
		273,000
Current assets		
Stock	250,000[9]	
Debtors	80,000[13]	
Cash	25,000	
	355,000	
Current liabilities		
(or Creditors: due		
within 1 year)		
Trade creditors	120,000[14]	
Taxation payable	27,000	
Dividend payable	30,000	
	177,000	
Net current assets		178,000
Total assets less		
current liabilities		451,000
Creditors: due after		
more than 1 year		
Mortgage debenture		100,000[12]
		351,000
Capital and reserves		
Ordinary share capital		300,000
Reserves (retained profits)		51,000
Ordinary shareholders' funds		351,000[18]

Chapter 2

FINANCIAL REPORTING STANDARDS AND PRINCIPLES

THE PRESENT STRUCTURE

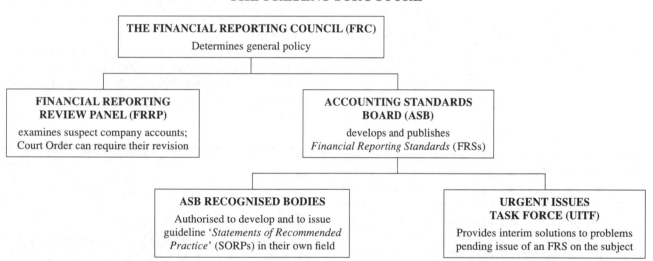

THE FINANCIAL REPORTING COUNCIL (FRC)
Determines general policy

FINANCIAL REPORTING
REVIEW PANEL (FRRP)
examines suspect company accounts;
Court Order can require their revision

ACCOUNTING STANDARDS
BOARD (ASB)
develops and publishes
Financial Reporting Standards (FRSs)

ASB RECOGNISED BODIES
Authorised to develop and to issue
guideline '*Statements of Recommended
Practice*' (SORPs) in their own field

URGENT ISSUES
TASK FORCE (UITF)
Provides interim solutions to problems
pending issue of an FRS on the subject

THE PREVIOUS REGIME

Until 1990 the Accounting Standards Committee (ASC) was the authority on the treatment and pre-sentation of company accounts.

It was made up of representatives from the main accounting Institutes and Associations in the UK and Ireland, and exercised its authority by issuing State-ments of Standard Accounting Practice (SSAPs).

The system had three serious drawbacks:

1. As the unanimous agreement of all members was required before an SSAP was issued, there was often compromise.
2. There were no legal sanctions to compel com-panies to comply with SSAPs.
3. The ASC's attempt to introduce Current Cost Accounting (CCA) had ended in an ignominious climb down, making a very big dent in the ASC's credibility. See Chapter 29, *Inflation accounting.*

Competition for business was rife between the leading firms of accountants, who became prepared to take a very flexible view of the rules in order to retain their existing clients and acquire new ones.

Barry Riley summed up the situation pretty succinctly in the *Financial Times* in December 1990:

FINANCIAL TIMES *Extract from article on accountants December 1990*

Essentially the external auditor has ceased to devote himself primarily to presenting the users of accounts with the truth, but instead has come to help the financial director of his client company to show his results in the best possible light, taking due advantage of all the loopholes.

THE PRESENT REGIME

Following the Dearing Report the government set up a new structure for setting and enforcing accounting standards, headed by the *Financial Reporting Council* (FRC).

It also included a definition of 'accounting standards' in the Companies Act and, where a company's accounts do not comply with the requirements of the Act, the court is given the power to order the preparation of revised accounts at the expense of the directors. **It is this that gives accounting standards their teeth.**

The Financial Reporting Council (FRC)

The FRC is constituted as a company limited by guarantee, and its constitution provides for a council whose function is to determine general policy.

The chairman and three deputy chairmen of the council are appointed jointly by the Secretary of State for Trade and Industry and the Governor of the Bank of England. The aim is that the Council should include a wide and balanced representation at the most senior level of preparers, auditors and users of accounts and others interested in them.

Reporting to the FRC are two bodies, the *Financial Reporting Review Panel* (FRRP) and the *Accounting Standards Board* (ASB).

The Financial Reporting Review Panel (FRRP)

The FRRP enquires into financial statements where it appears that the requirements of the Companies Act, principally that the financial statements show a true and fair view might have been breached. The FRRP is autonomous in carrying out its function.

The role of the Panel is to examine departures from the accounting requirements of the Companies Acts or accounting standards, and, if necessary, to seek an order from the court to remedy them.

It does not scrutinise on a routine basis all company accounts falling within its ambit; it acts upon matters drawn to its attention, either directly or indirectly. Experience shows that it is both able and willing to take on Britain's larger groups and professional firms, and is able to make them toe the line. Companies publicly examined include BRITISH GAS (now BG), FOREIGN & COLONIAL (the UK's biggest investment trust), ROYAL BANK OF SCOTLAND and SECURICOR.

Where a company has to revise its accounts, its reputation can be severely damaged. For example ASSOCIATED NURSING SERVICES, which had been in trouble with the Review Panel in 1992, was in serious trouble five years later, as the *Investors Chronicle* reported in February 1997:

ASSOCIATED NURSING SERVICES *Extract from Investors Chronicle 21 February 1997*

OFF BALANCE

An accounting watchdog this week fired a warning shot at the property industry when it told Associated Nursing Services (ANS), a nursing home operator, to revise its accounts for 1995 and 1996.

After an 18-month investigation the Financial Reporting Review Panel said the way ANS had treated the sale and leaseback of its nursing homes did not comply with accepted accounting standards. For the year ending March 1997, ANS's earnings per share will be reduced by 45 per cent.

The *Investors Chronicle* followed this up in July 1998 with a piece entitled 'Accounting policies still not care-free' and gave a Sell recommendation. As shown in Figure 2.1, the share price movement was a clear indicator of the loss of confidence.

Subsequently under fire for capitalising opening costs on new nursing homes, the management grew weary of being criticised and, having changed the company's name to ANS, organised an MBO in January 2000.

The Accounting Standards Board (ASB)

The ASB develops, issues and keeps accounting standards up to date. In addition, the ASB has set up an *Urgent Issues Task Force* (UITF).

The Urgent Issues Task Force

The main role of the UITF is to assist the ASB in areas where an accounting problem exists by providing an interim solution on the subject, called an *Abstract*, pending the development and issue of an accounting standard.

Financial Reporting Standards (FRSs)

The Companies Act 1985 includes the definition of 'accounting standards', and requires that directors of companies (other than most *small* or *medium-sized* companies) disclose in the accounts:

(a) whether the accounts have been prepared in accordance with applicable accounting standards;
(b) particulars of any material departure from those standards; and
(c) the reasons for the departure.

Accounting standards issued by the ASB are known as Financial Reporting Standards (FRSs) and Exposure Drafts as Financial Reporting Exposure Drafts (FREDs).

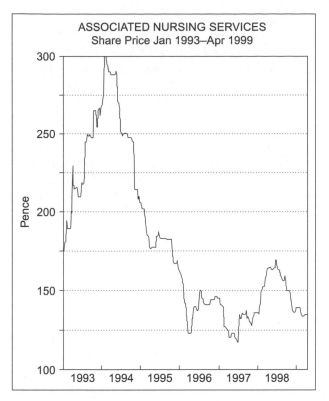

Figure 2.1 Associated Nursing Services: loss of confidence

Where an area is particularly important or controversial, ASB's practice is to issue a Discussion Paper which, after taking account of comment by interested parties, leads to a FRED.

Nineteen FRSs have so far been published, including FRS 1, which requires the annual report and accounts to contain a cash flow statement, and FRS 3, which requires a statement of total recognised gains and losses.

In addition, at its first meeting, the ASB unanimously agreed to adopt all the extant SSAPs published by its predecessor, the ASC, thereby giving them statutory clout. The financial reporting standards currently in force are listed in Appendix 1.

Statements of Recommended Practice

Statements of Recommended Practice (SORPs) are developed by bodies recognised by the ASB to provide guidance on the application of accounting standards to specific industries, e.g. the British Bankers' Association's SORP on the treatment of securities. Companies are encouraged to comply with SORPs, but they are not mandatory, unless specifically required by legislation or other regulations.

International accounting standards

Certain aspects of the traditional body of UK accounting principles are, in the words of the ASB, 'becoming increasingly out of step with developments internationally'. To help facilitate international co-operation and harmonisation, the Board is working with other leading national standard-setting bodies, as well as the International Accounting Standards Board (IASB). But 'if the Board is to participate meaningfully and credibly in international debates about financial reporting, it must move closer to the conceptual frameworks of other leading standard-setters'.

For a comparison of UK, US and international accounting standards, see Chapter 30.

PRINCIPLES OF FINANCIAL REPORTING

Need for a conceptual framework

One criticism that had for a long time been levelled at UK accounting standards was the absence of agreement on the fundamental principles of accounting and reporting. This made it difficult to produce a consistent and coherent standards framework.

Fundamental accounting concepts

Prior to the formation of the ASB, four fundametal accounting concepts had been laid down by the ASC in SSAP 2 *Disclosure of accounting policies*:

1. The *going concern concept*: the accounts are compiled on the assumption that there is no intention or need to go into liquidation or to curtail the current level of operations significantly.
2. The *accruals (or matching) concept*: revenue and costs are accrued (accounted for) as they are earned or incurred, not as the money is received or paid, and revenue and profits are matched with associated costs and expenses by including them in the same accounting period.
3. The *consistency concept*: accounting treatment of like items is consistent from one period to the next.
4. The *concept of prudence*, which is the overriding concept, demands that:

   (a) revenue and profits are not anticipated;
   (b) provision is made for all known liabilities (expenses and losses), whether the amount is known with certainty or has to be estimated.

FRS 18 *Accounting policies*

FRS 18, which replaced SSAP 2, retains SSAP 2's four concepts, stressing the key status of *going concern* and *accruals*, which play a pervasive role in the selection of accounting policies, but placing less importance on the concepts of *consistency* and *prudence*.

In FRS 18 the key objectives are *relevance, reliability, comparability* and *'understandability'* (their word, not ours), while

- consistency is viewed against the objective of comparability, which can be achieved through a combination of consistency and disclosure;
- prudence is viewed against the objective of reliability. FRS 18 emphasises that it is not necessary to exercise prudence where there is no uncertainty.

Statement of Principles for Financial Reporting
After an Exposure Draft in 1995, a revised Exposure Draft in March 1999 and much discussion, the *Statement of principles for financial reporting* (StoP) was finally published in December 1999.

The ASB took the view that a common set of principles was necessary to achieve further harmonisation in international accounting practice.

For that reason, the UK Statement of Principles was based on the International Accounting Standards Committee's *Framework for the Preparation and Presentation of Financial Statements* (the IASC Framework), which was itself derived from the *Statements of Financial Accounting Concepts* issued in the USA by the Financial Accounting Standards Board (FASB).

As well as several fairly obvious truisms – the need for reliability, relevance, consistency, completeness, neutrality and understandability to the user – the StoP also spells out a number of further accounting concepts:

- *'Substance over form'*: This concept was introduced by FRS 5. It requires items to be accounted for so as to reflect their commercial substance rather than their legal form, if these differ. For example, where a company is for all practical purposes the owner of an asset, but is not technically the *legal* owner, the asset should be included in the company's balance sheet. This could occur where a company was already deriving virtually all the commercial benefit from an asset, and had an indefinite option to buy it from its owner for a nominal sum (StoP paras. 3.12 and 3.13).
- *Materiality*: If any information is not material it does not have to be included in financial statements (StoP paras. 3.28 to 3.32).

  Although the StoP doesn't give a definition of materiality, SSAP 3 *Earnings per share* (subsequently replaced by FRS 14) did so in the context of fully diluted earnings per share, which only had to be disclosed if dilution was

material; dilution of 5% or more was considered material.

A trick we came across in a company that went bust in the early 90s was to treat its various activities as *divisions* where, in most groups, they would have been *subsidiaries*. This enabled the company to treat quite significant matters as immaterial, as they were under 5% in the context of the whole Group, when they might have reduced the profits of a subsidiary by more, and often much more, than 5%.

- *Comparability*: Users need to be able to compare an entity's financial information over time in order to identify trends in its financial performance and financial position.

  They also need to be able to compare the financial information of different entities in order to evaluate their relative financial performance and financial position (StoP paras. 3.20 and 3.21).

In practice comparability over time is distorted unless figures are adjusted to allow for the effects of general inflation. This is demonstrated in Chapter 29.

Comparability over time can also be distorted if a company changes its accounting policies. For example the videotape hire company CITYVISION, before it was taken over by BLOCKBUSTER, a US company in the same business, revised the estimated useful life of its tape libraries, depreciating them over 30 months instead of 15 months. This increased reported profits by nearly 60%.

Comparability between companies can be distorted if their accounting policies are different; for example CABLE & WIRELESS and BRITISH TELECOM depreciate similar equipment over different useful lives.

Comparability between companies can also be distorted by differences in the way assets are financed. For example, a retailer which owns all its outlets cannot be fairly compared with a similar retailer that rents all its outlets, unless the analyst adjusts the figures to allow for the difference. Adjustments are also needed if the companies' financial years are not coterminous.

- *Financial adaptability*: This is a recent concept, defined as a company's ability 'to take effective action to alter the amount and timing of its cash flows so that it can respond to unexpected needs or opportunities' (StoP para. 1.19).

  This may include whether the company is in a position to issue more equity, to increase borrowings or to sell off surplus assets.

What financial statements comprise
The annual report of the auditors to the company's shareholders often begins 'We have audited the

financial statements on pages xx to yy', i.e. the pages containing the financial statements (but nothing else unless specifically stated).

These include four primary financial statements:

- Profit and loss account
- Statement of total recognised gains and losses
- Balance sheet
- Cash flow statement.

Financial statements also include

- The notes to the financial statements
- The statement of accounting policies.

The notes and the primary financial statements form an integrated whole, and should be read as such to obtain a complete picture.

The need to read the notes
The role of the notes is to amplify and explain the primary financial statements, and it can be very misleading to read the primary financial statements in isolation.

Although the 1995 ED says 'disclosure of information in the notes to the financial statements is not a substitute for recognition [in the financial statements], and does not correct or justify a misrepresentation or omission in the primary financial statements' (para. 6.13), some companies have certainly tried it on in the past, and will probably do so in the future. Let us give you two examples from the accounts of now defunct companies:

1. A year or so before its demise the Southampton-based golfing and tennis hotel company LEADING LEISURE's P & L account showed a pre-tax profit of £6.7m. Note 1 to the accounts reported that trading profit generated by the disposal of properties to joint ventures amounted to £10m. Note 12 revealed additions to loans to related companies of £35.8m.

    A sceptical analyst might suspect that Leading Leisure had loaned its joint venture partner the money to buy a 50% stake in the properties, and that the price of the 50% stake had been pitched to give Leading Leisure a £10m trading profit.

    Amongst other little gems in the notes, note 6 showed an extraordinary item of £1.3m 'Reorganisation and aborted fund raising costs'. There was obviously more than one Doubting Thomas about. In the next twelve months or so the share price fell from 96p to 2p, at which point the shares were suspended. A week later the banks called in administrative receivers.

2. RESORT HOTELS provides our second cautionary tale about the dangers of not reading the notes. As well as running its own hotels, Resort had management contracts to run a number of hotels financed by Business Expansion Schemes (a tax break to encourage investment in young and expanding companies).

    Resort charged these BES-financed hotels management fees. The hotels weren't profitable enough to be able to pay the fees. But the unpaid fees were counted as income by Resort, thus bolstering Resort's profits and, at the same time, producing an ever increasing debtor item of management fees due in Resort's balance sheet. Eventually the bubble burst.

    In the last report and accounts before its demise, Resort's balance sheet did give a warning clue: an alarming rise in 'Amounts due from managed companies' from £8.646m to £12.987m, an increase of £4.341m.

    But you had to read the notes to find out what was actually going on. Note 1 showed a breakdown of turnover between Hotel operations £11.874m and Hotel management fees £4.219m, almost exactly the increase in the amounts due from managed companies.

The objective of financial statements
The objective of financial statements is to provide information about the financial position and performance of an enterprise that is useful to a wide range of users for assessing the stewardship of management and for making economic decisions (StoP Chapter 1).

Users and their information needs
Financial information about the activities and resources of an entity is typically of interest to many people. Although some of these people are able to command the preparation of special purpose financial reports in order to obtain the information they need, the rest – usually the vast majority – will need to rely on general purpose financial reports (StoP para. 1.1). As the StoP points out, Annual Reports and Accounts and Interim Reports are of interest not only to investors, but to

- lenders (although banks demand and get a lot more timely and detailed information than is generally available);
- suppliers and other trade creditors (to decide how much credit to allow a company);
- customers (a retailer to assess the financial strength of a potential supplier);
- employees (whether to buy some shares, or to start looking for another job);
- governments and their agencies (a nosey lot at the best of times) and

- the general public (for example where a company makes a substantial contribution to a local economy by providing employment and using local suppliers).

What users look for

Economic decisions often require *an evaluation of the enterprise's ability to generate cash* and the timing and certainty of its generation. To do this users focus on the enterprise's (i) financial position, (ii) performance and (iii) cash flows; and use these in predicting expected cash flows.

The *financial position* of an enterprise encompasses the economic resources it controls, its financial structure, its liquidity and solvency, and its capacity to adapt to changes in the environment in which it operates. Much, but not all, of the information on financial position needed is *provided by the balance sheet*.

The *performance* of an enterprise comprises the return obtained by the enterprise on the resources it controls, including the cost of its financing. Information on performance is *provided by the profit and loss account* and *the statement of total recognised gains and losses*.

Recognition

At the heart of any statement of principles lie questions of recognition:

- When exactly *is* something (i) an asset; (ii) a liability?
  and
- Just when *does* one recognise (i) a gain; (ii) a loss?

For example, a well known construction and house-building company used to have an accounting policy which said that the profit on building houses should only be recognised when all the houses in a development had been sold. This gave the directors wonderful flexibility: they could (and did) build an estate of say 200 houses, sell 199 of them, and keep one unsold until they wanted to bring the profit on the whole estate into their accounts. This may have been extremely *prudent*, but it was hardly *true and fair*.

Chapter 5 of the StoP deals at length with *recognition in financial statements* (StoP pp. 57–74). Recognition is required if 'sufficient evidence exists that the new asset or liability has been created . . . and can be measured at a monetary amount with sufficient reliability' (StoP p. 59).

But, inevitably, there will be scope for subjective judgement of what is '*sufficient evidence*' and what is '*sufficient reliability*', and there will also be variations in the accounting policies of individual companies.

Accounting policies

FRS 18 requires the accounting policies used in the preparation of the accounts to be disclosed. They are usually shown after the accounts proper, either immediately before the notes to the accounts or as the first note. A few companies, like BRITISH TELECOM, show them at the beginning of the accounts, immediately before the profit and loss account.

As an illustration of accounting policies we have chosen extracts from the notes to the accounts of THE BODY SHOP, a company which we will be looking at in detail in Chapter 31. Our comments are in square brackets, and the italics are ours.

THE BODY SHOP *Extracts from the notes to the 2001 accounts*

Note 1 Accounting policies

The financial statements have been prepared under the historical cost convention and in accordance with applicable accounting standards . . .

Accounts are prepared to the Saturday nearest the end of February in each year. On that basis the 2001 accounts are prepared for a 53 week period ending 3 March 2001; comparatives are for the 52 week period ended 26 February 2000.

[Figures in the 2001 P & L account will need to be multiplied by 52/53 to be comparable with 2000 figures.]

The principal accounting policies are:

Basis of consolidation

. . . The Group uses the *acquisition method* of accounting to consolidate the results of subsidiary undertakings, and the results of subsidiary undertakings are included from the date of acquisition to the date of disposal.

[The other method, the *merger method*, which may only be used in very limited circumstances, takes in the acquired company's results for the *whole year* in which two companies combine.]

Goodwill

Goodwill arising on the acquisition of a subsidiary or business is the difference between the consideration paid and the fair value of the assets and liabilities acquired.

Goodwill arising on acquisitions *prior to 28 February 1998* was set off directly against reserves and has not been reinstated on implementation of FRS 10.

Positive goodwill arising on acquisitions from *1 March 1998* is capitalised, classified as an asset on the balance sheet and amortised on a straight line basis over its useful economic life up to a presumed maximum of fifteen years.

It will be reviewed for impairment at the end of the first full financial year following the acquisition and in other periods if events or changes indicate that the carrying value may not be recoverable.

Any goodwill previously eliminated to reserves will be charged/credited to the profit and loss account on disposal of the related business.

Valuation of investments
Investments held as fixed assets are stated at cost less any provision for impairment.

Depreciation
Depreciation is provided to write off the cost, less estimated residual values, of all tangible fixed assets, except for freehold land, over their expected useful lives . . .

Stocks
Stocks are valued at the lower of cost and net realisable value . . . Net realisable value is based on estimated selling price less further costs to completion and disposal.

The Body Shop International Employee Share Trust
The Body Shop is deemed to have control of the assets, liabilities, income and costs [of the Trust, which] has therefore been included in the financial statements of the Group and Company . . .

Foreign currency
The results of the foreign subsidiaries have been translated using the average monthly exchange rates . . .

Foreign currency monetary assets and liabilities are translated at the rates ruling at the balance sheet dates and any differences arising are taken to the Profit and Loss account.

Research and development
Research and development expenditure is charged to the profit and loss account in the year in which it is incurred.

Etc.

The full significance of the company's accounting policies will become clear in subsequent chapters.

Chapter 3

FORMING A COMPANY

 The key purpose of forming a company is to limit the liability of shareholders

Before the first Companies Act introduced the Company as a separate legal entity in 1862, the *Proprietor* of a business had **unlimited liability**. If his business failed, he was personally responsible for settling the debts of the business and, if he had no other means of doing so, could have to sell his home and personal possessions.

Not only was his liability unlimited but, if he took in partners, they would have unlimited liability too.

As the industrial revolution gathered momentum, *individual proprietors* found it increasingly difficult to raise enough capital to keep pace, or to find partners to share the increasing risk. Growth achieved by ploughing back profits was simply too slow.

The limited company
If a limited company goes bust, the shareholders will lose all the money they invested in the company but, providing their shares are fully paid up, will have no further liability. Their liability is **limited** to their investment, and not one penny more.

Incorporation of a company
When a company is formed by incorporation under the Companies Acts a Certificate of Incorporation is issued and the company assumes a legal identity separate from its shareholders.

Before incorporation can take place, a Memorandum of Association and Articles of Association have to be drawn up and filed with the Registrar of Companies in England and Wales or with the Registrar of Companies in Scotland.

Memorandum of Association
The Memorandum lays down the rules which govern the company in its relations with the outside world. It states the name of the company; the country in which the Registered Office will be situated; the objects of the company (i.e. activities the company may pursue); the authorised share capital; the nominal value of the shares; a list of initial subscribers and whether the liability of members (shareholders) is limited. An example is given in Table B of the First Schedule to the Companies (Tables A to F) Regulations 1985.

Articles of Association
The Articles lay down the internal rules within which the directors run the company. The main items covered are:

(a) the issue of shares, the rights attaching to each class of share, the consent required for the alteration of the rights of any class of shareholders, and any restrictions on the transfer of shares;
(b) the procedure for board and general meetings and for altering the authorised share capital;
(c) the election and retirement of directors, their duties and their powers, including borrowing powers;
(d) the declaration of dividends;
(e) the procedure for winding up the company.

A model set of Articles is given in Table A of the Schedule to the Companies (Tables A to F) Regulations 1985.

Members' (shareholders') liability
The liability of members (shareholders) of a company can either be limited by shares or by guarantee, or the liability can be unlimited.

Limited by shares

This is the method normally used for a company engaged in business activities. If the shares are fully paid, the members' liability is limited to the money they have put up: the maximum risk a shareholder runs is to lose all the money he has paid for his shares, and no further claim can be made on him for liabilities incurred by the company. If the shares are only partly paid, shareholders (and to a limited extent former shareholders) can be called upon to subscribe some or all of the unpaid part, but no more than that.

Limited by guarantee

This method is used for charitable and similar organisations, where funds are raised by donations and no shares are issued. The liability is limited to the amount each member personally guarantees, which is the maximum each member may be called upon to pay in the event of liquidation. This form of incorporation is not normally used for a business.

Unlimited

This method is used by professional firms that want the tax advantages of being a company; the members have joint and several liability in the same way as a partnership (each member can individually be held entirely responsible).

Public company

Reference: Companies Act 1985, Sections 1 (3), 11 and 25.

A public company is defined as one:

(a) which is limited by shares or guarantee, with a minimum issued share capital of £50,000, or such other sum as specified by statutory instrument (the shares must be at least 25% paid up, with any share premium fully paid up); and

(b) whose Memorandum states that it is a public company; and

(c) which has been correctly registered as a public company.

All other companies are private companies.

A public company registered as such on incorporation cannot do business until the Registrar of Companies has issued a certificate that he is satisfied that the share capital requirements have been met.

The name of a public company must in all cases end either with the words 'Public Limited Company' or with the abbreviation 'PLC', neither of which may be preceded by the word 'Limited'.

A public company does not automatically have its shares listed on the Stock Exchange, but the process of obtaining a listing (see Chapter 4) is often referred to as 'going public', as a private company cannot obtain a listing on The Stock Exchange.

Private company

A 'private company' is a company that is not a public company (CA 1985, s. 1 (3)).

A company limited by shares or by guarantee (not being a public company) must have 'Limited' as the last word in its name (CA 1985, s. 25).

Chartered company

Companies may also be established by Royal Charter, the method used before any Companies Acts existed; for example, the PENINSULAR & ORIENTAL STEAM NAVIGATION COMPANY was incorporated by Royal Charter in 1840. The legal position of a chartered company is similar to that of an incorporated company, except that any change to the Articles involves a petition to the Privy Council.

Small and medium-sized companies

Small and medium-sized companies are defined by the Companies Act 1985 as companies meeting two or more of the following criteria:

	Small company	Medium-sized company
Turnover not exceeding	£2.8m*	£11.2m*
Total assets not exceeding	£1.4m*	£5.6m*
Number of employees not exceeding	50	250

* Updated periodically to take account of inflation.

Small and medium-sized private companies are permitted to file abbreviated accounts but they are still required to send full accounts to their members.

Chapter 4

ADMISSION TO LISTING

Stock Exchange listing – 'quoted companies'
In April 2000, responsibility for UK Listing was transferred from the Listing Department of the London Stock Exchange (LSE) to the UK Listing Authority (UKLA), a division of the Financial Services Authority (FSA).

UKLA's Listing Rules are known as 'The Purple Book', from the colour of its cover.

Provided that it meets certain criteria, a public company may have its shares and/or debentures, unsecured loan stocks and warrants 'listed', i.e. included in The Stock Exchange Official List, so that a market is 'made' in the securities. Although it is usual for all the securities of a company to be listed, it is possible for this not to be the case. For example, SAINSBURY's preference shares were listed for many years before its ordinary shares were offered to the public.

Companies which have securities that are listed are often referred to as 'quoted companies', 'having a quotation' or 'being listed', although it is the company's securities that are listed, not the company itself. 'Having a quotation' is simply the old term for being 'listed'.

Requirements for listing
The minimum legal requirements that a company has to meet before any of its securities can be listed are contained in Part 4 of the Financial Services Act 1986, which implements in the United Kingdom four European Union directives, known as the Admission directive, the Listing Particulars directive, the Interim Reports directive, and the Mutual Recognition directive on the UK listing of EEC companies listed elsewhere in the EEC.

These requirements are incorporated in the UKLA's Listing Rules (The Purple Book).

Listing Particulars (prospectus)
Chapter 6 of The Purple Book contains details of the contents of Listing Particulars, which have to be supplied for approval prior to listing, and which have to be included in any prospectus inviting initial public subscription for the company's shares.

Companies wishing to have their securities admitted to the LSE's markets for listed securities have to complete a two-stage admission process: firstly, the securities need to be admitted to the Official List by UKLA; secondly, the securities must be admitted to trading by the LSE.

The Listing Particulars are designed to ensure that the company makes available sufficient information on its history, current position and future prospects to enable the general public to assess the value of the company's shares as an investment, and they are very comprehensive. The prospectus issued by a company when it goes public is therefore a most valuable source of information.

Minimum size of issue
The Stock Exchange has to satisfy itself that sufficient dealings are likely to take place in the class of security for which application is being made to make a realistic market, and thus justify a listing. The Listing Rules lay down two minimum criteria for listing – the expected market value of the securities for which listing is sought (the expected market price multiplied by the number of shares issued and to be issued: currently a minimum of £700,000 for shares and £200,000 for debt securities), and the proportion of shares to be held by the public (currently 25% of any class of share).

Keeping the public informed
The Stock Exchange also has to ensure that the general public will be kept satisfactorily informed of the

company's activities and progress in the future, and that the shareholders' interests will be adequately protected: this is done by requiring an applicant for listing to accept 'Continuing Obligations' as a condition of admission to and subsequent maintenance of listing.

Continuing Obligations

Chapter 9 of The Purple Book deals with the Continuing Obligations of listed companies, designed to protect shareholders and to keep them properly informed. Additional continuing obligations are contained in Chapters 10 to 16.

Companies are required to submit to the Stock Exchange through the company's official sponsors, normally brokers, drafts for approval of all circulars to holders of securities, notices of meetings, forms of proxy and notices by advertisement to holders of bearer securities.

Companies are also required to notify the Stock Exchange of profit announcements, dividend declarations, material acquisitions, changes of directors, proposed changes in the nature of the business and any other information necessary to enable holders of the company's listed securities and the public to appraise the position of the company and to avoid the establishment of a false market in its listed securities.

In particular a company must notify the Company Announcements Office, by way of a warning announcement, of information which is likely to lead to substantial movements in the price of its securities if at any time the necessary degree of confidentiality cannot be maintained, or that confidentiality has or may have been breached.

In addition, amongst various requirements on interim reports, proxy voting, registration of securities and several other topics, The Purple Book requires companies to include in the annual report and accounts:

(a) if the results for the period under review differ by 10% or more from any published forecast or estimate by the company for that period, an explanation of the difference;

(b) the amount of interest capitalised;

(c) particulars of the waiving of emoluments by any director, and of the waiving of dividends by any shareholder;

(d) details of each director's beneficial and non-beneficial interests in the company's shares and options;

(e) information on holdings, other than by directors, of 3% or more of any class of voting capital;

(f) details of any authority for the purchase by the company of its own shares, and details of any purchases made otherwise than through the market;

(g) details of shares issued for cash other than pro rata to existing shareholders;

(h) where a company has listed shares in issue and is a subsidiary of another company, particulars of the participation by the parent in any placing;

(i) particulars of significant contracts during the year in which any director is or was materially interested;

(j) a statement by the directors that the company is a going concern;

(k) for a company incorporated in the UK, a statement of how it has applied the Principles of the *Combined Code on Corporate Governance* (the '*Appliance*' statement) and a statement as to whether or not it has complied throughout the period with the Code (the '*Compliance*' statement), which should also specify any departures from the provisions of the Combined Code.

(l) a report to the shareholders by the Board, containing details of each director's remuneration, share option and pension arrangements.

Listed companies are also expected to issue their report and accounts within six months of their year end, but may apply for the six-month period to be extended if they have significant overseas interests.

Methods of obtaining a listing

Chapter 4 of The Purple Book describes the ways in which a company can obtain a listing. Briefly, they are as follows:

1. *Offer for sale*

   An offer for sale is the most common method of obtaining a listing. Both new and/or existing securities can be offered to the public. The issuing house or the sponsoring broker purchases the securities from existing securities holders and/or from the company, and offers them on to the public at a slightly higher price.

2. *Offer for subscription*

   An invitation is made to the public by, or on behalf of, an issuer to subscribe for new shares or other securities.

3. *Offer for sale by tender*

   This is a variation of methods 1 or 2, in which applicants are invited to bid for securities at or above a minimum issue price. The securities are then all sold at one price, the 'striking price', which may be the highest price at which all the securities can be sold, or a little lower, if this is necessary to ensure a good spread of holders.

4. *Placing*

   Securities are placed with specified persons or clients of the sponsor or any securities house assisting in the placing. There is no offer to the public and no general offer to existing holders.

5. *Intermediaries offer*
Securities are offered by, or on behalf of, the issuer to intermediaries for them to allocate to their own clients.

6. *Introduction*
An introduction is used where the company's securities are already widely held and/or are already listed outside the United Kingdom, or where a new holding company issues its securities in exchange for those of one or more listed companies; there is no formal offer of securities, but a listing is obtained for existing securities.

Methods 1 to 5 are referred to broadly as 'new issues', because the company's securities are new to the stock market, although only method 2 necessarily involves the issue of any new securities.

Alternative Investment Market

Reference: The Stock Exchange Rules, Chapter 16 – AIM Admission Rules.

The Alternative Investment Market, AIM, was set up in 1995 to provide an alternative source of capital and a trading platform for companies unable or unwilling to join the official list.

The entry requirements are less demanding than for a full listing:

* no requirement for a minimum trading record;
* no minimum levels of capitalisation;
* no requirement for any given percentage of the share capital of the company to be in public hands.

Although entry documentation has been kept as simple as possible, entrants to AIM must provide a prospectus or similar document which meets European Union directives, and audited accounts set out under company law. Companies must arrange for a member firm to support trading. They must also meet certain ongoing obligations including publication of unaudited interim figures and of all directors' dealings.

Price sensitive information must be published promptly; and trading on AIM is subject to the same level of surveillance and supervision as the official list. AIM has proved extremely popular; a huge variety of companies have joined, with market capitalisations ranging from about £1m to more than £100m.

By the end of 2000 more than 500 companies were trading on AIM.

Chapter 5

SHARE CAPITAL AND RESERVES

SHARE CAPITAL

A key point to check is whether shares in a company are widely held or whether the company is under the control of one person, or of a number of people, e.g. family controlled.

The normal means of control is to have at least 50% of the votes. This is simple if there is only one class of share, and each share carries one vote.

But there are complications when there is more than one class, with different voting rights, or there is a 'golden share' which carries an all powerful vote in certain circumstances.

Control

If a company is under the control of one person or group of persons, the other investors can be on a hiding to nothing. Check directors' holdings and look out for any note on substantial shareholdings, e.g.:

MAXWELL COMMUNICATION CORPORATION *Paragraph in the 1990 Report of the Directors*

Substantial shareholdings
As at the date of this report, pursuant to Section 198 of the Companies Act 1985, the Company had been advised of the following interests of 3% or more in the ordinary share capital of the company:

Name	*Number of shares*	*% of issued share capital*
Maxwell Foundation and its subsidiaries	202,558,076	31.34%
Robert Maxwell, his family and companies controlled by him and his family	155,912,928	24.14%

In 1990 Maxwell Communication Corporation was one of the world's top ten publishers, capitalised at about £1.4 billion. But the tyrannical management style of the controlling shareholder drove the company into administrative receivership less than two years later.

Authorised and issued share capital
When a company is formed, the authorised share capital and the nominal value of the shares are established and written into the company's Memorandum of Association, and the procedure for increasing the authorised share capital is included in the company's Articles of Association. This usually requires the approval of the shareholders.

Thereafter the directors of the company cannot issue new shares in excess of the authorised number, nor can they issue securities carrying rights to new shares that would exceed that number (e.g. convertibles and warrants: see below).

Both the authorised and the issued share capital are shown in the company's accounts, divided into equity and non-equity shares, e.g.

BELLWAY *Extract from 2000 Group balance sheet*

	2000 £000	1999 £000
Capital and reserves		
Equity share capital		
Ordinary shares	13,652	13,622
Non-equity capital		
Preference shares	20,000	20,000
Called up share capital	33,652	33,622
. . .		

Details of the authorised share capital are normally shown in a note to the accounts.

Types of share capital

Although all shares are referred to generally as 'risk capital', as the shareholders are the first investors to lose if the company fails, the degree of risk can vary within the same company from hardly any more than that of an unsecured lender to highly speculative, with prospects of reward usually varying accordingly.

The main types of share, in increasing order of risk, the order in which they would rank for distribution in the event of liquidation, are:

(a) preference shares
(b) ordinary shares
(c) deferred shares
(d) warrants to subscribe for shares.

Unlike interest paid on loan capital, distributions of profits to shareholders are not an 'allowable expense' for company taxation purposes; i.e. dividends have to be paid out of profits *after* Corporation Tax has been deducted.

Preference shares

Preference shares carry a fixed rate of dividend, normally payable half-yearly, but unlike the holders of loan capital, who can take action against a company in default of interest payments, preference shareholders have no legal redress if the board of directors decides to recommend that no preference dividends should be paid. However, if no preference dividend is declared for an accounting period, no dividend can be declared on any other type of share for the period concerned, and the preference shareholders usually become entitled to vote at shareholders' general meetings. (Provided their dividends are paid, preference shares do not normally carry a vote.)

Varieties of preference shares can include one or a combination of the following features:

- *Cumulative*. If the dividend on a cumulative preference share is not paid on time, payment is postponed rather than omitted. When this happens, the preference dividend is said to be 'in arrears', and these arrears have to be paid by the company before any other dividend can be declared. Arrears of cumulative preference dividends must be shown in a note to the accounts.
- *Redeemable*. The shares are repayable, normally at their nominal (par) value, in a given year, e.g. 2002, or when the company chooses within a given period, e.g. 2001/04.

- *Participating*. In addition to receiving a fixed dividend, shareholders participate in an additional dividend, usually a proportion of any ordinary dividend declared.
- *Convertible*. Shareholders have the option of converting their preference shares into ordinary shares within a given period of time, the conversion period.

Where a company has a large proportion of non-equity shares, it is important to check whether a significant number are due for redemption in the near future.

Golden shares

Where nationalised industries have been privatised, the government has, in some cases, retained a 'golden share' to prevent takeover and/or has placed limits on the maximum size of any one holding or on the percentage that can be held by foreigners, e.g. the Secretary of State for Transport holds a Special Rights redeemable preference share of £1 in BAA, and BAA's articles of association limit the holding of any one shareholder to 15% of the ordinary shares.

Another example of control by a single share is REUTERS, where there is a single Founders £1 share designed to preserve Reuters' independence. The share is held by a Trust, and may be used to outvote all ordinary shares if other safeguards fail and there is an attempt to seize control of the company.

Ordinary shares

Ordinary shares usually form the bulk of the share capital of a company. Ordinary shareholders are normally entitled to all the profits remaining after tax and preference dividends have been deducted although, as explained later, not all these attributable profits are likely to be distributed. Ordinary shareholders are entitled to vote at general meetings, giving them control over the election of directors.

However some companies put a clause in their articles of association to allow them to disenfranchise a shareholder where the shares are held in a nominee name and the nominee holder fails to respond to a request for information on the underlying holder. This protects the company against the building up of anonymous holdings prior to a possible bid.

Under the Companies Act 1985 companies are allowed to issue redeemable ordinary shares, provided they also have shares in issue which are not redeemable; i.e. the share capital of a company cannot consist solely of redeemable shares. A company may now also purchase its own shares, subject to a large number of conditions, including the prior approval of its shareholders (see page 29).

Partly paid shares

When a company raises money, but doesn't need it all at once, for example an oil exploration company with a long drilling programme, it may issue partly paid shares, making calls on the unpaid part as and when required. The buyer of partly paid shares is legally obliged to pay the call(s).

Ordinary stock

Ordinary stock is a historical legacy from the days when every share in issue had to be numbered; some companies used to convert their shares into stock when they became fully paid (as this avoided the bother of numbers), and a few companies continue to use the term.

Ordinary stock can, in theory, be transferred in any monetary amount, while shares can only be bought and sold individually; in practice ordinary stock is normally traded in multiples of £1, so the terms 'ordinary share' and 'ordinary stock' are effectively synonymous.

Non-voting shares

A number of companies have more than one class of share (other than preference shares), with differing rights on voting and/or dividends and/or on liquidation. The most common variation is in voting rights, where a second class of share, identical in all other respects to the ordinary class, either carries no voting rights (usually called N/V or A shares), or carries restricted voting rights (R/V shares).

The trend over the last few years has, however, been towards the abolition of non-voting shares, and it is becoming increasingly difficult (if not actually impossible) to raise new money by the issue of non-voting shares. Several companies, led by MARKS & SPENCER in 1966, and including more recently, in 2000, the construction group JOHN LAING, have enfranchised their non-voting shares, giving scrip (free) issues to voting shareholders by way of compensation, but there are still a few exceptions. For example GLENMORANGIE, the Scotch whisky company, (formerly MACDONALD MARTIN) has a two-tier structure in which the founding family retain the majority of the B shares:

GLENMORANGIE *Extract from 2000 accounts*

Called up share capital	£000
A Ordinary Shares	
(one vote per share) of 10p each	1,165
B Ordinary Shares	
(5 votes per share) of 5p each	200

Investing in shares that have fewer votes than another class of share, or have no votes at all, is very much a case of *caveat emptor* (buyer beware).

You may find yourself investing in a company like C.H. BAILEY, where the B ordinary shares, largely family owned, carry 100 times the votes of the more widely held ordinary shares.

The chairman, Mr C.H. Bailey, has taken full advantage of his controlling position by paying himself over £1.4m in the last ten years, while shareholders have had only two dividends in the same period.

The company discourages them from complaining by holding the AGM at Alexandra Docks in Newport, Gwent, in the middle of winter, inconveniently close to Christmas. In 2000 it was held on 14 December.

Another company with non-voting shares is the electro-components and power supplies company BULGIN, which also illustrates another key point:

The jigsaw

As with doing a jigsaw (or in any intelligence-gathering organisation), the analyst often needs to put together several pieces of information to get the picture.

A.F. BULGIN *Note 23 to the 1997 accounts*

Called up share capital	£000
Authorised . . .	
Allotted, called up and fully paid	
2,000,000 Ordinary shares of 5p each	100
26,340,000 A Non-Voting shares of 5p each	1,317
	1,417

Extract from Report of the Directors

Directors and their interests

Beneficial interests	Ordinary	A Ordinary
R.A. Bulgin [Chairman/MD*]	307,200	645,087
R.E. Bulgin	201,800	96,059
G.A. Stone [Company Sec.*]	2,000	5,387
R.A.R. Bulgin	86,200	259,201
C.S. Bulgin (Resigned		
29 April 1997)	6,002	21,000
C.M. Leigh [FD*]	2,000	1,000

Non-beneficial interests . . .
* As shown in the list of Directors and Advisers

The Bulgin family directors hold a shade over 30% of the voting shares. Are there any other substantial shareholdings? Yes, and very interesting they are too (as we show at the top of the next page).

A.F. BULGIN *Extract from Report of the Directors 1997*

Substantial shareholdings
The Company is advised of the following interests in the issued voting ordinary shares of 5p each at 23 May 1997:

	Ordinary	%
National Westminster Bank Plc (mainly as managing trustees of certain settlements executed by the late Mr A.F. Bulgin)	658,500	32.9
Mars UK Pension Fund	65,000	3.3
Specialist Holdings Limited	260,000	13.0
G.M. Barber	74,500	3.7

Bulgin directors' holdings and the late Mr A.F. Bulgin's settlements together give voting control.

A.F. BULGIN *Note 9 to the 1997 accounts*

Directors' emoluments

	Salary £000	Benefits £000	Pension contrib. £000	Total £000
R.A. Bulgin	125	25	50	200
R.E. Bulgin	70	20	57	147
G.A. Stone	66	10	52	128
R.A.R. Bulgin	55	24	10	89
C.S. Bulgin	55	12	6	73
C.M. Leigh	55	20	8	83
	426	111	183	720

The Bulgin share of the total remuneration of the directors was £509,000, more than 70% of the total. Set this against a pre-tax profit for the year of £238,000 and one is led to ask: 'Are the shareholders happy?' and 'What do the non-executive directors think?'

'Has the Company any non-executive directors?' At the 1997 year end the answer was 'No'.

Two were appointed after the year end:

A.F. BULGIN *Extract from Report of the Directors*

On 17 February 1997 the following non-executive directors were appointed:
J.A.D. Skailes (59) – until he retired, a stockbroker at Vivian Gray . . . taken over by Gerrard & National.
A.S. Winter (50) – a management consultant specialising in corporate finance. Previously a Vice President of investment bankers Bear Stearns and before that of Chase Manhatten Bank.

So something was happening.

The company's stockbrokers are Gerrard Vivian Gray. Stockbrokers largely earn their living by telling clients what they want to hear, not necessarily what they ought to hear. That is rather different from the role of an effective non-executive director, which in four words is to provide 'independent and objective counsel'.

We continued our intelligence gathering:

A.F. BULGIN *Extract from Report of the Directors 1997*

Results and dividends
The profit for the year after taxation was £151,000 (1996: £691,000). The Directors recommend a final dividend of 0.50 pence per share amounting to £142,000 (1996: £127,000) and that £9,000 (1996: £564,000) be transferred to reserves.

No interim dividend had been paid for some years, so the total dividend increased by 11.8% in a year in which profits fell by 78.1%.

Another substantial shareholder
Turning back to the list of substantial shareholders, we asked ourselves: 'Who are Specialist Holdings Limited? Where do they come into the picture?' There is a clue in a note to the accounts:

A.F. BULGIN *Note 4 to the 1997 accounts*

Net operating expenses	£000
Exceptional administrative expenses comprise:	
Redundancy costs	71
Requisitioned extraordinary meetings costs	55
Defalcation	89
	215

So dissident shareholders have been requisitioning EGMs. 'What is the betting', we asked ourselves, 'that they included Specialist Holdings Limited – whose 13.0% holding would go a long way to mustering enough votes to requisition an EGM?' We could not find any amplification in the report and accounts, so we checked elsewhere:

INVESTORS CHRONICLE *17 Jan 1997 'Smaller Companies'*

Dyson tactics at Bulgin
Electronic components maker A.F. Bulgin will be expected to appoint an independent consultant to examine enfranchising its non-voting shares if, as expected, a seemingly anodyne resolution put forward by dissident shareholder Specialist Holdings is passed at next week's EGM.

SPECIALIST HOLDINGS are, in fact, renowned for stirring things up in companies, not so much in an altruistic crusade for the fair treatment of non-voting shareholders, but to make money.

We sympathise to some extent with the long-term non-voting shareholders, but they really have only themselves to blame for buying N/V shares in the first place: you do so at your own peril.

Let's see what disparity in price there is between voting and non-voting shares. It's no good looking in the *FT*, which typically only shows the N/V price (companies have to pay the *FT* an annual fee to have their share price listed each day, and Bulgin wouldn't be over keen to publicise the disparity between the two classes of share). The *IC* is more informative:

INVESTORS CHRONICLE *24 Oct 1997 'Smaller Companies'*

BULGIN
Electronic Components, power supplies

A N/V Ord price:	13^1/$_2$p	Market value:	£3.56m
Ord price:	77^1/$_2$p	Market value:	£1.77m

But that did not necessarily rule out the non-voting shares as an investment. Something was changing and if one is in on a change before everyone else, it *can* be profitable.

A year later, we read:

A. F. BULGIN *Extract from the statement of Mr A. S. Winter* [recognise the name?] *in the 1998 accounts*

Chairman's Statement
. . .
Management changes
During the course of the year four members of the Main Board either resigned or retired. A substantial element of the resulting cost savings has been reinvested in the recruitment of new sales and marketing staff at each of the operating companies
. . .

We are also actively studying the effect of our current capital structure on our share price. Moreover, the current capital structure, by limiting our ability to raise fresh funds on the Stock Market, is likely to prevent us from making a major strategic acquisition. This will become a more pressing matter over the next twelve to twenty four months.

So it came as no surprise when, in June 1999, the Chairman wrote to shareholders:

BULGIN *Extracts from letter to shareholders*

ENFRANCHISEMENT PROPOSALS

Introduction
. . . institutional investors will not invest in companies which have a two-tier capital structure.

. . . This current limitation on raising new capital makes the company reliant on organic growth.

In order to achieve sustainable growth the Company must have the ability to fund . . . substantial acquisitions with new debt and/or equity.

Summary of the proposals and their effect
. . . for each [voting] share – 13 new [voting] shares

. . . 'A' share to be converted into voting shares . . .

If the proposals are approved: the present Ordinary shareholders, who now hold about **7 per cent** of the Company and **100 per cent** of the voting rights, will own about **50.7 per cent** of the Company and of the voting rights . . .

Intentions to vote in favour of the Proposals
The Directors intend to vote in favour . . .

Specialist Holdings and shareholders associated with it have indicated that they intend to vote in favour of the Proposals (13 for 1).

The circular went on to explain that, although an independent adviser had recommended that the bonus issue should be in the range of 5 to 8 new shares for every voting share held, it would not have been possible to obtain the 75% majority for a bonus within that range.

But Specialist Holdings were being too greedy. At a heated meeting the non-voting shareholders firmly rejected the proposals. Nine months later proposals for enfranchisement on a 1 for 8 basis went through unopposed. So the non-voting shareholders were enfranchised in the end, but it was at the cost of substantial dilution, and they nearly got really ripped off by the 13 for 1 proposal.

Be very wary of buying shares that have no voting rights, or have only limited voting rights

As we said at the beginning, it is a case of c*aveat emptor*. The same warning applies to companies where all shares (other than preference shares) carry equal voting rights, and one person effectively controls more than 50% of the votes; other shareholders are relying very heavily on that one person, but at least the controlling shareholder doesn't enjoy power that is disproportionate to his stake in the company.

Deferred shares

Another class is the deferred share, where no dividend is payable either:

(a) until ordinary shareholders' dividends have reached a certain level; or
(b) until conversion into ordinary shares.

In the 1970s and 1980s, when the top rate of Income Tax was much higher than the rate of Capital Gains Tax (CGT), there were a number of issues.

For example, in 1989 LONDON MERCHANT SECURITIES made a scrip (capitalisation) issue of 1 Deferred Ordinary share for every 3 Ordinary shares held. The Deferred Ordinary shares do not rank for any dividend but they will be converted automatically into Ordinary shares after the AGM held in 2004.

While the current top rate of UK Income Tax remains at 40%, the same as CGT, further issues of deferred shares seem unlikely.

Warrants

Warrants are transferable options granted by the company to purchase new shares from the company at a given price, called the 'exercise price'. The warrant is normally exercisable only during a given time period, the exercise period, although one or two perpetual warrants have been issued.

Warrants can be issued on their own, for example HANSON used warrants plus cash in its acquisition of Kidde Inc. in 1987, of Consolidated Goldfields in 1989 and of Beazer in 1991.

They can also be issued attached to new issues of loan stock or bonds to give the holder an opportunity of subsequently participating in the equity of the company; the warrant element makes the issue more attractive and is sometimes referred to as the 'sweetener' (see Chapter 6).

Warrants provide a high risk/high reward form of equity investment. For example, if the ordinary shares of a company stood at 100p, warrants with an exercise price of 75p would then be worth a minimum of 25p. If the ordinary shares doubled to 200p then the warrants would be worth a minimum of 125p, a fivefold increase. In practice warrants command a premium over the ordinary price minus exercise price, although this premium tends to fall over the life of the warrant, reaching zero at the end of the exercise period.

Warrants are comparatively rare in the United Kingdom. Most recent issues have been made by investment trusts, which have attached them to issues of ordinary shares.

Exercise rights

Details of a warrant's exercise rights should be shown in the report and accounts. For example:

SCHRODER ASIA PACIFIC FUND *Note to 2000 accounts*

Share capital

There were 27,994,495 warrants remaining in issue at 30 September 2000. Each warrant entitles the holder to subscribe for one ordinary share of 10p at a price of 100p, on 31 January in any of the years from 2001 to 2006 inclusive.

Accounting for warrants

FRS 4 *Capital instruments* requires the net proceeds from the issue of warrants to be credited to shareholders' funds (FRS 4 para. 45). See, for example, SCHRODER ASIA PACIFIC FUND below.

SCHRODER ASIA PACIFIC FUND *Note to 2000 accounts*

Warrant Reserve	2000	1999
	£000	£000
Warrant reserve at 30 September	8,701	8,704

In accordance with the accounting standard on Capital Instruments (FRS 4) the premium arising on the issue of shares where there are warrants attached has been apportioned between the shares and the warrants as part of shareholders' funds on the basis of the market value of the shares and warrants as on the first day of dealing. The warrant element is referred to as the 'warrant reserve'.

Warrant price behaviour

Although one or two hefty and rather expensive books have been compiled about warrants, the clearest and most concise explanation we have found of the behaviour of warrant prices in practice is given in Chapter 16 of R.A. Brealey's book *Security Prices in a Competitive Market.*

The book was published by The M.I.T. Press in 1971, following Dick Brealey's statistical work on the behaviour of common stock prices on Wall Street. The chapter on warrants describes the empirical method, based on the graph of Warrant Price divided by Exercise Price plotted against Share Price divided by Exercise Price; i.e. WP/EP against SP/EP.

ADRs

ADRs (American Depositary Receipts) are used in the USA to simplify the holding of securities in non-US companies. The securities purchased on behalf of the American investor are deposited abroad in a custodian bank, and the corresponding ADR certificates are issued by a US depository bank. The ADR bank then acts both as depositary and stock transfer agent, dealing with the payment of dividends and the handling of proxies and rights issues for the American investor. ADRs can be unsponsored, normally traded on the Over-The-Counter (OTC) market, or sponsored by the non-US company. Sponsored ADRs can be traded on the New York and American stock exchanges, but the non-US company must register with the Securities and Exchange Commission (SEC) and meet the specific requirements of the exchange, including the filing of an annual report (usually Form 20-F).

SHARE SCHEMES FOR DIRECTORS AND EMPLOYEES

A number of companies have encouraged share ownership amongst their staff for many years (ICI, for example, introduced a profit-sharing scheme as long ago as 1954, under which employees received a salary-related allocation of shares each year, according to the profitability of the company), but it is only since the 1970s that governments have actively encouraged wider share participation by the introduction of substantial tax concessions.

Current share incentive arrangements fall into three categories:

- the granting of options
- the award of shares
- phantom share schemes.

Granting of options

Employers grant their employees share options (the right to acquire shares) at a given price, the *exercise price*, at a given future date or period, the *exercise period*.

At the exercise date or during the exercise period, the employees may exercise their options if the exercise price is *below* the share price at the time, but may let the options lapse if the share price in the market is *above* the exercise price.

Options may be granted in various schemes:

- executive share option schemes
- unapproved share option schemes
- Enterprise Management Incentives
- Save-As-You-Earn (SAYE) schemes.

The tax rules are complex, and we can only give readers an overview of the main tax implications.

Executive share option schemes

The Inland Revenue's prior approval is required. Approval will only be given if various conditions are met:

(a) The exercise price must be not less than the market price at the date of granting.
(b) The option may only be exercisable between 3 and 10 years of the date of grant.
(c) The value of the underlying shares at the exercise price must not exceed £30,000 per person.

Tax position: No Income Tax or National Insurance is payable when the option is exercised except where it is exercised within three years of the exercise of another approved option. On subsequent disposal of the share, normal CGT rules apply.

Unapproved share option schemes

These are not subject to Inland Revenue restrictions, but they do not qualify for any tax concession.

Enterprise Management Incentives (EMI)

Compared with other share option schemes, EMI schemes have very significant tax advantages.

Providing the exercise price was not set below the market price of the shares at the time the option was granted, no employer's National Insurance or employee's Income Tax will be payable. On subsequent disposal, normal CGT rules apply.

EMI schemes used to be limited to £100,000 total share value per employee and restricted to no more than 15 employees; but Budget changes announced in 2001 propose to replace these restrictions by an aggregate limit of £3 million on the value of shares under option.

Save-As-You-Earn (SAYE) share options

SAYE schemes, which require Inland Revenue approval, enable share options to be offered to all employees.

To provide the sum required to exercise their options (exercise price set when the options are granted × number of shares under option), regular deductions are made monthly from the employee's net pay. The monthly contribution must be at least £5 and not more than £250 and deductions must be made for between three and five years.

At the end of the period, employees can choose between exercising their option *or* taking the cash in their SAYE account. Heads they win; tails they can't lose.

Tax position: No Income Tax or National Insurance is payable when the options are granted or exercised. On the subsequent disposal of shares taken up, normal CGT rules apply.

All employee share ownership plans (AESOPs)

Employers may *give* up to £3,000 worth of shares a year to each employee free of Income Tax and National Insurance contributions.

Each employee may also buy up to £1,500 worth of shares from their pre-tax salary, free of Income Tax and National Insurance contributions.

HERCULES PROPERTY SERVICES took three pages of their annual report for 2000 to summarise the main features of AESOP:

HERCULES PROPERTY SERVICES

Summary of main features . . .
There are four different methods of acquiring shares under AESOP permitted by the legislation:

Free shares provided by the Company to employees, up to a limit of £3,000 in any tax year.

Partnership shares purchased by employees out of pre-tax and NIC salary, up to a limit of £125 per month (or 10% of their overall salary, if less).

Matching shares to match employees' purchase of Partnership shares, up to a limit of 2 for each Partnership share purchased.

Dividend shares. Up to £1,500 of dividends paid under AESOP can be reinvested in shares *tax free* each year . . .

Performance share plans

In this type of plan, also known as LTIPs (Long Term Incentive Plans), selected executives are granted the right to receive a fixed number of shares in the company at some future date, subject to one or more criteria.

For example, SCHRODERS has a plan in which the number of shares issued at the end of a five year period depends on where the Total Shareholder Return (TSR) of Schroders' shares rank in the FT-SE 100 Index:

Below 50th place	no shares issued
41st to 50th	40% of the shares issued
31st to 40th	60%
21st to 30th	80%
20th or above	100%.

The issue is also subject to a minimum average post-tax real return on equity of 7.5% per annum.

Employees are liable to Income Tax on shares received.

LTIPs have been open to criticism firstly because they are complicated and, more importantly, because research has shown that they do little or nothing to enhance the share price. In contrast, with share options, the interests of executives and shareholders coincide.

Phantom share schemes

These are cash bonus schemes where the performance of the share price determines the amount of the bonus. For example ELECO:

ELECO *Extract from Report and Accounts 2000, Remuneration Committee Report*

Note 6 Phantom Share Option Scheme
The scheme was devised for J.H.B. Ketteley in connection with his appointment as Executive Chairman . . . An option was granted over a maximum of 1,500,000 notional shares of the Company . . . The exercise of the option gives rise to the payment of a bonus based upon the number of shares notionally acquired, multiplied by the amount by which the market value of one ordinary share exceeds 10 pence.

Summary of schemes

Type (see Note)	Current limit on value of shares awarded per employee
Executive share option	£30,000
Unapproved share option	None
EMI (Options)	£100,000
SAYE share option	£22,968
AESOP (Shares)	£7,500
LTIP (shares)	None

Note: Schemes in italics benefit from tax breaks

The investor's viewpoint

Companies that encourage employee share participation on favourable terms are generally regarded as more likely to prosper than those which do not. In particular, companies that grant options to executive directors and key senior staff, on whose efforts the success of a company largely depends, can expect better than average performance. In short, giving the directors and employees a 'slice of the action' should be regarded as a plus point for investing in a company, providing the directors aren't being too greedy. Avoid companies where the boardroom's total rewards are high in comparison with pre-tax profits.

Effect of inflation

At times of high inflation there is a serious flaw in share schemes for directors and employees:

SHARE SCHEMES *Effect of high inflation*

Options are granted at the current share price of 100p, exercisable in between 3 and 7 years.

After 7 years the value of money has halved, and the share price has gone up to 200p. The real value to the shareholder is unchanged, but the option holders have doubled their money.

The fair thing would be to index the exercise price by the RPI.

THE ISSUE OF FURTHER EQUITY

There are three limitations to the issue of further equity:

1. As already mentioned, there must be sufficient share capital authorised.
2. The UK Listing Authority, in its Continuing Obligations for listed companies, forbids the issue of equity, convertibles, warrants or options for cash, other than to the equity shareholders of the company, except with the prior approval of ordinary shareholders in general meeting, and the approval of the Stock Exchange. The Stock Exchange normally restricts issues of equity capital by way of placings to protect the interests of existing shareholders (see The Purple Book, Chapter 9, para. 18), but these restrictions can be relaxed when market conditions or the individual circumstances of a company justify doing so.
3. Section 100 of the Companies Act 1985 prohibits the issue of shares at a discount, i.e. for less than their nominal value.

Rights issues

A rights issue is an issue of new shares offered to shareholders in proportion to their existing holdings at a discount to the current market price. Shareholders who do not wish to subscribe can sell their rights 'nil paid'. The discount varies according to the 'weight' of the rights issue; 1 new share offered for every 8 or 10 shares already held would be regarded as a 'light' issue, probably requiring a discount of not more than 15%, while more than 1-for-4 would be 'heavy' and likely to need nearer 20% discount, or more if the company is in poor health. At these discounts underwriting would be arranged to ensure buyers for any shares not taken up by shareholders, but companies occasionally choose to make a rights issue at very much below the market price, the lowest price normally permitted being the par value of the shares.

The effect on the balance sheet of an issue at par is to add the total nominal value of the shares being issued to the issued share capital, and to show the cash received on the assets side. The expenses of the issue would normally be written off against the share premium account.

If the new shares are issued above par, the nominal value of the shares issued is added to the issued share capital and the difference between the issue price and the nominal price of each new share, i.e. the premium at which the shares were issued, is added to the share premium account.

For example, in 1999, WASTE RECYCLING GROUP made a 7-for-20 rights issue of 30,308,859 ordinary 25p shares at 406p. The issue added £7.6m to the ordinary share capital (30.308m × 25p nominal value) and £111.5m (30.308m × 381p premium), less expenses, to the share premium account, as illustrated below.

WASTE RECYCLING GROUP *Rights issue*

	Pre-rights £m	Post-rights £m
Issued share capital		
Ordinary share capital	11.7	19.3
Share premium		
Pre-rights	27.7	27.7
Premium on shares issued		111.5
Expenses of rights issue		(2.6)
	39.4	155.9

There are two methods of dealing with convertible stock in a rights issue. Either the holders are offered new shares on the basis of the number of ordinary shares they would hold on full conversion, or the stock has its conversion terms adjusted to allow for the rights issue, whichever method is laid down in the convertible's trust deed (see Chapter 6). Similarly, either warrant holders are offered new shares or the warrant's terms are adjusted.

Placing and open offer

This method, colloquially known as a placing with clawback, is an alternative to a rights issue, and is usually done in conjunction with an acquisition. For example, in January 1999 the loss-making steel wire manufacturer ASW HOLDINGS raised £17m by an Open Offer to fund the acquisition of its main UK competitor CO-STEEL SHEERNESS.

Shareholders were invited to subscribe for the new ordinary 10p shares at 14p, on the basis of 73 new ordinary shares for every 50 ordinary shares held, and the issue was underpinned by the Birmingham stockbrokers Albert E Sharp and Candover Investments. There was a 53.8% take-up.

The main advantage of a placing with open offer is that it either is done at a much tighter discount than a rights issue, under 10%, or can be done, as in ASW's case, when a rights issue would have been difficult if not impossible to underwrite.

The disadvantage is that shareholders who do not want to subscribe cannot sell their rights nil paid.

Scrip issues

A scrip issue, also known as a bonus or capitalisation issue, is a free issue of additional new shares to existing shareholders, made by capitalising reserves. For example, HALMA made a 1-for-3 scrip issue in August 1997. The effect on the balance sheet is shown below.

HALMA *Effect of 1-for-3 scrip issue*

	Pre-scrip £000	Post-scrip £000
Ordinary share capital	26,919	35,905
Share premium account	2,479	614
Profit and loss account	52,283	45,136
Shareholders' funds	81,681	81,655*

* Fall in shareholders' funds due to £26,000 scrip issue costs, which were charged to the share premium account.

As a scrip issue is basically a bookkeeping transaction, the share price would normally be expected to adjust accordingly (e.g. would fall from 240p to 180p with a 1-for-3), and it is open to debate as to whether scrip issues serve any useful purpose.

The main arguments in favour of scrip issues are the following:

(a) Scrip issues are popular with the investing public, and therefore enhance share prices. Research shows that shares tend to outperform the market after the announcement of a scrip issue, but that companies make scrip issues only when they are doing well, i.e. when their share price would be expected to outperform just as much without the scrip issue.

(b) A 'heavy' share price in the market, say over £2, tends to make the shares harder to trade and artificially depresses the price. Scrip issues can be used to scale the price down.

(c) A scrip issue, being 'paid for' out of reserves, enables retained profits and/or the increased value of assets to be reflected by an increased share capital.

(d) The rate of dividends, expressed as a percentage of an unrealistically small share capital, can look excessive.

(e) An issued share capital of at least £1m is needed for Trustee status.

The last argument appears to be the only factual one in favour of scrip issues; the remainder are psychological, although only a sound and flourishing company is likely to be able to make substantial scrip issues every few years. HALMA's record illustrates this well: the company also made a 1-for-3 scrip issue in 1985, a 1-for-2 scrip issue in 1987 and 1989, and 1-for-3 scrip issues in 1991, 1993 and 1995. Thus an investor who purchased 1,000 Halma shares in 1984 would now have a holding of 9,473 ordinary shares.

The arguments against scrip issues are firstly the administrative costs incurred and secondly the increased risk of the share price subsequently falling close to or below par, thus precluding a rights issue. The cost is small, but reducing the market price can cause serious embarrassment if the company wants, at a later date, to make a rights issue only to find that its share price is too low to do so.

Share splits

Where a company feels its share price is 'heavy' but does not want to capitalise reserves – i.e. it does not want to make a scrip issue – it can split its shares into shares with a smaller par value. For example, in 1998 MITIE GROUP split its 10p shares, which were standing at around 240p at the time, into 5p shares, and the share price adjusted to around 120p.

Scrip (stock) dividends

The company allows shareholders to elect to receive new shares, i.e. a *scrip dividend*, in lieu of a cash dividend.

Each shareholder is sent a form of election in advance of each dividend payment, giving them the opportunity to opt for a scrip dividend, although some companies also pay a nominal cash dividend at least once each year in order to preserve 'wider range' investment status under the Trustee Investment Act 1961. The number of shares is calculated to give the same value as the net dividend payable, and counts as income, so there is no tax advantage, and a positive disadvantage for 'gross' funds (pension funds and charities, which pay no tax).

Scrip dividends are popular with private shareholders, because they can add to their holding at middle market price without paying stockbrokers' commission.

From the company's point of view, it is able to raise additional equity capital from its existing shareholders without the expense of a rights issue.

Further information on shares

Details of shares and debentures issued during the year should be given in a note to the balance sheet. The terms for redemption of all redeemable shares and the details of all outstanding rights to acquire shares either by subscription or conversion should also be given.

In addition, FRS 4 requires a brief summary of the rights of each class of share, other than ordinary shares, to be given, including: (i) the rights to dividends; (ii) date at which redeemable, and amount payable on redemption; (iii) priority and amount receivable on a winding up; (iv) voting rights.

This information will usually make it clear why a class of share has been classified as equity or non-equity, but additional information should be given, if necessary. Where rights vary according to circumstances, these circumstances and the variation should be described (FRS 4, paras. 56–57).

Company purchasing its own shares

Under Sections 162 to 169 of the Companies Act 1985, a company may purchase its own shares, providing it doesn't buy in all its non-redeemable shares. General authority may be given for market purchases up to a maximum number of shares, within a given price range and within a maximum of 18 months from the date the resolution is passed.

Most companies pass a resolution each year at their AGM giving the directors authority, until the next AGM, to purchase the company's shares, normally up to a maximum of 10% of the shares issued at up to 5% above the middle market price.

Where a company wishes to purchase shares outside the market, the transaction must be authorised in advance by a special resolution. For example in December 1992 FROGMORE ESTATES called an EGM (Extraordinary General Meeting) to authorise the purchase of 13.1% of its issued share capital from another property company at a discount of around 7% to the market price. The EGM was required firstly because the purchase was by private treaty, i.e. 'off-market', and secondly because the purchase was of more than 10% of its issued share capital, the maximum of the general authority approved at the previous AGM.

To protect investors, Chapter 15 of the UK Listing Authority's 'Purple Book' lays down various rules about the purchase of own securities.

Several property companies, including FROGMORE, took advantage of the 1985 Act to purchase their ordinary shares at a price below asset value, thus increasing the asset value of the remaining shares. More recently there has been a spate of companies falling over themselves to return 'spare cash' to their shareholders. This can be done

(a) by a company buying its own shares. Shares bought in have, by law, to be cancelled, or
(b) by, in effect, giving cash back to shareholders. In order to avoid the returned cash being treated as a distribution for tax purposes,

the return is achieved by a bonus issue of B shares, which are then redeemed by the company, or
(c) by a combination of (a) and (b), which is what W.H. SMITH did:

W.H. SMITH GROUP *Circular to shareholders April 1998*

Proposed Return of Capital to Shareholders
On 30 March 1998 the Company announced that it had successfully completed the sale of Waterstone's [a chain of bookshops] for £300m and that it proposed to return approximately £250m of capital to shareholders.

Approximately £153m will be returned by way of a bonus issue of one B share for each Existing Ordinary Share. The Company will subsequently offer to redeem the B shares. The balance of the £250m is intended to be returned to Shareholders by way of a rolling programme of on-market purchases.

Reduction of share capital
Under Section 135 of the Companies Act 1985 a company may, with court approval, reduce its share capital in any way and, in particular, may

(a) reduce or extinguish liability on share capital not fully paid up;
(b) cancel any paid-up share capital which is lost or unrepresented by available assets; and
(c) repay any paid-up share capital in excess of its requirements.

Where the net assets no longer exceed the paid-up value of the issued share capital, the reserves will appear negative in the balance sheet.

Take, for example, a company which has 1 million £1 ordinary shares in issue and negative reserves of £831,000. It might, with court approval, reduce its capital to $1^1/_2$ million 25p shares and eliminate share premium account to remove the accumulated losses (see Example 5.1).

Example 5.1 Effect of share capital reduction on the balance sheet

	Before reduction £000	After reduction £000
Issued share capital	1,000	375
Share premium account	206	–
Other reserves	(831)	–
Shareholders' funds	375	375

Arrangements and reconstructions

A company may make an arrangement with its creditors or shareholders. One possibility is a reorganisation of the company's share capital by consolidation of different classes and/or division into different classes, under Section 425 of the Companies Act 1985.

A meeting has to be called for each class of creditor or shareholder concerned, at which a resolution to make the arrangement requires at least three-fourths by value of those present and voting to vote in favour; after subsequent sanction by the court, the arrangement is then registered with the Registrar of Companies and becomes binding on all creditors and shareholders concerned.

Documentation in connection with arrangements and reconstructions is generally both lengthy and complex but it often provides 'new' material, i.e. information which was never reported in the accounts. But most shareholders are so disappointed by the outcome of their original investment that they devote neither the time nor the trouble to study the information and so, possibly, to learn by the mistake.

RESERVES

Where reserves come from

Reserves can arise in several ways:

(a) by the accumulation of profits, either by retained profits from the profit and loss account or from the sale of assets;
(b) by the issue of shares at a premium, i.e. at more than their nominal value: the issue can be either for cash or as consideration (payment) in an acquisition;
(c) by the issue of warrants;
(d) by upward revaluation of assets (see pages 56–8);
(e) by the acquisition of assets at below their balance sheet value.

They can be reduced by losses, share issue and share redemption expenses, revaluation deficits and the writing off of goodwill. In addition, foreign currency translation differences are taken direct to reserves (see Chapter 23).

The balance sheet formats in Schedule 4 of the Companies Act 1985 require reserves to be shown in three main subdivisions:

Share premium account,
Revaluation reserve, and
Other reserves.

Reserves should not include provision for deferred taxation, or any other provision.

Capital and revenue reserves

Under Section 264 (2) of the Companies Act 1985, a company's *undistributable reserves* are:

(a) the share premium account;
(b) the capital redemption reserve;
(c) unrealised profits (i.e. the revaluation reserve);
(d) any other reserve that a company is prohibited from distributing by its memorandum or articles.

Share premium account

Reference: Companies Act 1985, s. 130.

When shares are issued at a premium over their nominal value, the premium element must, by law, be credited to the share premium account, unless the rules of merger accounting apply (see page 172).

The share premium account has to be shown separately on the balance sheet and no part may be paid out to shareholders except on liquidation or under a capital reduction scheme authorised by the court.

It is permissible, however:

(a) to capitalise the share premium account to pay up unissued shares for distribution to shareholders as a scrip issue (otherwise known as a bonus or capitalisation issue), for instance:

	£
Ordinary share capital	100,000
Share premium account	85,000
Company makes 1-for-2 scrip issue:	
Ordinary share capital	150,000
Share premium account	35,000

(b) to charge to the share premium account
(i) the preliminary expenses of forming a company,
(ii) the expenses and commissions incurred in any issue of shares.

Revaluation reserve

The surplus (or shortfall) on the revaluation of assets should be credited (or debited) to a separate reserve, the revaluation reserve. The amount of the revaluation reserve shall be shown 'under a separate sub-heading in the position given for the item "revaluation reserve" in the balance sheet formats, *but need not be shown under that name*' (our italics; CA 1985, Sch. 4, para. 34.)

Capital redemption reserve

Shares may only be redeemed or purchased by the company out of distributable profits or out of the proceeds of a new issue of shares. Where redemption or purchase is out of distributable profits, an amount equal to the amount by which the company's issued share capital is diminished must, by law, be transferred to a reserve, called the capital redemption reserve. This reserve is shown separately under Other reserves. The idea behind the law is to prevent a company's overall share capital plus non-distributable reserves from being reduced when share capital is repaid: the reserve can never be distributed except upon liquidation or in a capital reduction scheme, but it can be capitalised by a bonus issue, as in Example 5.2.

Example 5.2 Capital redemption reserve

1. Initial position:

Issued share capital	£
30,000 £1 Redeemable preference shares	30,000
100,000 £1 Ordinary shares	100,000
	130,000
Reserves	
Revenue reserve (retained profits)	75,000

2. Company then uses retained profits to redeem all the preference shares:

Issued share capital	£
100,000 £1 Ordinary shares	100,000
	100,000
Reserves	
Capital redemption reserve	30,000
Revenue reserve (retained profits)	45,000

3. Company then decides to make a 3-for-10 scrip issue, which brings the issued share capital back to £130,000.

Issued share capital	£
130,000 £1 Ordinary shares	130,000
	130,000
Reserves	
Revenue reserve (retained profits)	45,000

Chapter 6

LOAN CAPITAL

The advantages of borrowing

If a company confidently expects that its return on capital (i.e. the trading profit expressed as a percentage of the capital the company employs) will exceed the cost of borrowing, then borrowing will increase the profit attributable to the ordinary shareholders. There are, however, various limitations on the amount a company can borrow, which we will discuss later in this chapter, and borrowing also increases risk.

The risk of borrowing

The risk of borrowing is twofold: firstly the interest on most borrowings has to be paid promptly when due (unlike dividends on shares, which can be deferred or omitted altogether) and secondly most borrowings have to be repaid by a certain date (unlike most share capital, which is only repayable on liquidation).

In a poor year, interest charges can drastically reduce the pre-tax profits of a heavily borrowing company. Take, for example, two companies that are identical except that one, Company A, is financed entirely by shareholders while the other, Company B, is financed half by shareholders and half by borrowing, which bears a rate of interest of 10% per annum.

The table in Example 6.1 on the next page shows the profitability of the two companies with varying rates of return on capital employed: in an average year Company B earns 15% on money borrowed at 10%, and so gains 5% on £2,000,000, adding £100,000 to pre-tax profits. This extra profit, after tax, adds 3.5p to the earnings attributable to each of the 2,000,000 shares that Company B has issued, making the earnings per share 14.0p compared with 10.5p for Company A.

In a good year the advantage of borrowing will enhance Company B's earnings per share even more (28p compared with 17.5p for Company A) but in a poor year, as our table shows, all the trading profit is used servicing the borrowings of Company B, while Company A still manages to earn £140,000 after tax for its shareholders.

The point at which the two companies do equally well as far as their shareholders are concerned is shown in the graph below. Their earnings per share are both 6.7p when the return on capital employed is 10% per annum; as one would expect, borrowing at 10% to earn 10% neither adds to nor detracts from Company B's profits. As the graph also shows, borrowing makes a company's profits more volatile and the risk of borrowing is further increased when money is borrowed at a variable rate of interest (e.g. on overdraft). If interest rates had risen above 10% in our example's 'poor year', Company B would have actually made a loss.

We will come back to the effects of borrowing later in this chapter, but let us now look in detail at various types of borrowing.

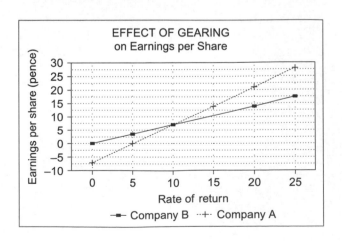

Example 6.1 Financing by share capital and by borrowing

	Company A				**Company B**		
Issued equity (£1 shares)	£4,000,000				£2,000,000		
Borrowings (10% interest)	Nil				£2,000,000		
	Good year	*Average year*	*Poor year*		*Good year*	*Average year*	*Poor year*
Rate of return	25%	15%	5%		25%	15%	5%
	£000	£000	£000		£000	£000	£000
Trading profit	1,000	600	200		1,000	600	200
Interest	–	–	–		200	200	200
Pre-tax profit	1,000	600	200		800	400	0
Taxation (30%)	300	180	60		240	120	0
Profit after tax	700	420	140		560	280	0
Earnings per share	17.5p	10.5p	3.5p		28.0p	14.0p	0p

Types of borrowing

There are many ways in which a company can borrow money, the main characteristics of different types of debt being:

(a) the length of time for which the money is borrowed;
(b) the rate of interest paid;
(c) the security offered to the lender by way of charges on the assets of the company;
(d) the negotiability of the debt instrument (i.e. does the lender receive a piece of paper which he can sell if he wishes to disinvest before the date of repayment?);
(e) the flexibility to the company and to the lender in the timing of borrowing and repayment;
(f) any deferred equity option given to the lender.

A company's borrowings fall broadly into three categories:

1. Debentures and unsecured loan stock, issued on the UK market, and bonds, issued on the Eurobond and other markets. These can be held by the general public, and can be bought and sold in the same way as shares.
2. Loans from banks and other financial institutions.
3. Bank overdrafts (described in Chapter 13).

Categories 1 and 2 are shown separately in the balance sheet, with a note describing the terms on which each loan is repayable and the rate of interest, dividing them into secured and unsecured loans.

An analysis of the maturity of debt should be given, showing amounts falling due:

(a) in one year or less, or on demand;
(b) between one and two years;
(c) between two and five years; and
(d) in five years or more.

 A loan which is soon due for repayment may significantly weaken a company's position

This can be a very serious threat to a company that is already short of funds if it is likely to have any difficulty refinancing the loan.

Security given to the lender

When a company wishes to issue loan capital it can offer the lender some specific security on the loan. If it does so, the loan is called a debenture (£100 units) or debenture stock (usually units of £1); if not it is unsecured loan stock (ULS), and these are the two main types of loan capital raised in the UK from the general public (often referred to as corporate bonds).

Debentures

Debentures can be secured by fixed and/or floating charges described below, the most common type of debenture being one that is secured on specific land or buildings, sometimes called a mortgage debenture.

Fixed charge

A fixed charge is similar to a mortgage on a house. The company enters into a debenture deed which places a charge on specific identifiable assets. This gives the debenture holder a legal interest in the assets concerned as security for the loan, and the company cannot then dispose of them unless the debenture holder releases the charge (which he is unlikely to do unless offered some equally good alternative security). If the company defaults or falls into arrears on interest payments or capital repayments, the debenture holder can either

(a) appoint a receiver to receive any income from the assets (e.g. rents) or

(b) foreclose, i.e. take possession and sell the assets, using the proceeds of the sale to repay the debenture holders in full; any surplus remaining is then paid to the company, but if the proceeds of selling the assets charged are insufficient to repay the debenture holders in full, the debenture holders then rank equally with unsecured creditors for the shortfall.

Floating charge

This is a general charge on the assets of a company. But the debenture holder has no legal interest in the assets unless and until an event specified in the debenture deed occurs; for example, if the company goes into liquidation or ceases trading, or falls behind with interest payments or capital repayments, or exceeds specified borrowing limits. In the event of default the debenture holder can then appoint a Receiver, who takes physical possession of the assets of the company. The Receiver can also be appointed as the Manager or a separate Manager can be appointed to continue running the company, or the Receiver can sell off the assets; the former course is adopted if possible, because a company can normally be sold as a going concern for more than the break-up value.

The ranking of ULS and bonds

In a liquidation the holders of unsecured loan stock and bonds rank equally with other unsecured creditors, that is after debenture holders and preferential creditors (tax, rates and certain obligations to employees). In practice trade creditors often restrict a company to 'cash with order' terms if they see it running into difficulties, and to that extent ULS and bonds tend to rank behind suppliers.

Typical characteristics of debentures and ULS

Interest

Most debentures, ULS and bonds carry a fixed annual rate of interest (known loosely as the 'coupon') which is payable (normally half-yearly) regardless of the company's profitability. Interest is deductible before the company is assessed for tax, i.e. it is an allowable expense for tax purposes, and therefore costs the company less than the same amount paid out in dividends on shares.

Redemption

Each issue is normally for a given term, and is repayable at the end of the term (at the redemption date) or, where there is a redemption period (e.g.

2002/04), it is repayable when the company chooses within that period. A few irredeemable stocks do exist, but they are rare, except in the case of water companies.

Liquidation

In the event of liquidation, debenture holders are entitled to repayment in full from the proceeds of disposal of the charged assets. Then the ULS and bond holders and other unsecured creditors, and the fixed charge debenture holders if not already fully satisfied, rank equally after preferential creditors, and have to be repaid before the shareholders are entitled to anything.

The trust deed

Where a debenture, loan stock or bond is to be issued to more than a very small number of holders, and particularly when it is going to be listed on the Stock Exchange, a trustee or trustees are appointed to represent the holders collectively, and the company enters into a trust deed rather than a debenture deed.

For listing, the Stock Exchange also requires that at least one trustee must be a trust corporation which has no interest in or relation to the company which might conflict with the position of the trustee. A large insurance company or the specialist LAW DEBENTURE CORPORATION is often appointed as trustee.

The deed contains all the details of the issue, except the issue price, including:

(a) details of fixed and floating charges, together with provision for substitution (securing further assets to replace secured assets which the company may subsequently wish to dispose of during the term of the loan). Provision may also be made for topping up (securing further assets if the value of secured assets falls below a given limit);

(b) redemption price and redemption date or period, and details of any sinking fund;

(c) conditions under which the company may repurchase in the market, by tender and from individual holders;

(d) redemption price in the event of liquidation;

(e) conditions for further pari passu (equal ranking) issues, restrictions on prior borrowings and, for ULS and bonds, overall borrowing limits;

(f) minimum transferable unit;

(g) powers to approve modifications to the terms and conditions.

The trust deed may also include restrictive clauses:

(h) to prevent the nature of the company's business being changed; this is known as a 'Tickler' clause, after the celebrated case of the jam manufacturer who was taken to court by the holders of an unsecured loan stock;

(i) to prevent major disposals of the company's assets – a 'disposals' clause;

(j) to restrict the transfer of assets between charging subsidiaries (those within the charging group, i.e. included in the charge on assets) and other subsidiaries – sometimes known as a 'ring fence' clause.

Accounting for finance costs

There are three elements to finance costs. The first is the interest payable each year. The second and third are the issue expenses and the difference between the issue price and the amount payable on redemption, i.e. the premium or discount on issue if redeemable at par. These two are amortised and charged against profits at a constant rate over the life of the debt instrument.

So the carrying amount, the amount at which the debt instrument is shown in the balance sheet at any time, starts off as the net proceeds of the issue and ends up at the redemption date as the amount payable on redemption.

Repurchase of debt

Where the cost of repurchase or early settlement of debt differs from the carrying amount in the balance sheet, the difference is taken to the profit and loss account in the accounting period of repurchase or early settlement.

Deep discount issues

Some companies issue loan capital at a substantial discount to par value in order to reduce the coupon, i.e. to reduce the amount of interest they have to pay during the life of the security concerned. The investor is compensated for receiving less interest by getting back appreciably more than he or she paid when the security is redeemed.

For tax purposes, a *deep discount security* is one

(a) where the discount on issue represents more than 15% of the capital amount payable on redemption, or

(b) where the discount is 15% or less but exceeds half the number of complete years between issue and redemption.

The income element is calculated as the percentage rate at which the issue price would have to grow on a compound basis over each income period to equal the redemption price at the date of redemption. The income element is treated as income of the holder and as a deductible expense of the issuer, as CGU shows in its accounting policies.

CGU *Extract from accounting policies*

Debenture loans

Borrowings issued at a discount are included in the balance sheets at their proceeds, net of expenses, together with amortised discount to the balance sheet date. The discount, amortised on a compound basis, and expenses are charged to loan interest in the profit and loss account over the term of the borrowing.

Sinking funds

Some debenture and loan stock issues make provision for part or all of the stock to be redeemed gradually over a period of time by means of a sinking fund, e.g. LAND SECURITIES' mortgage debentures.

The normal method for a sinking fund to redeem stock is by annual or six-monthly drawings (lotteries of stock certificate numbers), with the company in some cases having the option of purchasing stock in the market if it can do so at or below the drawing price. The company may also be allowed to invite holders to tender stock for redemption.

There are three types of sinking fund:

1. Original concept – no early redemptions

The sinking fund or redemption reserve fund, as originally conceived, was a fund into which a company put a given sum each year, the money being invested in government or other safe fixed interest securities rather than being used to make early redemptions. The sums, together with interest earned, went on accumulating in the balance sheet year by year until the redemption date. This method is now rarely used.

2. Non-cumulative

Each year in which the sinking fund is in operation the company normally sets aside enough cash to redeem a fixed amount of stock, expressed as a given percentage of the total issue, and uses it to redeem stock on or by the date of the second interest payment (see Example 6.2).

Example 6.2 Non-cumulative sinking fund

A 25-year stock with a 2% sinking fund starting at the end of the 5th year would be redeemed at the rate of 2% per annum at the end of years 5 to 24, leaving 60% of the stock to be redeemed at redemption date.

Provided redemptions each year are by drawings at par, the average life of a stock can be calculated by working out the average life of the stock redeemed by the sinking fund, in this case $14\frac{1}{2}$ years, and then weighting it by the percentage redeemed by the sinking fund, in this case 40%:

$$\text{Average life} = \frac{(14.5 \times 40\%) + (25 \times 60\%)}{100\%}$$

Example 6.3 Cumulative sinking fund

If our previous example had been a £10m issue of a 25-year stock with a 10% coupon and a cumulative sinking fund starting at the end of year 5, and with all redemptions made by drawings at par, the annual redemptions would be

End of year	Fixed amount of cash	Variable amount (interest saved)	Stock redeemed in year	Total stock redeemed	Stock remaining
	£	£	£	£	£
4	Nil	Nil	Nil	Nil	10,000,000
5	200,000	Nil	200,000	200,000	9,800,000
6	200,000	20,000	220,000	420,000	9,580,000
7	200,000	42,000	242,000	662,000	9,338,000
8	200,000	66,200	266,200	928,200	9,071,800

and so on. The average life can be calculated by time-weighting each year's redemption, e.g. 200,000 × 5 years plus 220,000 × 6 years, etc. ÷ 10,000,000. However, if redemptions are made by purchases in the market or by tender at below the redemption price, the amount redeemed will be greater, the amount of interest subsequently saved will be larger and the whole process of redemption will accelerate.

3. Cumulative

In a cumulative sinking fund the cash used for redemption each year is variable and normally consists of a fixed amount of cash plus the amount of interest saved by prior redemption (see Example 6.3 above).

Yields

The yield on an irredeemable security is the gross amount of income received per annum divided by the market price of the security. Redeemable securities have two yields, their running yield and their gross redemption yield.

Running yield

The running yield is the same as the yield on an irredeemable security: it measures income and is concerned purely with the annual gross interest and the price of the stock; for instance, an 8% unsecured loan stock issued at £98% will yield 8% ÷ 0.98 = 8.16% at the issue price, or a $4\frac{1}{2}$% debenture purchased at £50% will give the purchaser a yield of 9%, ignoring purchase expenses.

Redemption yield

The gross redemption yield is rather more complicated, as it measures 'total return'; i.e. it takes into account both the stream of income and any capital gain (or loss) on redemption. It is not just the sum of the running yield and the capital gain per annum, but is obtained by discounting the future interest payments and the redemption value at a rate that makes their combined *present value* equal to the current price of the stock. (The concept of discounting to obtain present value is explained in Appendix 2.) The rate required to do this is the gross redemption yield (see Example 6.4).

Typical gross redemption yields for a well secured debenture are $\frac{3}{4}$% to $1\frac{1}{2}$% above the yield on the equivalent gilt-edged security (i.e. a UK government stock of similar life and coupon), and 1% up to 5% or more for ULS, depending very much on the quality of the company and the amount of prior borrowings (borrowings that would rank ahead in a liquidation).

Example 6.4 Gross redemption yield

A 6% debenture due for redemption at £105% in four years' time is standing in the market at £90. Interest is payable in the normal manner, half-yearly in arrears (at the end of each six months). The present value of the stock is the sum of the present values of the eight future six-monthly interest payments discounted at $(1 + i)$ per half-year (where i expressed as a decimal = gross redemption yield).

$$\frac{3}{(1 + i)^{0.5}} + \frac{3}{(1 + i)^{1.0}} + \ldots + \frac{3}{(1 + i)^{4.0}}$$

plus the present value of the sum received on redemption in four years' time:

$$\frac{105}{(1 + i)}$$

Solving for i by trial and error:

Value of i	Present value of income	Present value of redemption	Total
10% =	19.48 +	71.72	= £91.20
11% =	19.09 +	69.15	= £88.24

Inspection suggests that the gross redemption yield on a market price of £90 is about $10\frac{1}{2}$%, and a more accurate figure can be obtained by further manual calculation or by computer. Alternatively, the yield can be obtained from Bond Tables.

Net redemption yields (i.e. the yields after tax) vary with the individual holder's rate of Income Tax payable on the stream of interest payments and the rate of tax on any capital gain on redemption.

Redemption date
When a stock has a final redemption period, e.g. 1999/2004, it is assumed in computing redemption yields that the company will choose the earliest date for redemption, 1999, if the stock is currently standing above par, otherwise the latest date, 2004. When there is a sinking fund which allows redemptions only by drawings, the average life can be calculated accurately and should therefore be used as the number of years to redemption in calculating redemption yields. However, if the company is allowed to redeem by purchase in the market or by inviting tenders, the stockholder can no longer be sure that early drawings at par will take place, and the average life is therefore ignored.

Bonds
A bond is the generic name given to loan capital raised in the Eurobond market and in the US and other domestic markets. Issues in the Eurobond market may be denominated in sterling or in a foreign currency, and are normally of between 7 and 10 years' duration.

The Eurobond market began with the issue of Eurodollar bonds – US$ denominated securities issued outside the United States. It now encompasses offshore issues in a variety of currencies, but it is still mainly a US$ market. An increasing number of UK companies make use of this market, e.g. PEARSON:

PEARSON *Note to the 1999 accounts*

Borrowing by instrument

Unsecured (£ million)	1999	1998
10.75% Sterling Bonds 2002	100	100
9.5% Sterling Bonds 2004	120	117
4.625% Euro Bonds	345	–
10.5% Sterling Bonds 2008	100	100
7% Sterling Bonds 2014	251	–
...		

Notes and loan notes
These are promissory notes issued to one or a small number of other companies or individuals, and are normally of between 1 and 10 years' maturity on issue. They are often issued to individuals in an acquisition in lieu of cash to defer the individuals' liability to Capital Gains Tax.

Commercial paper (CP)
This is a short-term loan vehicle between the borrower (the issuer) and the purchaser (the investor);

the issuer can sell direct to the investor or use banks as intermediaries.

Commercial paper takes the form of negotiable unsecured promissory notes. In the sterling CP market notes have a maximum maturity on issue of 1 year and a minimum of 7 days; they are usually for $£^1/_2$m or £1m. Although short-term, CP is often bought as part of a company's medium-term borrowing programme, backed by medium-term banking facilities, e.g. RIO TINTO:

RIO TINTO *Note on medium and long-term borrowings*

	1999 US$m
Commercial paper	
US commercial paper	1,866
Canadian commercial paper	267
Australian commercial paper	133
	2,266

In accordance with FRS 4, all commercial paper is classified as short-term borrowings though US$1,200 million backed by medium-term facilities. Under US and Australian GAAP these amounts would be grouped within non-current borrowings.

We agree with the US and Australian view. The notes are bearer securities issued at a discount to allow for interest, i.e. there is no separate payment of interest.

Rates are very competitive for companies with good credit ratings; commercial paper is easy to administer and costs are low.

By far the largest CP market is in the United States, where about $550 billion is outstanding.

The amount a company can borrow
The amount a company can borrow may be limited by the following:

(a) *its borrowing powers*. The directors' borrowing powers are normally limited by a company's Articles of Association, and cannot be altered except with the approval of shareholders at a general meeting. Borrowing powers are usually expressed as a multiple of shareholders' funds (issued share capital plus reserves, excluding intangible assets such as goodwill, although some companies, e.g. CADBURY SCHWEPPES, now include purchased goodwill in defining the directors' borrowing powers);

(b) *restrictions imposed by existing borrowings*. The terms of the trust deeds of existing loan capital may restrict or preclude the company from further borrowing. In particular the terms of an unsecured loan stock may include a clause preventing the company from issuing loans that rank ahead of the stock concerned, and unduly

Example 6.5 Capital cover

Capital	Amount	Cumulative total	Simple cover	Rolled-up cover
	£000	£000		
6% Debenture	15,000	15,000	4.0	4.0
8% ULS	10,000			
10% ULS	5,000	30,000	3.0	2.0
Ordinary shares	12,000			
Reserves (less goodwill)	18,000	60,000		
Total capital		60,000		

Example 6.6 Income cover

A company has £5.76m of earnings before interest and tax, and the following loan capital, with the ULS and the CULS ranking equally:

Nominal value of issue	Annual interest	Cumulative interest	Times covered	Priority percentage
£12m of 6% Debenture	£0.72m	£0.72m	8.0	0–12$\frac{1}{2}$%
£10m of 8% ULS	£0.80m			
£8m of 5% CULS	£0.40m	£1.92m	3.0	12$\frac{1}{2}$–33$\frac{1}{3}$%

restrictive clauses are often the reasons for companies redeeming loan capital in advance of the normal redemption date;

(c) the lender's requirement for *capital and income covers*;

(d) *the lender's general opinion* of the company and its overall borrowing position.

Capital and income covers

These are two standard measures that the intending purchaser of a debenture or loan stock may use to assess the security of his or her investment.

The *capital* or asset cover can be calculated in two ways, on a simple basis or on a 'rolled-up' basis.

Using the simple basis, the cover is the total capital less all prior-ranking stocks, divided by the issued amount of the stock in question. Using the 'rolled-up' basis, the cover is the total capital divided by the stock in question plus all prior-ranking stocks.

As Example 6.5, above, shows, the two equal-ranking ULS issues are three times covered on a simple basis (£60m total capital less £15m prior-ranking debenture, divided by the total of £15m ULS), but only twice covered on a rolled-up basis. The more conservative rolled-up basis is normally used for assessing capital covers.

For a floating charge debenture a rolled-up capital cover of at least 3 or 4 is expected by the lender, and 2$\frac{1}{2}$ times is the normal minimum for an unsecured loan stock, but both depend on the quality of the assets, i.e. the likely realisable value of the assets on the open market in the event of a liquidation.

The *income cover* is normally worked out on a rolled-up rather than a simple basis: i.e. it is the number of times the interest on a stock plus the interest on any prior-ranking stocks could be paid out of profits before interest and tax. This cover can also be expressed as a priority percentage, showing the percentile ranking of a stock's interest, with earnings before interest and tax representing 100% (see Example 6.6 above).

Convertible loan capital

Convertible loan capital, which is usually convertible unsecured loan stock (CULS) or convertible bonds rather than convertible debentures, entitles the holder to convert into ordinary shares of the company if he or she so wishes (see also convertible preference shares, Chapter 5).

The coupon on a convertible is usually much lower than the coupon needed for the issue of a straight unsecured loan stock with no conversion rights. This is because a convertible is normally regarded by the market as deferred equity, valued on the basis of the market value of the shares received on conversion plus the additional income enjoyed before conversion (the coupon on issue being higher than the yield on the ordinary shares).

Because convertibles are a form of deferred equity, listed companies can issue them without shareholders' prior approval only as a rights issue or as part or all of the consideration in an acquisition. In a takeover situation the bidder can use a suitably pitched convertible to provide the shareholders of the company being acquired with a higher initial income than they would receive from an equivalent offer of the bidder's ordinary shares. This is particularly useful when a bidder with low-yielding shares wants to avoid the shareholders of the company he wishes to acquire suffering a fall in income if they accept his offer.

CULS is attractive to investors seeking higher income, for example to an income unit trust, and it also provides greater security than ordinary shares for both income and capital. From a company's point of view, CULS is cheaper to service than convertible preference shares, as the interest on the former is deducted in the assessment of Corporation Tax, but this advantage has been considerably eroded by the reduction in the rate of Corporation Tax. Most companies now prefer to issue convertible preference shares rather than CULS in order to reduce rather than increase their gearing.

Terms of a convertible loan

The holder has the option of converting into ordinary shares during a given period in the life of the loan stock or bond (the conversion period), at a given conversion price per share, expressed as so many shares per £100 of stock, or as so much nominal stock per ordinary share (see Example 6.7).

Example 6.7 Convertible loan: GREAT PORTLAND ESTATES

In January 1988 GREAT PORTLAND ESTATES made a rights issue of a $9^1/2\%$ convertible loan stock 2002 at par, on the basis of £1 nominal of CULS for every 4 ordinary 50p shares held. The stock, when issued, was convertible into 30.303 ordinary shares per £100 stock (equivalent to a price of 330p per share when issued at par) in the August of any year between 1992 and 2002 inclusive; these conversion terms will be adjusted for any scrip issues to the ordinary shareholders in the meantime. The terms were subsequently adjusted twice, to give a conversion price of 273p.

Any rights issues to ordinary shareholders will *either* be made to the holders of the convertible as if they had been converted, *or* an adjustment will be made to the conversion terms (most CULSs specify only one method).

In the event of a bid the company will endeavour to ensure that a like offer is made to the CULS holders as if they had converted; they would, however, lose any income advantage they enjoyed over the ordinary shareholders. This is a risk you have to take if you buy the CULS rather than the ordinary shares.

If more than 75% of the stock is converted, GREAT PORTLAND has the right to force remaining stockholders to convert or redeem straight away; this is a fairly standard condition, enabling the company to clear a convertible off its balance sheet once most of it has been converted. Stock that remains unconverted at the end of the conversion period will be redeemed by GREAT PORTLAND at par on 1 December 2002.

The period between issue and the first date for conversion is sometimes called the 'rest period', and the period from the last date for conversion to the final redemption date the 'stub'. Diagrammatically the GREAT PORTLAND convertible can be shown as:

		Stub ↓
Rest period	Conversion period	
1988	1992	2002

A rest period of two or three years is normal, and most conversion periods run for at least four or five years. Some convertibles have a stub of several years, which is more prudent because if convertible holders decide not to exercise their conversion rights the company concerned is probably not doing very well and would not want to be faced with having to redeem the stock almost as soon as the conversion rights lapsed.

To protect investors the terms of some convertible debt (and some convertible preference shares) include what is known as *bid protection*, a fairly recent innovation. This protection can be either an enhancement of the conversion terms, or compensation based on the average premium over the preceding year, in the event of a takeover.

Another piece of convertible jargon is the *conversion premium*. This is the premium one pays by buying the ordinary shares via the convertible rather than buying them direct. For example, if the GREAT PORTLAND convertible in Example 6.7 was standing at 120% (per £100 nominal) and the ordinary shares were standing at 300p, the cost of getting into the ordinary shares through the convertible would be £120 ÷ 36.63 (£30.303 adjusted for subsequent scrip issues) = 327.6p, a conversion premium of just over 9%.

A good indication of the likely market price of a convertible can be obtained by discounting the future income advantage to present value and adding it to the market value of the underlying equity. One caveat to this method is that if the price of the ordinary shares is very depressed, the price of the convertible in the market can become mainly dependent on its value as a fixed-interest security, particularly if the conversion period has not long to run.

Convertibles with 'put' options

In the euphoria before the market fall in October 1987, several companies were so confident that their share price was going on up for ever that they agreed to the innovation suggested by fee-hungry US investment banks to include a 'put' option in the terms of their convertibles. This 'put' option gave the convertible bond holders the option to redeem after four or five years at a substantial premium, which was calculated to give a specified gross redemption yield.

From an investor's point of view, an early 'put' option is a 'heads I win, tails I can't lose' situation (unless the company goes bust). But from a company's point of view it is asking for trouble: if the ordinary share price is depressed when the date for exercising the 'put' option approaches, it is unlikely to be a good time for the company to have to redeem the convertible.

In addition, the market may become worried about whether the company has the financial resources to meet the repayment; this may further depress the share price, increasing the likelihood of investors exercising their 'put' options, e.g. the fashion retailer NEXT.

Next had one £50m and one £100m convertible with conversion prices of 286p and 430p respectively, and 'put' options to redeem in 1992. Next's share price peaked in 1987 at 378p, but fell to under 100p in 1989 as the company was hit by the recession and moved into loss. By this time the market became anxious about whether Next could fund redemption, and the share price tumbled to $6^1/_2$p at one point.

Next did survive, but only by selling off its mail order subsidiary Grattan in 1991 to pay for the 'put' options which were, of course, exercised. As the result of Next and several other companies burning their fingers badly, the drawbacks of 'put' options are now well appreciated, and companies issuing convertibles have stopped giving them. However, they may appear again in the euphoria of the next roaring bull market; if they do – beware.

Warrants

A warrant gives the holder the right to subscribe at a fixed price for shares in a company at some future date. Where a company is reluctant to raise loan capital, e.g. when very high long-term interest rates prevail, or investors are reluctant to commit themselves to purely fixed-interest securities, loan capital can be raised with a lower coupon by attaching warrants to issues of stock.

Warrants issued in this way are normally detachable and exercisable as soon as the stock to which they are attached is fully paid, and in some issues stock can be surrendered at its nominal value as an alternative to cash payment when the warrants are exercised.

For accounting purposes, when a debt instrument is issued with warrants attached, the proceeds of the issue should be allocated between the debt and the warrants (FRS 4, para. 22).

In a takeover situation, warrants can provide a more flexible way for the bidder to give loan stock an equity interest than convertibles, because the number of warrants, sometimes called the equity 'kicker', can be varied as the company wishes, while the quantity of ordinary shares to which convertible holders are entitled is defined within a narrow range by the limit the market will accept on the conversion premium.

On the other hand, a drawback to warrants is that they will seldom be exercised until close to the final exercise date, because they are bought by investors who want the gearing they provide, so the future flow of money into the company's equity is more chancy than with a convertible.

Mezzanine finance

Mezzanine finance is the term used to describe a form of finance that lies between straight debt and share capital. It is used in situations, e.g. management buyouts (MBOs) and institutional purchases, where the amount of debt that can be raised is limited, and the amount of cash available to subscribe for shares is insufficient to make up the total required.

It is usually in the form of a loan that ranks after the normal debt (the 'senior' debt) and, because of the higher risk, bears a higher rate of interest and either carries an option to convert part of the loan into equity or has a warrant to subscribe for equity.

For example in BBA's sale of its automotive products businesses in the spring of 1995, the purchase by the new company AUTOMOTIVE PRODUCTS GROUP LTD. was arranged by leading venture capital company CINVEN, financed as follows:

AUTOMOTIVE PRODUCTS GROUP *Financing of institutional purchase*

	£000	
Senior debt	90,000	(Note 1)
Mezzanine finance	20,000	(Note 2)
Senior management investment	1,244	
Cinven investment	62,956	(Note 3)
Opening revolving credit	4,435	
	£178,635	

Notes:
1. Medium-term loan at 2% over LIBOR, reducing to 1.5% providing certain profit targets are met. Final repayment date December 2001.
2. 8-year term loan at 3.5% over LIBOR. Carries warrants to subscribe for an additional 9% of the ordinary share capital.
3. Equity underwritten by Cinven's clients, who also underwrote a further £1.5m share offer to the remaining employees.

Highly geared (leveraged) deals are high risk; hence the need for the mezzanine debt to have an equity 'sweetener'.

Complex capital issues

There is almost no limit to the ingenuity of companies and their financial advisers in devising innovative terms for the issue of loan capital. In addition to the deep discount bonds and convertibles with 'put' options that we have described, complex capital issues include

(a) *Stepped interest bonds*, where the interest payable increases by fixed steps over the life of the bond e.g. CANARY WHARF's £120m stepped fixed interest tranche (part) of a £555m first mortgage debenture, where interest was paid at 5% until October 1999. From October 1999 the interest then increases in steps to 9.535%, which is payable from October 2006. In these cases the profit and loss account should be charged at a constant rate computed over the anticipated life of the bond, irrespective of the amount of interest paid each year (FRS 4, para. 28).

(b) *Bonds with variable payments*, where the interest payments and the amount payable on redemption are adjusted by the Retail Price Index or some other index. An annual charge should be made against profits to reflect the variations caused by the movement in the relevant index during the year (FRS 4, para. 31), e.g. ANGLIAN WATER's 5.125% Index Linked Loan Stock 2008, where the value of the capital and interest elements are linked to movements in the Retail Price Index.

Off balance sheet financing

The problem of what became known as 'off balance sheet financing' became evident in the 1980s. In that period a number of complex arrangements were developed which, if accounted for in accordance with their legal form, resulted in accounts that did not report the commercial effect of the arrangement; in particular, they did not show the finance as a liability on the balance sheet.

This was, of course, precisely what the devisers of these schemes intended. These developments raised fundamental questions about the nature of assets and liabilities and when they should be included in the balance sheet – questions which, lacking a fundamental theory of accounts, the accountancy profession found it difficult to answer. Although generally termed 'off balance sheet' some of the transactions also affected the profit and loss account and/or the cash flow statement.

Substance over form

In response to the problem, the concept of 'substance over form' was developed. Freely translated this means 'report the substance of the transaction and ignore the legal position. Accounts should reflect the reality of the situation.' This led to the publication of FRS 5.

FRS 5 *Reporting the substance of transactions*

We cover FRS 5 in this chapter, on the ground that it is largely concerned with borrowing, but it applies to all transactions or arrangements of a reporting entity whose financial statements are intended to give a true and fair view except

1. forward contracts and futures (such as the use of foreign currencies or commodities);
2. foreign exchange and interest rate swaps;
3. contracts where a net amount will be paid or received based on the movement in a price or an index (called 'contracts for differences');
4. expenditure commitments (such as purchase commitments) and orders placed, until the earlier of delivery or payment;
5. employment contracts.

Essentially the Standard is very simple: 'A reporting entity's financial statements should report the substance of the transactions into which it has entered. In determining the substance of a transaction, all its aspects and implications should be identified and greater weight given to those more likely to have commercial effect in practice.'

The effect of FRS 5 can be considerable in individual companies: GREAT UNIVERSAL STORES used to include finance advances and related unearned service charges in their sales figures. When, in 1995, in compliance with FRS 5, it excluded them, the reported figure for turnover was reduced by £700m. The accounting policy is now:

GREAT UNIVERSAL STORES *Accounting policies 2000*

Instalment and hire purchase debtors
The gross margin from sales on extended credit terms is recognised at the time of sale. The finance charges relating to these sales are included in the profit and loss account as and when instalments are received. The income in the Finance Division under instalment agreements is credited to the profit and loss account in proportion to the reducing balances outstanding.

Quasi-subsidiaries

Under FRS 5 a quasi-subsidiary is 'a company, trust, partnership or other vehicle that, though not fulfilling the definition of a subsidiary, is directly or indirectly controlled by the reporting entity and gives benefits for that entity that are in substance no different from those that would arise were the vehicle a subsidiary'.

'Where the entity has a quasi-subsidiary, the substance of the transactions entered into by the quasi-subsidiary should be reported in the consolidated financial statements.'

BRITISH AIRWAYS accounts explain in a note:

BRITISH AIRWAYS *Note on Accounting Policies 2000*

Basis of consolidation

Where an entity, though not fulfilling the legal definition of a subsidiary, gives rise to benefits for the Group that are, in substance, no different than those that would arise were the entity a subsidiary, that entity is classified as a quasi-subsidiary.

In determining whether the Group has the ability to enjoy the benefits arising . . . regard is given as to which party is exposed to the risks inherent in the benefits and which party, in practice, carries substantially all the risks and rewards of ownership.

Sale and leaseback

Sale and leaseback is an arrangement where the owner of an asset, typically a property, sells the asset and then leases it back. Under FRS 5, the accounting treatment of the transaction will depend on its substance:

- If the '*seller*' retains the risks and rewards of ownership (e.g. would benefit/suffer from any subsequent increase/decrease in the value of the property) *the transaction is treated as a financing transaction*.

  The property would remain on the seller's balance sheet, and the cash received would be regarded as a loan.

- On the other hand, if the '*purchaser*' benefits from any subsequent increase in value, and the seller pays rentals subject to periodic review, *the transaction is treated as a sale*.

  The property would be removed from the seller's balance sheet, and the profit/loss on sale would be taken to the seller's profit and loss account.

Linked presentation

The FRS employs a 'linked presentation' to deal with a limited class of non-recourse finance arrangements (including most securitisations) which shows, on the face of the balance sheet, the finance deducted from the gross amount of the asset it finances. Strict conditions attaching to its use require, inter alia, that the finance is repaid from the asset it finances and that there is no provision for the asset to be kept on repayment.

It will be seen that FRS 5 is very broadly drawn and should bring disclosure or put an end to most if not all existing forms of off balance sheet finance. But merchant banks and other financial advisors have long earned substantial fees from devising this sort of scheme and will not give up easily.

Other aspects of FRS 5

FRS 5 *Reporting the substance of transactions* covers a number of other transactions. Two important ones are consignment stocks, dealt with in Chapter 10, and debt factoring, discussed in Chapter 11.

GEARING RATIOS

Financial ratios fall into two broad groups, gearing ratios and liquidity ratios.

Gearing is concerned with the proportion of capital employed that is borrowed, the proportion provided by shareholders' funds and the relationship between the two, while liquidity ratios (see page 97) are concerned with the company's cash position.

Financial gearing

Financial gearing can be defined in a multiplicity of ways, the two most common being:

(a) the Debt/Equity ratio, shown as Borrowings/Shareholders' Funds in the *Investors Chronicle*, and called 'leverage' in the United States and elsewhere; and

(b) the percentage of capital employed represented by borrowings.

Whatever method is used to compute gearing, a company with 'low gearing' is one financed predominantly by equity, whereas a 'highly geared' company is one which relies on borrowings for a significant proportion of its capital.

To illustrate (see Example 6.8), let us take the bottom half of three different companies' balance sheets, adjusting them to include bank overdraft and any other borrowings falling due within one year (these are normally netted off against current assets in a company's balance sheet, but are just as much a part of capital employed as long-term borrowings are). As you can see, Debt/Equity ratio is a more sensitive measurement of gearing than Debt/Capital Employed, and it also gives a better indication of the effect of gearing on equity income, known across the Atlantic as the 'leverage effect'. But it can be distorted by the treatment of deferred tax under provisions varying from company to company, or varying within a

Example 6.8 Calculation of gearing and Debt/Equity ratios

		Company		
		A	B	C
		£000	£000	£000
Ordinary share capital		600	500	250
Reserves		850	550	300
Ordinary shareholders' funds	[A]	1,450	1,050	550
Redeemable preference share capital (3.5%)	[B]	–	100	–
Minorities	[C]	150	150	150
Provisions		400	400	400
Loan stock (10%)	[D]	–	150	400
Overdraft (currently 12%)	[E]	–	150	500
Capital employed	[F]	2,000	2,000	2,000
		A	B	C

Debt/Equity (Leverage) =

$$\left(\frac{B + D + E}{A + C} \right) \qquad 0\% \quad 33\% \quad 128\%$$

Debt/Capital Employed =

$$\left(\frac{B + D + E}{F} \right) \qquad 0\% \quad 20\% \quad 45\%$$

Gearing	None	Low	High

[B] The treatment of preference shares is a problem: although they are not debt they do carry a *fixed* rate of dividend that is payable ahead of ordinary dividends. On balance we favour treating them as debt if redeemable in the reasonably near future, say in less than 10 years, but otherwise as equity when looking at capital (because it would be misleading to ascribe the same Debt/Equity ratio to a company with, say, 60 debt/40 equity as one with 60 pref./40 equity).

[C] Minorities have been included as equity in the calculation of Debt/Equity ratios, on the assumption that minority interests in subsidiaries are all pure (non-redeemable) equity.

company from year to year under SSAP 15 (see page 128).

Leverage effect

The effect of leverage can be expressed as a ratio: percentage change in earnings available to ordinary shareholders brought about by a 1% change in earnings before interest and tax (EBIT).

Suppose each of the three companies in Example 6.9 has a Return On Capital Employed (ROCE) of 10%, and that the rate of Corporation Tax is 30%; then earnings before interest and tax (EBIT) will be as shown in Example 6.9.

Example 6.9 Calculation of leverage effect

		Company		
		A	B	C
		£000	£000	£000
EBIT		200.00	200.00	200.00
Less				
Loan stock interest		–	(15.00)	(40.00)
Interest on overdraft		–	(18.00)	(60.00)
Pre-tax profits		200.00	167.00	100.00
Tax at 30%		(60.00)	(50.10)	(30.00)
Profits after tax		140.00	116.90	70.00
Preference dividends		–	3.50	–
Available for minorities and ordinary shareholders	[G]	140.00	113.40	70.00
1% change in EBIT		2.00	2.00	2.00
Tax		0.60	0.60	0.60
Available for minorities and ordinary shareholders	[H]	+ 1.40	+ 1.40	+ 1.40

Leverage ratio

$$\frac{H}{G} \times 100 \qquad 1.00 \quad 1.23 \quad 2.00$$

Leverage, of course, works both ways; if EBIT fell by 50% then earnings available to ordinary shareholders would fall to £70,000 (Company A) and to £43,400 (Company B); and Company C would be on the point of making a loss.

Interest rate sensitivity

A simple calculation can be made to see the sensitivity of a company's profits to interest rates: if, in Example 6.9, the rate charged on overdrafts rose to 16% (or fell to 8%), Company C's pre-tax profit would be reduced (or increased) by 20%.

Operational gearing

In assessing what level of financial gearing might be reasonable for a company, we must first look at the volatility of profits. This depends to a large extent on the sensitivity of profits to turnover, which we will call operational gearing (although the term 'operational gearing' is sometimes used in the sense of overall gearing to include the effects of financial gearing as well).

The operational gearing of a company can be described as the ratio of the percentage change of trading profit which results from 1% change in turnover, and depends on the relationship between fixed costs, variable costs and net profit, where fixed costs

Example 6.10 Effects of operational gearing

	Turnover	Fixed costs	Variable costs	Trading profit	Operational gearing
	£m	£m	£m	£m	
Company D	100	20	70	10	3:1 (100 – 70:10)
Company E	100	70	20	10	8:1 (100 – 20:10)

If turnover increases by 10%:

	£m	£m	£m	£m	Change in profits
Company D	110	20	77	13	+ 30%
Company E	110	70	22	18	+ 80%

This is fine for both D and E, especially for E, which is much more highly geared operationally than D. But, as with high financial gearing, high operational gearing works against a company when turnover falls. Assume a 10% fall in turnover:

	£m	£m	£m	£m	Change in profits
Company D	90	20	63	7	– 30%
Company E	90	70	18	2	– 80%

are costs that are incurred regardless of turnover, and variable costs are directly proportional to turnover:

Operational gearing =
(Turnover − Variable costs) ÷ Trading profit

or

(Trading profit + Fixed costs) ÷ Trading profit

Example 6.10 demonstrates this.

Profit/volume chart

The effect of gearing can also be illustrated graphically on a 'profit/volume chart', as shown in Example 6.11. A profit/volume chart is constructed by plotting two points:

(a) trading profit against actual turnover;
(b) fixed costs against zero turnover;

and joining the two points together. The point where this line crosses the horizontal 'zero profit' line represents the level of turnover at which the company 'breaks even', i.e. makes neither a profit nor a loss. The steeper the gradient of the line the higher the operational gearing of the company.

The break-even point can also be calculated:

Break-even turnover

$$= \text{Fixed costs} \times \frac{\text{Turnover}}{\text{Turnover} - \text{Variable costs}}$$

$$\text{e.g. Company D} = 20 \times \frac{100}{100 - 70} = £66.67\text{m}$$

$$\text{e.g. Company E} = 70 \times \frac{100}{100 - 20} = £87.50\text{m}$$

Example 6.11 Profit/volume chart

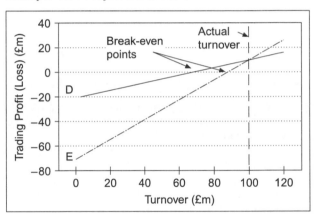

Aggravating the problem

It is fairly obvious that a company with high operational gearing aggravates the problem by gearing up financially. Suppose, for instance, that Company E has borrowings that incurred interest charges of £3m p.a.; Example 6.12 shows the effect on profits.

Example 6.12 Effect of high financial gearing coupled with high operational gearing

Turnover	Net trading profit	Interest charges	Pre-tax profits
£m	£m	£m	£m
100	10	3	7
110	18	3	15
90	2	3	−1

But the directors of a property company with mainly completed developments let to substantial clients will know that they have an assured rental income coming in each quarter, and they would not be considered imprudent to borrow heavily (i.e. gear up) provided the level of interest payments plus running expenses could not exceed the stream of rental income. We say 'could not exceed', because one of the ways property companies get into trouble is by borrowing short-term with a variable interest rate (e.g. on bank overdraft), rather than at a fixed rate; they then get caught out when interest rates go up faster than rental income.

Fixed charges cover

This is a very useful ratio, not often shown in company reports and accounts. An exception is W H SMITH.

W H SMITH *Extracts from Financial review 2000 and from Notes to the 2000 accounts*

Fixed charges cover

A key measure of financial strength for the businesses is fixed charges cover. The fixed charges comprise operating lease rentals, property taxes, other property costs and interest. They were covered 1.73 times by profits before fixed charges, a slight reduction from the previous year when the ratio was 1.81.

Note 11 Fixed charges cover

	2000 £m	1999 £m
Interest income	(6)	(14)
Operating lease rentals	154	141
Property taxes	32	30
Other property costs	11	9
Total fixed charges	**191**	**166**
Profit before tax	**140**	**134**
Profit before tax and fixed charges	**331**	**300**
Fixed charges cover	**1.7x**	**1.8x**

Fixed charges cover is calculated by dividing profit before tax and fixed charges by total fixed charges.

Chapter 7

INTANGIBLE FIXED ASSETS

Schedule 4 to the Companies Act 1985 requires fixed assets to be presented in the balance sheet under three headings: intangible assets, tangible assets and investments. We deal with the intangible assets in this chapter, with tangible fixed assets in Chapter 8 and with investments in Chapter 9.

Intangible fixed assets
Intangible fixed assets comprise:

(a) capitalised development costs;
(b) what we will call 'rights' (e.g. licences, concessions, patents and trademarks); and
(c) purchased goodwill.

Capitalised development costs
Under SSAP 13 *Research and development* all expenditure on R & D should normally be written off in the year in which it is incurred.

However, where development is for clearly defined projects on which expenditure is separately identifiable and for which commercial success is reasonably certain, companies may if they wish defer charging development expenditure 'to the extent that its recovery can reasonably be regarded as assured'. Capitalised development expenditure should be separately disclosed. However the trend amongst companies which capitalise development is to change to the more prudent policy of immediate write-off. For example ML LABORATORIES:

ML LABORATORIES *Extracts from 1998 Directors' report and accounts*

Research & Development
The Group is engaged in the research into, and the development of, a diverse portfolio of pharmaceutical, medical and other novel products.

During the year the Group has changed its accounting policy of capitalisation and subsequent amortisation to one of immediate write-off. Full details of this change are in notes 1 and . . .

The loss for the year [£8,442,697] is stated after charging research and development expenditure of £7,719,642.

Note 1. Change in accounting policy
The comparative results for the year to 30 September 1997 have been adjusted as follows:

	£
Profit as originally reported	683,810
Change in treatment of R & D	(5,671,095)
Restatement of minority interest	437,427
Loss as restated	(4,549,858)

> ## TERMINOLOGY
> ### Fixed assets
>
> **Assets** are things which a business owns and on which a value can be placed.
>
> **Fixed assets** are assets held not for resale but for use by the business. Schedule 4 to the Companies Act 1985 requires fixed assets to be presented in the balance sheet under three headings:
>
> * intangible assets,
> * tangible assets and
> * investments.

Rights
Intangible assets purchased separately from a business, i.e. not part of an acquisition, should be capitalised at cost. They include:

(a) copyright and similar publishing rights;
(b) licenses;
(c) patents;
(d) trademarks.

Copyright and similar publishing rights

Copyrights provide the holder with the exclusive right to produce copies of, and control over, an original musical, artistic or literary work. For literary (including compilations and computer programs), dramatic, musical and artistic works, copyright expires 70 years from the end of the calendar year in which the author died. The sums involved can be considerable. For example EMI GROUP's balance sheet at the year end 31 March 2001 showed music copyrights of £546.8m after a £42.6m amortisation charge for the period.

Licences

Licences are agreements that a company enters into with government or with a third party which enables it to carry out certain trading functions. Examples are brewers which operate licensed premises, or bookmakers, who are required to obtain a licence for each bookmaking shop.

Companies may also purchase licences which allow them to use software or technology developed by third parties, and licences from government authorities, as with VODAFONE:

VODAFONE *Extracts from 2000 accounts*

Statement of accounting policies
INTANGIBLE FIXED ASSETS
Purchased intangible fixed assets, including licence fees, are capitalised at cost.

Network licence costs are amortised over the periods of the licences. Amortisation is charged from commencement of service of the network. The annual charge is calculated in proportion to the expected usage of the network during the start up period and on a straight line basis thereafter.

Note 8 Intangible fixed assets

	Licence and spectrum fees £m
Cost	
1 April 1999	173
Exchange movements	(26)
Reclassification – associated undertakings	326
Additions	251
	724
Amortisation	
1 April 1999	17
Exchange movements	–
Charge for the year	12
31 March 2000	29
Net book value	
31 March 2000	695
31 March 1999	156

Patents and trademarks

A patent is in effect a document granted by the government assuring an inventor of the sole right to make, use and sell his invention for a determined period. For example LATCHWAYS, a small producer and distributor of industrial safety products, is heavily dependent on world-wide patents to protect its inventions. The 2000 balance sheet showed intangible assets of £306,000, and details were contained in a note:

LATCHWAYS *Note to the 2000 accounts*

Intangible fixed assets
Patents, trademarks and registered designs

	£000
Cost	
At 1 April 1999	362
Additions in the year	88
Amounts written off	(2)
At 31 March 2000	448
Amortisation	
At 1 April 1999	123
Charge for the year	21
Amounts written off	(2)
At 31 March 2000	142
Net book value	
At 31 March 2000	306
At 31 March 1999	239

Registering a trademark provides legal protection to the name or symbol used to differentiate the products supplied by a manufacturer or authorised distributor from those of competing manufacturers and dealers. Given their identifiable cost and their value to businesses over long periods in terms of income stream generation, it is not unreasonable to capitalise those costs and amortise them over their useful lives; but that decision is one for the directors. BASS does not capitalise costs of this nature.

Purchased goodwill

The difference between the fair value of the consideration paid for an acquired entity and the aggregate of the fair values of that entity's identifiable assets and liabilities is termed purchased goodwill. For example ML LABORATORIES:

ML LABORATORIES *Note to the 2000 accounts*

Note 1. Acquisitions
During the year the Company acquired a new subsidiary, Cobra Therapeutic Limited . . .

Net book value and fair value of net assets

	£
Tangible fixed assets	964,504
Debtors	253,887
Cash	4,389,095
Creditors	(1,169,359)
	4,438,127
Fair value of share consideration	10,059,194
Costs of acquisition	300,000
	10,359,194
Goodwill	5,921,067

Purchased goodwill – old rules

Until the end of 1998 the normal way of dealing with purchased goodwill was to write it off immediately against reserves.

This was thoroughly unsatisfactory for two main reasons:

1. Millions and millions of pounds of shareholders' money disappeared from the balance sheet without trace. Well, almost without trace: the Companies Act required the cumulative amount of goodwill written off against reserves to be shown in the accounts.

    But it was usually put in some obscure note, and very few analysts paid any attention to it, except when an acquisition was subsequently disposed of, where the goodwill written off in the acquisition had to be reinstated. This often turned a handsome profit on disposal into a thumping loss.

2. Reducing the size of shareholders' funds played merry hell with some ratios. Two key ones that most investors still clung to with touching, almost childlike, faith were Return On Capital Employed (ROCE), and Gearing (Debt to Equity ratio). Due to 'immediate write-off', both were often grossly misleading.

Hardly surprising, when some companies actually reported negative shareholders' funds.

Purchased goodwill – FRSs 10 and 11

Under FRS 10 *Goodwill and intangible assets* and *FRS 11 Impairment of fixed assets and goodwill*, purchased goodwill and intangible assets must be capitalised and either

(a) amortised over their useful economic lives, or
(b) where their useful economic lives exceed 20 years, or they are not amortised, their value must be reviewed annually for impairment.

CADBURY SCHWEPPES *Extract from accounting policies 2000*

(o) Intangibles
Intangibles represent significant owned brands acquired since 1985 valued at historical cost. No amortisation is charged as the annual results reflect significant expenditure in support of these brands and the carrying values are reviewed on an annual basis for any impairment in value.

Under transitional arrangements, any goodwill which had previously been written off to reserves could remain there, until such time as the related business is disposed of.

Companies have, however, the option to reinstate as an asset old goodwill previously written off to reserves. If they do this, either all old goodwill or all post-FRS 7 goodwill should be reinstated.

Impairment

FRS 11 *Impairment of fixed assets and goodwill* requires assets not to be recorded in the balance sheet at more than their *recoverable amount*, which is the higher of

- net realisable value – what an asset could be sold for, and
- value in use – the present value of the cash flows which the asset is expected to generate.

FRS 11 only requires assets to be reviewed for impairment, that is for a reduction in their recoverable amount below book value, in specific circumstances. For goodwill or other intangibles, these are:

1. When goodwill or intangibles appear in the balance sheet and are not amortised over 20 years or less.
2. Where there are indicators of impairment that suggest that the company's assets may not be fully recoverable, e.g. persistent operating losses; negative operating cash flows; a significant fall in an asset's market value; an asset being physically damaged, or becoming obsolete; a significant adverse change in the competitive or regulatory environment; a reorganisation; or even loss of key employees.
3. Where an acquisition took place in the previous year, a review should take place at the end of the first full year following the acquisition.

Past impairment losses can only be reversed subsequently if the recovery in value is due to the reversal of the reason which gave rise to the impairment in the first place. So previous impairment losses will rarely be reversed.

The standard applies not only to any goodwill that is recognised as an asset but to most fixed assets, except derivatives and oil exploration expenditure.

TERMINOLOGY
Intangible fixed assets

Intangible fixed assets are non-monetary fixed assets that have no physical substance but are identifiable and are controlled by the entity (company) through legal rights or physical custody.
They include:

- purchased goodwill
- capitalised development costs
- concessions, patents, licences, trademarks and similar rights and assets.

Purchased goodwill represents the difference between the consideration paid for an acquisition and the aggregate of the fair values of that acquisition's net assets.

Fair value is the amount at which an asset could be exchanged in an arm's length transaction between informed and willing parties, other than in a forced or liquidation sale.

Positive goodwill arises when the consideration exceeds the aggregate fair values of the identifiable assets and liabilities. **Negative goodwill** arises when the aggregate fair values exceed the consideration paid.

Carrying value is simply another term for book value (which avoids suggesting that the balance sheet is a valuation statement).

Impairment is a reduction in the recoverable amount of an asset below its carrying value.

Recoverable amount is the higher of net realisable value of an asset and its value in use.

The **useful economic life** of an intangible asset is the period over which the entity expects to derive economic benefit from it. The useful economic life of purchased goodwill is the period over which the value of the underlying business is expected to exceed the values of its identifiable net assets.

Value in use is the present value of the future cash flows obtainable as a result of an asset's continued use, including those resulting from its ultimate disposal.

Chapter 8

TANGIBLE FIXED ASSETS

Reference: FRS 15 *Tangible fixed assets*

Tangible fixed assets

Tangible fixed assets are items used in a company to earn revenue. They may include:

- land and buildings
- plant and machinery
- fixtures, fittings and tools
- vehicles
- office and computer equipment.

Depreciation

Depreciation is a measure of the loss of value of an asset due to use, the passage of time and obsolescence, including the amortisation of fixed assets whose useful economic life is predetermined (e.g. leases) and depletion of wasting assets. In an example from BLUE CIRCLE:

BLUE CIRCLE INDUSTRIES *Accounting policies 2000*

Depreciation

Depreciation is provided from the date of original use or subsequent valuation by equal annual amounts over the estimated lives of the assets, except for freehold and leasehold mineral lands where it is provided on the basis of tonnage extracted.

Traditionally fixed assets are shown in the balance sheet at cost less accumulated depreciation to date (i.e. at net book value). This book value is not, and does not purport to be in any sense, a valuation, though fixed assets, particularly land and buildings, are often revalued. In UK practice, sometimes, but by no means always, the valuation is taken into the books.

Companies Act requirements

The requirements of the Companies Act 1985 with regard to fixed assets are complex. In summary:

COMPANIES ACT REQUIREMENTS

Tangible fixed assets

Accounting bases

Fixed assets may be shown on

- a historical cost basis, *or*
- at valuation, *or*
- at current cost (described in Chapter 29, *Inflation accounting*).

Historical cost

Assets are stated in the balance sheet at depreciated actual cost. Amounts must be shown under the following headings:

(i) cost;
(ii) cumulative provision for depreciation;
(iii) book (or carrying) value (i minus ii).

At valuation

The amount included must be shown, together with the years and amounts of the valuations. If valued during the year, the names of the valuers and the basis of valuation must be given (see page 57 on QUEENS MOAT HOUSES). Historical cost details must also be given.

Modified historical cost

In practice, UK companies frequently adopt the **modified historical cost convention**, under which historical cost is employed, but certain assets are revalued.

> *Current cost*
> Assets are stated at their value to the business (sometimes called 'alternative accounting rules'). Historical cost details must also be given.
>
> *Under all bases*
>
> 1. Assets should be classified under headings appropriate to the business.
> 2. Land must be analysed into freehold, long (over 50 years unexpired) and short leaseholds.
> 3. Details must be given of *acquisitions* and *disposals* made during the year.

FRS 15 requires companies to disclose the method of depreciation used for each category of asset, together with the effective useful lives assumed.

Rates of depreciation

The following are typical rates (using the straight line method of depreciation, described below):

Freehold land	Nil
Freehold buildings	2% = 50-year life
Leasehold property:	
Long leases (over 50 years)	2% = 50 years
Short leases	Over life of the lease
Tenants' improvements	Over life of the lease
Plant and machinery	10% = 10 years
Vehicles	20% = 5 years
Ships, according to type	4–10% = 10–25 years
Furniture and equipment	10% = 10 years

Where there is a wide range of estimated useful lives within a single classification, some companies also show an *average life*, which is much more informative. An example is CABLE & WIRELESS:

CABLE & WIRELESS *Accounting policies 2000*

Tangible fixed assets and depreciation

	Lives	*Average*
Telephone cables and repeaters – analogue	12 to 20 years	14 years
digital	15 years	15 years
Plant	2 to 40 years	10 years

Subnormal depreciation charges

Where a company charges a subnormal rate of depreciation, or does not charge depreciation on assets (other than freehold land), it will report higher pre-tax profits than it would otherwise have done.

For example, a few companies in the retail sector, for example KINGFISHER, do not provide depreciation on their freehold and long leasehold properties, and explain why in their accounts:

KINGFISHER *Note on accounting policies 2000*

Depreciation
Depreciation of fixed assets is provided where it is necessary to reflect a reduction from book value to estimated residual value over the useful life of the asset . . . It is the Group's policy to maintain its properties in a state of good repair to prolong their useful lives. The directors consider that, in the case of freehold and long leasehold properties occupied by the group, the estimated residual values at the end of their useful economic lives . . . are not materially different from their current carrying values. The lives of these properties and their residual values are such that no provision for depreciation is considered necessary. Any permanent diminution is charged to the profit and loss account . . .

Analysts sometimes make allowances for differing depreciation policies when making comparisons between companies.

Useful economic life

Determination of useful economic life (the period over which the present owner expects to derive economic benefit from the asset's use) is a matter for management and depends on business circumstances. For example, in the Chairman's Statement of THE JERSEY ELECTRICITY COMPANY, he refers to a site redevelopment that will allow relocation of the company's head office and provision of commercial retail and other office space. A note to the accounts discloses that the site has been examined in relation to FRS 11 *Impairment of fixed assets and goodwill*. As a result of this examination, depreciation has been accelerated to ensure that the assets will be written off during the development period. As a consequence, additional depreciation of £0.7m has been charged in 1998. It seems that this charge relates principally to buildings which will be demolished to allow completion of the development.

Where depreciation is shown in the accounts

Depreciation appears in several places. HALMA, in the extracts shown below, provides an example of what a good set of accounts shows:

- the note on *Accounting policies*;
- Note 3 and Note 22: the depreciation charge for the year;
- Note 12: disposals and the cumulative amount of depreciation to date;
- Note 12 also illustrates several other requirements of the Companies Act 1985, e.g. the analysis of land into freehold, long leasehold and short leasehold.

HALMA *Extracts from the 2000 accounts*

Accounting policies:
Depreciation
With the exception of freehold land, depreciation is provided on all tangible fixed assets on the straight line method, each item being written off over its estimated life.

The principal annual rates used for this purpose are:

Freehold buildings	2%
Leasehold properties	
more than 50 years unexpired	2%
less than 50 years unexpired	Period of lease
Plant, machinery and equipment	8% to 20%
Motor vehicles	20%
Short-life tooling	$33^1/_3\%$

Note 3 to the profit and loss account:

	2000 £000	1999 £000
Operating profit is arrived at after charging:		
Depreciation	6,252	5,748

Note 22 Reconciliation of operating profit to net cash inflow from operating activities:

Operating profit	42,136	40,501
. . .		
Depreciation	6,252	5,748

Note 12
[Fixed assets – tangible assets]

Group			Land and buildings			Plant,	
			Freehold	Long	Short	equipment	
Cost			properties	leases	leases	& vehicles	Total
At 3 April 1999			20,438	1,503	1,797	47,540	71,278
Assets of businesses acquired			–	–	30	3,370	3,400
Additions at cost			96	14	161	8,027	8,298
Disposals			(830)	(150)	(3)	(4,921)	(5,904)
Exchange adjustments			(48)	–	(14)	(266)	(328)
At 1 April 2000	**(a)**		19,656	1,367	1,971	53,750	76,744
Accumulated depreciation							
. . .							
At 1 April 2000	**(b)**						
			2,500	234	831	30,965	34,530
Net book amounts							
At 1 April 2000	**(a–b)**		17,156	1,133	1,140	22,785	42,214

DEPRECIATION METHODS

The most common method or basis of depreciation, used by over 80% of major companies, is the straight line (or fixed instalment) method.

Other methods include:

(a) the declining (or reducing) balance method;
(b) the sum of the years' digits method;
(c) the renewals method;
(d) the production unit method;
(e) the annuity method;
(f) the sinking fund method.

As will be seen, the different methods of depreciation affect:

(i) net asset values
(ii) net profit
(iii) return on capital employed.

The straight line or fixed instalment method
Depreciation under the fixed instalment method is computed as follows (see also Example 8.1 at the top of the next page):

$$\text{Annual depreciation} = \frac{\text{Cost} - \text{Residual value}}{\text{Useful economic life}}$$

Example 8.1 Straight line depreciation

If a machine having a useful economic life of five years is purchased for £10,000, and is expected to have a residual value of £1,000 at the end of that life, depreciation will be:

$$\frac{£10,000 - £1,000}{5} = \frac{£9,000}{5} = £1,800 \text{ per annum}$$

and the accounts will show:

End of year	Depreciation for the year shown in the P & L account	Cost	Provision for depreciation to date	Net book value
	£	£	£	£
1	1,800	10,000	1,800	8,200
2	1,800	10,000	3,600	6,400
3	1,800	10,000	5,400	4,600
4	1,800	10,000	7,200	2,800
5	1,800	10,000	9,000	1,000

←————————— shown in the balance sheet —————————→

TERMINOLOGY

Tangible fixed assets

Tangible fixed assets are long-lived assets held for the purpose, directly or indirectly, of earning revenue. They include not only items like **plant and machinery**, which are actually used to provide the product, but assets used to house or support operations, such as **land, buildings, furniture, computer equipment and motor vehicles**.

They may be owned by the company or financed by finance leases.

Depreciation is the measure of the cost or revalued amount of the economic benefits of the asset that have been *consumed* during the period.

Consumption includes the wearing out, using up or other reduction in the useful economic life of a tangible fixed asset whether arising from use, efflux- ion of time or obsolescence through changes either in technology or in demand for the goods and ser- vices produced by the asset.

Useful economic life of a tangible fixed asset is the period over which the company expects to derive economic benefit from that asset.

Residual value is the realisable value of an asset at the end of its useful economic life.

The straight line method is ideal where the service provided by the asset continues unabated throughout its useful economic life, as might be the case with a 21-year lease of a building. It is the method generally used wherever the equal allocation of cost provides a reasonably fair measure of the asset's service, for example, for buildings, plant, machinery, equipment, vehicles and patents. A key advantage is that it is easy to calculate, and con- ceptually simple to understand.

The reducing balance method

The reducing balance (or declining balance) method used to be the most popular method of depreci- ation; but, except for tax purposes, it has largely been supplanted in recent years by the straight line method.

Under the reducing balance method, the annual depreciation charge represents a fixed percentage of the net book value brought forward (i.e. cost less accumulated depreciation). The calculation of the annual charge is simple enough once the appropriate percentage has been determined, but this requires the use of tables or a calculator:

Depreciation rate = $1 - (\text{Residual value} \div \text{Cost})^{1/n}$

where n = useful economic life in years and depre- ciation rate is a decimal.

Example 8.2 illustrates the calculation.

Among the disadvantages of the reducing bal- ance method are these:

(a) most users do not calculate the rate appropriate to each particular item of plant, but use standard percentages, which tend to be too low rather than too high;

(b) unless notional adjustments are made to cost and residual value, it is impossible to calculate satisfactorily a reducing balance rate if the residual value is nil: the net book value can never get to nil, as it can only be reduced by a pro- portion each year;

Example 8.2 Reducing balance depreciation

The rate for the machine in Example 8.1 would be computed as follows:

Depreciation rate (as a decimal) = $1 - (£1,000/£10,000)^{1/5} = 1 - 0.631 = 0.369$ (i.e. 36.9%)

Thus the rate to apply is 36.9%.

End of year	Depreciation for the year (shown in the P & L account)	Cost	Provision for depreciation to date	Net book value
		←————————	shown in the balance sheet ————————→	
	£	£	£	£
1	3,690	10,000	3,690	6,310
2	2,328	10,000	6,018	3,982
3	1,470	10,000	7,488	2,512
4	927	10,000	8,415	1,585
5	585	10,000	9,000	1,000

(c) even if the asset is assigned a nominal scrap value (say £1 so that it is not overlooked in the books) or if there is some residual value but it is small in relation to cost, the method is unlikely to be satisfactory without notional adjustments, because it leads to such high charges in the early years, as Example 8.3 shows.

The sum of the years' digits method

The sum of the (years') digits method is not commonly found in the United Kingdom, though it is used a good deal as a method of allowing accelerated depreciation in the United States (where accounting depreciation, provided it is computed by an acceptable method, is used for tax purposes too). It is occasionally found in the United Kingdom in connection with activities like leasing which involve heavy outlays in early years.

In this method, the cost less any residual value is divided by the sum of the years' digits to give

Example 8.3 Reducing balance depreciation, small residual value

Taking our previous example of plant costing £10,000, but with a residual value of £200 instead of £1,000, we get:

Year	Depreciation with residual value	
	£200	£1,000
	£	£
1	5,425	3,690
2	2,482	2,328
3	1,135	1,470
4	520	927
5	238	585
Accumulated depreciation at the end of year 5	9,800	9,000
Residual value	200	1,000

Example 8.4 Sum of the years' digits method of depreciation

Taking our example of a machine costing £10,000, with an estimated life of five years and a residual value estimated at £1,000: the sum of the year's digits is 15, and a unit of depreciation is thus (£10,000 − £1,000) ÷ 15 = £600, so:

End of year	Depreciation for the year (shown in the P & L account)	Cost	Provisions for depreciation to date	Net book value
		←————————	shown in the balance sheet ————————→	
	£	£	£	£
1	3,000	10,000	3,000	7,000
2	2,400	10,000	5,400	4,600
3	1,800	10,000	7,200	2,800
4	1,200	10,000	8,400	1,600
5	600	10,000	9,000	1,000

what, for the purpose of this explanation, may be termed a unit of depreciation. In the last year of expected life, one unit of depreciation is provided; in the next to last, two; in the one before that, three; and so on.

The sum of the years' digits is simply the sum of the series: $(1 + 2 + 3 + 4 \ldots + n)$, where n represents the expected life of the asset.

The formula for computing the sum of the digits is $n(n + 1) / 2$, where n is the number of years. Thus, to apply the sum of the digits to an asset having a life of 5 years, the divisor (i.e. the sum of the years' digits) is $5 (5 + 1) / 2 = 15$, and the first year's depreciation is 5/15 of (cost minus residual value), the second year's 4/15, and so on.

Comparison of methods

It is interesting to compare the balance sheet value of this asset year by year under sum of the digits (SD) with the value under the straight line (SL) and the reducing balance methods (RB£1,000 for a residual value of £1,000 and RB£200 for one of £200), as shown in Example 8.5 below.

The value under the sum of the digits method, on the other hand, is reduced in decreasing steps, year by year, reaching residual value at the end of

Example 8.5 Balance sheet values compared for four methods of depreciation

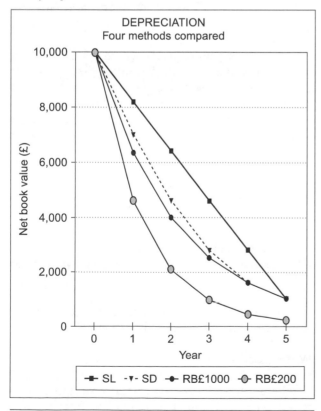

the asset's expected life, regardless of the size of the residual value, if any.

The renewals method

Definable major assets or components within an infrastructure or network with determinable finite lives should be treated separately and depreciated over their useful economic lives.

For the remaining tangible fixed assets within the system or network, renewals accounting may be used as a method of estimating depreciation (FRS 15, para. 97).

Where renewals accounting is adopted, the level of annual expenditure required to maintain the operating capacity of the infrastructure asset is treated as the depreciation charged for the period (FRS 15, para. 98). For example the SOUTH STAFFORDSHIRE GROUP:

SOUTH STAFFORDSHIRE GROUP *Accounting policies 2000*

Infrastructure assets
Infrastructure assets comprise a network of systems that, as a whole, is intended to be maintained in perpetuity at a specified level of service by the continuing replacement and refurbishment of its components . . .

The depreciation charge for infrastructure assets is the level of annual expenditure required to maintain the operating capability of the network . . .

Change in expected useful life

The useful economic life of a tangible fixed asset is reviewed as part of the normal end of period reporting procedures. If it is revised, the carrying amount of the tangible fixed asset at the date of revision should be depreciated over the revised life (FRS 15, para. 93).

Changes in useful life can have a significant effect on profits. For example STORM, the cartoon character licensing group, changed its accounting policy on film costs in its 1992 accounts to reflect a change in group strategy, as the chairman explained.

STORM GROUP *Extract from Chairman's statement*

It was decided that Storm would no longer utilise its own funds to invest in animated cartoon film productions . . . all production work would be funded from commissions, external funding or pre-sales revenue.

As a result of this change in strategic focus, the Board elected to adopt a revised accounting policy in respect of film costs and to write them off to the profit and loss account as incurred. The total sum involved was £2.289m, of which £1.538m was charged in 1992 and the balance treated as a prior year item.

The effect of the change in accounting policy was the major cause of the group reporting a pre-tax loss of £2.1m. But the chairman's statement went on to say:

STORM GROUP *Second extract from Chairman's statement*

It is, however, vitally important to emphasise that the write-off of film production costs should not be seen to detract from the inherent value of the animation programmes to which they relate. Animated cartoons have traditionally generated revenues over a long period . . .

Storm claimed that the revised policy had been adopted on the grounds of prudence, but does it necessarily provide 'a true and fair view'? Future profits will be enhanced by hundreds of thousands of pounds per annum for several years, because animation programmes will no longer have to be depreciated.

Writing down of asset values

As explained in Chapter 7, FRS 11 *Impairment of fixed assets and goodwill* calls for the writing down of fixed assets if they are judged to have become permanently impaired. The standard introduces the implication that assets must be stated in the balance sheet at amounts that are expected to earn at least a satisfactory rate of return. Companies earning a poor rate of return, even though profitable, will have to write down their assets (see pages 48–9 regarding impairment reviews).

The useful economic life of a tangible fixed asset should be reviewed at the end of each reporting period and revised if expectations are significantly different from previous estimates. If a useful economic life is revised, the carrying amount of the tangible fixed asset at the date of revision should be depreciated over the revised remaining useful economic life (FRS 15, para. 93).

What is more, where the residual value is material that review has to take account of reasonably expected technological changes based on prices prevailing at the date of acquisition (or revaluation). A change in its estimated residual value should be accounted for prospectively over the asset's remaining useful economic life, except to the extent that the asset has been impaired at the balance sheet date (FRS 15, para. 95).

Changing method

A change from one method of providing depreciation to another is permissible only on the grounds that the new method will give a fairer presentation of the results and of the financial position. Such a change does not, however, constitute a change of accounting policy; it does not give rise to an exceptional item: the carrying amount of the tangible fixed asset is depreciated using the revised method over the remaining useful economic life, beginning in the period in which the change is made (FRS 15, para. 82).

Freehold land and buildings

Traditionally, neither freehold land nor buildings were depreciated, though the majority of companies had been depreciating freehold buildings in years before accounting standards were introduced.

Under FRS 15 companies are normally required to depreciate freehold and long leasehold buildings.

If, however, no depreciation charge is made on the grounds that it would be immaterial, or on the grounds that the estimated remaining useful life of the asset is over 50 years, tangible fixed assets should be reviewed for impairment at the end of each reporting period.

THE REVALUATION OF ASSETS

Background

Under historical cost accounting, assets appear at cost less depreciation, and they are not revalued to show their current worth to the company. But because of the effects of inflation, the practice grew up in the United Kingdom of revaluing assets, particularly freehold land and buildings, from time to time.

Indeed, Schedule 7 para. 1 of the Companies Act 1985 requires the difference between the market value of property assets and the balance sheet amount to be disclosed in the directors' report if, in the opinion of the directors, it is significant. UK companies thus face the choice; they must either

(a) incorporate any revaluation in the accounts, or
(b) disclose it in the directors' report.

Where assets are revalued and the revaluation is incorporated in the accounts, both 'sides' of the balance sheet are affected, and depreciation from then on is based on the revalued amounts, as Example 8.6 illustrates.

Example 8.6 Effects of revaluation

A company has freehold land which cost £10m and buildings which cost £4.2m, have a useful life of 50 years and were 10 years old on 31 December 1999. Depreciation to that date would therefore be 2% p.a. for 10 years on £4.2m = £840,000, so the balance sheet would show:

	£m
Freehold land and buildings at cost	5.200
less depreciation to date	0.840
Book value at 31 December 1999	4.360

On 1 January 2000 the land was revalued at £3.8m and the buildings at £8.1m. After the revaluation the accounts would show freehold land and buildings at the valuation figure of £11.9m, an increase of £7.54m. On the other side of the balance sheet the reserves would normally be increased by £7.54m. (If, however, the company has entered into a binding agreement to sell the buildings, FRS 19 para. 14 requires a provision to be made out of the revaluation surplus for the tax which would be payable on disposal, and this would be credited to deferred tax, the remainder of the surplus being credited to reserves.)

The 2000 accounts would be required to disclose the basis of valuation used and the name or qualification of the valuer (CA 1985, Sch. 4, para. 43 (b)).

The revaluation will affect the company in several ways:

1. The annual depreciation charge on the buildings, based on the new value and the current estimate of the remaining useful life (40 years), will increase from £84,000 to £202,500 ($2^1/2\%$ p.a. on £8.1m), thus directly reducing the pre-tax profits by £118,500 in each future year.
2. The overall profitability of the company, as measured by the ratio Return On Capital Employed (ROCE, described in Chapter 16), will also appear to deteriorate because the capital employed will have increased by £7.54m. For instance, if the company in our example went on to make £3m before interest and tax in 2000, and had £20m capital employed before the revaluation, the 2000 return on capital employed would be:

No revaluation $\dfrac{3,118,500}{20,000,000} = 15.6\%$ *Revaluation* $\dfrac{3,000,000}{27,540,000} = 10.9\%$

3. The borrowing powers of most companies are expressed as a multiple of share capital and reserves, so the increase in reserves will raise the borrowing limits, and improve the capital cover of existing lenders.
4. The higher property value may give more scope for borrowing on mortgage.
5. The increase in reserves will also increase the n.a.v., the net asset value per share, described in Chapter 24.

The arguments for and against valuations

On the one hand, valuations can produce figures that fluctuate wildly, and a lot may depend on the valuer, and whether he thinks his client wants a 'very full' valuation, or a parsimonious one. He who pays the valuer calls the tune.

For example, at the end of 1991 the hotel group QUEENS MOAT HOUSES had its properties independently valued by a well known firm of chartered surveyors at a figure of £2,000 million.

At the end of the following year a different but equally reputable firm of chartered surveyors valued the same portfolio of hotels at £861 million.

The *new* chairman explained what had happened:

QUEENS MOAT HOUSES *Extract from Chairman's statement*

At 31 December 1991, the group's properties were valued by Weatherall Green & Smith (WGS) at £2.0 billion, a valuation which was incorporated in the 1991 audited balance sheet . . .

In June the previous board appointed Jones Lang Wootton (JLW) to value the group's hotel portfolio in place of WGS. They have valued the portfolio of properties as at 31 December 1992 at £861 million . . .

After careful consideration the board accepted the JLW valuation and it has been incorporated into the group's balance sheet at 31 December 1992. In the UK and Continental Europe there was considerable hotel expansion in the late 1980's fuelled by the abundant availability of capital. Circumstances have changed materially over the past few years and the recent market place for hotels in the UK has been dominated by distressed sale values. On the continent, the declining profitability has lagged the UK but the market place has shown similar adverse developments. It is this adverse context of declining profitability and limited purchasers' interest in hotels in which the valuation has been prepared . . .

On the other hand, as the chairman of the ASB, Sir David Tweedie, has pointed out, it is nonsense to have a property shown in the balance sheet at £10m if the bank, valuing it at £50m, has accepted it as security for a £40m loan.

We rather agree with Sir Adrian Cadbury, who said at his last AGM as chairman of CADBURY SCHWEPPES that the only time the real value of a brand [or any other asset] is known is when it changes hands.

FRS 15 *Tangible fixed assets*

The ASB has now grasped the nettle somewhat cautiously. Under FRS 15, in force for financial periods ending on or after 23 March 2000, revaluing tangible fixed assets remains optional.

But, where a policy of revaluation is adopted, it must be applied to a whole class of assets and the valuations kept up to date. This will generally be achieved by a five-yearly full valuation of an asset with a qualified external valuer, and an interim valuation in year 3. Valuations in the intervening years are only required where there is likely to have been a material change in value.

Revaluation gains should be recognised in the profit and loss account only to the extent that they reverse valuation losses on the same asset that were previously recognised in the profit and loss account. All other revaluation gains should be recognised in the statement of total recognised gains and losses (FRS 15, para. 63).

Revaluation losses caused by a clear loss of economic benefit should be recognised in the profit and loss account. Other revaluation losses should normally be recognised in the statement of total recognised gains and losses until the carrying amount reaches its depreciated historical cost (FRS 15, para. 65).

Sales and other disposals of fixed assets

Where fixed assets are disposed of for an amount which is greater (or less) than their book value, the profit or loss on disposal should be shown separately on the face of the profit and loss account after operating profit and before interest, and attributed to continuing or discontinued operations (FRS 3, paras. 19 and 20), e.g. TESCO at the top of the next column.

Where assets which have been revalued are subsequently disposed of, the gains or losses are to be calculated against the carrying value (valuation amount less any subsequent depreciation).

TESCO *Extract from profit and loss account 1999*

	£m	£m
Operating profit	934	849
Loss on disposal of discontinued operations	–	(8)
Net loss on disposal of fixed assets	(8)	(1)
Share of operating profit/ (loss) of joint ventures	6	(6)
Profit on ordinary activities before interest	932	834
Net interest payable	(90)	(74)
Profit on ordinary activities before taxation	842	760

Investment properties

Currently, while FRS 15 requires annual depreciation charges to be made on fixed assets, and makes it clear that an increase in the value of a fixed asset does not remove the necessity to charge depreciation, a different treatment is applied to fixed assets held as disposable investments.

Under SSAP 19, 'investment properties' (i.e. properties held as investments rather than for use in a manufacturing or commercial process) are not depreciated, but are revalued each year at their open market value, and the valuation is reflected in the balance sheet. Changes in the value of investment properties should be treated as a movement on an 'investment property revaluation reserve'. The cumulative amounts credited to reserve can be very large; see leading property company LAND SECURITIES on the next page. If, however, there is a fall in value that exceeds the balance in the investment property revaluation reserve, the excess should be charged to the profit and loss account; i.e. the reserve cannot 'go negative'.

GOVERNMENT GRANTS

Reference: SSAP 4 *Accounting for government grants*

Capital-based grants
Capital-based grants are grants made as a contribution towards specific expenditure on fixed assets. SSAP 4 requires capital-based grants to be credited to revenue (i.e. to the profit and loss account) over the expected useful life of the asset concerned.

Revenue-based grants
These include grants to finance the general activities of an enterprise over a specific period, which SSAP 4 requires to be credited to the profit and loss account in the period in which they are paid.

RMC GROUP *Extract from accounting policies 1999*

Grants
Grants received from government and similar agencies, where they relate to expenditure on fixed assets or are to finance the activities of the group over a number of years, are recognised in the profit and loss account over the expected useful economic lives of the related assets or over that number of years, and to the extent not so recognised are treated as deferred income. Grants which are intended to give immediate financial support or assistance or which are made to reimburse costs incurred are included in the profit and loss account so as to match with those costs in the period in which they become receivable.

LAND SECURITIES *Extracts from notes to 2000 financial statements*

1. Accounting policies

(e) DEPRECIATION AND AMORTISATION In accordance with SSAP 19, no depreciation or amortisation is provided in respect of freehold or leasehold properties held on leases having more than 20 years unexpired . . .

Properties are included in the financial statements at their open market value.

Note 11 Properties

| | | Leasehold | | |
	Freehold £m	Over 50 years to run £m	Under 50 years to run £m	Total £m
GROUP				
At 1 April 1999; at valuation	5,394.0	1,463.4	53.1	6,910.5
Additions	216.3	185.9	1.3	403.5
Sales	(246.8)	(61.9)	(5.6)	(314.3)
	5,363.5	1,587.4	48.8	6,999.7
Unrealised surplus on valuation	348.4	99.4	6.2	454.0
At 31 March 2000; at valuation	5,711.9	1,686.8	55.0	7,453.7

Note 21 Reserves

	Share premium account £m	Capital redemption reserve £m	Revaluation reserve £m	Other reserves £m	Profit and loss account £m	Total £m
GROUP						
At 1 April 1999	284.0	–	3,286.5	632.0	713.6	4,916.1
Premium arising on issue of shares	22.0					22.0
Purchase and cancellation of own shares	–		(194.4)		(55.4)	(249.8)
Cancellation of shares on buybacks		36.0				36.0
Unrealised surplus on valuation of properties			454.0			454.0
Realised on sale of properties			(158.1)			(158.1)
. . .						
Retained profit for the year					86.3	86.3
At 31 March 2000	305.2	36.0	3,582.4	141.2	1,194.6	5,259.4

Where the amounts involved are material, grants will appear

(i) separately in the profit and loss account or notes as a contribution to profit and
(ii) in the balance note on creditors and deferred income.

Hybrid grants
With some grants, e.g. Regional Selective Investment Grants, which are made to help generate jobs in Assisted Areas, it is debatable whether they should be treated as capital grants or as revenue grants.

RATIOS

Ratios may be useful in looking at a manufacturing company's *tangible fixed assets*. For example, on plant and machinery:

Question 1: **Is it being kept well renewed?**

$$\text{Ratio 1} = \frac{\text{Additions each year}}{\text{Annual depreciation charge}}$$

Question 2: **Is it reasonably up to date?**

$$\text{Ratio 2} = \frac{\text{Cumulative depreciation}}{\text{Cumulative cost}}$$

For example LOCKER GROUP (see below):

Ratio 1 line (d) / line (k)
shows an increasing amount being spent each year on additions, compared with the annual depreciation charge.

LOCKER GROUP *Plant and equipment*

	Year to 31 Mar:	1996	1997	1998	1999	2000
		£000	£000	£000	£000	£000
	Cost					
(a)	At beginning of year	8,256	18,983	19,653	19,627	21,633
(b)	Exchange differences	272	(808)	(948)	21	(346)
(c)	Subsidiary acquired	10,078	–	–	760	–
(d)	Additions	611	1,855	1,543	1,847	2,307
(e)	Disposals	(234)	(377)	(621)	(622)	(975)
(f)	At end of year	18,983	19,653	19,627	21,633	22,619
	Depreciation					
(g)	At beginning of year	5,100	9,917	10,755	11,162	12,637
(h)	Exchange differences	149	(439)	(545)	9	(226)
(j)	Subsidiary acquired	3,966	–	–	436	–
(k)	Depreciation charge for year	880	1,573	1,490	1,587	1,736
(l)	Disposals	(178)	(296)	(538)	(557)	(666)
(m)	At end of year	9,917	10,755	11,162	12,637	13,481
	Ratios					
(d/k)	Additions / Depreciation charge	69.4%	117.9%	103.6%	116.4%	132.9%
(m/f)	Cu. depreciation / Cu. Cost	52.2%	54.7%	56.9%	58.4%	59.6%
(l/e)	Disposals: Depreciation / Cost	76.1%	78.5%	86.6%	89.5%	68.3%

Ratio 2, line (m) / line (f)
shows that cumulative depreciation is becoming a larger percentage of cumulative cost.

But ratios can be much more interesting if looked at in the context of what's happening in the company. For example, the 1996 column of the table shows that the Locker Group made a very large acquisition in that year.

The company acquired was called Pentre, and it was, in fact, a reverse takeover, in which the Chairman and the Chief Executive of Pentre (both founder directors of Pentre, aged 44 and 48 respectively) replaced Locker's elderly Chairman and its Chief Executive.

It is interesting to look at Ratio 2 of Pentre when acquired, and of Locker at the beginning of 1996:

£000		Pentre	Locker
Cu. Depreciation		3,966	5,100
Cumulative cost	=	10,078	8,256
Ratio 2		39.3%	61.8%

In other words, Pentre's plant and equipment was pretty up to date, while Locker's was getting a bit old, like the previous chairman.

Many companies in the service sectors have no significant amount of tangible fixed assets but where they do, for example with hotels, these ratios may be useful. For example the London restaurant chain GROUPE CHEZ GERARD:

GROUPE CHEZ GERARD *Fixtures and fittings*

Year end	Cumulative cost £000	Cumulative depreciation £000	Percentage depreciated
1994	1,323	944	71.4%
1995	1,533	1,085	70.8%
1996	1,980	1,271	64.2%
1997	3,049	1,586	52.0%
1998	4,050	2,031	50.1%

The improving trend was due partly to the opening of new restaurants, with brand new fixtures and fittings.

Chapter 9

FIXED ASSET INVESTMENTS

Types of investment

Investments may be fixed assets or current assets. This chapter considers only investments which are fixed assets, i.e. held long-term, rather than for resale or as a temporary store of value.

Fixed asset investments fall into four categories:

(a) investment in subsidiaries
(b) investment in associates
(c) investment in joint ventures
(d) other investments.

Investment in subsidiaries

In simple terms, a subsidiary undertaking is a company, partnership, or unincorporated association, where the company owning the investment (the holding company) is able to control the board of directors, either by virtue of its voting power or in some other way. A holding company is required by law to produce group accounts, in which the profits, assets and liabilities of the subsidiary are combined with those of the holding company, as described in detail in Chapters 20 and 21.

A company which is a holding company thus publishes two balance sheets: one for the company itself and a group balance sheet. This is demonstrated in the extract from the accounts of RMC shown below. The figures in the columns headed Parent are for investments owned directly by RMC itself.

The composition of *group* figures, which are clearly quite different, is explained in Chapters 20 to 22.

Investment in associates

Where an investing company or group holds a *participating interest* in a company *and exercises significant influence*, that company is deemed to be an **associate**.

A *participating interest* is an interest held by the investor on a long-term basis to secure a contribution to its activities by the exercise of control or influence. A holding of 20% or more is presumed to be a participating interest unless shown to the contrary.

To *exercise significant influence* the investor must be actively involved and influential in the making of policy decisions on strategic issues: for

---

RMC *note to the 1999 accounts*

Note 13 Fixed asset investments

	Parent			Group	
	1999	1998		1999	1998
Note 13 Fixed asset investments	£m	£m		£m	£m
Group undertakings	**1,938.8**	1,101.1		–	–
Joint ventures	**1.0**	9.3		**78.2**	61.9
Associated undertakings	–	–		**31.4**	39.8
Other investments	**278.6**	7.2		**287.8**	25.5
Total	**2,218.4**	1,117.6		**397.4**	127.2

example, on the expansion or contraction of the business, and on dividend policy.

Associates are covered in detail in Chapter 22.

Investments in joint ventures

Where the investor holds a long-term interest in a company and shares control under a contractual arrangement, that company is deemed to be a **joint venture**.

Joint ventures are covered in detail in Chapter 22.

Other fixed asset investments

Whereas at first sight it may seem that these will consist entirely of investments of less than 20% this is not always the case. However, where a company has a holding of 20% or more in another undertaking, but does not treat it as an associated undertaking or as a participating interest, it should explain why. For example:

TT GROUP *Extract from note to 1998 accounts*

Fixed asset investments
The UK listed Investments of the Group . . . include a 26.39% holding in the ordinary shares of Prestwick Holdings plc which has not been treated as an associated undertaking because the Group did not participate in the direction of its investment during the year and had no board representative.

Other investments may include works of art (as with CORDIANT, formerly SAATCHI & SAATCHI). Investments in works of art, other than by art dealers, should be viewed with distinct suspicion; directors should not indulge their artistic tastes with shareholders' money. In the past it has often been a warning sign of an arrogant top management.

They may also include life assurance policies and the company's own shares held for employee share option schemes:

DIAGEO *Extracts from the notes to the 2000 accounts*

14. Fixed assets – investments
Investment in associates comprises the cost of shares, less goodwill written off on acquisitions prior to 1 July 1998, of £962 million plus the group's share of acquisition reserves of £268 million. Investment in associates includes £901 million in respect of Moet Hennessey.

Investment in own ordinary shares comprised 25.1 million in respect of longer term incentive plans . . . and 7.3 million in respect of savings-related share option schemes. The market value of these shares at 30 June 2000 was £192 million.

The net book value of other investments listed on UK stock exchanges was £12 million, and on other stock exchanges was £39 million. These investments had a market value of £45 million.

TERMINOLOGY

Fixed asset investments

Fixed asset investments fall into four categories:

- investments in subsidiaries
- investments in associates
- investments in joint ventures
- other investments

A **subsidiary undertaking** is a company, partnership, or unincorporated association, where the company owning the investment (the **holding company**) is able to control the board of directors, either by virtue of its voting power or in some other way.

A holding company and its subsidiaries are termed a **group**.

An **associate** is an investment where the investor holds a participating interest and actually exercises significant influence.

A **joint venture** is an investment where the investor holds a long-term interest, and shares control under a contractual arrangement.

A **participating interest** is an interest held by the investing group or company on a long-term basis to secure a contribution to its activities by the exercise of control or influence. A holding of 20% or more of the shares of an undertaking is presumed to be a participating interest unless the contrary is shown.

Other investments should be shown separately:

KINGFISHER *Extract from note to 2000 accounts*

Fixed asset investments

Other Investments	Listed in the UK £m	Listed Overseas £m	Unlisted £m
At 30 January 1999	0.4	4.4	13.9
Additions	–	–	4.2
Disposals	–	–	(12.2)
Effect of foreign exchange rate changes		(0.6)	(1.1)
At 31 January 2000	0.4	3.8	4.8

The aggregate market value should also be shown where it differs from cost (CA 1985, Sch. 4, para. 45). Unlisted investments should be shown at cost or valuation.

Disclosures on significant holdings

Where a company holds *either* 20% or more of any class of share in another company, *or* the book value of the holding is more than one-fifth of the other company's assets, the accounts must show

- the name of the other company;
- country of incorporation if not Great Britain;
- if unincorporated, the address of the business;
- identity of each class of share held;
- the proportion held.

Balance sheet presentation

The Companies Act 1985 requires that where investments are shown as fixed assets, a further breakdown should be given, if individual amounts are material, either in the balance sheet itself or in notes:

(a) shares in group undertakings;
(b) loans to group undertakings;
(c) interests in associated undertakings;
(d) other participating interests;
(e) loans to undertakings at (c) and (d);
(f) other investments other than loans;
(g) other loans;
(h) own shares.

Points to watch

A holding may indicate

- the possibility of an eventual bid, particularly if the holder is predatory by nature;
- a blocking position taken by the holder to protect his trade interests from the risk of the company concerned being taken over by some (larger) competitor.

There is no hard and fast rule about which is which, and a holding could indicate a blocking position pending a possible bid in the distant future.

In this context it is worth checking whether directors have substantial holdings and, if so, whether any are nearing retirement age.

If the holding is of *20% or more* and the company is not treated as an associate, the chances are probably more in favour of a bid than a blocking position – the unwelcome holder of a substantial stake being unlikely to be given a seat on the board.

If the holding is of *25% or more* the holder is in the strong position of being able to block any arrangements and reconstructions that the company might wish to make with creditors and members under Section 425 of the Companies Act 1985, which require three-fourths to vote in favour.

Interlocking holdings

Where a number of companies under the same management have substantial holdings in each other or in another company, the holdings may be entirely innocent; but interlocking holdings can give scope for manipulation to the detriment of outside shareholders and should be viewed with caution.

A classic illustration of the dangers of interlocking holdings was provided by the affairs of several companies in the LOWSON GROUP, which came under investigation by the Department of Trade in 1973.

The appointed inspectors found that a number of defaults in the management 'were knowingly committed by Sir Denys [Lowson] and constituted grave mismanagement of the affairs of the companies concerned' and that in some transactions 'his motive was to obtain a very substantial gain for himself and his family'.

Take care where a chairman or chief executive's private interests seem difficult to distinguish from those of the group he manages.

As Robert Maxwell showed in connection with PERGAMON and MAXWELL COMMUNICATION CORPORATION, danger lies in wait for shareholders, employees, pensioners, and for the reputations and profits of city institutions and auditors alike, once private and public interests become intertwined.

We have more to say about related party transactions in Chapter 22.

Chapter 10

STOCKS AND WORK IN PROGRESS

Different classes of stock

Most manufacturing companies have traditionally shown stocks as a single figure under current assets, described either as 'stocks', as 'inventories' or as 'stocks and work in progress', but these terms cover three very different classes of asset:

(a) items in the state in which they were purchased; these include raw materials to be used in manufacture, components to be incorporated in the product and consumable stores (like paint and oil) which will be used in making it;
(b) items in an intermediate stage of completion ('work in progress', or in the United States 'work in process');
(c) finished goods.

For wholesalers and retailers, stocks are almost entirely goods purchased for resale.

Subclassification

The balance sheet formats in Schedule 4 of the Companies Act 1985 require stocks to be analysed under the following subheadings:

(a) raw materials and consumables;
(b) work in progress;
(c) finished goods and goods for resale;
(d) payments on account (for items of stock not yet received).

SSAP 9 calls for the accounts to show the subclassification of stocks and work in progress 'in a manner which is appropriate to the business and so as to indicate the amounts held in each of the main categories'. For example, GLENMORANGIE's stock is mostly whisky:

GLENMORANGIE *Note to the 2000 accounts*

Note 15 Stocks

	2000 £000	1999 £000
Group		
Whisky	63,995	59,112
Other stocks	2,327	2,009
	66,322	61,121

The matching principle

Expenditure on stocks which remain unsold or unconsumed at the balance sheet date (or upon work in progress which is incomplete) is carried forward into the following period and set against the revenue from the stocks when it arises. This is an application of what accountants term the matching principle, i.e. matching cost and revenue in the year in which the revenue arises rather than charging the cost in the year in which it is incurred.

Dead stock

Stocks and work in progress should be valued at the lower of cost and net realisable value, and any irrecoverable cost (e.g. due to deterioration or obsolescence) should be charged to revenue.

Allowing 'dead' stock to be carried forward at cost is a classic way of boosting profits.

Consistency

The method of valuing stock should be consistent, and most sets of accounts include a brief statement in the notes on how stocks have been valued:

THE BODY SHOP *Extract from accounting policies 2001*

Stocks are valued at the lower of cost and net realisable value. Cost is calculated as follows:

Raw materials	Cost of purchase on a first-in first-out basis.
Work in progress and finished goods	Cost of raw materials and labour together with attributable overheads.

Net realisable value is based on estimated selling price less further costs to completion and disposal.

DIAGEO *Extract from accounting policies 2000*

Stocks are stated at the lower of cost and net realisable value. Cost includes raw materials, direct labour and expenses, and an appropriate proportion of production and other overheads.

A particular point to look for is any statement of a change in the basis between year ends and, when one is made, why, and whether any indication is given of how much difference the change has made to the year-end stock figure and, hence, to profits.

The importance of stock valuation
The accurate valuation of stock on a consistent basis is important, because quite small percentage variations can very significantly affect profits:

Example 10.1 Stock valuation

	£000	£000
Sales		2,000
Cost of goods sold:		
Opening stock	600	
Purchases in period	1,500	
	2,100	
Closing stock	400	
		1,700
		300
Wages, overheads, etc.		200
Operating profit		100

Had the opening stock been overstated by 10% (at £660,000) and the closing stock undervalued by 10% (at £360,000), the cost of goods sold would appear £100,000 higher and the operating profit would have been wiped out.

Problems in valuing stock
Three main problems arise in valuing stock:

(a) the price to be used if an item has been supplied at varying prices;

(b) the value added in manufacture both to incomplete items (work in progress) and to completed items (finished goods);

(c) the assessment of net realisable value.

Stocks in a large retail business
Having defined the main principles and problems, let us now look at stocks in practice, beginning with the control of stocks in a large retail business, where virtually all stocks are goods purchased for resale and the complications of work in progress (WIP) and finished goods do not arise.

The central management of most supermarkets controls the efficiency and honesty of local stores by charging goods out to those stores at selling price, and by maintaining overall stock control accounts in terms of selling price by broad product groups. By suitably analysing takings it will then be possible, for each of these product groups, to compare theoretical stock with actual stock:

$$\begin{array}{l}\text{Opening} \\ \text{stock at} \\ \text{selling} \\ \text{price}\end{array} + \begin{array}{l}\text{Deliveries} \\ \text{at selling} \\ \text{price}\end{array} - \text{Takings} = \begin{array}{l}\text{Theoretical} \\ \text{closing stock at} \\ \text{selling price}\end{array}$$

With this sort of operation, it is usual for the purpose of monthly, quarterly, half-yearly and annual accounts to deduct from the value of stock at selling price the normal gross profit margin:

TESCO *Extract from accounting policies* 2000

Stocks comprise goods held for resale and development properties, and are valued at the lower of cost and net realisable value. Stocks in stores are calculated at retail prices and reduced by appropriate margins to the lower of cost and net realisable value.

SSAP 9 requires that before such a figure is used for the purposes of the annual accounts, it be tested to ensure that it gives a 'reasonable approximation of the actual cost'.

Stocks in a manufacturing business
Most manufacturing businesses employ a system of cost accounting. They do so

(a) as an aid to price fixing, so that they can charge the customer with the materials used and the time actually taken to complete the job – as is the case with a motor repair garage, or jobbing builder;

(b) in order to provide the estimating department with information on which to base future estimates or tenders; and/or

(c) as a means of controlling operating efficiency.

The type of record employed varies widely, from a few scribblings on the back of an envelope, to a cost system parallel to the normal financial system, reconciled with it but not part of it, right up to a completely integral cost and financial accounting system. In all but the first of these there is normally some form of stock record.

Methods of pricing issues from stock

Several different methods of pricing issues from stock are commonly employed, and the value of the stock remaining depends to some extent on the pricing method used.

FIFO (First In, First Out)

Good storekeeping demands that goods should, so far as is possible, be used in the order in which they are received; it merely assumes for accounting purposes that the normal rules of good storekeeping have been followed.

Average or weighted average price

When an organisation receives a number of deliveries during an accounting period at a series of different prices, it is reasonable to take the average price or, for more accuracy, the weighted average price.

Replacement cost and NIFO (Next In, First Out)

In the past, items in stock were occasionally stated in the accounts at replacement cost when this was lower than both cost and net realisable value. The effect of this was to increase the cost of goods sold for the period, and thus reduce reported profits. The statement of stocks at the lowest of cost, net realisable value and replacement cost is not (under SSAP 9) an acceptable basis of stock valuation.

LIFO (Last In, First Out)

Another method of valuation, permitted by the Companies Acts and commonplace in the United States but unacceptable under SSAP 9, is the last in, first out (LIFO) basis in which issues are charged at the latest price at which they could conceivably have come. This has the advantage of charging the customer with the most recent price; but in the balance sheet stocks appear at the price of the earliest delivery from which they could have arisen. The basic rule of good storekeeping is (in theory only) reversed, and goods received latest are assumed to be used first.

Thus, in a time of rising prices LIFO has the effect of

(a) showing stocks in the balance sheet at a cost appropriate not to recent purchases but to those many months or even years earlier; and, consequently,

(b) reducing profit made on holding stock.

Taxation of stock profits

Suppose that a company has an opening stock of raw materials of £10m at the beginning of the year. At the end of the year the closing stock comprises exactly the same material quantities as the opening stock but, because of inflation and/or rising commodity prices, the value under FIFO has risen to £11m:

Opening stock of raw materials	£10,000,000
Closing stock of raw materials	11,000,000
Increase in value of stock	1,000,000

This increase in value of £1m reduces the cost of goods sold by £1m, which adds £1m to pre-tax profit. This stock profit, although unrealised, bears Corporation Tax at 30% = £300,000 tax, which has to be paid even though the physical amount of stock is unchanged.

The problems of stocks in an inflationary situation will be discussed further in Chapter 29.

Requirements of the Companies Act 1985 and of SSAP 9 on stocks and WIP

The Companies Act 1985 allows the use of FIFO, LIFO, weighted average price or any other similar method to be used for fungible assets (assets substantially indistinguishable from one another) but, where the amount shown differs materially from the replacement cost (or the most recent purchase price or production cost), the amount of that difference must be disclosed (Sch. 4, para. 27).

The inclusion of overheads in cost

It was at one time accepted that companies should be free to choose whether to value work in progress and finished goods

(a) at prime cost: that is to say, to exclude all overheads; or

(b) at variable (or marginal) cost: that is to say to exclude all fixed overheads, but include prime cost plus variable overheads; or

(c) at the full cost of purchase plus the cost of conversion (including fixed overheads too).

The Companies Act 1985 and SSAP 9 both regard (c) as the only proper method. The classification of overheads between fixed and variable is regarded as an unsuitable one for determining whether or not they should be included in the cost of conversion: the dividing line is too imprecise.

Costs of general management, as distinct from functional management, are excluded unless directly related to current production (as they may be to some extent in smaller companies), but the Companies Act 1985 does allow a reasonable proportion of interest on capital borrowed to finance production costs to be included in the value of stock; however, if this is done the amount must be disclosed (Sch. 4, para. 26).

Net realisable value
Net realisable value is 'the actual or estimated selling price (net of trade but before settlement discounts) less:

(a) all further costs to completion; and
(b) all costs to be incurred in marketing, selling and distributing'.

Consignment stocks

Consignment stocks are stocks held by one party, **'the dealer'**, but legally owned by another party, **the manufacturer**. The terms of the agreement between them give the dealer the right to sell the stock in the normal course of his business or, at *his* option, to return it unsold to the legal owner.

FRS 5 *Reporting the substance of transactions* requires the agreement to be analysed to decide how it actually works in practice.

If it can be shown that the benefits and risks remain with the manufacturer until transfer of legal title, the stock will not be included in the dealer's balance sheet. For example CAFFYNS:

CAFFYNS *Note to the 2001 accounts*

Note 14 Stocks

	2001 £000	2000 £000
Group		
Vehicles	11,773	11,241
...		
Vehicles on consignment	3,777	2,247
...		
	22,096	21,647

In addition, non-interest bearing consignment vehicles excluded from the balance sheet at 31 March 2001 had a cost of £2,804,000 (2000 – £5,754,000)

The danger of rising stocks

Although SSAP 9's requirement to include production overheads in arriving at the cost of finished goods gives a fair picture when stocks are being maintained at prudent levels in relation to demand, when a manufacturer leaves production unchanged in periods of

---

TERMINOLOGY

Stocks

Cost, in relation to stocks, is expenditure which is incurred in the normal course of business in bringing the product or service to its present location and condition. It includes, in addition to cost of purchase, costs of conversion that are appropriate to that location and condition.

Cost of purchase comprises purchase price including import duties, transport and handling costs and any other directly attributable costs, less trade discounts, rebates and subsidies.

Cost of conversion comprises:

(a) costs which are specifically attributable to units of production, e.g., direct labour, direct expenses and sub-contracted work;
(b) production overheads;
(c) other overheads, if any, attributable in the particular circumstances of the business to bringing the product or service to its present location and condition.

Production overheads are overheads incurred in respect of materials, labour or services for production, based on the normal level of activity, taking one year with another.

Net realisable value is the actual or estimated selling price (net of trade but before settlement discounts) less

(a) all further costs to completion; and
(b) all costs to be incurred in marketing, selling and distributing.

Unit cost is the cost of purchasing or manufacturing identifiable units of stock.

Average price is the price computed by dividing the total cost of the item by the total number of units. This average price may be arrived at by means of continuous calculation, a periodic calculation or a moving periodic calculation.

FIFO (first in, first out) represents the calculation of the cost of stocks on the basis that quantities in hand represent the latest purchases or production.

LIFO (last in, first out) represents the calculation of the cost of stocks on the basis that quantities in hand represent the earliest purchases or production.

Replacement cost is the cost at which an identical asset could be purchased or manufactured.

lower demand their inclusion can produce unduly optimistic profits (see Example 10.2). In practice, the profit from full production would be likely to be reduced by interest charges to finance carrying increased stock, but even so management may try to bolster profits in the short term by continuing high production in the face of falling demand. Rising stocks unmatched by rising turnover may give some warning here, and this can be monitored by the ratio stocks/turnover.

Here is an example of a rising stocks/turnover ratio giving warning of trouble. It illustrates two key points. See if you can spot them.

SPRING RAM *Extract from chairman's statement 1991*

A most satisfying result was achieved for the year under review, despite a generally very difficult economic climate. Group profits before tax advanced to a record £37.6m (1990 £30.1m), an increase of 25% on the previous year. Consolidated turnover of £194.2m (1990 £145.3m) ... Earnings per share were 7.1p (1990 5.4p).

But in market conditions described by the chief executive of one housebuilder, BELLWINCH, as 'certainly the worst in post-war years', Spring Ram's results seemed too good to be true. The sharp rise in the ratio 'finished goods and goods for resale/turnover', to the unprecedented level of 13.5%, was a warning signal.

The 1992 interim results showed further growth in turnover, profits and earnings per share. It wasn't until the week before the 1992 final figures were due to be announced that Spring Ram issued a profit warning and asked for its shares to be suspended.

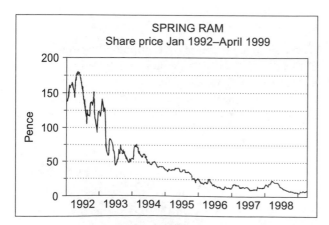

SPRING RAM
Share price Jan 1992–April 1999

Profits at a bathroom manufacturing subsidiary had been overstated by £5.6m, mainly through the inflation of stock values and sales.

Example 10.2 Rising stocks

A company with a single-product factory faces a year in which demand is forecast to fall by 30% due to an economic recession.

> Production overheads (rent of factory, etc.) = £1m
> Production capacity = 100,000 units per annum
> Variable costs = £10 per unit
> Selling price = £25 per unit
> Sales last year = 100,000 units

The management is faced with the decision of whether

(a) to continue at full production, hoping that demand will pick up sharply the following year if not sooner, and that it possibly won't fall quite as sharply as forecast; or

(b) to cut production by up to 30%.

Under SSAP 9, assuming demand does fall by 30%, the figures that will be reported at the end of the year under these two choices will be:

	(a) Full production Units	(b) Production cut by 30% Units
Opening stock	20,000	20,000
Units manufactured	100,000	70,000
	120,000	90,000
Units sold	70,000	70,000
Closing stock	50,000	20,000
Fixed costs	1,000,000	1,000,000
Variable costs (£10 per unit)	1,000,000	700,000
Total costs	2,000,000	1,700,000
Costs per unit manufactured	£20	£24.285

Profit and loss account

	£	£
Sales (£25 per unit)	1,750,000	1,750,000
Cost of goods sold:		
Opening stock (£20 per unit)	400,000	400,000
Cost of units manufactured	2,000,000	1,700,000
less Closing stock by FIFO method	1,000,000 (£20)	485,700 (£24.285)
Cost of goods sold	1,400,000	1,614,300
Gross (or Trading) profit	350,000	135,700

NOTE: A watchful auditor would require to be satisfied (i) as to the net realisable value of the closing stock under (a); and (ii) that the requirements of SSAP 9 regarding spreading of overheads on the basis of 'normal production' were met.

SPRING RAM *Extracts from 1987–1991 accounts*

	1987 £000	1988 £000	1989 £000	1990 £000	1991 £000
Turnover	60,785	85,173	121,017	145,285	194,173
Stocks					
Raw materials	3,296	6,386	8,035	8,813	12,984
Work in progress	297	927	1,160	1,277	1,787
Finished goods and goods for resale	4,508	10,041	10,984	15,019	26,255
Total stocks	8,101	17,354	20,179	25,109	41,026
Ratios (%)					
Raw materials/turnover	5.4	7.5	6.6	6.1	6.7
WIP/turnover	0.5	1.1	1.0	0.9	0.9
Finished goods and goods for resale/turnover	7.4	11.8	9.1	10.3	13.5
Total stocks/turnover	13.3	20.4	16.7	17.3	21.1

Key point 1

When a sector of the market is going through hard times, and the management of a company in that sector tells you 'we are going to buck the trend', be highly sceptical. Our experience is that they are about to run into very serious trouble.

Key point 2

If a company's results seem too good to be true, don't believe them.

LONG-TERM CONTRACTS

A long-term contract is defined by SSAP 9 as 'a contract entered into for manufacture or building of a single substantial entity or the provision of a service where the time taken to manufacture, build or provide is such that a substantial proportion of all such contract work will extend for a period exceeding one year'.

Shipbuilders, constructional engineers and the like frequently engage in long-term contracts. Because of the length of time such contracts take to complete, to defer taking profit into account until completion would result in the profit and loss account reflecting not a true and fair view of the activity of the company during the year, but rather the results of those contracts which, by the accident of time, were completed by the year end.

It is normal with long-term contracts to have an arrangement under which the contractor receives payment on account on the basis of the 'work certified' by an architect or surveyor. Traditionally, there are two ways of computing the profit to be taken. The 'work certified' is an essential piece of information whichever of the two ways of arriving at the profit to date is adopted.

Under the first method, profit to date is computed as follows:

$$\text{Work certified at balance sheet date} - \text{Costs incurred on contract to date} = \text{Profit to date}$$

The second method takes the overall profit expected:

$$\text{Total contract price} - \text{Total costs incurred on contract to date} - \text{Total estimated further costs to completion}$$

and multiplies it by $\dfrac{\text{Work certified to date}}{\text{Total contract price}}$

to arrive at the profit to date.

If the first formula is used it is still necessary to have regard to the costs likely to be incurred in completing the job, for it is clearly wrong to take a profit on the first stage of a contract if the profit is likely to be lost at a later stage. In either case, in considering future costs, it is necessary to allow for likely increases in wages and salaries, in the price of raw materials and in general overheads, in so far as these items are not recoverable from the customer under the terms of the contract: inflation can play havoc with the profitability of fixed-price or inadequately protected contracts, as many companies have learned to their cost.

In neither case is it usual to take up the entire profit to date. Some companies take only two-thirds, others only three-quarters.

Many multiply by a further fraction:

$$\frac{\text{Amount received to date}}{\text{Work certified to date}}$$

Where the customer is entitled (as is usually the case) to retain, say, 10% of the amount certified as 'retention monies', so as to ensure satisfactory rectification of any defects, the use of this further fraction of, in this case, 9/10, has the effect of disregarding that part of the profit appropriate to the amount retained.

The amount reflected in the year's profit and loss account will be the appropriate proportion of the total profit by reference to the work done to date, less any profit already taken up in prior years on the contracts still on hand. The aim of using a multiplying factor of two-thirds or three-quarters is to ensure that unless the remaining work on a contract is disastrous, some profit remains to be taken when the contract is finally completed.

The second formula relies on an estimate of future costs and is therefore open to subjective judgement. Results should be viewed with caution if the overall profitability margin is estimated to be higher than the margin to date; i.e. if the second formula allows a higher profit to be taken now than the first formula would allow.

Example 10.3 Long-term contracts: COMMERCIAL CONTRACTS LTD

COMMERCIAL CONTRACTS LTD is engaged in a long-term bridge-building contract.

		£000
Work certified to 31 December 1999	W	1,250
Total contract price	P	2,000
Costs incurred on contract to 31 December 1999	C	1,025
Estimated further costs to completion	E	575
Amount received from customer by 31 December 1999	R	1,125
Profit taken on the contract in 1998	T	45

The company takes up three-quarters of the profit earned to date, reduced by the fraction:

amount received to date ÷ work certified to date.

What profit will be taken up on the contract in 1999?

Using the first formula:
Profit to date = W − C = £225,000

Of which $^3/_4 \times R \div W = ^3/_4 \times 1,125,000 \div 1,250,000 = 67^1/_2\%$ (£151,875) will be taken as profit by 31 December 1999.

But £45,000 of this was taken up in 1998, so only £106,875 remains to be taken in 1999.

Using the second formula:
Profit to date = (P − C − E) × W ÷ P = (£2,000,000 − £1,025,000 − £575,000) × 1,250,000 ÷ 2,000,000 = £250,000.

Of this £250,000 profit, $67^1/_2\%$ will be taken up (as before), i.e. £168,750, less the £45,000 already taken up in 1998 = £123,750.

The difference between the two figures for profit to date is due to the difference between the profit margin on that part of the contract completed to date (£225,000 on £1,250,000 in the first formula = 18%) and that estimated on the contract as a whole (£400,000 on £2 million in the second formula = 20%).

SSAP 9 requirements on long-term contracts

In the past, accounting treatment of long-term contracts has varied enormously from company to company. BOVIS, for example, in its 1972 accounts noted that 'no provision is made for anticipated future losses' and a year later had to be rescued by P. & O. At the other end of the scale companies like JOHN LAING pursued policies of extreme prudence: all losses were taken when they were foreseen, but no account was taken of profits on contracts unfinished at the end of the year.

SSAP 9 requires that 'The amount at which long-term contract work in progress is stated in periodic financial statements should be cost plus any attributable profit, less any foreseeable losses and progress payments received and receivable', and the amount of attributable profit included should be disclosed. Attributable profits on contracts are, however, only required to be taken up when 'it is considered that their outcome can be assessed with reasonable certainty before their conclusion'; if the outcome cannot be reasonably assessed, 'it is prudent not to take up any profit', so management is still left with a certain latitude, and the key point to watch for is undue anticipation of profits.

SSAP 9 also requires balance sheets to show how the amount included for long-term contracts is reached by stating:

(i) the amount of work in progress at cost plus attributable profit (i.e. profit or loss taken to date), less foreseeable losses;

(ii) cash received and receivable at the accounting date as progress payments on account of contracts in progress, as Example 10.4 illustrates:

Example 10.4 Long-term contracts: COMMERCIAL CONTRACTS LTD (continued)

If the bridge contract we discussed in Example 10.3 was the only contract of Commercial Contracts Ltd to appear in the balance sheet at 31 December 1997, and if the first formula was used, it would appear in the balance sheet as follows:

	£000	£000
Work in progress, at cost		
plus Profit taken to date	1,176	
Less Cash received from customer	1,125	
		51

The MACLELLAN GROUP, whose activities include the design, supply and installation of specialist welded and fabricated products in stainless steel, provides an actual example:

MACLELLAN GROUP *Extracts from Financial statements 2000*

Accounting policies – Long term contracts

. . . Turnover is calculated on the basis of the work done, and, when a profitable outcome to the contract can be assessed with reasonable certainty, includes attributable profit.

Attributable profit is calculated on a prudent basis for each contract by reference to the contract's cumulative turnover, total contract value and total profit estimated for the completed contract.

Full provision is made for any foreseen losses on contracts. . . .

Note 11 Stocks

	2000 **£000**	1999 £000
Long term contracts		
Net cost less foreseeable losses	13,565	8,039
Payments on account	(10,136)	(6,712)
	3,429	1,327
Raw materials and consumables	428	178
	3,857	1,505

STOCK RATIOS

Except when stocks are built up in anticipation of sharp price rises, well-run companies usually try to carry the minimum stock needed for the satisfactory running of their business. They do so

(a) to minimise interest charges on the money tied up in stocks;
(b) to save unnecessary storage costs (including pilferage); and
(c) to reduce the risk of being left with goods that can't be sold due to deterioration, becoming obsolete or going out of fashion.

Although some distortion can occur with accelerating growth, because stock is a year-end figure while sales occur throughout the year (on average several months earlier), a rising stock ratio without any special reason is regarded as bad news, reflecting lack of demand for goods and/or poor stock control.

Stocks/Turnover ratio

The most generally used stock ratio (as shown in our Spring Ram example on page 68) is

$$\frac{\text{Stocks}}{\text{Turnover}} \text{ expressed as a percentage}$$

Stocks/Turnover ratios vary enormously with the nature of a business. At one end of the scale, and apart from advertising agencies and other service industries, ready-mixed concrete companies probably have one of the lowest Stocks/Turnover figures of any industry: aggregates are extracted from the ground when required and the product is delivered the same day, so all that is needed in stock is a supply of fresh cement and fuel, giving a typical Stocks/Turnover figure of 5%. At the other end of the scale a company which maintains depots of finished goods and replacement parts world-wide, like a power transmission and mechanical handling systems manufacturer, can reasonably be expected to have a ratio as high as 35% in order to maintain a first-class service to its customers all over the world. Nevertheless, a high ratio in comparison to similar companies is undesirable.

For an average manufacturing company a Stocks/Turnover ratio of around 15–20% would be reasonable, increasing the larger and more complex the goods made; for instance, an aircraft manufacturer might have stocks and WIP representing 30–35% of turnover and this level could be subject to sharp fluctuations, depending on whether completed aircraft had been delivered to clients just before or just after the end of the year; in contrast, a company

71

making a limited range of nuts and bolts could probably run on a few weeks' stock, though if supplies were subject to interruption and/or shortages it might be prudent to carry more raw materials, and if orders tended to be erratic a higher stock of finished goods would be needed.

Stocks/Cost of sales ratio

P & L accounts using Format 1 (see page 106) show the *cost of sales*. Where this is available it can be used to compute the average amount of stock held during the year, which can be expressed as so many months' stock, or so many days' stock. Many analysts take the average of the opening and closing stocks, which has a smoothing effect, and dampens the effect of a major change in stocks over the period.

$$\text{Stock (months)} = \frac{(\text{Opening stock} + \text{Closing stock}) \div 2}{\text{Cost of sales}} \times 12$$

$$\text{Stock (days)} = \frac{(\text{Opening stock} + \text{Closing stock}) \div 2}{\text{Cost of sales}} \times 365$$

Cost of sales/Stock ratio

The previous ratio can be inverted, Cost of sales/Stock, to give the number of times the stock has been turned over in the year, the **stockturn**:

$$\text{Stockturn} = \frac{\text{Cost of sales}}{(\text{Opening stock} + \text{Closing stock}) \div 2}$$

Example 10.5 Calculation of stock ratios

Extracted from accounts:

	1998	1999	2000
	£m	£m	£m
Year-end stock	2.10	2.20	3.00
Sales		10.00	12.00
Cost of sales		7.50	8.00

Ratios:

	1999	2000
Stocks/Sales	22.0%	25.0%
Stock (days)	104.6 days	118.6 days
Stockturn	3.49 ×	3.08 ×

Chapter 11

DEBTORS

TRADE DEBTORS AND OTHER DEBTORS

Introduction

Debtors (also known as 'receivables') are a current asset, representing amounts owing to the business.

The Companies Act 1985 require debtors to be subdivided into

- trade debtors – those arising from the sale of goods on credit;
- amounts owed by group undertakings – see Chapter 20;
- amounts owed by undertakings in which the company has a participating interest – see Chapter 22;
- other debtors – for example debts due from the sale of fixed assets or investments; and
- prepayments and accrued income – for example rent or rates paid in advance.

The amount falling due after more than one year should be shown separately for each item included under debtors. Other items which may be found shown separately under debtors (and which are not trade debtors for the purpose of computing collection ratios) include

(a) Corporation Tax recoverable (in respect of loss relief etc. – see Chapter 17);
(b) deferred taxation (see Chapter 17);
(c) pension prepayments (see Chapter 16);
(d) amounts receivable under finance leases (see Chapter 16);
(e) loan notes (see Chapter 6).

Most companies show a single figure for debtors in their balance sheet, and give the required details in a note, as illustrated here.

THE BODY SHOP *Extract from note to the accounts*

Debtors	2001 £m	2000 £m
Amounts falling due within one year		
Trade debtors	30.3	30.3
Other debtors	12.8	10.1
Prepayments	4.7	5.5
	47.8	45.9
Amounts falling due after more than one year		
Other debtors*	6.7	6.0
	54.5	51.9

* Included in 'Other debtors' is £6.0 million relating to the deferred payment arrangement on the sale of manufacturing to Creative Outsourcing Solutions International Ltd. Payments of £0.6 million are due each February until 2010.

Bad debts and doubtful debtors

The granting of credit inevitably involves some risk that the debtor will fail to pay, that is, will become a bad debt. When a business recognises that a debt is bad, the debt is written off to the profit and loss account. That is to say, the balance appearing as 'debtors' falls by the amount of the debt, and 'bad debts' appears as an expense. But this expense is shown separately in the published accounts only if the amount is material.

In addition, it is normal to set up a 'provision for doubtful debtors'. To do so a charge is made to the profit and loss account and, in the balance sheet, the cumulative provision for doubtful debtors is deducted from the total debtors. It is disclosed separately in the published accounts only if it is material. A provision for doubtful debtors may be specific, that is to say where management estimate the probable loss, studying each debt in turn; for instance, there is a 10% probability that Tin Pott plc will fail to pay its debt of £121,000, they must therefore provide £12,100; or it may be general, e.g. $2^1/_2$% of total debtors; or a combination of the two.

The importance of debtors

Companies such as supermarket chains, whose turnover is almost entirely for cash, will have very few debtors; the figure appearing in the balance sheet is likely to be largely prepayments and non-trade debtors. Trade debtors may have little significance. SAINSBURY, for example, with sales excluding VAT of £14,500m, showed trade debtors of a mere £50m in its 1998 accounts. At the other extreme are companies whose entire turnover is on credit terms, in which case very large amounts of working capital may be tied up in debtors. Here the efficiency with which credit accounts are handled, and the timing of the taking of profit where payments are by instalment, are of considerable interest to the analyst.

Debt collection period

The ratio Trade debtors/Sales can be used to monitor a company's credit control. Logically it should be sales including VAT, because the debtors include VAT, but the VAT inclusive figure is not usually available.

Analysts often feel that a more meaningful measure is that expressed in terms of time, as the debt collection period (or, simply, the collection period) in days or months:

$$\text{Debt collection period (days)} = \frac{\text{Trade debtors}}{\text{Sales}} \times 365$$

$$\text{Debt collection period (months)} = \frac{\text{Trade debtors}}{\text{Sales}} \times 12$$

But it may be expressed simply as a percentage of sales:

$$\frac{\text{Trade debtors}}{\text{Sales}} \times 100$$

For example, given Trade debtors of £8.219m and Sales of £50m:

$$\text{Collection period} = \frac{£8.219m}{£50m} \times 365 = 60 \text{ days}$$

$$\text{Collection period} = \frac{£8.219m}{£50m} \times 12 = 1.97 \text{ months}$$

$$\frac{\text{Trade debtors}}{\text{Sales}} = \frac{£8.219m}{£50m} \times 100 = 16.4\%$$

Trade debtors/Sales has the advantage of stating the percentage of the year's sales which were outstanding at the balance sheet date (which is correct) rather than suggesting that the business' debtors represent 60 days' sales (which we cannot say).

Apart from 'strictly cash' businesses like supermarkets, with virtually zero debtors, normal terms tend to be payment at the end of the month following delivery, so with 100% prompt payment the average credit given would be between 6 and 7 weeks, making debtors about 12% of turnover. In practice, a figure of 15–20% is quite normal although some companies may, as a matter of policy, give more generous credit in order to give themselves a competitive edge, while others may factor their debts (see pages 78–9) and so possibly show abnormally low debtors.

A falling collection period is generally a good sign – an indication of effective financial control – but it could reflect a desperate need for cash, involving extra discounts for cash and undue pressure on customers.

On the other hand, a marked rise in the ratio can be a warning signal. For example BOOSEY & HAWKES:

BOOSEY & HAWKES *Extracts from 1999 accounts*

	1999 £000	1998 £000
Profit and loss account		
Turnover	96,766	98,895
Note on debtors		
Trade debtors	25,568	20,699
Ratio (calculated)		
$\dfrac{\text{Trade Debtors}}{\text{Turnover}} =$	**26.4%**	**20.9%**

The huge jump in the ratio suggested that there might be 'something nasty in the woodshed'. And so there was:

BOOSEY & HAWKES *Extracts from 2000 Interim report*

CHAIRMAN'S STATEMENT

. . .

North American bad debt provision

Earlier this year the Board made a decision to investigate possible securitisation of trade debt . . . As part of this process, we instigated a review of the sales ledger of our Chicago-based distribution company, Boosey & Hawkes Musical Instruments Inc. The results of this review indicated that, for the past two years, the level of bad debt provisioning was significantly inadequate and that some of these debts are irrecoverable.

. . . the directors have made a provision of £3.52m which has been fully charged as an exceptional item. Further investigations are being conducted into the levels of stock . . .

The Chairman commented: 'Having regard to the underlying trading performance of the Group and our confidence for the remainder of the year the directors have declared an interim dividend of 2.395p (1999: 2.395p)'.

But his confidence was misplaced. There was worse to come:

BOOSEY & HAWKES *Extracts from Trading statement November 2000*

. . .

These investigations [conducted by Ernst & Young, the Group's auditors] are now nearing completion. A write-down of a further £10m will be required, which has arisen mainly in the areas of stock and prepayments as a result of a long series of misleading and incorrect accounting entries . . . The personnel responsible have been dismissed and the evidence supporting a legal action against them is being evaluated . . . A final dividend is therefore unlikely to be paid.

What we would like to know

The analyst can tell comparatively little about debtors unless a significant proportion of debtors are due after more than one year or unless the company discloses more than the minimum information required by law. Among the things which one would like to find out (and should be on the look out for any hint about in the chairman's statement or financial review) are the following:

1. Is an undue proportion due from one major customer, or from customers in one industry?
2. Would failure of one or two customers have a material effect upon the company's future?
3. What is the age pattern of debtors? Are some unduly old?
4. Is there adequate provision for bad and doubtful debts?
5. Are any of the debts which fall due after more than one year very long-term in nature? In the United Kingdom debtors appear at their face value regardless of when they are due. In the United States, if a debt is not due within one year, it is usually necessary to discount it, i.e. to take account of imputed interest. Thus, a debt of $1m due three years hence might appear, taking interest into account at 10%, as $751,300.

Factors affecting the debt collection period

A short debt collection period is, other things being equal, preferable to a longer one; but as with many ratios one has to qualify this general principle. For by restricting credit and selling entirely for cash, a business can have a zero debt collection period; but if this drives its customers into the arms of competitors it is scarcely an improvement so far as the business as a whole is concerned. Subject to that

qualification, any improvement in collection period, since it represents a reduction in overall debtors, means that more capital is available for other purposes, or that there is less need to borrow money from the bank.

At first sight it may seem that an increase in collection period represents a fall in the efficiency of the debt collection section. This is likely to be the case, but it is not necessarily so. The debt collection period may increase (decrease) between one period and another for a number of reasons:

- if there is a policy change with regard to:

  (a) credit terms to existing customers; if, for example, the board of directors, to obtain a valuable order from a major customer, offers two months' credit instead of one;
  (b) the granting of credit; for instance, if potential customers whose credit ratings were formerly insufficient for them to be granted credit, are granted credit – for such customers are unlikely to be among the fastest payers;

- where there is poor credit management or accounts administration, e.g.:

  (a) if credit is given to unsatisfactory customers;
  (b) if the invoicing section falls behind; customers will not pay until they receive an invoice and, in general, pay at a fixed time determined by the date on which they receive it, e.g. at the end of the month in which they receive the invoice;
  (c) if statements are late – while some businesses ignore statements, others wait until they receive one;
  (d) if there is no consistent follow-up of overdue debts, by letter and/or telephone, or as a last resort in person;

- if a subsidiary with an atypical debt collection period is disposed of or acquired, e.g. BASS's sale of the CORAL betting business and over 300 managed pubs in 1998 increased the group's debt collection period by several days;
- if factoring or invoice discounting is introduced or discontinued (see pages 78–9).

Although it is necessary for most businesses to offer some credit, any unnecessary credit is bad management because it ties up money which (normally) earns no return, and which is subject to increased risk. The customer who is short of money, and who finds he can order things from a company without having to pay for them at the end of the month, tends to place more and more of his orders with that company; if he later goes into liquidation, he may do so owing a hefty amount.

Debtors due after more than one year

Traditionally, liabilities were regarded as current if they were expected to fall due within one year. Similarly, assets were treated as current if it was expected that they would be turned into cash within one year. The Companies Act 1985 changed that. Debtors are shown under current assets whenever they fall due, though the amount falling due after more than one year is required to be shown separately for each item. The inconsistency is clearly evident in the accounts of the leisure management group KUNICK (see next column), where the figure for net current liabilities of £6.866m. in 2000 included as a current asset the item 'Debtors; falling due after more than one year' of £2.957m. The Act does not require companies to show the split on the face of the balance sheet (like KUNICK does), but UITF Abstract 4 requires this where the amount is material in the context of net current assets. But the misdescription 'net current assets' usually remains, leading the unwary to compute a false current ratio (see p. 98).

Where long-term debtors seem an important factor in assessing a group's future, considerable research may be necessary. Companies are sometimes so keen to get rid of an unprofitable activity (perhaps an unwanted part of an acquisition) that they will sell to anybody who is willing to take the activity off their hands, regardless of their financial weakness, and give them extended credit.

And it's not unknown for companies to guarantee borrowings the acquirer has made to help finance the deal, which is simply asking for trouble (see pages 103–4 on contingent liabilities). Debts which persist long after a subsidiary is sold should raise suspicions.

Similarly, advances to a company which later becomes a subsidiary raise the question of whether the acquisition itself was in some way forced (to maintain supplies, or custom), and whether the advance has become in the nature of capital.

It would also be worth asking about the £1.692m of properties that KUNICK was holding for resale. Were the properties surplus in a reorganization after acquisitions or disposals? How much is a carry forward from 1999's figure of £2.285m? Has it not been possible to find buyers?

KUNICK *Extract from 2000 consolidated balance sheet*

	Notes	2000 £000	1999 £000
Current assets			
Assets held for resale	18	1,692	2,285
Stocks		2,734	5,602
Debtors			
Falling due within one year	20	28,471	29,561
after more than one year	20	2,957	3,953
		31,428	33,514
Cash at bank and in hand		7,985	4,066
		43,839	45,467
Creditors			
Amount falling due within one year		(50,705)	(65,302)
Net current liabilities		(6,866)	(19,835)
Note 18 Assets held for resale			
Properties		1,692	2,285
Note 20 Debtors: amounts falling due after more than one year			
Prepayments and accrued income		2,957	3,953

HIRE-PURCHASE AND CREDIT SALE TRANSACTIONS

Reference: SSAP 21 *Accounting for leases and hire purchase contracts.*

Definitions

A *hire-purchase transaction* is a transaction in which the hirer agrees to hire goods from their owner in return for which he pays (usually) a deposit and a series of weekly, monthly, quarterly or yearly payments. The intention is that when the hiring period comes to an end, the ownership of the goods will pass to the hirer, sometimes on the payment of a nominal sum, sometimes with the final instalment; ownership, therefore, does not pass to the hirer until all payments have been made.

A *credit sale* is an outright sale (usually by a retailer) where payment by instalments is agreed in writing as a condition of the sale. Under a credit sale arrangement the property in the goods passes immediately to the purchaser, who becomes the owner of the goods, but payment is required to be made over a period.

Interest is normally charged by the seller both in credit sale and hire-purchase arrangements; the great difference between them is that in a credit sale the 'purchaser' owns the goods from the outset, whereas in the case of a hire-purchase sale, they do not become his until the final payment is made. Thus the seller cannot reclaim the goods in the case of a credit sale if the purchaser defaults, whereas, subject to the terms of the agreement and the law on hire purchase, he can in the case of a hire-purchase transaction.

Amounts due under credit sale transactions are debtors, and normally appear with other trade debtors, though they may be shown separately. In the case of a hire-purchase transaction, there has, strictly speaking, been no sale, and the goods involved are still an asset of the seller; but, adopting the principle of 'substance over form', most companies refer to 'hire-purchase debtors' or 'instalments due under hire-purchase agreements'.

Timing of profit taking

Whether the sale is a credit sale or on hire purchase, there are two elements of profit: the profit on the sale of the goods themselves and interest upon the amounts outstanding. There are a number of ways in which these two forms of profit can be spread over the accounting periods involved; but essentially these break down into two methods:

1. Take all the profit on the sale immediately, and spread only the interest element.
2. Spread both the profit on the sale and the interest over the life of the agreement.

Although method 1 is permissible for credit sales, method 2 is the more prudent. Method 1 is not recommended for hire purchase, as the goods have not actually been sold.

Where a credit sale is made on truly 'interest free' terms, there is no interest to spread, though logically there is an interest cost so far as the selling company is concerned. This is not normally taken into account, though it could be, by taking into account imputed interest. But it is always necessary to make provision for collection costs. Such a provision might, for instance, be 10% of the credit sale account debtors outstanding on balance sheet date.

The rule of 78

Finance companies frequently apply the 'rule of 78' in spreading either the interest alone, or the whole profit and interest, over the life of the agreement. This is simply a form of the 'sum of the years' digits method' already discussed in connection with depreciation in Chapter 8. What happens is this: the period of the agreement is set down in months (or it could be weeks in the case of a weekly agreement, or years where payments were on an annual basis), and the sum of the digits represents the sum of $1 + 2 + 3 + 4 \ldots$ to n, where n is that number of months (or weeks or years). It is called the rule of 78 because for a year's agreement, the sum of $1 + 2 + 3 + \ldots + 12$ is 78. Any interest charge

is then spread as follows (in this case a year's agreement):

First month 12/78 of total interest
Second month 11/78
Third month 10/78
... Twelfth month 1/78.

Many companies take the profit immediately and spread the interest in respect of hire-purchase transactions, though it was at one time considered more prudent to spread both profit and interest over the life of the transaction (see Example 11.2 below), rather than to take profit at the outset. This could be said to be an example of 'substance over form' (see page 41).

The rule of 78 is a simple, though not totally accurate, way of spreading interest or profit over the period of an agreement. Some companies use more sophisticated techniques, spreading interest or profit by what is termed the 'actuarial method', taking into account interest (at the true effective rate payable) on the balance outstanding period by period.

Example 11.2 Taking of profit on hire-purchase transactions

The hire-purchase trading account of DEFERRALS LTD for 1999 is as follows:

Hire-purchase sales	£120,000
less Cost of goods sold	80,000
Gross profit on HP sales ($33^{1}/_{3}$%)	£40,000

Receipts from 1999 HP sales =	£36,000	
Profit to be taken in 1999		
£36,000 × $33^{1}/_{3}$% profit margin =	£12,000	
Provision for unearned profit carried forward on 1999 HP sales = £40,000 − £12,000 =	£28,000	
HP sales in 1999		£120,000
less Cash received		36,000
		84,000
less Provision for unearned profit		28,000
Hire-purchase debtors (from 1999 sales)		£56,000

If, say, £63,000 is received in 1999 in respect of transactions from 1998 and £42,000 from 1997, when the profit margins were 30% and 35% respectively, the total profit from HP sales to be taken in 1999 would be:

From 1999	£12,000
From 1998 (30% of £63,000)	18,900
From 1997 (35% of £42,000)	14,700
Total profit	£45,600

GREAT UNIVERSAL STORES *Information on hire purchase*

Note on debtors	**2000** **Due within** **one year** **£m**	**2000** **Due after more** **than one year** **£m**	1999 *Due within* *one year* *£m*	1999 *Due after more* *than one year* *£m*
Trade debtors				
Instalment and hire purchase debtors	**1,119.5**	**290.2**	1,385.5	541.1
Provision for unearned finance charges	**(104.5)**	**(30.5)**	(153.7)	(53.4)
	1,015.0	**259.7**	1,231.8	487.7
Other trade debtors	**265.8**	–	320.1	–
Total trade debtors	**1,280.8**	**259.7**	1,551.9	487.7

. . .

Accounting policies

Instalment and hire purchase debtors
The gross margin from sales on extended credit terms is recognised at the time of sale. The finance charges relating to these sales are included in the profit as and when instalments are received. The income in the Finance Division under instalment agreements is credited to the profit and loss account in proportion to the reducing balances outstanding.

Hire-purchase information given in accounts
A good set of accounts will give quite a lot of information on hire-purchase and credit sale business, e.g. how profit is taken and how interest is brought in. See GREAT UNIVERSAL STORES above.

Some companies (like Great Universal Stores) arrange for some or all of their credit sales and hire-purchase transactions to be handled by a separate finance company, so that they receive payment for goods at once and thus reduce their requirements for working capital.

In the absence of any provision for recourse by the finance company, the amounts outstanding are then of no concern to the selling company and do not appear in its accounts. Transactions which potentially involve recourse to the seller are required by FRS 5 *Reporting the substance of transactions* to be accounted for (a) as a debtor; and (b) as a corresponding liability.

FACTORING

Factoring involves the sale of a company's trade debtors to a factoring house. Factoring houses offer three facilities:

1. The provision of finance for working capital.
2. A credit management and sales accounting service.
3. Bad debt protection.

The provision of finance
This is the main reason why companies use factoring. The factor assesses the client's trade debtors and agrees the level of 'prepayment' that he will provide; this is normally between 70% and 80% of the value of the invoices. The client may then sell his existing trade debts to the factor and receive prepayment immediately; the debtors are informed that the debts have been factored, and are asked to make payment direct to the factor.

All new invoices then carry an assignment notice, asking the debtors to make payment direct to the factor. Copies of all invoices are sent to the factor, who will make the agreed prepayment. If the agreed level of finance is 75%, the client will receive the balance of 25%, less the factor's charges, as his debtors settle each invoice. The factor provides credit advice and runs the sales ledger, sending statements and reminders.

Service charge
A service charge is made, usually between 1% and 3%, depending on the number of customers and invoices involved. The factor also makes a finance charge on any funds drawn under the prepayment arrangement, usually at rates similar to bank overdraft rates of interest. Because factoring finance is based on the trade debtors, it fluctuates automatically with the level of business, and is thus more flexible than an overdraft.

Bad debt protection
There are two types of factoring agreement: 'with recourse' and 'without recourse' to the client. Under

a with recourse agreement, the client takes the risk of bad debts, and the factor will pass the debt back to his client if the debtor has not paid within 90 or 120 days.

Most factors offer bad debt protection as an optional extra, providing cover on all *approved* invoices. The cover is for 100%, which compares favourably with the 80% offered by most credit insurance companies. Factors usually add between $^1/_4$% and $^3/_4$% to their service charge for bad debt protection, depending on the industry involved.

International factoring
An increasing proportion of British goods go to Western Europe, North America and other markets. Many exporters use factors primarily to obtain credit advice and bad debt protection, although prepayment finance is available.

Factors handling exports send correspondence and make telephone calls in the language of overseas customers, and know the local business practices; this usually enables them to obtain faster collection of export debts.

Invoice discounting
This is similar to factoring except that, under an invoice discounting arrangement, the client continues to run his sales ledger and collect the payments, which he banks to the account of the discounting company. When each debtor's payment is banked, the discounter deducts the prepayment already made to the client, plus charges, and pays the balance into the client's bank account.

Most invoice discounting agreements are with recourse, i.e. the client takes the risk of bad debts. Because the client goes on running the ledger and collecting payments, it is sometimes called *confidential invoice discounting*.

Factoring in the accounts
In the past it has not always been possible to tell from the accounts whether a company was using factoring or invoice discounting. However, under FRS 5 *Reporting the substance of transactions*, companies are normally required to disclose factoring and invoice discounting and the degree of debt protection.

Debt factoring is considered in Application Note C of FRS 5, which also covers invoice discounting. Accounting treatment depends upon the precise terms of the contract. If the debts are sold at a fixed price, with no recourse, the seller has no further interest in the debts which no longer appear in the balance sheet; but an interest charge will normally appear in the profit and loss account. See, for instance, PIC INTERNATIONAL (formerly DALGETY) at the top of the next column.

PIC INTERNATIONAL *Extract from 1998 accounts*
Note 4 Interest

	1998 £m	1997 £m
Interest payable and similar charges:		
On bank loans and overdrafts	15.2	20.6
Non recourse finance	1.4	2.0

In respect of the prior year non recourse finance, the Group was not obliged to support any losses and did not intend to do so. The providers of this finance . . . confirmed that they would not seek recourse from the Group.

However, when the factor or invoice discounter has full recourse in the event of bad debts, the substance of the transaction is that the company is taking all the risk, and the factor or invoice discounter is merely providing finance. The company's accounts would therefore show (where £80m was advanced by a factor, with full recourse, on debtors of £100m):

	£m
Current assets:	
Debtors	100
Current liabilities:	
Finance from factor	80

rather than debtors of £20m, as was long the case.

Linked presentation
What is termed a linked presentation may be adopted where there is limited recourse by the factor (FRS 5, paras. 26–28). The accounts of pharmacy supplier ALLIED UNICHEM provide an illustration:

ALLIED UNICHEM *Extract from 1999 accounts*
Note 13 DEBTORS
Amounts falling due within one year

	1999 £m	1998 £m
Trade debtors subject to discounting arrangements	191.1	224.8
Non-returnable amounts received	(165.0)	(193.8)
	26.1	31.0
Other trade debtors	678.4	700.5
Other debtors . . .		

Certain amounts receivable from French pharmacies have been discounted on a non-recourse basis, under a 5 year facility entered into in 1997. The Group is not obliged to support any losses in respect of the amounts advanced under the discounting arrangement, nor does it intend to do so.

Chapter 12

CURRENT ASSET INVESTMENTS, CASH AT BANK AND IN HAND

Types of investment

As explained in Chapter 9, investments may be held as fixed assets or as current assets. This chapter considers only investments which are current assets, i.e. held short-term, either for resale or as a temporary store of value; and not intended for use on a continuing basis in the company's activities.

Types of current asset investment

Current asset investments include:

1. Short-term government and other listed securities:

    (a) intended to be held to maturity;
    (b) not intended to be held to maturity (but for trading).

2. Certificates of deposit.
3. Certificates of tax deposit.
4. Commercial paper.
5. Short-term deposits, e.g. money market deposits.
6. Short-term local authority bonds.
7. Options.
8. Other unlisted investments.

Accounting for current asset investments

A current asset investment is initially recorded at its purchase cost, including expenses, and is normally included in the balance sheet at the lower of cost and net realisable value. It must be written down to its net realisable value at the balance sheet date if that is less than its cost, and the loss taken to the P & L account. If at a subsequent balance sheet date the net realisable value has increased again, that higher value (up to the purchase cost) must be taken as the balance sheet value and any increase credited to the P & L account.

Under the Companies Act 1985 historical cost principles can be replaced by alternative accounting rules to allow for revaluations and current cost accounting (see Chapter 29). The provisions allow investments of any description to be shown either at market value determined at the date of their last valuation or at a value ('fair value') determined on any basis which appears to the directors to be appropriate in the circumstances of the company. The method of valuation and the reasons for adopting it must be shown in the notes to the accounts.

In theory this makes a variety of treatments possible, including the occasionally used practice known as '*marking to market*', where investments are written up to market value and the profit taken to the profit and loss account. So any note in the accounting policies on current asset investments should be read carefully. For example GLAXOSMITHKLINE:

GLAXOSMITHKLINE *Extract from the note on accounting policies in the 2000 accounts*

Current asset investments

Current asset investments are stated at the lower of cost and net realisable value.

In the case of securities acquired at a significant premium or discount to maturity value, and intended to be held to redemption, cost is adjusted to amortise the premium or discount over the life to maturity of the security. Floating rate bonds are stated at cost . . .

Equity investments are included as current assets when regarded as available for sale.

Current asset investments in practice

Many listed companies only have cash and short-term deposits. Some, like THE BODY SHOP, seem to prefer to hold cash. But there are groups which do have very large amounts of current asset investments. e.g.:

GLAXOSMITHKLINE *Extracts from the 2000 accounts*

Note 26 Net debt

Liquid investments

	Market value		Book value	
	2000	1999	2000	1999
	£m	£m	£m	£m
Government and equivalent investments	**177**	238	**177**	238
Other investments	**1,508**	1,345	**1,504**	1,342
Deposits at banks	**457**	200	**457**	200
	2,142	1,783	**2,138**	1,780

At the balance sheet date the Group's liquid investments included listed investments of £142 million (1999 – £161 million) with an aggregate market value of £143 million (1999 – £162 million).

Some companies, like REUTERS, draw a distinction between government securities and other listed investments and, within unlisted securities, between CDs (certificates of deposit), term deposits and other investments:

REUTERS GROUP *Extract from the notes to the 2000 accounts*

Note 19. SHORT-TERM INVESTMENTS		2000	1999
		£m	£m
Listed			
Government securities:	UK	–	2
	Overseas	127	180
Other deposits:	Overseas	48	–
		175	182
Unlisted			
Certificates of deposit		2	1
Term deposits:	UK	67	156
	Overseas	8	100
Other deposits:	UK	9	21
	Overseas	269	30
		355	308
		530	490

Significance of short-term investments

Cash rich companies like GLAXOSMITHKLINE and REUTERS have a significant part of their assets in short-term investments, but they are not central to the operation of the company.

But in a few companies they are. For example C.H. BAILEY, a company we have mentioned before in the context of voting and non-voting shares (see page 21):

C.H. BAILEY *Extracts from 2000 accounts*

Group balance sheet	2000	1999
	£	£
Fixed assets . . .		
Current assets:		
Stocks and WIP	75,279	165,443
Debtors	794,737	762,625
Current investments	7,821,838	7,816,789
Cash at bank and in hand	748,407	859,950
	9,440,261	9,604,807
. . .		
Net assets	15,789,974	15,821,829

In 2000 the Group made a pre-tax loss of £265,661, while income from current asset investments was reported as £351,754, and profit from sale of investments £673,521.

As we pointed out earlier, the controlling shareholder of a company can do very much what he likes within his own personal feifdom. Many do, though some less patently than others.

Availability of short-term investments

Do not assume that current asset investments are necessarily available to meet current liabilities; read the small print, e.g. TATE & LYLE:

TATE & LYLE *Note from 2000 accounts*

Current asset investments	2000	1998
	£m	£m
Listed on overseas exchanges	37	73
Unlisted investments	1	1
Loans, short-term deposits and unlisted fixed interest securities	172	111
	210	185

Cash at bank and in hand

The last item among current assets in the standard formats is Cash at bank and in hand. Apart from this, the Companies Acts contain no specific requirements on cash balances; and while the sums involved can be considerable, most companies do not explain the amount shown either by way of note or in their accounting policies:

DIAGEO *Extract from the consolidated balance sheet as at 30 June 2000*

	2000 £m	1999 £m
. . .		
Cash at bank and in hand	1,063	1,097
. . .		

Cash at bank and in hand forms part of Cash as defined in FRS 1. It is closely related to Current asset investments; indeed while many companies previously treated deposits as Current asset investments, others treated them as bank balances.

Cash at bank and in hand is shown on the face of the balance sheet, but the formats are inconsistent: loans and overdrafts, as we shall see in Chapter 13, are relegated to a note.

Where a group has both credit balances and overdrafts with the same bank, the question arises as to the extent to which one can be set off against the other (and how this should be reflected in the accounts). Many groups have cash pooling arrangements with their bank.

Guidance on offsetting is provided by FRS 5 *Reporting the substance of transactions*.

Disclosure requirements

Disclosure requirements, which are the same whether an investment is a fixed asset or a current asset, are as follows:

1. the amount relating to listed investments;
2. the aggregate market value of listed investments must be shown if different from the book value, and the stock exchange value if it is less than the market value;
3. various details must be provided where the investment is 'significant', i.e. where
   either it is 20% or more of the nominal value of the shares of that class in the investee,
   or it represents more than 20% of the investor's own assets; the details to be disclosed are:

   (a) the name of the investee;
   (b) its country of incorporation (if outside Great Britain), and
   (c) a description of the investment and the proportion of each class of share held.

Chapter 13

BANK LOANS AND OVERDRAFTS

Bank facilities

There are three main methods by which a company can borrow money from a bank:

(a) by overdrawing on its current account;
(b) by loans; and
(c) by the use of acceptance credits.

The bank normally agrees with a company the maximum amount that can be borrowed under each method, and this is called granting a facility. For example, a company that has the bank's permission to run an overdraft of up to £1m has overdraft facilities for that amount.

What is shown in the balance sheet is, however, only the amount actually borrowed from the bank at the balance sheet date, although the average amount overdrawn during the year can be estimated from the interest charged to the profit and loss account.

The bank facilities available to a company do not have to be disclosed, but broad statements may be made about the company having 'ample overdraft facilities', and the trend is towards being more specific, e.g. BLUE CIRCLE:

BLUE CIRCLE *Extract from note to 2000 accounts*

19. Financial instruments: Liquidity risk profile
The group had undrawn committed facilities available at 31 December 2000 in respect of which all conditions precedent had been met as follows:

	£m
Expiry in one year or less	123.9
Expiry in more than one year but not more than two years	35.3
Expiry in more than two years	555.8
	715.0

Bank loans and overdrafts fall in the formats under the headings Creditors: amounts falling due within one year and Creditors: amounts falling due after more than one year, and are often grouped with finance leases.

Where security has been given (see p. 33), the amounts secured and a general indication of the security must be stated For example, ICI:

ICI *Extract from note to 1999 accounts*

21. Loans	*Repayment dates*	1999 £m	1998 £m
Secured loans:			
US dollars	2000/2016	6	25
Taiwanese dollars	2000/2001	–	5
Other currencies	2000/2004	86	89
Total secured		92	119
Secured by fixed charge – bank loans		78	85
– other		13	27
Secured by floating charge – bank loans		1	7
		92	119

For each item the following amounts must be shown separately:

(a) amounts payable otherwise than by instalments five years hence;
(b) those payable by instalment, any of which are due more than five years hence;
(c) the total of such instalments.

In addition listed companies must disclose amounts which are payable between one and two years, and those payable between two and five years. ICI more than meet this requirement, disclosing year by year up to 5 years:

ICI *Extract from note to 1999 accounts*

Loan maturities	1999	1998
...	£m	£m
Total loans		
Loans or instalments repayable:		
After 5 years	738	1,181
From 4 to 5 years	494	164
From 3 to 4 years	151	667
From 2 to 3 years	620	228
From 1 to 2 years	249	714
Total due after more than one year	2,252	2,954
Total due within one year	647	585
Total loans	2,899	3,539

Where any part of the debt is repayable after more than five years, the terms of repayment and rates of interest payable should be shown. If the information is excessive, a general indication of terms and rates of interest is permitted.

Overdrafts

The traditional method of clearing bank lending is to allow the customer to overdraw on his current account. It was originally designed to cover fluctuations in the company's cash during the year and gives the company complete flexibility of drawing within a given limit, which is normally reviewed annually.

Bank advances on overdraft are technically repayable on demand and, although this is seldom enforced, the bank when granting overdraft facilities may expect the customer to produce budgets and cash flow forecasts to show the purposes for which the facilities are intended and the plans for eventual repayment. Bank lending on overdraft is traditionally short-term in character, designed to cover fluctuations in working capital requirements rather than to provide permanent capital for the company.

When long-term interest rates were driven high by inflation, few finance directors were willing to commit their companies to long-term fixed interest rate debt, especially if they expected interest rates to fall in due course. Instead they resorted more and more to borrowing from their banks, where interest on an overdraft is charged at an agreed percentage over the clearing bank's base rate (see below), which they hoped would average less than the long-term rate at the time, and where the company is free to reduce its borrowing whenever it wishes.

Although it is now quite common for companies to finance a large part of their working capital in this way, clearing banks are usually reluctant to let companies increase their overdraft ad lib, even against a floating charge, preferring their clients to convert any 'hard-core' borrowing that has built up on overdraft into loans (see under bank facilities on page 83).

The cost of borrowing on overdraft

The interest a company has to pay on its overdraft is usually set at a given percentage above its bank's base rate, depending on the standing of the customer; a financially stable, medium-sized company might pay a fixed $1^{1}/_{2}\%$ above base.

The base rate, the datum on which the rates of interest are based, is adjusted up and down to reflect fluctuations in short-term interest rates. Each bank sets its own base rate, though in practice the clearing banks' base rates keep very much in line with each other.

Fluctuations in amount

As we have said, the overdraft figure given in the balance sheet is the amount the overdraft facility is being used at the year end. Companies normally choose their year end to fall when business is at its slackest, and the balance sheet figure is most unlikely to be the maximum amount the company has overdrawn during the year.

For example, a company in a seasonal business, with peak sales in the summer, could be expected to build up stocks from early spring and to carry high debtors across the summer. With an annual turnover of, say, £15m, £200,000 in the bank at its year end (31 December) and £120,000 bank interest paid (reflecting an average overdraft of £1.5m during the year, bearing interest on average at 8%), the amount the company was actually overdrawn during the year would be likely to fluctuate with the sales cycle as shown in Example 13.1.

Example 13.1 Annual fluctuation in sales and overdraft

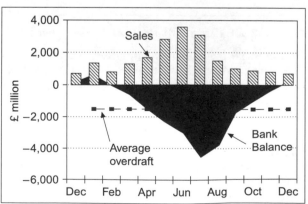

In practice, profit on sales and depreciation on assets would accumulate during the year, steadily improving the overdraft position, but sharp increases would be expected with the payment of dividends and Corporation Tax, and capital expenditure would also have an immediate effect on the overdraft position.

Vulnerability

Companies which rely heavily on borrowing on overdraft and on floating-rate loans (see below) are vulnerable to rising interest rates, particularly if their profit margins are small, and those which let their overdrafts steadily increase year by year without raising further equity or fixed-interest capital are steadily increasing their interest rate risk. Another hazard of financing on overdraft is that the amount a bank can lend has in the past been subject to Bank of England controls, which were tightened from time to time without much warning.

Banks are also liable to restrict credit on their own account when they find themselves up against their own overall lending limits or too heavily lent in the particular sector in which the company operates. As credit restrictions often come when conditions are unfavourable for capital raising, a company which is financed extensively by overdraft can all too easily find its operations severely constrained by its immediate cash position.

Bank loans

The simplest type of bank loan is one where the full amount is drawn by the borrower at the outset and is repaid in one lump sum at the end of the period. The duration (or 'term') of the loan is seldom more than seven years but, unlike an overdraft, a bank loan cannot be called in before the end of the term unless the borrower defaults on any condition attached to the loan.

Interest is charged either at a fixed rate or, more frequently, at a floating rate: an agreed percentage over base rate, or over London Inter-Bank Offer Rate (LIBOR). Where LIBOR is used, an interest period is agreed between the borrower and the bank, and the bank then, on the first day of each interest period, determines the rate at which deposits are being offered in the inter-bank market for the relevant period.

For example, if a rate of $1/2\%$ over LIBOR and a three-month interest period have been agreed and the three-month LIBOR rate is 5.7% at the start of the period, the borrower will pay 6.2% for the next three months, and the rate will then be redetermined. Banks frequently allow borrowers to vary their choice of interest period – one month,

three months or six months – during the life of a loan.

Where the borrower doesn't need all the money at once, the bank may allow the loan to be drawn down in tranches (specified instalments). Repayments may also be arranged in instalments, which may often be a stipulation of the lender; banks like to see money coming back gradually to make repayment easier for the borrower and to give early warning of a borrower getting into difficulties over repayment. Details of drawing down and repayment are agreed in advance, together with the rate of interest payable and the security to be given, although any of these features can be altered subsequently by mutual agreement.

Security

Bank loans are sometimes secured on assets acquired by the loan or on other assets of the company, but a floating charge is more usual. If the loan is not secured at all, the company may be required to give a *negative pledge*, i.e. to undertake not to give security to any new or existing creditor or to borrow further amounts under existing security without the bank's prior agreement in writing.

Flexible loan facilities

There is an increasing trend, particularly in European banking, to provide companies with more flexible financing than term loans by granting loan facilities, usually for periods of between 3 and 5 years. Drawing down (usually with a minimum limit on any one drawing) can be allowed at any time given a little notice, repayment is flexible, and subsequent redrawing is often allowed, but the borrower will be charged for this flexibility by a commitment commission payable on any unused portion of the facility for as long as the facility is left open. Facilities giving this flexibility are called revolving, and can be single- or multi-currency.

Some companies, like UNIGATE, give details:

UNIGATE *Extract from note to 2000 accounts*

18 Borrowings and Finance Leases

. . .

At 1 April 2000, the Group had revolving credit facilities of £460m (1999: £260m) under which it may repay amounts borrowed at its option while retaining the flexibility to re-borrow under the facilities. These facilities expire during the period from 1 June 2001 to 1 June 2003.

BILLS OF EXCHANGE

Definition

A bill of exchange is, briefly, an order in writing from one person (the *drawer*) to another (the *drawee*) requiring the drawee to pay a specified sum of money on a given date. When the drawee signs the bill he becomes the *acceptor* of the bill, and the person to whom the money is to be paid is the *payee*. The main legislation on bills is contained in the Bills of Exchange Act 1882, and their use in practice is clearly and concisely described in a book, *The Bill on London*, produced by Gillett Brothers, one of the discount houses.

Primary purpose

The primary purpose of a bill of exchange is to finance the sale of goods when the seller or exporter wishes to obtain payment at the time the goods are despatched and the buyer or importer wants to defer payment until the goods reach him, or later.

In these circumstances A, the supplier of goods to B, would draw a bill of exchange for the goods, which B 'accepts', acknowledging the debt and promising payment at some future date, often three months ahead. Bills of this type are called trade bills.

A can then sell the bill to a third party, C, at a discount to the face value of the bill; and C in turn can endorse it and sell it on to D. In this case if B subsequently defaults, D can claim payment from A, and if A also defaults D can then claim on C.

Alternatively A can retain the bill, which gives a legal right to payment at a given date in the future (the date of maturity), or the bill can be deposited at a bank as a security against borrowings.

Balance sheet presentation

If Company A's year ends before the bill has reached maturity, then:

(a) if A still holds the bill, it would be shown separately under current assets as Bills receivable or included in debtors; or
(b) if A discounted the bill, traditionally it would not appear in the balance sheet, but would be shown as a contingent liability recognising the possibility that B may subsequently default. FRS 5 *Reporting the substance of transactions* has changed that. Most companies now show bills of exchange discounted as a liability until the time for payment has passed (i.e. there has been no recourse).

In Company B's balance sheet the outstanding bill would be shown under creditors as a bill of exchange payable.

Discounting

When a bill of exchange is discounted, i.e. sold to a third party at a discount to its face value, this is usually done through one of the discount houses, which will trade it in the money market. The discount on a trade bill depends on prevailing interest rates, on the creditworthiness of the drawer, the acceptor and any subsequent endorsers, and on the nature of the underlying transaction. In the case of a bank bill, that is one where a bank is the acceptor of the bill, or has endorsed it, the discount rate will be less than on a trade bill. The finest rates are obtained in discounting bills drawn against exports or imports and accepted by 'eligible banks' (i.e. those banks whose acceptances are eligible for rediscount at the Bank of England).

When it was in a tight spot in 1998 engineering group BRUNEL made extensive use of discounting:

BRUNEL HOLDINGS *Extract from note to 1998 accounts*

18. Creditors	1998
	£000
Amounts falling due within one year:	
Bank loans and overdrafts	4,957
Payments received on account	3,807
Trade creditors	13,789
Bills of exchange discounted with recourse	2,794
Proposed dividends	1,302
. . .	

Acceptance credits

Many eligible banks specialise in accepting bills for customers. They provide this type of short-term finance by granting the client an acceptance credit facility up to a given limit for an agreed period, and the client can then draw bills of exchange on the bank as he wishes, provided the running total of bills outstanding does not exceed the prescribed limit (in other words, it is a revolving credit facility). The bank 'accepts' the bills, which can then be discounted in the money market at the finest rate, and the customer receives the proceeds of the sale, less the acceptance commission he has to pay to the accepting house (normally between $3/8\%$ and $1/2\%$ p.a. for good-quality borrowers). When the bill falls due for payment (usually three months later), the customer pays the bank the full face value of the bill and the bank in turn honours the bill when it is presented by the eventual purchaser. The bank has to honour the bill even if the customer defaults, because it had 'accepted' responsibility for meeting the bill when it fell due. The acceptance of bills by banks is related to commercial transactions, either specifically matched or linked to the general volume of business, so that the bills are self-liquidating.

Unlike an overdraft, the interest on discounted bills is paid in advance by the deduction of discount charges from the face value of the bill and, in addition, if the bills have been accepted by a bank, the company will also have to pay the acceptance commission in advance. In spite of these extra costs,

variations of interest rates often make the use of acceptance credit facilities cheaper than an overdraft or a bank loan.

The future obligation of a company to provide cash cover to meet bills that have yet to mature under an acceptance credit facility must, if material, be shown separately in a company's balance sheet under creditors as 'Bills of exchange payable' as illustrated by BRUNEL HOLDINGS on page 86.

THE BIG PICTURE

As we have seen in this chapter, amounts borrowed from the bank do not normally appear on the face of the balance sheet but fall within Creditors as Amounts due within one year or Amounts due after more than one year, and are detailed in the notes to the balance sheet.

There is thus no netting of amounts owed by banks and amounts owing to banks; but while this might be important to an economist, as such it is not particularly significant either to the company or to analysts and investors.

The key question is;

> Is there enough cash or credit available to meet the debts and obligations of the business when they fall due?

The balance sheet and the notes to it do not answer either of these questions.

The balance sheet and the notes to it do not answer either of these questions.

This is largely due to the British system of operating with an overdraft. Although theoretically an overdraft is repayable on demand, in practice a limit is agreed for a specific time and normally adhered to by the bank. But as we have seen, that limit does not have to be disclosed. If it is not disclosed, one has no way of assessing how much is available.

Imagine two companies, A and B, much the same size. Each owes wages and other creditors due tomorrow £1.5m. A has an overdraft of £27m, B has £1m in the bank. At first sight, B looks more solvent than A. But if A has an overdraft limit of £50m, £23m of which remains unused, and B, having a poor reputation for past dealings and a low credit rating, cannot raise an overdraft or borrow elsewhere, we would not normally be able to tell from the balance sheet.

'Going concern' assurances required in the directors' report or the corporate governance statement (see page 211), offer a safeguard, although a somewhat limited one.

Cash flow statements
Chapter 19 is devoted to FRS 1 *Cash flow statements*. Nevertheless, because of its close relationship to the content of this chapter, it is perhaps right to say a few words here.

Cash is defined in FRS 1 to be:

(a) cash in hand and deposits repayable on demand with any qualifying financial institution (i.e. an entity that as part of its business receives deposits or other repayable funds and grants credits for its own account); less
(b) overdrafts from any qualifying financial institution repayable on demand.

To qualify as 'cash' the deposits must be capable of being withdrawn at any time without notice and without penalty. They count as 'on demand' if a maturity or period of notice of not more than 24 hours or one working day has been agreed. Cash includes cash in hand and deposits denominated in foreign currencies.

It will be seen that the definition of 'cash' for the purposes of FRS 1 is extremely narrow.

This chapter has looked at something quite different: at all forms of bank borrowing, not just those that count as negative 'cash' for purposes of FRS 1.

Nevertheless, FRS 1 does also take in the big picture. It requires (para. 33) a note reconciling the movement of cash in the period with the movement in net debt (i.e. all capital instruments which are classified as liabilities under FRS 4 *Capital instruments* plus related derivatives and obligations under finance leases). And this reconciliation provides another place to look for information on bank borrowings and debt more generally.

The Body Shop's reconciliation below shows how a company, for many years with no debt at all, went from net funds of £5.1 million at the beginning of one year [A] to a net debt of £48.2 million at the end of the following year [B].

Below the reconciliation, the *Analysis of changes in net debt* shows Debts due within one year had risen from £35.0 million at the beginning of the year [C] to £57.9 million at the end of the year [D].

THE BODY SHOP *Extracts from 2001 accounts*

Consolidated cash flow statement

	2001 £m	2000 £m
For the 53 weeks ended 3 March 2001		
Net cash inflow from operating activities	21.4	31.4
. . .		
Decrease in cash	(2.8)	(8.5)

Reconciliation of Net Cash Flow to Movement in Net Debt

	2001 £m	2000 £m
Decrease in cash in the year	(2.8)	(8.5)
Cash inflow from decrease in debt and lease financing	(18.5)	(7.7)
Cash inflow from decrease in liquid resources	(3.8)	(6.6)
Increase in net debt resulting from cash flows	(25.1)	(22.8)
Redeemable convertible loan notes	(4.1)	–
Translation difference	(1.2)	(0.1)
Movement in net debt in year	(30.4)	(22.9)
Opening net (debt)/funds	(17.8)	5.1[A]
Closing net debt	[B] (48.2)	(17.8)

Note 22 Analysis of changes in net debt

	At 27 Feb 2000 £m	Cash flows £m	Exchange movements £m	Other non-cash changes £m	At 31 March 2001 £m
Cash in hand, at bank	11.2	(2.4)	0.7	–	9.5
Bank overdraft	(0.3)	(0.4)	–	–	(0.7)
	10.9	(2.8)	0.7	–	8.8
Debt due within one year	[C] (35.0)	(18.4)	(1.8)	(2.7)	(57.9)[D]
Debt due over one year	(1.7)	(0.1)	(0.1)	(1.4)	(3.3)
	(36.7)	(18.5)	(1.9)	(4.1)	(61.2)
Short term deposits	8.0	(3.8)	–	–	4.2
Total	(17.8)	(25.1)	(1.2)	(4.1)	(48.2)

Chapter 14

DERIVATIVES AND OTHER FINANCIAL INSTRUMENTS

Introduction

The complexity of this subject is reflected by the length of FRS 13 *Derivatives and other financial instruments*. Complete with its Summary and its Appendices, it runs to 165 pages.

Disclosure requirements depend on whether you are a Bank (Part B), an Other financial institution (Part C), or neither (Part A). Parts B and C are, appropriately, printed on pink paper.

In this chapter we will concentrate on non-financial institutions, and the disclosures required of them, which fall broadly into:

- *Narrative Disclosures*, usually contained in the Operating and Financial Review (OFR) or the Directors' report; and
- *Numerical Disclosures* in the notes to the accounts.

Derivatives can seriously damage your wealth

Although much of the business done by companies in this market is for the prudent reduction of risk – primarily interest rate risk, currency risk and commodity risk – much is sheer speculation: the unacceptable face of capitalism, doubled and redoubled.

Let us be quite clear about two things:

1. In business school parlance, derivatives are a 'zero sum game'. If anybody is going to 'make a bomb', somebody else is going to 'lose a bomb'. The overall outcome is zero.
2. This is cowboy country. As the *Daily Telegraph* reported on 6 October 1995:

DAILY TELEGRAPH *Extracts from article by Banking correspondent*

P & G accuses Bankers Trust of racketeering

Proctor & Gamble . . . alleges that 'a culture of greed and duplicity', permeated through Bankers Trust. 'Fraud was so pervasive Bankers Trust employees used the acronym ROF – short for rip-off factor – to describe one method of fleecing clients.'

. . .

Proctor and Gamble highlights one taped conversation in which a Bankers Trust employee describes a deal he has just concluded with the company as 'a massive gravy train' . . .

Another tape related to massive profits made by Bankers Trust on a leveraged derivatives transaction sold to Proctor & Gamble. 'They would never know,' said one saleswoman. 'They would never be able to know how much money was taken out of that.' A colleague replied 'Never, no way. That's the beauty of Bankers Trust.'

'Funny business, you know,' said one salesman in a taped conversation. 'Lure people into that calm and then just totally f*** them.'

Definition of a derivative

A derivative financial instrument is a financial instrument that derives its value from the price or rate of some underlying item.

Underlying items include equities, bonds, commodities, interest rates, exchange rates and stock market and other indices.

They include futures, options, forward contracts, interest rate and currency swaps, interest rate caps, collars and floors, forward interest rate agreements, and commitments to purchase shares or bonds (FRS 13, para. 2).

Risk management and derivative trading

Most large companies, and particularly multinationals, use derivatives to reduce exposure to various types of risk. This is a perfectly normal and usually fairly safe activity, providing you choose your counterparties carefully; i.e. don't deal with cowboys.

Other companies also *trade* in derivatives; this can be a very dangerous activity unless it is

- run by experienced and responsible staff, and
- tightly controlled.

Disclosure requirements

FRS 13 requires both narrative and numerical disclosures on the use of financial instruments.

Narrative disclosures

GLAXOSMITHKLINE makes it clear that it wouldn't touch derivatives trading with a bargepole:

GLAXOSMITHKLINE *2000 accounting policies*

Derivative financial instruments

- The group does not hold or issue derivative financial instruments for trading purposes.
- Derivative financial instruments are used to manage exposure to market risks from Treasury operations. The derivative contracts are treated from inception as an economic hedge . . .
- Currency swaps and forward exchange contracts are used to fix the value of the related asset or liability in the contract currency . . .
- Interest differentials under interest swap and cap agreements are recognised . . . by adjustment of interest expense over the life of the agreement.

SHELL, on the other hand, has always been in the business of trading in oil, as its full name, Shell Transport & Trading implies, and has a huge depth of experience in the management of trading:

SHELL TRANSPORT AND TRADING *Extract from 2000 Operational and financial review*

Treasury and trading risks

. . . Apart from forward foreign exchange contracts to meet known commitments, the use of derivative financial instruments by most Group companies is not permitted by their treasury policy.

Some Group companies operate as *traders* in crude oil, natural gas and oil products using commodity swaps and options as a means of managing price and timing risks . . . the use of derivatives is generally confined to specialist oil trading and central treasury organisations which have appropriate skills, experience, supervision, and control and reporting systems.

Numerical disclosures show how the company's objectives and policies were implemented in the period and provide supplementary information for evaluating significant or potentially significant exposures: see page 93.

Common types of derivative

The most common types of derivative that the ordinary investor is likely to come across are:

(a) options;
(b) futures and forward contracts; and
(c) currency and interest rate swaps.

An *options contract* is a contract giving the holder the right, but not the obligation, to buy ('call'), or sell ('put'), a specified underlying asset at a pre-agreed price, at either a fixed point in the future (European-style), or a time chosen by the holder up to maturity (American-style). Options are available in exchange-traded (e.g. on LIFFE, the London International Financial Futures Exchange) and over-the-counter (OTC) markets (shorthand for anywhere else, between any two parties).

A *futures contract* on the other hand is an agreement (obligation) to buy or sell a given quantity of a particular asset, at a specified future date, at a pre-agreed price. Futures contracts have standard delivery dates, trading units, terms and conditions.

In a *forward contract* the purchaser and its counterparty are obligated to trade a security or other asset at a specified date in the future. The price paid for the security or asset is either agreed upon at the time the contract is entered into, or determined at delivery. Forward contracts are generally traded over-the-counter.

In a *currency swap* a company borrows foreign currency for a given period, and lends the equivalent sterling for the same period. In an *interest rate swap* the company swaps a fixed rate of interest with a bank for a floating rate, or vice versa.

While these are the most common types of derivative that ordinary investors are likely to come across, the range of derivatives possible is limited only by the imagination of investment banks. New types of derivative are being created all the time.

It is convenient to classify derivatives as either

(a) commodity related, or
(b) financial.

Commodity related derivatives

Manufacturers whose business depends upon a particular key commodity (like sugar or cocoa) may well 'hedge', i.e. buy or sell options or futures contracts or employ forward contracts to fix the price of the underlying raw material, or the sales proceeds of a product.

TATE & LYLE discloses its policy on commodity derivatives in its OFR:

TATE & LYLE *Extract from 2000 Operating and financial review*

Commodities

Derivatives are used to hedge movements in the future prices of commodities in those domestic and international markets where the Group buys and sells sugar and maize.

Commodity futures and options are used to hedge inventories and the costs of raw materials for unpriced and prospective contracts not covered by forward product sales.

The options and futures hedging contracts generally mature within one year and are all with organised exchanges.

Tate & Lyle added in a note to the accounts: 'Changes in the fair value of instruments used as hedges are not recognised in the financial statements until the hedged position matures.' This is known as *hedge accounting* (FRS 13, para. 58).

In other words, whatever the total cost of acquiring the raw material this way, that is its 'cost'; and whatever the net sales proceeds are as a result of the future, those are the sales proceeds.

Providing the management lays down limits to the amount of hedging, and has control systems in place to ensure that these limits are not exceeded without permission, then hedging is a perfectly normal and reasonable business activity.

Where things go wrong is when you get a *rogue trader*. This happened some years ago in a chocolate manufacturer, where a commodity dealer started to gamble on cocoa futures and went way beyond the company's requirement for cocoa, thinking he could make a lot of money for the company.

When it was noticed that he was over the limits set for him, management stood over him while he closed all his positions. The moment they were out of the room, he opened them all up again.

When he was finally rumbled, a very substantial loss was incurred covering all his positions. In the aftermath of this débâcle the company's share price fell by more than 80%.

Reducing the risks of trading in derivatives

One secret of good management with any trading or dealing in derivatives is to ensure that the functions of confirmation and of settlement are kept entirely separate from the dealing department. In the celebrated case of currency swaps that brought down BARINGS, all these functions in Barings' Singapore office came under one person: Leeson.

Investors should also be wary when a company's dealers are 'earning' huge bonuses. Greed comes before a fall.

Financial derivatives

Companies have traditionally borrowed in foreign currencies to help finance overseas investment and reduce exposure to currency risk. In this modern day and age the mobility of capital in most of the developed countries of the world – exchange controls are still prevalent in LDCs – and the increasing sophistication of the financial markets, has led to the development of a wide range of financial instruments to hedge against both currency and interest rate risk.

It no longer follows that you borrow French francs long-term at fixed rates of interest to finance long-term investment in France; it may be advantageous to borrow variable rate in sterling and do a currency swap and an interest rate swap.

Currency swaps

A currency swap is, in effect, the same as a reciprocating or back-to-back loan: the company borrows foreign currency for a given period and, in the same transaction, lends an equivalent amount of sterling for the same period.

For example, a UK company wants to borrow US dollars, but also wants to avoid the currency risk on the principal amount borrowed, i.e. it wants to hedge the currency risk. So it raises, say, £100m by a 7-year 10% Eurobond issue and swaps it for 7 years with a bank for, say, $160m at $7\frac{1}{2}$%. During the 7 years the company pays interest to the bank in dollars at $7\frac{1}{2}$% per annum on the $160m and the bank pays interest to the company in sterling at 10% per annum on the £100m. At the end of the 7 years the swap is reversed, so the company gets its £100m back regardless of the sterling/US$ exchange rate and in time to redeem the Eurobond issue.

Currency swaps normally appear either in a note to the accounts or in the financial review, e.g. BP AMOCO:

BP AMOCO *Extract from financial review 2000*

Financial risk management

. . .

The main underlying economic currency of the Group's cash flows is the US dollar and the Group's borrowings are predominantly in US dollars. Our foreign exchange management policy is to minimise economic and material transactional exposures arising from currency movements against the US dollar.

Interest rate swaps

An interest rate swap can be used by a company to protect itself against the impact of adverse fluctuations in interest rates on the interest charge it has to pay on its floating rate debt. The company agrees a fixed rate with the bank on a nominal sum for a given period; the company then pays the bank the fixed rate and the bank pays the company the floating rate; as, for example, GLAXOSMITHKLINE:

GLAXOSMITHKLINE *Extract from note to the 1998 accounts*

26. Financial instruments and related disclosures
Interest rate risk management
INTEREST RATE SWAP The Group has agreed with a commercial bank to exchange, at specified intervals, the difference between the fixed and floating rate interest amounts calculated by reference to a total principal amount of £500m, exchanging sterling floating interest rate for a fixed rate of 8.61 per cent.

When used in conjunction with a currency swap, an interest rate swap enables a company to lock in at a fixed rate of interest in one currency to cover floating-rate interest charges in another currency.

Companies may also use interest rate swaps in the reverse direction to reduce the proportion of their fixed-rate interest charges if they take the view that interest rates will fall. In neither case is there any transfer of principal.

The swap market has grown in recent years for another reason: to exploit the differences that exist between the fixed rate and the extremely competitive floating-rate credit markets in order to reduce the cost of borrowing, as illustrated in Example 14.1 at the next column.

Interest rate caps
Another way for a company with floating-rate debt to hedge against increases in interest rates is to buy a *cap*. A cap is a contract in which a counterparty, in exchange for a one-time premium, agrees to pay the bond issuer if an interest rate index rises above a certain percentage rate, known as the cap or *strike rate*. It is also called a *ceiling*.

The advantage of a cap over an interest rate swap from floating to fixed is that a cap not only protects the company from the effect of rising interest rates, but allows it to benefit from any fall in interest rates.

A *collar* is the simultaneous purchase of a cap and sale of a floor by the issuer, in which it trades any benefits from a potential fall in the interest rate index for protection against an excessive rise. Under a collar agreement, the issuer defines a specific range for its interest rate payments.

Caps and collars protect issuers from having to pay higher interest rates on variable rate debt if market rates increase beyond the cap rate.

Example 14.1 Use of swaps to reduce the cost of borrowing

Two companies both want to borrow money for five years. One has an AAA Standard & Poor's credit rating and wants to borrow floating rate, while the other, rated BBB, wants to borrow fixed. Market conditions are:

Company rating	AAA	BBB
Cost of 5-year fixed rate bond	10%	$11\frac{1}{2}\%$
Cost of 5-year bank loan	LIBOR + $\frac{1}{8}\%$	LIBOR + $\frac{5}{8}\%$
Cost of a swap:		
Company pays	LIBOR	$10\frac{1}{2}\%$
Company receives	$10\frac{3}{8}\%$	LIBOR

The AAA company, wanting to borrow floating, would issue 5-year bonds at 10% and swap; cost of borrowing floating = 10% + LIBOR – $10\frac{3}{8}\%$ = LIBOR – $\frac{3}{8}\%$ compared with the 5-year bank loan's cost of LIBOR + $\frac{1}{8}\%$.

Similarly the BBB company, wanting to borrow at a fixed rate, would take out a bank loan at LIBOR + $\frac{5}{8}\%$ and swap; cost of borrowing fixed = LIBOR + $\frac{5}{8}\%$ – LIBOR + $10\frac{1}{2}\%$ = $11\frac{1}{8}\%$, which is cheaper than issuing bonds at $11\frac{1}{2}\%$.

A *floor* is the mirror image of a ceiling. With a floor contract, the bond issuer receives an up-front fee from a counterparty. If the interest rate index falls below the floor or strike level, the issuer makes payments to the counterparty. Similarly to a cap agreement, if the floating index rate does not fall below the strike level, the issuer pays nothing.

One company that uses a mixture of caps, swaps and forward agreements is SHELL:

SHELL *Note to the 2000 accounts*

26. Financial instruments
(b) Interest rate risk
Some Group companies, primarily those with specialist treasury operations, use derivatives to manage their exposure to movements in interest rates.

The total contract/notional amounts and estimated fair values of Group companies interest rate swaps/forward rate agreements and interest rate caps at 31 December were:

	Contract/ notional amount	Estimated fair value
	\$m 2000	
Interest rate swaps/ forward rate agreements and interest rate caps	3,113	(26)

The amount of hedging gains or losses on these instruments which had been deferred at 31 December 2000 in respect of firm commitments was not significant.

TATE & LYLE *Note to the 2000 accounts*

30. Currency and interest rate exposure of financial assets and liabilities

After taking into account the various interest rate and cross currency interest rate swaps entered into by the Group, the currency and interest rate exposure of the financial liabilities of the Group as at 25 March 2000 was:

Currency	*Total*	*Fixed rate*	*Floating rate*	*Non-interest bearing*
	£m	£m	£m	£m
Sterling	150	166	(18)	2
United States Dollars	708	256	452	–
Canadian Dollars	21	–	21	–
Australian Dollars	16	–	16	–
EU currencies (excl. Sterling)	163	78	84	1
Others	10	–	10	–
Total	1,068	500	565	3
of which – gross borrowings	1,066	500	565	1
– working capital	–	–	–	–
– non-equity shares	2	–	–	2
Total	1,068	500	565	3

Interest rates	*Average interest rate (%) of fixed rate liabilities*	*Average years to maturity of fixed rate liabilities*	*Average years to maturity of non-interest bearing liabilities*
Sterling	10.8	1	–
United States Dollars	6.8	1.3	
EU currencies (excl. Sterling)	5.6	6.5	2.7
Average	6.9	1.9	2.7

Numerical disclosures

These give an overall picture of a company's currency and interest rate exposure, as TATE & LYLE'S accounts illustrate at the top of the page.

Counterparty risk

Companies which use derivatives are subject to *counterparty risk*, i.e. the risk that the counterparty defaults. The counterparty is simply the party with which one does the transaction.

Some companies with large exposure to derivatives, like REUTERS, describe the risk:

REUTERS *Note to the 2000 accounts*

All derivative instruments are unsecured. However, Reuters does not anticipate non-performance by the counterparties who are all banks with recognised credit ratings of 'A' or higher.

Concern about derivatives

What is disturbing about derivatives is that:

1. It is likely that anyone who today has funds invested will, usually unwittingly, be indirectly exposed to derivatives. Many major companies use them in one way or another; investment trusts, unit trusts and pension funds employ them in an effort either to protect themselves or to boost returns; so do some local authorities.

2. The sums involved are astronomical. For instance, BARCLAYS alone reported that at the end of 1998 it held or had issued:

	Contract or underlying principal amount
	£m
Foreign exchange derivatives	434,452
Interest rate derivatives	1,111,858
Equity and stock index derivatives	38,303
Commodity derivatives	12,941

3. Dealings are international and controls have yet to be agreed internationally.

There has been a series of derivative-based disasters in various countries – BARINGS was no isolated case – which have alerted management to the risks, but there is still plenty of ignorance around.

How can you blame the ignorant when a team of 'big hitters', as they call them in the United States, including the winner of a Nobel Prize for his research work on derivatives, set up an outfit called LTCM, Long Term Credit Management, got backing to the tune of $600 billion, turned out in practice to be Short-term Catastrophic Asset Mismanagement (SCAM), but a scam of such gigantic proportions that it had to be rescued by the Fed (The U.S. Federal Reserve Bank)?

But why bother with derivatives?

You may well ask 'Why do companies go to all this trouble to complicate matters, when they would probably do just as well in the long run to carry the risk themselves?' Good question. Plenty of companies would agree with you, e.g. RIO TINTO:

RIO TINTO *Extract from 2000 financial review*

Exchange rates, reporting currencies and currency exposure

. . . the Group does not generally believe that active currency hedging would provide long term benefits to shareholders . . .

Rio Tinto's business is mining, not commodity trading. The Group does not generally undertake transactions in products other than those it has produced itself . . . the Group does not generally believe a commodity price hedging programme would provide long term benefit to shareholders.

We can think of three reasons why companies and others use derivatives:

1. The real professionals, like SHELL and TATE & LYLE, have an enormous amount of in-house expertise and long experience of making profits on trading.
2. Although year-on-year currency risk and interest rate risk would probably be a case of swings and roundabouts, companies prefer to minimise the risk of a big hiccough in their reported profits. Investors don't like them, and in a bad year a sharp drop in profits due to adverse movements in currencies and/or interest rates could leave a company open to predators.
3. There is much international competition in banking these days and the traditional business of taking deposits and lending is much less profitable than it used to be. So bankers turn to other means of earning a crust and *some* aren't too particular how they do it.

Benefits of disclosure

There is a great deal of work involved in collecting and disclosing the information required by FRS 13, and the information is likely to be beyond the average investor. But the very process of collecting and reviewing the required information brings to the attention of directors and managers the nature and amount of risk which the company is running, and helps them meet their responsibilities. And most of the problems we have seen over derivatives, whether financial or commodity-based, have been due to weakness of controls and lack of higher management attention.

Chapter 15

CREDITORS, PROVISIONS, CONTINGENT LIABILITIES AND CONTINGENT ASSETS

CREDITORS

Presentation

Most companies use balance sheet Format 1 (set out in the Companies Act 1985), which nets out Creditors falling due within one year (also known as current liabilities), against Current assets to produce Net current assets (liabilities).

Amounts falling due after one year are then deducted from Total assets less current liabilities to give Net assets; see THE BODY SHOP in the next column.

Types of creditor

The following items are required to be shown, if material:

(a) debenture loans (see Chapter 6);
(b) bank loans and overdrafts (see Chapter 13);
(c) payments received on account;
(d) trade creditors;
(e) bills of exchange payable (see Chapter 13);
(f) amounts owed to group undertakings (see Chapter 20);
(g) amounts owed to undertakings in which the company has a participating interest (see Chapter 22);
(h) other creditors, including taxation and social security;
(i) accruals and deferred income.

Details of creditors are usually given in the notes rather than in the balance sheet itself.

THE BODY SHOP *Extract from 2001 Group balance sheet*

	Note	2001 £m	2000 £m
Fixed assets			
Intangible assets		33.6	31.5
Tangible assets		71.8	68.4
Investments		5.2	4.8
		110.6	104.7
Current assets			
Stocks		51.3	44.7
Debtors		47.8	45.9
Debts due after more than one year		6.7	6.0
Cash at bank and in hand		13.7	19.2
		119.5	115.8
Creditors: amounts falling due within one year	16	102.1	96.4
Redeemable convertible loan notes		2.7	–
Net current assets		14.7	19.4
Total assets less current liabilities		125.3	124.1
Creditors, amounts falling due after more than one year	17	1.9	1.7
Redeemable convertible loan notes		1.4	–
Provisions for liabilities and charges		0.3	0.7
[Net assets]		121.7	121.7

THE BODY SHOP *Extract from 2001 accounts*

16. Creditors: Amounts falling due within one year

	2001 £m	2000 £m
Bank loan	55.0	35.0
Bank overdraft	0.7	0.3
USA loans	0.2	–
Trade creditors	10.7	20.5
Corporation tax	1.6	8.0
Other taxes, social security costs	5.5	3.7
Proposed dividend	7.3	7.3
Other creditors	9.6	6.0
Accruals	11.5	15.6
	102.1	96.4

Note 17 (not shown) is mainly concerned with bank and other loans falling due after more than one year.

Trade creditors represent money owed for goods supplied. The size of trade creditors shows the extent to which suppliers are financing a company's business. For example, TESCO's suppliers finance not only its stock and debtors, but also its money market investments, earning interest for Tesco, not for its suppliers:

TESCO *Extracts from 2000 accounts*

	2000 £m	1999 £m
Current assets		
Stocks	744	667
Debtors	252	151
Investments	258	201
	1,254	1,019
Creditors: Amounts falling due within one year		
...		
Trade creditors	1,248	1,100

Taxation and social security are each shown separately. Taxation due within 12 months will normally include one year's Corporation Tax (but see Chapter 17 re large companies), and any foreign tax due.

An *accrual* is an apportionment of a known or determinable future liability in respect of a service already partly received. Thus, a business paying rent of £60,000 half-yearly in arrears on 30 June and 31 December would, if it had an accounting year ending 30 November, show an accrual of £50,000 (the five months' rent from 1 July to 30 November unpaid at the end of its accounting year).

Dividends proposed: the directors' report must state any amount which the directors recommend be paid by way of dividend. Although the company cannot, in law, pay these proposed dividends until they have been approved at the annual general meeting, companies always show them as a liability.

Also under Creditors may appear various items that are not in the example from THE BODY SHOP:

Deferred income is money received by or due to the company but not yet earned. Companies like VODAFONE GROUP (shown below) which take a month's rental in advance may well have greater accruals and deferred income than trade creditors.

VODAFONE GROUP *Note to the 2000 accounts*

13. Creditors:

Amounts falling due within one year

	2000 £m	1999 £m
Bank loans and overdrafts	94	174
Commercial paper	700	203
Trade creditors	706	216
Amounts owed to associated undertakings	2	–
Taxation	535	252
Other taxes and social security costs	54	28
Other creditors	436	46
Dividends	417	100
Accruals and deferred income	1,497	511
	4,441	1,530

Other types of borrowing which include bonds, loan notes and commercial paper (see Chapter 6).

Deposits: in addition to deposits in respect of a contemplated purchase (included under payments received on account), deposits may have been charged where goods have been despatched in containers, drums, barrels or boxes, to ensure their return. The container, etc., remains part of the stock of the despatching company, until it becomes apparent that it will not be returned, e.g. when the return period has elapsed, when it is treated as having been sold.

In financial companies, where deposits are a major item, representing money deposited to earn interest, they are shown as a separate heading.

Payments received on account arise where a *customer* is asked as a sign of good faith to deposit money in respect of a contemplated purchase. If the purchase goes through, the deposit becomes a part payment and ceases to be a creditor. Should the sale not be consummated, the deposit would normally be returned, though it could conceivably be forfeited in certain circumstances.

WORKING CAPITAL AND LIQUIDITY RATIOS

Now that we have described stocks, debtors and creditors, this may be a good place to deal with working capital, the working capital ratio, and liquidity ratios.

Watch the working capital ratio

The working capital ratio is important for two reasons:

- Firstly, if it is high, expansion of the business, especially rapid expansion, is going to gobble up cash like crazy.
- Secondly, if it is not kept under control, the business will eat up more cash than it should.

Some types of business are well placed with working capital. Supermarkets do particularly well, as illustrated by the TESCO example we showed on the previous page. In contrast, in a sector like building materials, you may find the company *has* to keep large stocks in order to provide a really good service to its customers world-wide, and to give them plenty of credit to be competitive. For example BLUE CIRCLE, the international cement group:

BLUE CIRCLE *Working capital ratio 2000:*

	2000 £m	1999 £m
Stocks	327.8	217
+ Trade debtors	394.0	316.2
− Trade creditors	(178.0)	(134.2)
= Working capital	543.8	399.0
Turnover	2,127.3	2,038.6
Working capital ratio	**25.6%**	**19.6%**

Had the ratio remained at the 1999 level in 2000, only £2,127.3m × 0.196 = £416.9m would have been tied up in working capital, rather than £543.8m. Having £126.9m less tied up would have saved about £10m interest on borrowings.

Let's see how well THE BODY SHOP has controlled its figure over the last five years:

THE BODY SHOP *Working capital 1996 to 2001*

Year end	1996 £m	1997 £m	1998 £m	1999 £m	2000 £m	2001 £m
Stocks	37.6	34.8	47.7	38.6	44.7	51.3
+ Trade debtors	27.5	31.7	31.3	27.8	30.3	30.3
− Trade creditors	7.7	10.2	11.0	13.0	20.5	10.7
Working capital	57.4	56.3	68.0	53.4	54.5	70.9
Turnover (Sales)	256.5	270.8	293.1	303.7	330.1	374.1
RATIOS						
Stocks/Sales	14.7%	12.9%	16.3%	12.7%	13.5%	13.7%
Trade debtors/Sales	10.7%	11.7%	10.7%	9.2%	9.2%	8.1%
Trade creditors/Sales	3.0%	3.8%	3.8%	4.3%	6.2%	2.9%
Working capital/Sales	22.4%	20.8%	23.2%	17.6%	16.5%	19.0%

Comment on The Body Shop's ratios

Stocks/Sales

In 1998 the ratio jumped sharply to 16.3%. If stocks had increased in 1998 in line with the increase in sales, they would have been £37.7m at the 1998 year end, instead of £47.7m.

The company had plenty of cash at the year end, so the £10m extra stock wasn't increasing the overdraft. But even so it could have earned a useful £0.5m on deposit. Stock levels returned to a more normal level in the following years.

Trade creditors/Sales

This ratio is surprisingly small, suggesting that The Body Shop pays its suppliers more quickly than most.

Working capital/Sales

After peaking at 23.3% in 1998, this overall ratio was brought below 20%.

Liquidity ratios

The two ratios most commonly used in assessing a company's liquidity are concerned with current assets (stocks and WIP, debtors and cash) and current liabilities (creditors, bank overdraft and any debts due to be settled within the next 12 months):

1. **Current ratio**

$$= \frac{\text{Current assets}}{\text{Current liabilities}}$$

2. **Quick ratio**

$$= \frac{\text{Current assets} - \text{Stock}}{\text{Current liabilities}}$$

The Companies Act 1985 requires all amounts owing by the company to be included under creditors, with amounts due within one year and after one year being shown separately. When they can be identified, provisions for amounts due within one year should be included in current liabilities.

Current ratio

The current ratio is a broad indicator of a company's short-term financial position: a ratio of more than 1 indicates a surplus of current assets over current liabilities. A current ratio of 2 or more used to be regarded as prudent in order to maintain creditworthiness, but in recent years a figure of about 1.5 has become quite normal, and a higher figure isn't necessarily a good sign: it may be due to excessive stocks or debtors, or it may mean that the directors are sitting on an unduly large amount of cash which could be more profitably invested.

When looking at an individual company's current ratio, there is no simple rule of thumb on what the company's ratio 'ought' to be, because it so much depends on a number of different factors, including the following:

1. *The nature of the company's business.* If large stocks and the giving of generous credit terms are normal to the business, the current ratio needs to be higher than the general average, whereas a retail business with only cash sales, no work in progress and stocks financed mainly by suppliers (i.e. creditors a large item) may be expected to have a lower than average current ratio.
2. *The quality of the current assets.* Stocks, for example, may be readily saleable, e.g. gold, or virtually unsaleable, e.g. half-completed houses in a property slump.
3. *The imminence of current liabilities.* A large loan due for repayment very soon could be embarrassing. It would be acutely embarrassing if gearing was already very high, there was no scope for an equity issue and neither cash nor further overdraft facilities were available. Even that is not perhaps as embarrassing as being unable to pay the wages next week, and next week's wages do not, of course, appear in the balance sheet.

    The key factor is whether a company has scope for further borrowings or is right up against its limits, but facilities available (as opposed to facilities being used) are not necessarily revealed in annual reports.
4. *The volatility of working capital requirements.* A company with a highly seasonal business pattern, for instance a Christmas card manufacturer or a UK holiday camp operator, may well make use of a much higher average level of borrowings during the year than the balance sheet shows, particularly as companies usually arrange their year end to coincide with low stocks and/or a low level of activity. When the interest charge in the P & L account is disproportionately large in comparison to the borrowings shown in the balance sheet, this is a clear indication that borrowings during the year have been significantly higher than at the year end.

Because of these individual factors, the most informative feature of a current ratio is its normal level and any trend from year to year. A drop below normal levels is worth investigating, and a continuing decline is a warning signal that should not be ignored.

Quick ratio or acid test

As we have said, not all current assets are readily convertible into cash to meet debts; in particular stocks and work in progress may be able to be run down a certain amount, but not eliminated if the business is to continue. The quick ratio recognises this by excluding stocks from current assets and applies the 'acid test' of what would happen if the company had to settle up with all its creditors and debtors straight away: if the quick ratio is less than 1 it would be unable to do so.

Some companies whose normal terms of trade allow them to sell goods for cash before paying for them habitually operate with a quick ratio of well under 1 (0.2 is typical for a supermarket); so it is a poorer than average figure compared with other companies in the same industry, coupled with a declining trend, that signals possible trouble ahead. A feature that a low and declining ratio often highlights is a rising overdraft: the question then is, 'Are

their bankers happy?' Fears in this direction may be allayed by a statement in the annual report about operating well within the facilities available, or by a statement at the time that new money is raised confirming that working capital will be adequate.

A large difference between the current ratio and the quick ratio is an indication of large stocks:

$$\text{Current ratio} - \text{Quick ratio} = \frac{\text{Stocks}}{\text{Turnover}}$$

Bathroom and kitchen unit manufacturer SPRING RAM, which has had a very chequered time over a ten-year period, provides an interesting example:

THE SPRING RAM CORPORATION *Current ratio and Quick ratio*

	1990 £m	1991 £m	1992 £m	1993 £m	1994 £m	1995 £m	1996 £m	1997 £m
Current assets	91.1	128.8	128.0	91.3	109.5	130.1	83.8	72.1
Current liabilities	54.9	79.4	95.1	90.5	65.7	105.1	70.6	72.2
Current ratio	1.66	1.62	1.35	1.01	1.67	1.24	1.20	1.29
Stocks	25.1	41.0	52.4	45.4	47.7	64.7	38.8	33.1
Current assets – Stock	66.0	87.8	75.6	45.9	61.8	65.4	45.0	37.0
Quick ratio	1.20	1.11	0.79	0.51	0.94	0.62	0.64	0.51
See Note	1	2	3	4				

NOTES:

1. *Chairman's statement:*
   Bonus issue The strength of the Group's balance sheet is such that, on 26 April 1991, shareholders approved a one for one bonus issue, the fifth since flotation in 1983 . . .
   Management The number and quality of the Corporation's management teams continues to grow. There are now 47 directors managing 16 autonomous operating companies.
2. Stock increased by more than 60%, although Turnover was marginally down from £194m to £191m. Invested £37.1m in buildings and plant. Spent £12.8m on Stag furniture acquisition.
3. *New chairman's statement:* The five months of 1993 since the new team was installed have been used to stabilise the financial position of the company . . . severe recession in the UK housing market. Prompt action was necessary to eliminate the excessive decentralization which had led both to the Group's businesses competing with each other and to the duplication of overheads and stockholdings . . . the number of businesses operated by the company was reduced from 22 to 11.
4. Rescue rights issue; 2 for 9 to raise £42.1m net.

We would like to tell you that, after the rescue rights issue, the company was soon restored to good health. Sadly not. As the ratios continue to indicate, this company is still a sick chick. Its share price bottomed at 4p, down from 188p in the heyday of the first chairman.

The wounds were deep. Due to the unbounded optimism of the first chairman in the face of a recession, the company had gone from cash at bank of £45.8m at the beginning of 1992 into net bank borrowings of £37.8m by the end of August 1993.

But worse still was the damage done to the integrity of the company by some serious creative accounting. As the *Investors Chronicle* wisely warned its readers:

INVESTORS CHRONICLE *Extract from 26 March 1993*

Battered Ram
Cautious investors would be right to avoid Spring Ram shares until credibility is restored.

Investors have good reason to be angry with the former market darling Spring Ram . . .

First there was last November's debacle at Balterley Bathrooms. The problem is believed to have been the result of huge pressure on the divisional finance director to perform. He apparently overvalued stocks to produce the figures that head office wanted to see.

Although the group sought to reassure shareholders that this was an isolated incident this week's shocks have undermined its attempt.

Last week, trading in its shares was suspended ahead of a profit warning. Management blamed more stringent accounting policies.

PROVISIONS

Reference: FRS 12 *Provisions, contingent liabilities and contingent assets.*

Background

Before FRS 12 the making of provisions gave imaginative companies enormous scope for enhancing profits. All you had to do was this:

- Year 1 make a huge provision, so large that analysts would ignore it in their calculation of that year's earning per share, and forget about it in subsequent years.
- Year 2 and in subsequent years, offset against the provision costs that you would prefer not to hit the profit and loss account, until such times as the 'kitty' is used up.
- Then scratch around for another suitable provision.

The two classics were ICI's provision of several hundred million for 'Restructuring' and Unilever's £800m for 'Entry into Europe'.

We are sure that both these companies were scrupulous in choosing what costs to offset against these Jumbo provisions, but the scope for creative accountancy was enormous. FRS 12 severely curtails the scope for this particular dodge.

Definition

A *provision* is a liability that is of uncertain timing or amount. A provision should be recognised when a company has an obligation which it will probably be required to settle, and a reliable estimate can be made of the amount of the obligation. Unless these conditions can be met, no provision should be recognised.

A 'provision' (as defined by CA 1985) is either:

(a) any amount written off by way of providing for depreciation or diminution in the value of assets (in which case it is deducted from the fixed asset); or

(b) any amount retained to provide for any liability or loss which is either likely to be incurred, or certain to be incurred but uncertain as to the amount or as to the date on which it will arise (it then appears among provisions for liabilities and charges).

FRS 12 (see below) sets out more demanding conditions than those in (b) above, and it is those in FRS 12 which have to be applied in practice.

Provisions for liabilities and charges are frequently made for:

(a) pensions and similar obligations (see page 115);
(b) taxation, including deferred taxation (see Chapter 17); and
(c) other provisions.

Pension schemes can be either funded, i.e. contributions paid away to separate funds (see page 115), or unfunded. In an unfunded scheme, which is the norm in some foreign countries, the company makes a provision for future liabilities in its accounts.

Particulars should also be given of any pension commitments for which no provision has been made.

The item Taxation will normally only include deferred taxation (see Chapter 17), as other taxation will be shown under Creditors, unless the amount is uncertain.

When to make provisions

Under FRS 12 a provision – a liability that is of uncertain timing or amount – should *only* be recognised when:

- a company has an *obligation* which it will probably be required to settle; and
- a *reliable estimate* can be made of the amount of the obligation.

Unless these conditions can be met, no provision should be recognised. A provision should be *used* only for expenditure for which the provision was originally recognised.

Annual review and disclosure

Provisions should be reviewed at each balance sheet date and adjusted to reflect the current best estimate.

If it is no longer probable that a transfer of economic benefits will be required to settle the obligation, i.e. if it looks as though the company is no longer likely to have to cough up, the provision should be reversed.

As SMITHS GROUP (see opposite) illustrates, the company's annual report should disclose:

- the carrying amount at the beginning and end of the period;
- additional provisions made in the period, including increases to existing provisions;
- amounts used (i.e. incurred and charged against the provision) during the period; and unused amounts reversed during the period.

Provisioning – the main areas

Provisions can involve huge sums of money. The main areas are:

SMITHS GROUP *Extract from notes to the 2001 accounts*

Note 25, Provisions for liabilities and charges

| | At 1.8.00 £m | Exchange adjustments £m | Profit and loss account | | Acquisitions £m | Utilisation £m | Disposals £m | At 31.7.01 £m |
			Provisions £m	Releases £m				
. . .								
Post-retirement healthcare	90.8	3.4	3.5			[3.5]		**94.2**
Service guarantees and product liability	36.5	1.1	15.2		0.2	[15.2]		**37.8**
Reorganisation	6.0	0.1	62.6			[24.9]		**43.8**
Property	14.6	0.2	10.2			[2.5]		**22.5**
Litigation	14.9	0.1	2.2	[5.2]		[3.1]		**8.9**
	162.8	4.9	93.7	[5.2]	0.2	[49.2]		**207.2**
Discontinued businesses	42.4	1.8	3.9			[10.7]	[37.4]	
	205.2	6.7	97.6	[5.2]	0.2	[59.9]	[37.4]	**207.2**

Deferred taxation [note 20 – not reproduced] **1.7**

Total provision for liability and charges **208.9**

. . .

Post-retirement healthcare
The company has contractual commitments to provide private healthcare after retirement to a significant number of employees, mostly in the US. The annual charge against profits and the amount of the provision carried forward are based on actuarial assessments of the company's discounted future obligations.

Service guarantees and product liability
Service guarantees and warranties over the company's products typically cover periods of between one and three years. Provision is made for the likely cost of after-sales support based on the recent past experience of individual businesses.

Reorganisation
Significant parts of the company's operations, especially in Aerospace and Sealing Solutions, have been undergoing a phased restructuring programme over the past four years. Full provision is made for schemes approved and committed by the end of each financial year. This year's balance relates mainly to Aerospace sites in the US, and Sealing Solutions businesses in the UK and Europe. This restructuring should be completed by July 2002.

Property
As stated in the Accounting Policies . . . where a property is vacant, or sub-let under terms such that rental income is insufficient to meet all outgoings, the company provides for the anticipated future shortfall up to termination of the lease. Provision is also made for the cost of reinstatement work on leased properties where there is an obligation under the lease, and the costs can be reasonably estimated. Where evidence of contamination is found on property in the company's occupation, provision is made for estimated remedial costs pending action on the affected site.

Litigation
The company has on occasion been required to take legal action to protect its patents and other business intellectual property rights against infringement, and to similarly defend itself against proceedings brought by other parties. Provision is made for the anticipated fees and associated costs, based on professional advice as to the likely duration of each case. Provisions totalling £5.2m were released relating to litigation settled at less than the anticipated cost.

- Environmental (SHELL opposite, $475m)
- Restructuring (BOC overleaf, £56.5m)
- Litigation (GKN overleaf, £266m).

Other areas include:

- Warranties
- Onerous leases
- Overhaul of items on operating leases.

SHELL *Operational and Financial Review 2000*

Environmental and decommissioning costs
At the end of 2000, the total provisions being carried for environmental clean-up were $475 million (1999 $505 million) . . .

Provisions being carried for expenditures on decommissioning and site restoration, including oil and gas platforms, amounted to $2,514 million (1999: 2,539 million).

BOC GROUP *Note to the 2000 accounts*

Note 11 Provisions for liabilities and charges

. . .

The restructuring provision represents expenditure to be incurred on the major reorganisation announced in August 1998. This year £35.5 million was spent including £12.8 million on redundancy costs and £8.0 million on consultancy . . . The remaining provision of £21.0 million consists mainly of redundancy costs and will be spent during 2001.

- A restructuring provision should include only the direct expenditures arising from the restructuring, which are those that are necessarily entailed by the restructuring.
- A restructuring provision does not include such costs as: (a) retraining or relocating continuing staff; (b) marketing; or (c) investment in new systems and new distribution networks.
- No obligation arises for the sale of an operation until the company is committed to the sale i.e. there is a binding sale agreement.

GKN *Note to the 1997 accounts*

Provisions for liabilities and charges

	1997 £m	1996 £m
Deferred taxation	2	7
Post-retirement and other provisions	174	173
Meineke litigation	266	270
	442	450

Meineke litigation
In the interests of prudence an exceptional litigation provision of $270m was made in the 1996 accounts following a judgment of the US District Court, Charlotte, North Carolina in respect of claims brought by certain of its franchisees against Meineke Discount Muffler Shops Inc. (owned by one of GKN's subsidiaries) alleging breach of contract and fiduciary duty . . . by Meineke . . . appeal with the US Court of Appeal . . .

The movement on the provision represents legal costs incurred in the year.

So GKN's lawyers took a cool $4m off the company in 1998. Litigation is a serious hazard in doing business in the US. (Rumour has it that US pharmaceutical and cosmetic companies are using lawyers rather than rats for testing new products. This is for two reasons: firstly there are more of them – and secondly you are less likely to get attached to them.)

Other Accounting Standards on provisions
Where another FRS or an SSAP deals with a more specific type of provision, that standard applies, rather than FRS 12. These include:

- long-term contracts (SSAP 9, see page 69);
- deferred tax (SSAP 15 and FRS 19, see page 127);
- leases (SSAP 21, see pages 104–5);
- pension costs (SSAP 24, see pages 115–17).

Other uses of the term 'provision'
The term 'provision' may also be used in the context of items such as depreciation, impairment of assets and doubtful debts: these are adjustments to the carrying amounts of assets, and are not covered by FRS 12.

What does all this mean to the investor?
Prior to FRS 12 the recognition (making) of a provision was based on management's intention, or possible intention, of making expenditures, rather than on any legal or moral obligation to do so.

In particular, as we have mentioned, there was the use of what Sir David Tweedie, chairman of the ASC, called *'big bath' accounting*. Several years of future expenditure, including items related to continuing operations, and possibly a sum to cover unforeseen costs, would be heaped together into one large provision, which would be reported as an exceptional item.

This gave enormous scope for earnings to be *'smoothed'*: large fluctuations in reported earnings being avoided by provisions being released in lean years.

The new rules should make management much more accountable. The hope is that companies will keep shareholders more closely informed about provisions and exceptional expenditure. Companies which haven't already adopted the Operational and Financial Review should do so to help achieve this better communication.

The danger is that management will become less inclined to 'grasp nettles' in continuing operations, for fear of causing a 'blip' in reported profits.

CONTINGENT LIABILITIES AND CONTINGENT ASSETS

Definition

A contingent liability is a potential liability which had not materialised by the date of the balance sheet. By their nature, contingent liabilities are insufficiently concrete to warrant specific provision being made for them in the accounts, and none is in fact made. However, the Companies Act 1985 requires a company to disclose by way of note or otherwise:

(a) any arrears of cumulative dividends (para. 49);

(b) particulars of any charge on the assets of the company to secure the liabilities of any other person, including, where practicable, the amount secured (para. 50 (1));

(c) the legal nature of any other contingent liabilities not provided for, the estimated amount of those liabilities, and any security given (para. 50 (2)).

Examples of contingent liabilities

Typical contingent liabilities include:

(a) bills of exchange discounted with bankers (where an FRS 5 linked presentation is not used (see page 42));

(b) guarantees given to banks and other parties;

(c) potential liabilities on claims (whether by court action or otherwise);

(d) goods sold under warranty or guarantee;

(e) any uncalled liability on shares held as investments (i.e. the unpaid portion of partly paid shares held).

Contingencies frequently arise in respect of an acquisition as the result of an 'earn-out', where part of the consideration is based on future profits.

Litigation, impending litigation and threatened litigation are popular breeding grounds for contingent liabilities; for example BP AMOCO:

BP AMOCO *Note to the 2000 accounts*

39. Contingent liabilities

Approximately 200 lawsuits were filed . . . arising out of the Exxon Valdez oil spill in Prince William Sound in March 1989.

Most of these suits named Exxon, Alyeska Pipeline Service Company (Alyeska), which operates the oil terminal at Valdez, and other oil companies which own Alyeska . . . BP owns a 50% interest in Alyeska . . .

Exxon has indicated that it may file a claim for contribution against Alyeska for a portion of the costs and damages which it has incurred.

How an oil terminal operator can be held responsible for a tanker running aground is way beyond our comprehension (unless Alyeska provided the pilot), but in the US it seems they'll try anything.

As explained below, companies are also required to disclose 'commitments'. It is often quite difficult to decide just what is a commitment and what a contingent liability; and many groups, like ICI, treat them in a single note.

ICI *Extract from note to the 1999 accounts*

42. Commitments and contingent liabilities

In 1995 ICI Explosives USA Inc and a former employee each admitted to a single offence in breach of US antitrust laws relating to the sale of certain commercial explosives between 1988–1992 and as a result ICI Explosives USA Inc paid a fine of US$10m.

The Company, as well as several other ICI companies were named as defendants in lawsuits, relating to the bombing of the A P Murrah Building in Oklahoma City, Oklahoma. . . . In November 1996 the District Court in Oklahoma granted ICI's motion to dismiss the complaint, holding that the ICI companies have no case to answer.

However, the plaintiffs in the Oklahoma bombing case then went to appeal, and the case dragged on for another two years until, on 9 November 1998, the Court of Appeal affirmed the dismissal of the case against the ICI defendants, and rejected the plaintiffs' request that it rehear the appeal.

The significance of contingent liabilities

In many cases notes on contingent liabilities are of no real significance, for no liability is expected to arise, and none does. Occasionally, however, they are very important indeed, and points to watch for are a sharp rise in the total sums involved, and liabilities that may arise outside the normal course of business.

To guarantee the liabilities of someone, or some company, over which one has no control entails undue risk, and calls into question the management's judgement if the sums involved are significant.

In particular, experience suggests that any contingent liability in respect of a subsidiary that has been disposed of can be extremely dangerous. For example, when COLOROLL took over JOHN CROWTHER it accepted more than £20m of contingent liabilities in order to help the MBO of Crowther's clothing interests, which it wanted to be shot of.

COLOROLL *Note to the accounts*

Contingent liabilities
At 31 March 1989 the group had contingent liabilities in connection with the following matters:

(a) the sale with recourse of £7,500,000 of redeemable preference shares and £14,250,000 senior and subordinated loan notes in RESPONSE GROUP LTD which were received as part consideration for the sale of the clothing interests of JOHN CROWTHER GROUP PLC;

(b) the guarantee of borrowings and other bank facilities of . . .

In February 1990 the Response Group called in the receivers, and Coloroll followed four months later!

Guaranteeing the borrowings of associated undertakings or joint ventures may also be dangerous.

Capital commitments
The Companies Act 1985 requires that, where practicable, the aggregate amounts or estimated amounts, if they are material, of contracts for capital expenditure (not already provided for) be shown by way of note. For example RANK:

RANK *Extract from note to the 1999 accounts*

33 Commitments
At 31 December 1999 commitments for capital expenditure amounted to £48m (1998 £190m).

Such a note provides some indication of the extent to which the directors plan to expand (or replace) the facilities of the group, and thus of the potential call upon its cash resources. It should be read in conjunction with the directors' report and chairman's statement and any press announcements by the company, but it is not a particularly helpful guide to future cash flows unless it gives some information on timing. Although the sums involved are material, it is impossible to tell from RANK's note how long the various facilities to which it is committed will take to build or deliver, and when payments will fall due.

Other financial commitments
The Companies Act 1985 requires particulars to be given of any other financial commitments which have not been provided for and which are relevant to assessing the company's state of affairs (Sch. 4, para. 50 (5)). This requirement covers such things as leasing commitments and long-term contracts,

where the sums involved can be very large indeed, as illustrated by SHELL TRANSPORT AND TRADING's note on commitments, shown here:

SHELL TRANSPORT AND TRADING *Note to the 2000 accounts*

16. Commitments
(a) Leasing arrangements
The future minimum lease payments under operating leases and capital leases, and the present value of net minimum capital lease payments at 31 December 2000 were as follows:

		$ million
	Operating leases	Capital leases
2001	1,401	49
2002	859	43
2003	711	61
2004	508	48
2005	399	46
2006 and after	2,056	209
Total minimum payments	5,934	456

The figures represent minimum commitments existing at December 31, 2000 and are not forecasts of future total rental expense.
(b) Long term purchase obligations . . .

The distinction between operating leases and capital (finance) leases is explained below.

Leases
SSAP 21 *Accounting for leases and hire purchase contracts* divides leases into two types, finance leases and operating leases, and requires quite different accounting treatment for each type.

A *finance lease* is defined as a lease which transfers substantially all the risks and rewards of ownership of an asset to the lessee. All other leases are *operating leases*.

Finance leases: the lessee
Prior to SSAP 21 a company could enter into a finance lease instead of borrowing the money to purchase an asset, and neither the asset nor the commitment to pay leasing charges would appear in the balance sheet. This was an example of what was known as 'off balance sheet financing', which produced 'hidden gearing', as the company had effectively geared itself up just as much as if it had borrowed the money to purchase the asset, except that it had to pay leasing charges rather than paying interest and bearing depreciation charges.

SSAP 21 requires a finance lease to be recorded in the balance sheet of the lessee as an asset and as an obligation to pay future rentals. The initial sum to be recorded both as an asset and as a liability is the present value of the minimum lease payments, which is derived by discounting them at the interest rate implicit in the lease. The method of accounting is illustrated in Example 15.1.

Example 15.1 Accounting for a finance lease

A company acquires a small computer system on a finance lease. Lease payments are £10,000 p.a. for five years, with an option to continue the lease for a further five years at £1,000 p.a. Payments are made annually in advance, i.e. the first payment is made on taking delivery of the computer. The interest rate implicit in the lease is 10%, and the estimated useful life of the system is five years.

The present value of the minimum lease payments discounted at 10% p.a. can be calculated using the table Present value of 1 in *n* years' time in Appendix 2:

Payment date	Present value of 1 (from table)	Present value of £10,000 payment £
On delivery	1.000	10,000
In 1 year	0.909	9,090
In 2 years	0.826	8,260
In 3 years	0.751	7,510
In 4 years	0.683	6,830
Present value of minimum lease payments		£41,690

The computer system will thus be recorded as an asset of £41,690 and the liability for future rental payments will also be recorded as £41,690. After the first year:

(a) The asset will be depreciated over the shorter of the lease term (the initial period plus any further option period, i.e. a total of ten years in this case), and its expected useful life (five years). Annual depreciation charge on a straight line basis is therefore one-fifth of £41,690 = £8,338, reducing the asset value to £33,352.

(b) The present value of the remaining minimum lease payments is recomputed. There is no longer a payment due in four years' time (£6,830 in our table above), so the present value of future payments is now £41,690 − 6,830 = £34,860. £6,830 is deducted from the future liability and the remaining £3,170 of the £10,000 payment made on delivery is shown as interest paid.

These calculations would then be repeated each subsequent year as shown in Example 15.2.

Example 15.2 Accounting for a finance lease – subsequent years

End of year	Balance sheet		P & L account	
	Asset value	Remaining payments	Interest charge	Depreciation charge
	£	£	£	£
1	33,352	34,860	3,170	8,338
2	25,014	27,350	2,490	8,338
3	16,676	19,090	1,740	8,338
4	8,338	10,000	910	8,338
5	Nil	Nil	Nil	8,338

Finance leases: the lessor

In the past the practice of 'front-ending', taking a high proportion of the profits on a lease in the first year, has got a number of companies into serious difficulties, e.g. SOUND DIFFUSION, which went into liquidation primarily as a result of taking 60% of profits on leasing electrical equipment – telephone switchboards, fire-alarm and public-address systems – in the first year.

Under SSAP 21, front-ending is not allowed. The amount due under a finance lease should be recorded as a debtor at the net investment after provisions for bad and doubtful rentals, etc., and the earnings in each period should be allocated to give a constant rate of return on the lessor's net investment (SSAP 21, paras. 38 and 39).

Operating leases

An operating lease is normally for a period substantially shorter than the expected useful life of an asset; i.e. the lessor retains most of the risks and rewards of ownership.

Under an operating lease the lease rentals are simply charged in the profit and loss account of the lessee as they arise. Leased assets and the liability for future payments do not appear in the balance sheet, even though companies can enter into operating leases of several years' length, as the extract from SHELL TRANSPORT AND TRADING's accounts illustrated on page 104.

While SSAP 21 sets out the distinction between an operating lease and a finance lease, FRS 5, *Reporting the substance of transactions*, looks behind the lease at the nature of the underlying transaction. But this application of 'substance over form' does not meet with universal approval.

Chapter 16

PROFIT AND LOSS ACCOUNT

INTRODUCTION

As described briefly in Chapter 1, the profit and loss account is a score-card of how the company did in the period reported on, normally the last year. The Companies Act 1985 offers companies the choice of four profit and loss account formats:

- Formats 1 and 2 are 'modern' single-page vertical formats;
- Formats 3 and 4 are 'traditional' two-sided formats, common in the UK until 50 years ago, still used in Europe and elsewhere, but rarely found among listed UK companies. They will not be considered further.

The upper parts of Formats 1 and 2 are shown in Examples 16.1 and 16.2 respectively. The difference between them is the way they show operating costs:

- Format 1 breaks down operating costs by function:
  Cost of sales (which will include all costs of production, such as factory wages, materials and manufacturing overheads, including depreciation of machinery);
  Distribution costs (costs incurred in getting the goods to the customer);
  Administrative expenses (e.g. office expenses, directors' and auditors' fees).
- Format 2 breaks down operating costs into:
  Raw materials and consumables
  Staff costs Wages and salaries; Social security costs; Other pension costs

Example 16.1 Profit and loss account: Format 1

	£000	£000
Turnover		7,200
Cost of sales		3,600
Gross profit		3,600
Distribution costs	1,100	
Administrative expenses	900	
		2,000
		1,600
Other operating income		50
[Operating or Trading profit]		1,650
Income from interests in associated undertakings		30
Income from other participating interests		10
Income from other fixed asset investments		5
Other interest receivable		120
		1,815
Amounts written off investments	15	
Interest payable	600	
		615
[Profit on ordinary activities before tax]		1,200

Depreciation and other amounts written off fixed assets
Other external charges
Change in stock of finished goods and work in progress.

Example 16.2 Profit and loss account: Format 2

	£000	£000
Turnover		7,200
Changes in stocks of finished goods and work in progress	160	
Other operating income		50
		7,410
Raw materials and consumables	1,700	
Other external charges	1,120	
Staff costs		
Wages and salaries	2,050	
Social security costs	300	
Other pension costs	120	
Depreciation and other amounts written off tangible and intangible fixed assets	400	
Other operating charges	70	
		5,760
[Operating or Trading profit]		1,650
Income from interests in associated undertakings		30
Income from other participating interests		10
Income from other fixed asset investments		5
Other interest receivable		120
		1,815
Amounts written off investments	15	
Interest payable	600	
		615
[Profit on ordinary activities before tax]		1,200

The formats reflect the disclosure requirements of the European Union Fourth Directive as incorporated in Schedule 4 of the Companies Act 1985. Items in square brackets, 'Trading profit' and 'Pre-tax profit', have been included because they are important to the analyst, although they do not actually appear in the formats in Schedule 4. Most companies now adopt Format 1, though some use a combination of Formats 1 and 2.

Comparatively few companies adopt Format 2. One which does, but puts most of the detail in the notes to its accounts (see page 108), is PIC INTERNATIONAL, the profit and loss account of which is shown below. We look at PIC International again later in this chapter in connection with audit fees, interest paid and Research & Development.

Profit before taxation
As shown in Examples 16.1 and 16.2:

- trading profit, *plus*
- income from interests in associated undertakings and from other participating interests (see Chapter 22), *plus*
- income from other investments and other interest receivable, *less*
- interest payable and any amounts written off investments,
- leaves the profit before tax, or 'pre-tax profit'.

PIC INTERNATIONAL is one of a growing number of companies which show the information required

PIC INTERNATIONAL *Extract from group profit and loss account for the year ended 30 June 2000*

	Operations before exceptional items £m	Exceptional items £m	2000 £m	1999 £m
Turnover				
Continuing operations				
Group and share of joint ventures	151.9	–	151.9	167.4
less: share of joint ventures	(11.7)	–	(11.7)	(16.4)
Group turnover	140.2	–	140.2	151.0
Group operating loss (Note 2 – see next page)	(3.5)	(1.3)	(4.8)	(17.1)
Share of operating profit of joint ventures	0.2		0.2	0.1
Loss before fundamental restructuring, interest and tax	(3.3)	(1.3)	(4.6)	(17.0)
Fundamental restructuring				
– Sale and closure of businesses	–	(6.7)	(6.7)	(7.5)
– Other consequential income		8.6	8.6	2.0
Net interest receivable	0.9	–	0.9	3.5
(Loss) profit on ordinary activities before tax	(2.4)	0.6	(1.8)	(19.0)

PIC INTERNATIONAL *Extract from note 2 to the accounts for the year ended 30 June 2000*

2. Operating loss
Operating loss is calculated as follows:

	Continuing operations 2000 £m	Continuing operations 1999 £m
Turnover	140.2	151.0
Charges		
Change in stocks of work in progress	(5.5)	(0.6)
Raw materials and consumables	78.2	79.8
Other external charges	30.4	36.8
Staff costs (note 7b – not shown)	33.2	41.2
Depreciation of tangible fixed assets	6.5	7.5
Impairment of tangible fixed assets	3.4	1.4
Hire of plant and machinery	0.1	1.0
Other operating lease rentals	4.3	3.2
Goodwill charged to P & L account	–	5.8
Total charges	150.6	176.1
Income		
Own work capitalised	–	0.2
Net profit on disposal of fixed assets	1.3	1.8
Other operating income	4.3	6.0
Total income	5.6	8.0
Operating loss	(4.8)	(17.1)

by one or other of the formats laid down not on the face of the profit and loss account but in the notes.

The three parts
Whatever format is used, the profit and loss account (sometimes referred to as the revenue account or statement of income) can conveniently be divided into three parts which show

- how the profit (or loss) was earned;
- how much was taken by taxation;
- what happened to the profit (or loss) that was left after taxation.

This chapter covers the first part. Chapter 17 is devoted to taxation and Chapter 18 considers profit after tax, dividends and earnings per share.

Additional disclosures
Profit and loss accounts of listed companies are rarely quite as simple as those shown in Examples 16.1 and 16.2.

The formats do not cover everything. Additional disclosures are required by

(a) the Companies Act itself;
(b) Accounting Standards; and
(c) UK Listing Authority (UKLA)'s Listing Rules

We focus separately on each of these in the sections which follow. Examples later in this chapter and in the chapters which follow illustrate

(a) how accounting standards and the requirements of UKLA affect the profit and loss account; and
(b) the use which the investor and analyst can make of that information.

DISCLOSURES REQUIRED BY THE COMPANIES ACT

Turnover
Turnover is the amount derived from the provision of goods and services falling within the company's ordinary activities (after deduction of trade discounts and before adding VAT and other sales-based taxes). Companies are required by the standard formats of the Companies Act 1985 to disclose turnover (i.e. total sales) in their profit and loss account. The following must also be given:

(a) Under Sch. 4, para. 55 (1)), if a company carried on two or more classes of business during

the year which in the directors' opinion differ substantially from each other, it should describe the classes and show each one's turnover and pre-tax profit.

(b) If in the year a company supplied geographical markets which in the directors' opinion differ substantially, the turnover attributable to each should be stated (Sch. 4, para. 55(2)).

However, this information need not be disclosed if, in the opinion of the directors, it would be seriously prejudicial to the interests of the company to do so;

but the fact that it has not been disclosed must be stated (Sch. 4, para. 55 (5)).

Segmental reporting (SSAP 25), is considered later in this chapter (see pages 123–4).

Other items in the profit and loss account

The Companies Act 1985 requires that the following be shown separately in the profit and loss account or in the notes:

1. *Directors' emoluments*: Schedule 6 of CA 1985 requires:

(a) aggregate, for all directors, of each of: emoluments (salaries, fees and bonuses); gains on exercise of share options; amounts in respect of long-term incentive schemes; employers' pension contributions under money purchase (defined contribution) schemes;

(b) number of directors accruing benefits under each of money purchase schemes and defined benefit (final salary) schemes;

(c) details of emoluments of highest paid director where aggregate of items in (a) above, excluding employers' pension contributions, exceeds £200,000;

(d) aggregate of excess retirement benefits;

(e) aggregate amount of compensation for loss of office;

(f) sums paid to third parties in respect of directors' services.

Note: The UKLA Listing rules require fully listed companies to provide detailed information on each director – see Chapter 26.

2. *Particulars of staff*: the average number employed during the year, and the aggregate amounts of their (a) wages and salaries, (b) social security costs, (c) other pension costs (CA 1985, Sch. 4, para. 56); see page 115.

3. *Auditors' remuneration* in their capacity as such, including expenses. Remuneration for services other than those of auditors should be shown separately (CA 1985, s. 390A and 390B)

A sharp increase in the auditors' remuneration (i.e. more than merely keeping pace with inflation) may be an indication of difficulties; for example SOCK SHOP paid their auditors £60,000 for the 17 months ended 28 February 1989 compared with £10,000 for the previous year, and went into receivership in 1990. Or to take a recent example:

PIC INTERNATIONAL *Extract from note 2 to the accounts for the year ended 30 June 2000*

	2000 £m	1999 £m
Audit fees: Group	0.5	0.5
...		
Non-audit fees: Group		
UK	0.1	2.8
Non-UK	0.5	0.3
	0.6	3.1

...

Non-audit fees relate to work in respect of accounting, tax and other financial advice, the majority of which are a consequence of the Group's fundamental restructuring which took place in 1998.

---

4. *Depreciation* and diminution in value of fixed assets (see Chapter 8). In Format 1 depreciation is not shown as a separate item, but in all formats the amount provided during the year will be found in the note on fixed assets.

5. *Interest paid*: the Companies Act 1985 (Sch. 4, para. 53(2)) requires the disclosure of the interest paid on bank loans and overdrafts, on loans repayable within five years and on other loans. Most companies show a single figure in their profit and loss account, giving details in a note which may include: (i) some netting out of interest received; (ii) discount amortisation of deep discount bonds; (iii) interest capitalised and other adjustments; as, for example the note explaining 'net interest' in PIC INTERNATIONAL's 2000 accounts:

PIC INTERNATIONAL *Extracts from the accounts for the year to 30 June 2000*

Note 4 Interest	2000 £m	1999 £m
Interest payable and similar charges:		
On bank loans and overdraft	(1.3)	(0.8)
Other interest payable	(0.7)	(2.3)
Unwind of discount on surplus property provision	(0.4)	(0.4)
Interest receivable	3.3	7.0
Net interest receivable	0.9	3.5

Other interest payable of £0.7m (£2.3m) includes interest paid to purchasers on the delayed settlement of purchase price adjustments and other residual liabilities connected with the disposal of businesses in 1998 which have yet to be settled.

Although all this information may be shown on the face of the profit and loss account, it rarely is. In general one finds it early in the notes to the accounts, in a note entitled something like 'Profit on ordinary activities before tax', though there is then usually a separate note on employment costs and/or directors' emoluments.

Parent company profit and loss account

If, at the end of a financial year, a company is a parent company, group accounts have to be prepared as well as individual accounts for the parent company (CA 1985, s. 227).

As will be explained in Chapter 20, group accounts comprise a consolidated balance sheet and profit and loss account dealing with the parent company and its subsidiary undertakings.

Under Section 230 (3) of the Companies Act 1985, the parent company's profit and loss account may be omitted from the consolidated accounts providing the parent company's balance sheet shows the parent company's profit or loss for the year. Since most listed companies are holding companies, i.e. have subsidiaries, in practice one seldom if ever sees the parent company's own profit and loss account; one sees only the profit and loss account of the group.

DISCLOSURES REQUIRED BY ACCOUNTING STANDARDS

A large number of Accounting and Financial Reporting Standards require the disclosure of information in the profit and loss account or the notes:

1. Segmental reporting

SSAP 25 *Segmental reporting* requires companies which have two or more classes of business or which operate in two or more geographical segments to report turnover (differentiating between external sales and sales to other segments), pre-tax profits and net assets for each class of business and for each geographical segment. A separate section of this chapter (pages 123–4) is devoted to the requirements of SSAP 25.

2. Research and development

SSAP 13 *Research and development* requires all expenditure on **research** to be charged to the P & L account in the same year. **Development** costs are normally charged to the P & L account in the same year, but providing there is a clearly defined project that is technically and commercially viable, and that related expenditure is separately identifiable, development expenditure may be capitalised and written off to the P & L account over a number of years.

PIC INTERNATIONAL *Extract from note 2 to the accounts for the year ended 30 June 2000*

Research and development expenditure This amounted to £5.4m (£4.7m), and related to enabling and development research.

---

3. Operating lease rentals

SSAP 21 *Lease and hire purchase contracts* requires rentals on operating leases to be charged to the P & L account on a straight line basis over the term of the lease.

4. Pension costs

SSAP 24 *Accounting for pension costs*, issued in 1988, required:

(a) Defined contribution (money purchase) schemes – contributions payable by the company to the pension scheme are charged to the P & L account.

(b) Defined benefit (final salary) schemes – the costs of the scheme are charged to the P & L account so as to spread the cost of pensions over the employees' expected working lives with the company.

In November 2000, the Accounting Standards Board issued FRS 17 *Retirement benefits*. Following a potentially lengthy transitional period, this Standard will eventually replace SSAP 24.

See pages 115–17 for a summary of the requirements of SSAP 24 and FRS 17.

5. Investment income

Under FRS 16 *Current tax*, dividends received from UK resident companies are shown at the actual amount received or receivable.

6. Substance over form

The influence of FRS 5 *Reporting the substance of transactions* has been considered in Chapters 6, 11, 12 and 13.

7. Foreign exchange

SSAP 20 *Foreign currency translation* gives a choice on the treatment of foreign currencies. In a group with overseas subsidiaries, profit and loss account items may be translated using either the *average rate* for the accounting period or the *closing rate*. The method chosen should be applied consistently.

As explained in Chapter 23, whether the average rate or the closing rate is used can make a considerable difference to reported profit.

8. Subsidiaries and groups
FRS 2 *Accounting for subsidiary undertakings*, FRS 6 *Acquisitions and mergers*, FRS 7 *Fair values in acquisition accounting*, FRS 10 *Goodwill and intangible assets*, and FRS 11 *Impairment of fixed assets and goodwill* all affect the P & L account in one way or another; see Chapters 20 and 21.

9. Associated undertakings
'Income from interests in associated undertakings' and 'Income from other participating interests' both appear in the formats but FRS 9 *Associates and joint ventures* calls for additional disclosures as explained in Chapter 22.

10. Provisions
The making of provisions and utilisation of provisions made in earlier years both affect profits. This is covered by FRS 12 *Provisions, contingent liabilities and contingent assets*. See Chapter 15.

11. Exceptional and prior year items
FRS 3 *Reporting financial performance* is concerned, amongst other things, with items disclosed as exceptional or prior year. It will be considered later in this chapter.

DISCLOSURES REQUIRED BY THE UKLA LISTING RULES

Purple Book requirements
Several Purple Book requirements (see Chapter 4) concern the profit and loss account:

(a) if the results for the period under review differ by 10% or more from any published forecast or estimate by the company for that period, an explanation of the difference must be given;

(b) a statement is required of the amount of interest capitalised;

(c) particulars must be given of the waiving of emoluments by any director, and of the waiving of dividends by any shareholder;

(d) details of remuneration for *each director* must be given. See Chapter 26.

WEEKS GROUP *Extract from note on Directors' emoluments*

Directors' emoluments

The emoluments of the directors who served during the year are set out below:

	Salary inc. fees £'000	Benefits £'000	Profit related pay £'000	Total 2000 £'000	Total 1999 £'000	Pension contributions 2000 £'000	Pension contributions 1999 £'000
Chairman:							
A G Weeks	24	10	–	34	52	–	–
Executive directors:							
P R Hill	51	2	1	54	–	4	–
R S Pugh	73	9	1	83	82	6	6
P B Griffith	69	5	1	75	73	6	6
J C Slack	33	1	–	34	–	3	–
Non-executive directors:							
BSL Trafford	8	–	–	8	8	–	–
Total	258	27	3	288	215	19	12

The pension contributions disclosed above were all made in respect of money purchase arrangements. The emoluments of P R Hill and J C Slack reflect only the period during the year ended 31 March 2000 after they were appointed directors of the company.

. . .

EFFECT OF ACCOUNTING POLICIES ON PROFITABILITY

Accounting policies

The company's accounting policies, which usually appear either as 'Note 1' to the accounts or as a separate statement, should be read carefully to see if there are any unusual features that might affect the company's reported profits.

Abnormal accounting policies which can materially alter the reported profits include:

1. *Valuation of stock.* The higher the value of stocks at the end of the period, the lower the cost of goods sold and the higher the profits. Stock valuation is to an extent subjective, so that when times are hard there is a temptation for management at the worst to inflate figures or at best simply to look through rose coloured spectacles at items which may prove to be unsaleable. To do this is to improve current results at the expense of the future.

2. *Depreciation.* The lower the charge for depreciation in a particular year, the higher the book value of fixed assets carried forward and the higher the profits. For example THORNTONS, the chocolate manufacturer and retailer, changed its policy on depreciation in 2000 and showed the effect of the change in a note:

THORNTONS *Note on Accounting policies 2000*

Tangible fixed assets and depreciation
... Following a change in strategic emphasis, which will result in fewer shop refits and shop openings, the useful life of Retail fixtures and fittings has been extended from 4 to 5 years. The effect in the period has been to reduce the depreciation charge for the Group by £1,966,000.

Without this change, Profit on ordinary activities before tax would have fallen from £11.085 million in 1999 to £3.546 million in 2000, rather than the reported figure of £5.512 million – a fall of 68% rather than a reported fall of 50%.

Thorntons had expanded their retail chain too fast, and were having to slow down. The new Chief Executive was refreshingly candid:

THORNTONS *Extract from Annual report 2000*

Chief Executive's review
Clearly we know that mistakes have been made in the past, but we understand how they arose and what we have to do to prevent their reoccurrence.
... our marketing and NPD investment was poorly targeted and uncoordinated ... over ambitious sales expectations for Easter ...

Selection of an appropriate method of depreciation, the estimation of the useful life of an asset, and its residual value are all matters for management judgement (FRS 15, paras. 77, 93 and 95). This may differ from company to company.

3. *Capitalising expenditure.* All expenditure incurred by a company must either add to the value of the assets in the balance sheet or be charged in the profit and loss account. In the sense that it would otherwise be a charge against profits, any amount that can be capitalised will increase profits directly by the amount capitalised at the expense of the profits in future years, when increased capital values will require increased depreciation.

What is it reasonable to capitalise?

Items which are sometimes capitalised include:

- research and development;
- finance costs;
- starting-up costs.

Research and development

As explained earlier, under SSAP 13 *Research and development* all expenditure on research and development should normally be written off in the year in which it is incurred. However, where development is for clearly defined projects on which expenditure is separately identifiable and for which commercial success is reasonably certain, companies may if they wish defer charging development expenditure 'to the extent that its recovery can reasonably be regarded as assured'. Capitalised development expenditure should be separately disclosed.

Finance costs

Capitalising interest on a project during construction is a normal and reasonable practice provided interest is not capitalised outside the planned time-scale of the project. There are, indeed, strong arguments in favour of capitalisation:

(i) finance costs are not intrinsically different from other directly attributable costs of constructing a tangible fixed asset;
(ii) capitalising finance costs results in a tangible fixed asset cost that more closely matches the market price of completed assets;
(iii) treating the finance costs as an expense distorts the choice between purchasing and constructing a tangible fixed asset.
(iv) the accounts are more likely to reflect the true success or failure of the project.

The ASB would like to make capitalisation of interest mandatory but was influenced by the argument that 'if capitalisation is to become mandatory, in theory notional interest should also be capitalised'. Otherwise, capitalisation of finance costs results in the same type of asset having a different book value, depending on the method of financing adopted by the enterprise. It is inconsistent to allow debt-funded entities to include interest costs in the cost of an asset, whilst prohibiting equity-funded entities from reflecting similarly the cost of capital in the cost of an asset.

But 'notional interest' would certainly be contentious. In the absence of international agreement, the ASB has maintained the optional capitalisation of finance costs (Appendix IV to FRS 15 *Tangible fixed assets*).

But FRS 15 tightens the rules. If a policy of capitalisation is adopted:

1. It must be consistently applied to all finance costs directly attributable to the construction of tangible assets.
2. The amount capitalised in any period may not exceed finance costs incurred in that period, so notional interest may not be capitalised.
3. Capitalised finance costs must be 'directly attributable', i.e. they must be incremental, avoidable if there had been no expenditure on the asset.
4. Finance costs are to be capitalised gross, i.e. before the deduction of any tax relief attributed.
5. All finance costs, as defined by FRS 4 *Capital instruments*, have to be capitalised, not just the interest on the debt. This means that issue costs that are deducted in arriving at the net proceeds of the debt instrument will be capitalised to the extent that they form part of the finance charge.
6. If a company borrows funds specifically to construct an asset, the costs to be capitalised are the actual finance costs during the period.
7. If the project has been financed from the company's general borrowings, a detailed calculation method is laid down.
8. Capitalisation should begin when:

   (a) finance costs are being incurred;
   (b) expenditures for the asset are being incurred; and
   (c) activities that are necessary to get the asset ready for use are in progress. Necessary activities can, in fact, start before the physical construction of the asset, for example technical and administrative costs such as obtaining permits.

9. Capitalisation must cease when the asset's physical construction is complete and ready for use, even if it has not yet been brought into use.

Stopping companies from continuing to capitalise interest after completion will close a loophole used widely in the past whenever properties have proved harder to let than was originally expected.

LAND SECURITIES, easily the largest of all UK property companies, won't be affected, because it is also probably the most prudent:

LAND SECURITIES *Accounting policies 2000*

Properties

. . .

Additions to properties include costs of a capital nature only; interest and other costs in respect of developments and refurbishments are treated as revenue expenditure and written off as incurred.

Unlike Land Securities most UK listed property companies do capitalise interest, and may need to revise their accounting policies. For example the well respected property company HELICAL BAR:

HELICAL BAR *Note to Accounting policies 1999*

Interest capitalised on development properties
Interest costs incurred on development properties are capitalised until the earliest of:

– the date when the development becomes fully let
– the date when the income exceeds outgoings;
– a date within two years of completion to allow for letting

The note to Helical Bar's 2000 accounts showed that the group had changed the third criterion above to '– the date of completion of the development'. The note added that the change, made to adopt the requirements of FRS 15, has had no material effect on the group.

The new rules will also require a change in accounting policy for many non-construction companies, e.g. SAINSBURY:

SAINSBURY *Accounting policies 2000*

Capitalisation of interest
Interest incurred on borrowings for the financing of specific property developments is capitalised.

Starting-up costs
FRS 15 does not permit capitalisation of start-up costs unless 'the asset is available for use but incapable of operating at normal levels without such a

start-up or commissioning period'. The costs of a commissioning period, necessary for running in of machinery or testing equipment, may be capitalised as part of the cost of the asset. But costs incurred when demand is low, for example in a new hotel or bookstore, do not meet the definition of being 'directly attributable': they have been incurred after physical completion and they are not necessary in order to use the asset.

In the past companies have sometimes capitalised starting-up costs when (or because) they were expanding faster than was prudent. When the new project failed to live up to expectations the company ran into serious trouble. SOCK SHOP provides a good example.

SOCK SHOP *Extracts from the 1988–89 accounts*

Accounting policies
Overseas subsidiary set-up costs
Costs incurred in establishing overseas operations in the first year are capitalised as intangible assets and amortised over 4 years on a straight-line basis commencing at the end of the first year.

Intangible assets	£000
Overseas subsidiary set-up costs:	
At beginning of period	–
Additions	354
At end of period	354

The capitalising of £354,000 was not, in itself, significant: it only represented 8% of reported pre-tax profits of £4.32m; but the overseas expansion proved disastrous: less than a year later the company

- reported an interim loss of £3.97m;
- announced heavy write-offs on the closure of 17 loss-making US outlets;
- went into receivership.

Changes of accounting policy
FRS 18 *Accounting policies* requires companies to flag up clear details of accounting policy changes:

- a brief explanation of why each new accounting policy is thought more appropriate;
- a prior year adjustment involving restatement of the previous year's figures (or a reason why this is not practicable);
- an indication of the effect of the change on the results for the current period (or a reason why this is not practicable).

Changes in accounting policies can have a dramatic effect on reported profits or losses, and result in a prior period adjustment (see page 145) as we showed in relation to ML LABORATORIES on page 46.

Often there will be no choice: the change of accounting policy is required by financial reporting standards. But it does help if exactly what is happening is spelled out:

Some companies change their accounting policies for no convincing reason other than to boost profits.

If this is spotted it is a danger signal, as with REGALIAN PROPERTIES:

REGALIAN PROPERTIES *Note to the 1998 accounts*

Change in Accounting Policy
The newly adopted accounting policy provides that sales and profits will be recognised when . . . the Group is contractually entitled to issue a notice requiring the purchaser to complete.

The effects of the change in policy are as follows:

	Turnover £000	*Profit before tax* £000
1998 – Prior accounting policy	40,167	2,629
Effect of change	17,812	4,083
1998 – As reported in accounts	59,979	6,712

Changes of presentation
Companies also change their minds upon how certain transactions should be treated and there is nothing sinister or unusual about that. They may not even tell you provided they consider the change is not 'material' and the auditors agree. BARCLAYS are specific:

BARCLAYS *Extract from accounting policies 1998*

Accounting presentation
Changes in accounting presentation
Within the classification other operating income, income from the long-term assurance business now includes amounts previously reported within other income (1997 £14m, 1996 £15m).

Following a reassessment, certain BGI managed funds, previously reported within life-fund assets attributable to policyholders, are now more appropriately classified as funds under management. Accordingly these funds, and their related liabilities, have been excluded from the consolidated balance sheet (1997 £2,228m).

RETIREMENT BENEFITS

SSAP 24 *Accounting for pension costs* requires the employer to 'recognise the expected cost of providing pensions on a systematic and rational basis' over the period of employment. Cash accounting is not permitted, and companies are required to disclose detailed information on their pension arrangements.

In November 2000 the ASB issued FRS 17 *Retirement benefits* which comes fully into force for accounting periods ending on or after 22 June 2003, although earlier adoption is encouraged.

In view of the complexity of FRS 17, and the problems of gathering together information for disclosure purposes, the ASB has given companies the option of phasing in the new Standard over a three-year transitional period, as described in FRS 17, para. 94.

In view of the lengthy transitional period, we will cover the requirements of both SSAP 24 and FRS 17.

Types of pension scheme
Pension schemes can be either funded or unfunded:

* In a *funded* scheme, the company's contributions (and the employees' contributions if it is a 'contributory' rather than a 'non-contributory' scheme) are paid away to be invested externally to meet future pension liabilities, and the assets of the scheme are held in trust outside the company.
* In an *unfunded* scheme, which is the norm in some foreign countries, the company makes a provision for future liabilities in its accounts.

There are three types of pension scheme in the UK:

1. SERPS, the State Earnings-Related Pension Scheme. Companies pay the employer contribution and have no further liability.
2. Defined contribution schemes.
3. Defined benefit schemes.

Defined contribution schemes and defined benefit schemes are invariably funded.

Defined contribution schemes
In a defined contribution or 'money purchase' scheme, the employer has no obligation beyond payment of the contributions he has agreed to make. The benefits may vary with the performance of the investments purchased by the contributions, but this risk is borne by the employees.

The cost of providing pensions is thus straightforward: it is the amount of contribution due for the period, and will be charged against profits, e.g. TESCO:

TESCO *Note on pension commitments 2000*

26. Pension commitments
. . .

The group also operates a defined contribution pension scheme for part-time employees which was introduced on 6 April 1988. The assets of the scheme are held separately from those of the Group, being invested with an insurance company. The pension cost represents contributions payable by the Group to the insurance company and amounted to £19m (1998 – £17m).

Smaller companies tend to run this type of scheme, or to contribute to SERPS or to employees' own Personal Pension Plans, in order to avoid taking on any open-ended future commitment. Indeed, a number of larger companies have in recent years closed defined benefit schemes and moved to defined contribution schemes to avoid this liability.

Defined benefit schemes
In a defined benefit or 'final salary' scheme, the pensions to be paid depend on the employees' pay, normally the pay in the final year of employment, so the employer's liability is open-ended.

Because of the complexities of estimating the contributions needed to provide for pensions based on wages or salaries often many years hence, consulting actuaries are used to carry out periodic valuations, usually every three years, and to determine the contribution rate required.

Where an actuarial valuation reveals a material deficiency or surplus in a defined benefit scheme, SSAP 24 requires that it should normally be taken into account by adjusting the current and future costs in the accounts over the remaining service lives of the current employees, or over the average life. See SSAP 24, paras. 81 to 83 for exceptions.

Actuaries use a number of techniques and assumptions in arriving at a valuation, and they do not all use the same ones. SSAP 24 explains the terminology, e.g. 'attained age' or 'projected unit' method. Where there are changes to the actuarial assumptions, or to the valuation method or to the benefits of the scheme, their effect on pension costs should also be spread over the remaining service lives or average life.

115

The disclosure requirements of SSAP 24 are very extensive. Items of particular interest to the analyst are:

- the accounting policy and, if different, the funding policy and any resulting provisions or prepayments;
- the pension cost charge and the reasons for any significant change from the previous year;
- details of the expected effects on future costs of any material changes in pension arrangements.

Because several schemes are often involved, sometimes in several countries, notes on pensions can be exceedingly long and complex. Most tend to be in narrative form, e.g. TESCO:

TESCO *Note on pension commitments 2000*

Pension commitments
The Group operates a funded defined benefit pension scheme for full-time employees in the UK, the assets of which are held as a segregated fund and administered by trustees. The total cost of the scheme to the Group was £60m (1999 – £55m).

An independent actuary . . . carried out the latest actuarial assessment of the scheme at 5 April 1999 . . . The key assumptions made were:

Rate of return on investments	7.25%
Rate of increase in salaries	4.50%
Rate of increase in pensions	2.75%

. . . the market value of the scheme's assets was £1.297m and the actuarial value represented 96% of the benefits that had accrued to members . . . The actuarial shortfall of £53m will be met by increased contributions over the period of 11 years, being the expected average service lifetime of employed members. . . .

The group operates a number of pension schemes world wide, most of which are defined contribution schemes. . . .

A defined benefit scheme operates in the Republic of Ireland. At the latest actuarial valuation . . .

TESCO is among a growing number of companies that operate a scheme offering post-retirement healthcare benefits. The cost of providing for these benefits is usually accounted for on a basis similar to that used for defined benefit pension schemes. Companies listed in the US are required to disclose the provision for such schemes, which can be massive, e.g. SHELL in its 1999 accounts provided $1,214m in respect of unfunded post-retirement benefits other than pensions.

What to look for
What is important to the analyst is:

- the regular cost of pensions, which represents a very long-term obligation;
- variations from regular cost, the reasons for them, and the time over which they are likely to persist;
- changes in actuarial assumptions, and the reasons for them;
- changes in benefits and their probable future cost.
- any very substantial increase in salary (often to a departing chief executive subject to a final salary scheme);
- any unfunded liability;
- any significant unexplained prepayment to the pension fund;
- Investment of the pension fund in assets used by the company.

A tabular presentation often makes funding assumptions easier to understand and interpret and goes some way to bring out that:

- Pension funding is a very long-term business.
- It is necessary to make assumptions about matters which are very difficult to predict (e.g. the rate of inflation over, say, the next 30–40 years, mortality over that period, and the performance of the stock market as a whole, and that of the fund's investment managers in particular).
- Benefits payable tend to improve over time.

Problems faced by actuaries and pension funds
On 2 July 1997 the Chancellor announced that 'payment of tax credits will be abolished for charitable companies on dividends paid on or after today'. This completely changed one key long-term assumption made by all funds: the assumed return on investments.

The National Association of Pension Funds (NAPF)'s Chairman estimated at the time that the Chancellor's move would require UK pension schemes to contribute an extra £50bn over the next 10 years. He went on: 'Even Robert Maxwell only took £400m.' The changes in the tax system could not have come at a more unfortunate time. Pension schemes are still relatively new. For the last 20–30 years, as funds built up, contributions, in general, exceeded outgoings. Only recently have we begun to see mature funds in which pensions and other benefits being paid exceed the contributions coming in, increasing the fund's dependence on investment income.

Wide awake companies like DIAGEO asked their actuaries what effect all this is likely to have. They seem undismayed.

DIAGEO *Extract from Note 5 to the 2000 accounts*

(i) Pension plans

. . .

Valuations were carried out in 1999 of the UK, US and Irish plans. All valuations were done by independent actuaries using the projected unit method to determine pension costs. The principal assumptions were: real rate of return on assets 4% . . . real annual increase in wages and salaries 2.0% to 2.5% . . . real rate of future dividend growth for UK equities 1% . . . and pension increases to be approximately in line with inflation . . . The market values of the assets of the principal funds . . . totalled approximately: UK fund – £3,068 million; US funds – 1,174 million; and Irish funds – £931 million.

Disclosure of information

By law most types of pension scheme must, within seven months after the end of the scheme year, make available an annual report, including audited accounts. Trustees who fail to do this are guilty of a criminal offence, and liable to a fine. A SORP, *Financial reports of pension schemes*, reflects the accounting requirements.

FRS 17 *Retirement benefits*

SSAP 24 was criticised on a number of grounds:

- it allowed preparers of accounts too many options, resulting in inconsistency in accounting practice;
- it resulted in poor disclosures, thus preventing users from making informed judgements on how companies had accounted for pension cost issues;
- it resulted in balance sheet prepayments and provisions which were almost impossible to explain or to interpret.

FRS 17 addresses these criticisms by introducing major changes in accounting and disclosure requirements for *defined benefit* pension schemes.

There are no changes in the requirements for *defined contribution* schemes.

The full requirements of FRS 17 will be reflected in the balance sheet, the profit and loss account, and the statement of total recognised gains and losses, as well as in the notes.

Key points are:

- Full actuarial valuations of pension scheme liabilities will be required at least three-yearly, with updates in other years.
- The balance sheet will include one-line items for pension fund asset (assuming a surplus) and pension fund reserve. The pension fund asset is the amount by which the total value of the scheme assets exceeds the present value of the scheme liabilities.
- The profit and loss account will include two charges or credits:

    (1) operating profit will be charged with current service cost and past service cost
    (2) finance income will be credited (debited) with the amount by which the expected return on scheme assets exceeds (falls short of) the interest on pension scheme liabilities.

- The statement of total recognised gains and losses will pick up actuarial gains and losses.
- Movement in surplus or deficit in schemes over the period will be analysed with reconciliation of surplus / deficit to the balance sheet asset / liability.
- A company will have to build up to a five-year statistical summary.

Main points of interest for users of accounts will be:

- The balance sheet will show the pension scheme's surplus or deficit to the extent that the employer company expects to benefit or suffer from it.
- The profit and loss account will show the ongoing service cost, interest cost and expected return on assets.
- The statement of total recognised gains and losses will record and reflect market fluctuations in interest rates and share prices.
- A trend picture will be highlighted by the disclosure of a five-year history of actuarial gains and losses – making users aware of when actuarial assumptions are consistently not being met.

EXCEPTIONAL ITEMS

Basic purpose of the profit and loss account

There are two conflicting views of the basic purpose of the profit and loss account:

(a) the current operating performance concept;
(b) the all-inclusive concept.

(a) Current operating performance concept

Advocates of the current operating performance concept believe that the profit and loss account should be designed to disclose the earnings of the business which arise from the *normal operating activities* during the period being reported upon;

anything exceptional, extraordinary or relating to prior years, and the effects of accounting changes, would be excluded.

A profit and loss account prepared in this way facilitates comparison both with those of the same business for earlier periods and with those of other companies for the current period.

(b) All-inclusive concept

Advocates of the all-inclusive concept, on the other hand, believe that the profit and loss account should include *all transactions* which bring about a net increase or decrease in net tangible assets during the current period, apart from dividend distributions and transactions such as the issue of shares.

There has been a shift of opinion towards the all-inclusive concept during the past few years, not only in the United Kingdom but also in the United States and Canada, although none of these countries adopts a pure all-inclusive basis.

Is it extraordinary or exceptional?

Prior to FRS 3 *Reporting financial performance*, published in 1993, companies were allowed to show *extraordinary items* 'below the line' in their profit and loss account, i.e. below the figure for profit attributable to ordinary shareholders, on which earnings per share were calculated, while *exceptional items* came 'above the line'.

This led to widespread abuse: companies tended to classify unusual losses as extraordinary and unusual profits as exceptional, in order to enhance their reported earnings per share. In some cases the questionable classifications of items more than doubled reported profits, e.g. in 1990 the hotel group STAKIS reported a pre-tax profit of £30.6m which included gains on the sale of properties of £18.5m. (Management was replaced in 1991.)

In order to stop what had probably become the most widespread form of creative accounting, FRS 3 not only produced a much tighter definition of an extraordinary item, so as to make them extremely rare, but also requires extraordinary (as well as exceptional) items to be included in the calculation of earnings per share.

FRS 3 definition

Extraordinary items are 'Material items possessing a high degree of abnormality which arise from events or transactions that fall outside the ordinary activities of the reporting entity and which are not expected to recur. They do not include exceptional items nor do they include prior period items merely because they relate to a prior period' (FRS 3, para. 6).

In practice extraordinary items are now virtually extinct.

Exceptional items are 'Material items which derive from events or transactions that fall within the ordinary activities of the reporting entity and which individually or, of a similar type, in aggregate, need to be disclosed by virtue of their size or incidence if the financial statements are to give a true and fair view' (FRS 3, para. 5).

One consequence of FRS 3 is that profits before taxation now have to include large 'one-off' items. This has led to much increased volatility, in some cases even turning a profit into a loss.

FRS 3 has not met with universal approval either among companies or analysts. Although the computation of earnings per share is explained in Chapter 18, this is nevertheless an appropriate point to consider the adjustments which analysts make. In order to focus on the profitability of the normal trading operations of a company (i.e. to move nearer to a current operating performance basis as described above), the Institute of Investment Management and Research (IIMR) has developed a standard approach to reported profits, which eliminates capital transactions and abnormal items. This produces what are called the *headline earnings*.

'Headline' or 'normalised' earnings

Headline earnings exclude the following items:

1. Profits or losses on the sale or termination of an operation.
2. Profits or losses on the disposal of fixed assets.
3. Expropriation of assets.
4. Amortisation of goodwill.
5. Bid defence costs.
6. Diminution in the value of fixed assets.
7. Profit or loss on the capital reorganisation of long-term debt.
8. Profits or losses on the disposal of trade investments.

The IIMR approach, focusing on the trading activities of a company, has been followed by most leading stockbrokers, to produce what are termed *normalised earnings*, but with some variations.

The main variation between brokers is that some follow the IIMR recommendation to include 'costs of a fundamental reorganisation or restructuring having a material effect on the nature and focus of the reporting entity's operations' (one of the items shown separately below operating profit), while others exclude it on the grounds of abnormality and of being unlikely to recur.

The trouble with excluding it is that doing so encourages companies to classify relatively minor reorganisations as 'fundamental' in order to avoid the costs reducing 'normalised' profits and earnings per share.

The other problems with adjusting or 'normalising' earnings are taxation and minority interests. With the three items that have to be disclosed separately after operating profit (sale or termination of an operation, fundamental reorganisation and restructuring, and disposal of fixed assets), FRS 3 requires relevant information on the effect of these items on the tax charge and on any minority interests (see Chapters 20 and 21) to be shown.

With the other items listed by the IIMR for stripping out, e.g. expropriation of assets, the effect on the tax charge may have to be estimated by the analysts. And the effect on minorities will not be known unless disclosed by the company.

FRS 3 *Reporting financial performance*
Besides greatly increasing the number and amount of items appearing on the face of the profit and loss account as exceptional, FRS 3 introduced two new and valuable features to the profit and loss account:

1. *Subdivision of results* down to operating profit level into Continuing operations; Acquisitions (considered in Chapters 20 and 21); and Discontinued operations.
2. *Separate disclosure*, after operating profit and before interest, of three important items:

   (a) profits or losses on the sale or termination of an operation,
   (b) costs of a fundamental reorganisation or restructuring having a material effect on the nature and focus of the reporting entity's operations, and

(c) profits or losses on the disposal of fixed assets.

Items (a), (b) and (c) are sometimes referred to as 'the paragraph 20 items', because they are contained in para. 20 of FRS 3.

The way exceptional items might be handled is illustrated in two examples in FRS 3:

*   a single-column format, and
*   a multi-column format.

Comparative figures
The analysis of comparative figures between continuing and discontinued operations is not required on the face of the profit and loss account. Nevertheless, experience suggests that most companies do show it there.

Whichever method is employed, the composition of the comparative figures needs to be understood. As para. 64 of the Explanations to FRS 3 explains:

'To aid comparison, the comparative figures in respect of the profit and loss account should be based on the status of an operation in the financial statements of the period under review and should, therefore, include in the continuing category only the results of those operations included in the current period's continuing operations. . . . the comparative figures for discontinued operations will include both amounts relating to operations discontinued in the previous period and amounts relating to operations discontinued in the period under review, which in the previous period would have been included as part of continuing operations.'

RATIOS

Most well-run companies of any size make extensive use of ratios internally, to monitor and ensure the efficient running of each division or activity.

In addition to the published report and accounts of a group, resort can be made to Companies House for accounts filed by subsidiaries, although these can be misleading

*   if goods and services have been transferred within the group at unrealistic prices; or
*   if major adjustments have been made on consolidation.

In any case, the accounts of subsidiaries are often not filed at Companies House until some time after the group accounts have been published.

Horizontal analysis
The simplest method of comparing one year's figures with another involves working out the percentage change from the previous year of each main component of the accounts, e.g. BRANDON HIRE, a company which employs the single-column format to display the effects of acquisitions in its profit and loss account.

Percentage changes in themselves may reveal a certain amount about a company's performance, but, like many ratios, they are of most value in prompting further enquiry. For example: What did Brandon Hire acquire in 1999? Why was the 23.0% margin so much higher than Brandon's own 13.5%?

Are they in areas where Brandon could expand?

BRANDON HIRE *Extract from 1999 P & L*

	1999 £000	1998 £000
Turnover		
Tool hire – Continuing operations	21,907	16,859
Acquisitions	1,596	3,465
	23,503	20,324
Catering hire		
– Discontinued operations	–	7,381
	23,503	27,705
Operating profit		
Continuing operations	2,947	2,252
Acquisitions	367	596
Total operating profit	3,314	2,848

BRANDON HIRE *Year-on-Year analysis*

Continuing operations

Turnover 1999/1998	21,907/20,324	=	+7.8%
Operating profit	2,848/2,947	=	+3.5%
Margins 1998	2,252/16,859	=	13.4%
1999	2,947/21,907	=	13.5%

Acquisitions

Margins 1998	596/3,465	=	17.2%
1999	367/1,596	=	23.0%

Comment

The company is making some high margin acquisitions, but they are relatively small, and will have little impact unless they can be expanded.

Vertical analysis

Year-on-year comparisons can be thought of as working across the page, comparing each item with the previous year to get the percentage change, or looking at several years to see the trend of an item.

If we work vertically, calling the total 100, we can construct what are termed 'common size' statements giving a percentage breakdown of an account item.

The advantages of this method are, firstly, that the items are reduced to a common scale for inter-company comparisons and, secondly, that changes in the financial structure of a company stand out more clearly.

Vertical analysis can be used over several years to show how the sales/profitability pattern or financial structure of a company is changing.

Operating ratios

The three main operating ratios are:

1. Profit margin.

2. Return on capital employed.
3. Sales to capital employed.

1. **Profit margin** $= \dfrac{\textbf{Trading profit}}{\textbf{Sales}}$ **as a %**

where:
Trading profit = profit before interest charges and tax. Investment income and the company's share of the profits of associated undertakings are not included.

Sales (Turnover) = Sales (excluding VAT and excluding transactions within the group).

This ratio gives what analysts term the profit margin on sales; a normal figure for a manufacturing industry would be between 8% and 10%, while high volume/low margin activities like food retailing can run satisfactorily at around 3%. This profit margin is not the same thing as the gross profit margin (the difference between selling price and the cost of sales, expressed as a percentage of selling price), which can be obtained only if the company reports cost of sales (as BRANDON HIRE does, in a note to the acounts).

Unusually low margins can be set deliberately by management to increase market share or can be caused by expansion costs, e.g. new product launching, but in general depressed margins suggest poor performance.

Somewhat better than average margins are normally a sign of good management, but unusually high margins may mean that the company is 'making a packet' and will attract competition unless there are barriers to entry (e.g. huge initial capital costs, high technology, patents or other special advantages enjoyed by the company).

The converse also applies: if a company has lower margins than others in the same sector, there is scope for improvement. For example, between 1985 and 1993 TESCO managed to more than double its margins as it shifted away from the 'pile it high and sell it cheap' philosophy of its founder, the late Sir Jack Cohen, towards SAINSBURY's quality image and better margins. As the table below shows, neither is now finding it easy to maintain margins, let alone to continue to increase them, and SAINSBURY's have tumbled.

Example 16.3 Comparison of margins

Year ended	1985	1993	1997	2000
TESCO	2.7%	6.5%	5.6%	5.1%
SAINSBURY	5.1%	8.1%	5.2%	3.9%

Trading profit margins are also important in that both management and investment analysts usually base their forecasts of future profitability on projected turnover figures multiplied by estimated future margins.

An alternative definition of trading profit, used by Datastream and some analysts, is before deducting depreciation, the argument being that different depreciation policies distort inter-company comparisons. If this approach is used, then trading profit should also be before deducting rental charges, to bring a company that leases rather than owns plant and premises on to a comparable basis. Our view is that depreciation is a cost and should be deducted in any calculation of profit; we therefore prefer to deal with cases where a company's depreciation charge seems unduly low (or high) by making an adjustment, rather than by adding back every company's depreciation charge. Datastream also excludes exceptional items.

2. Return on capital employed $= \dfrac{\textbf{Trading profit}}{\textbf{Capital employed}}$

Return on Capital Employed (ROCE), expressed as a percentage, is a traditional measure of profitability for several reasons:

- a low return on capital employed can easily be wiped out in a downturn;
- if the figure is lower than the cost of borrowing, increased borrowings will reduce earnings per share (e.p.s.) unless the extra money can be used in areas where the ROCE is higher than the cost of borrowing;
- it serves as a guide to the company in assessing possible acquisitions and in starting up new activities – if their *potential* ROCE isn't attractive, they should be avoided;
- similarly, a persistently low ROCE for any part of the business suggests it could be a candidate for disposal if it isn't an integral part of the business.

ROCE can be calculated either for the company overall or for its trading activities:
Capital employed (in trading) = Share capital + reserves + all borrowing including obligations under finance leases, bank overdraft + minority interests + provisions – associates and investments. Government grants are not included.
Capital employed (overall) Associates and investments are not deducted, while the overall profit figure includes income from investments and the company's share of the profits of associated companies, in addition to trading profit.

However, ROCE can be seriously distorted by intangible fixed assets and by purchased goodwill that has been written off directly to reserves (immediate write-off). Ideally, purchased goodwill that was written off direct to reserves should be added back in calculating ROCE but FRS 10 does not require this in the accounts; and information which would allow the analyst to do this for himself is not always available.

We suggest that intangible items shown in the balance sheet should be included in capital employed at their cost less any subsequent amortisation; e.g. patents, newspaper titles and brand names that have been purchased, but not newspaper titles and brand names that have been built up internally. As Sir Adrian Cadbury said, after RHM had put £678m of brands at valuation in its balance sheet: 'The market value of a company's brands can only be established objectively when their ownership is transferred. Any other form of valuation is by definition subjective.'

The figure for capital employed should, strictly speaking, be the average capital employed during the year, but for simplicity's sake it is normally satisfactory to use the capital employed at the end of the year unless there have been major changes. Some companies label the total at the bottom of their balance sheet as 'capital employed' (BRANDON HIRE shows Equity shareholders' funds). But using the balance sheet total can be deceptive, in that bank overdrafts and loans repayable within 12 months are netted out against current assets, giving a company that has perhaps an embarrassingly large short-term debt a better ROCE than a company whose debt is more prudently funded long-term.

Another variation used by some analysts is to deduct any cash from the overdraft or, where a company has a net cash position, to deduct net cash in calculating capital employed. Netting out cash against overdraft can be justified where cash and overdraft are both with the same bank and the bank is known to calculate interest on the net figure (overdraft – cash), but in general we accept the figures used for the purposes of FRS 5 *Reporting the substance of transactions* and FRS 1 *Cash flow statements*.

If a company feels it prudent to operate with a large cash margin it should be measured accordingly, and if the company's cash is locked up somewhere (for example, if it has arisen from retaining profits overseas to avoid UK taxation) the situation should be reflected in the ratio.

Any upward revaluation of property is likely to reduce ROCE in two ways:

(a) it will increase capital employed (the surplus on revaluation being credited to capital reserve), and

(b) it will probably increase the depreciation charge, and thus reduce profits.

See Chapter 8 regarding valuations under FRS 15 *Tangible fixed assets*.

3. $$\frac{\text{Sales}}{\text{Capital employed in trading}}$$

expressed as a multiple.

Improving the return on capital employed

A rising Sales/Capital employed ratio usually indicates an improvement in performance, i.e. the amount of business being done is increasing in relation to the capital base, but beware of an improvement in the ratio achieved when a company fails to keep its plant and machinery up to date; depreciation will steadily reduce the capital base and improve the ratio without any improvement in sales. Beware, too, of any rapid increase in the ratio, which may well be a warning signal of *over-trading*, i.e. trying to do too much business with too little capital.

In inter-company comparisons care should be taken to compare like with like: the ratio can be misleading unless the operations of the companies concerned are similar in their activities as well as in their products. For example, a television manufacturing group which is vertically integrated (makes the tubes, electronic circuits and the cabinets and then puts them together) will have much more capital employed than a company which merely assembles bought-in components.

A better measure of performance might be that of value added compared with capital employed, but value added is rarely included in published information.

The three ratios are, of course, interrelated:

$$\frac{\text{Trading profit}}{\text{Sales}} \times \frac{\text{Sales}}{\text{Capital employed}}$$

$$= \frac{\text{Trading profit}}{\text{Capital employed}}$$

as seen from BRANDON HIRE at the top of the next column.

BRANDON HIRE *Extracts from 1999 accounts*

	1999 £000	1998 £000
Sales (Turnover)	23,503	20,324
Operating profit	3,314	2,848
Capital employed	20,592	20,948

BRANDON HIRE *Ratios*

	1999	1998
Profit margin	14.1%	14.0%
Return on capital employed	16.1%	13.6%
Sales/Capital employed	1.14	0.97

In 1999 Brandon Hire managed to do more business than in 1998 on slightly less Capital employed, with maintained margins.

The ratio Trading profit/Capital employed helps to illustrate the four ways in which management can improve this ratio:

1. by increasing the first factor by:

   (a) reducing costs or
   (b) raising prices

   to produce higher profit margins;

2. by increasing the second factor by:

   (a) increasing sales or
   (b) reducing capital employed

   so raising volume of output per £1 of capital.

A healthy way of improving profitability is to dispose of low profitability/high capital parts of the business, provided this can be done without adversely affecting the remainder.

Massaging the figures

There was another way of producing the same optical effect other than by running down capital investment: by leasing rather than buying plant and machinery (or by selling and leasing back fixed assets already owned), but this loophole has largely been closed by SSAP 21 *Accounting for leases and hire purchase contracts*, which requires companies to capitalise financial leases in their balance sheet (see Chapter 15).

Two other ways in which companies used to be able to reduce their apparent capital employed were by factoring their debtors and by off balance sheet financing of stock. FRS 5 *Reporting the substance of transactions* requires both the debtors and the stock to remain on the balance sheet unless the risks and rewards have been transferred to the other party; i.e. unless the factor has no recourse to the company on bad debts, and the company has no obligation to repurchase the stock.

SEGMENTAL REPORTING

Accounting standard

SSAP 25 *Segmental reporting* requires companies which have two or more classes of business or which operate in two or more geographical segments to report turnover, profit and net assets for each class of business and for each geographical segment: e.g. DIAGEO:

DIAGEO *Extract from a note to the accounts for the year ended 30 June 2000*

2 Segmental analysis

	2000			1999		
	Turnover *£ million*	*Operating* *profit* *£ million*	*Net assets* *£ million*	*Turnover* *£ million*	*Operating* *profit* *£ million*	*Net assets* *£ million*
Class of business						
Spirits and wine	4,971	1,002	4,221	4,929	967	4,432
Beer	2,146	284	751	2,234	273	882
Packaged food	3,812	492	3,734	3,757	478	3,391
Quick service restaurants	941	202	1,356	875	185	1,226
	11,870	1,980	10,062	11,795	1,903	9,931
Investment in associates			1,230			1,113
Tax, dividend and other			(462)			(395)
Net borrowings			(5,545)			(6,056)
			5,285			4,593
Geographical area						
Europe	4,181	585	3,804	4,230	594	4,003
North America	5,639	956	5,696	5,656	936	5,266
Asia Pacific	886	170	183	777	131	248
Latin America	697	165	252	716	155	258
Rest of World	467	104	127	416	87	156
	11,870	1,980	10,062	11,795	1,903	9,931

Analysis of profitability

The analyst can work on a segmental analysis, calculating various ratios and using them to compare performance between classes of business and between geographical areas.

Return on capital employed (ROCE) is widely used internally for management decisions, but for the external analyst the ratio can have serious problems because of:

1. The different ways in which companies define capital employed.
2. The huge amounts of purchased goodwill that companies wrote off under earlier accounting rules (see Chapter 20).
3. The differences in the ways companies allocate central overheads and finance costs.

For these reasons many analysts no longer use ROCE, focusing instead on margins.

For example DIAGEO's margins (Operating profit/Turnover), using the figures in the table above, show:

DIAGEO *Margins in 1999 and 2000*

	2000	1999	Change
Class of business			
Spirits and wine	20.2	19.6	3.0%
Beer	13.2	12.2	8.2%
Packaged food	12.9	12.7	1.6%
Quick service restaurants	21.5	21.1	1.9%
Geographical area			
Europe	14.0	14.0	0.0%
North America	17.0	16.5	3.0%
Asia Pacific	19.2	16.9	13.6%
Latin America	23.7	21.6	9.7%
Rest of World	22.3	20.9	6.7%
OVERALL	16.7	16.1	3.7%

At the same time note should be taken of the Chairman's statement, the Chief Executive's report or review of operations and/or Financial review as, in a good set of accounts, these will contain comment on marked changes, they may indicate strategy, and they may give further details. e.g. DIAGEO:

DIAGEO *Extracts from 2000 report*

Operating and financial review

Economic recovery in Asia Pacific has led to a recovery in the premium spirits market.

. . .

Organic growth of Operating profit during the year, at a **level exchange rate**:

	£ million	growth
Spirits and wine	1,002	15%
Beer	284	14%
Packaged food	492	1%
Quick service restaurants	202	6%
	1,980	11%

Chairman's statement

. . .

Our strategy is to focus Diageo on beverage alcohol. We will drive growth through powerfully focused marketing of our global priority brands . . .

Non-disclosure

Segmental information need not be disclosed if doing so is considered by the directors to be seriously prejudicial to the interests of the company. e.g.:

WATERMARK *Note to the 2000 accounts*

Segmental analysis

In the opinion of the directors the segmental reporting of results would be seriously prejudicial to the business and accordingly it has not been disclosed.

Chapter 17

TAXATION

INTRODUCTION

A UK resident company is liable to Corporation Tax (CT) on its income and capital gains, and until 5 April 1999 had to pay Advance Corporation Tax (ACT) when it distributed dividends. If it has income taxable abroad, it will also suffer overseas tax. All this appears in the profit and loss account under the heading 'Taxation'.

VAT, Excise Duty, employee PAYE and other forms of taxation that the company may bear or be involved in are not normally shown (e.g. POWERGEN showed only by way of note that its figures for tax charge 'exclude the exceptional Windfall tax of £266m, of which the first instalment of £133m was paid in December 1997').

Tax in the profit and loss account
Schedule 4 of the Companies Act 1985 requires taxation to be shown in the profit and loss account under three headings:

1. Tax on profit or loss on ordinary activities.
2. Tax on extraordinary profit or loss.
3. Other taxes not shown under the above.

The notes to the accounts should give details of the basis of computation, any special circumstances affecting the tax liability, and under para. 54 (3):

(a) the amount of UK Corporation Tax;
(b) the extent of double taxation relief;
(c) the amount of UK Income Tax; and
(d) the amount of foreign tax charged to revenue.

The notes may also include details of:

(e) irrecoverable ACT;
(f) over/under-provision for prior years' taxation;

(g) deferred taxation;
(h) taxation on share of profit on associated undertakings.

Air charter company AIR PARTNER's P & L account illustrates a tax charge where overseas taxation is involved:

AIR PARTNER *note to the 2000 accounts*

7. Tax on profit on ordinary activities

	2000 **£000**	*1999* *£000*
The tax charge is based on the profit for the year and comprises:		
UK corporation tax	**762**	714
Prior year	**(50)**	(25)
Double taxation relief	**(89)**	–
Overseas taxation	**278**	268
	901	957

The taxation charge represents an effective tax rate of 33.8% (1999: 34.5%) compared to the applicable charging rate of 30.0% (1999: 30.7%) as a result of certain disallowable expenses and the higher rates of tax payable by some of the foreign subsidiary companies.

Tax in the balance sheet
In the balance sheet taxation will appear:

1. Under *Creditors falling due within one year*: the amount falling due within one year will, typically, include one year's Corporation Tax, and any foreign tax due. Large companies (i.e.

those with taxable profits of £1.5m or more) are required to make quarterly payments (due on the fourteenth day of months 7, 10, 13 and 16 following the start of the accounting period).

2. *Under* **provisions**: any provision for deferred taxation (see pages 27–9) and any provision for other taxation, shown separately (CA 1985, Sch. 4, para. 47).

Tax in the cash flow statement

FRS 1 *Cash flow statements* lays down that the cash flow statement should list cash flows for the period classified under eight standard headings, the third of which is 'Taxation'. In the past this item has normally represented one year's payment of Corporation Tax (that for the previous tax year) and, in the case of a group with foreign activities, one year's overseas tax (usually shown separately).

Is the tax charge 'normal'?

If not, WHY NOT?

The tax charge shown in the profit and loss account is unlikely to be 'normal', i.e. what the layman might expect, namely, pre-tax profits × average rate of Corporation Tax during the company's accounting year. It is important to understand why this is the case.

The amount of Corporation Tax payable does not depend purely on the company's pre-tax profit figure. The tax charge varies not only because of differences that arise between the taxable profit and the profit shown in the company's accounts (the 'book profit'), but because of differences in the rate charged on particular types of income.

The differences fall into two categories:

1. **Timing differences**, where the company may be liable to pay the full rate of tax at some time, but not in the year being reported upon (see below).
2. **Permanent differences** where expenses are disallowed or income is tax-free or is taxed at a rate other than that of UK Corporation Tax (see page 130).

One of the most important examples of a *timing* difference is capital expenditure, where capital allowances are allowed for tax purposes, but depreciation is charged for accounts purposes.

Example of a timing difference

A company pays less Corporation Tax than normal if the capital allowances received for the year are greater than the amount the company provides for depreciation, as Example 17.1 shows.

Example 17.1 Depreciation and capital allowances

If a large company invested £1m in plant and machinery in 2001 and used straight line depreciation spread over an expected ten-year life, the capital allowances and depreciation would be:

	Capital allowances £	Depreciation £
2001	250,000	100,000
2002	187,500	100,000
2003	140,625	100,000
2004	105,469	100,000
2005	79,102	100,000
2006	59,326	100,000
2007	44,495	100,000
2008	33,371	100,000
2009	25,028	100,000
2010	75,084	100,000
	1,000,000	1,000,000

Note: This assumes that trading ceased in 2010 and that the plant and machinery had no residual value. If the company continued trading, the allowances would continue ad infinitum at 25% a year on the declining balance, i.e. £18,771 in 2010, £14,078 in 2011 ... £334 in the year 2024, and so on.

The advantage of the reducing balance method is that it simplifies calculations.

If the company made taxable trading profits before capital allowances of £2m in each of the ten years and we ignore all other allowances for the purpose of illustration, the Corporation Tax payable, assuming a 30% rate throughout, would be:

	Taxable profit £		Corporation Tax liability £
2001	1,750,000		525,000
2002	1,812,500		543,750
2003	1,859,375		557,813
2004	1,894,531		568,359
2005	1,920,898		576,269
2006	1,940,674		582,202
2007	1,955,505		586,651
2008	1,966,629		589,989
2009	1,974,972		592,492
2010	1,924,916	(Note 1)	577,475
	19,000,000	(Note 2)	5,700,000

Notes:
1. Assuming trading ceases in 2010 and the plant and machinery has no residual value, to give capital allowances of £75,084 that year.
2. The reported profit before tax each year would be £1,900,000 (£2m less £100,000 depreciation), so the total taxable profit over the ten years would be the same as the total reported profit, and the total tax payable would be the same as a tax charge of 30% each year on reported profit.

Advance corporation tax from earlier years

Prior to 5 April 1999 a company, when it paid dividends to its shareholders, had to hand over to the Inland Revenue *Advance Corporation Tax* (ACT).

ACT was part payment of the company's Corporation Tax liability for the period in which the dividend was paid. (The remaining Corporation Tax payable was referred to as *Mainstream Corporation Tax*.)

Although ACT was abolished on 6 April 1999, some companies have ACT relating to earlier periods which they were unable to offset against the overall Corporation Tax liability because of offset restrictions. For tax purposes, this ACT can be carried forward indefinitely.

Where companies consider that ACT will be recoverable in a future accounting period, it may be included in the balance sheet as a debtor provided it can satisfy a number of demanding conditions (see FRS 16 *Current tax* and FRS 19 *Deferred tax*).

Depreciation and capital allowances

Different classes of asset have long been treated quite differently for tax and accounting purposes.

For some, like office buildings, there is no allowance at all for tax purposes for depreciation, or in Revenue terms: no 'capital allowances' are available, except in Enterprise Zones. Others have been treated generously (e.g. plant and machinery), and some more harshly, e.g. motor vehicles costing more than £12,000.

'Pooling'

The cost of all plant and machinery is put into a 'pool'. Each year the total in the pool qualifies for a 25% writing down allowance, on a reducing balance basis.

New assets are added to the pool at cost and the proceeds of asset disposals are deducted from the pool.

The advantage of the *reducing balance* method is simplicity: assets in the pool do not have to be accounted for individually.

Tax years

The *fiscal* (or *Income Tax*) *year* runs from 6 April of one year to 5 April the following year and is referred to by stating both years, e.g. *Income tax year* 2001/2002 is the year from 6 April 2001 to 5 April 2002.

The *financial year* (FY), used for Corporation Tax purposes, runs from 1 April to 31 March and is referred to by the year in which it *starts*, e.g. *Financial year* 2001 is the year from 1 April 2001 to 31 March 2002.

Rates of Corporation Tax

There are two rates of Corporation Tax, the *standard rate* and the *small companies' rate*. 'Small companies' in this context are those with taxable profits (income and capital gains) not exceeding £300,000 in the year.

There is marginal relief for companies with profits of between £300,000 and £1.5 million.

When Corporation Tax rates are set

The rates for each financial year are normally set in the Budget the previous November.

For the financial year 2002 the *standard rate* has been set at 30%, and the *small companies rate* at 19%.

DEFERRED TAXATION

Timing differences

The annual *depreciation charge* on an asset is determined by the company's accounting policy. The annual *capital allowance* on an asset is determined by the Chancellor of the Exchequer, and applied by the Inland Revenue. The two are seldom the same.

The difference is called a *timing difference*, as we have illustrated in Example 17.1.

Purpose of deferred tax

The purpose of deferred tax is to remove the effect that any timing differences would otherwise have on the annual tax charge.

Companies make a transfer to a *deferred tax provision* of an amount equal to the difference between

- the Corporation Tax actually payable on the company's taxable trading profit and
- the tax that would have been payable if the taxable trading profit had been the same as the accounting profit.

Accounting for deferred tax

The accounting rules for the treatment of deferred tax are in transition between SSAP 15 *Accounting for deferred taxation* and FRS 19 *Deferred tax*, which supersedes SSAP 15.

FRS 19 was issued in December 2000, and is mandatory for accounting periods ending on or after 23 January 2002; earlier adoption is encouraged. So in 2001 we are betwixt and between.

SSAP 15

The about to be superseded SSAP 15 required companies to account for deferred tax to the extent that it was probable that a liability would crystallise. If a company could show that it was probable that a liability would not crystallise in the foreseeable future, SSAP 15 ruled that no provision should be made for deferred tax.

For example, a company might be able to provide capital expenditure forecasts covering the next five years showing that, for each of these years, forecast capital allowances would exceed forecast depreciation charges i.e. timing differences were not expected to reverse, and the company would make no provision for deferred tax.

 SSAP 15 let companies *assume* that, with their future capex plans, there was no need to provide for deferred tax. FRS 19 allows no such assumption.

The assumption being made by companies under SSAP 15 is that, with a continuing investment programme, capital allowances would never be less than depreciation.

To show the dangers of that assumption, let's continue on from Example 17.1:

Example 17.2 Risks of not providing for deferred tax

To recap, in 2001 the company invested £1m in plant and machinery. With *Capital allowances* on a 25% reducing balance basis, and *Depreciation* on a straight line basis over an expected ten-year life, the annual charges and allowances would be:

	Capital allowances £	Depreciation £
2001	250,000	100,000
2002	187,500	100,000
2003	140,625	100,000
2004	105,469	100,000
2005	79,102	100,000
2006	59,326	100,000
2007	**44,495**	**100,000**
2008	33,371	100,000
2009	25,028	100,000
2010	75,084	100,000
	1,000,000	1,000,000

Let us suppose that, due to an economic downturn and over-capacity in its industry, the company puts a freeze on all capital expenditure in 2001, shortly after completing its £1m investment in plant and machinery.

By 2007, with still no capex (it must have been in steel making), the company struggled to make £150,000

EBITDA (earnings before interest, tax, depreciation and amortisation). Interest took £50,000, leaving £100,000, just enough to cover the annual depreciation charge.

Break even? Oh no, that's not how the Inland Revenue will see it. In their eyes the company made £100,000 before capital allowances.

In 2007, as our table shows, there will be capital allowances of £44,495 to offset against that £100,000. This will leave a taxable profit of £55,505, on which HMIT will make an assessment for Corporation Tax of £16,501.50 (30% on £55,005).

If no provision has been made for deferred tax, and the CT rate is 30%, the company will go into loss to the tune of around £16,500.

Reasons for introducing FRS 19

- FRS 19 is more prudent, because companies may have to curtail capital expenditure in a future economic downturn. When times get hard, capital expenditure is usually one of the first things to be cut back.
- The reliance on future capital expenditure plans is inconsistent with the now well established principle of basing liabilities on existing obligations arising from past transactions.
- In practice there had been wide variations in the application of SSAP 15.
- International harmonisation. FRS 19 is more in line with accounting rules in the United States and in countries adopting International Accounting Standards.

ASB Chairman comments on deferred tax

When FRED 19 *Deferred tax* was published, the ASB issued a Press Release, as is their wont:

ASB PRESS RELEASE *Publication of FRED 19*

Sir David Tweedie, ASB Chairman, commented that: 'The current proposals reflect the Board's commitment to harmonising its standards with international ones, except in areas of fundamental disagreement ... on deferred tax, we will not shift international opinion back to partial provision. Having consulted widely on an informal basis, we have concluded that **deferred tax is not one of the areas where there are grounds for flying in the face of international practice.**'

FRS 19

Deferred tax is the estimated future tax consequences of transactions and events recognised in the financial statements of the current and previous periods (FRS 19, para 2).

Deferred tax is required to be recognised for all timing differences that have originated but not reversed by the balance sheet date.

Example 17.3 shows how deferred tax appears in the accounts.

Example 17.3 Deferred tax in the accounts

An engineering company buys £2 million of plant and machinery at the beginning of the company's year, so:

1. For corporation tax purposes the company is entitled to a Writing Down Allowance (WDA) of 25% per annum on a reducing balance basis: £500,000 in Year 1, £375,000 in Year 2, ...
2. The company depreciates the plant and machinery on a straight line basis over 10 years, i.e. £200,000 each year.

The originating timing difference in Year 1 is £300,000 (£500,000 − £200,000). With a Corporation Tax rate of 30%, the deferred tax provision required by FRS 19 is £90,000, with a corresponding charge to the P & L account for deferred tax provided.

Year 1's accounts would show:

Profit and Loss account	£000
Pre-tax profit	1,200
Taxation (see Note 1)	360
Profit after tax	840

Note 1	£000
Corporation tax payable = 0.3(1200 + 200 − 500)	270
Transfer to Provision for deferred tax	90
Total tax charge (£1.2 million at 30%)	360

The changeover from SSAP 15 to FRS 19

Some companies have already adopted FRS 19 for accounts ending earlier than 23 January 2002, when adoption becomes mandatory.

In accounts prepared on an SSAP 15 basis the note on deferred tax will show both the amount of deferred tax provided and the *unprovided* amount, i.e. the amount which SSAP 15 did not require to be included in the provision because it was deemed to be probable no future liability would crystallise.

As a rule of thumb, the provision required under FRS 19 would be the sum of these two amounts.

The ST IVES example shown here is typical of a partial provision disclosure under SSAP 15.

ST IVES *Partial provision of deferred tax under SSAP 15*

18. Provisions for liabilities and charges

The amounts of deferred taxation provided and unprovided in the financial statements are as follows:

2000	*Amount provided*	*Amount unprovided*
Capital allowances in excess of depreciation	16,142	802
Gains deferred by rollover relief	–	946
Other timing differences	(3,395)	–
	12,747	1,748

Other timing differences

In addition to differences between capital allowances and depreciation, FRS 19 covers:

- Pension liabilities accrued in the accounts, but only allowed for tax when contributions are paid.
- Interest costs and development cost capitalised in the accounts, but allowed for tax purposes.
- Fixed assets revalued in the accounts; the gain only taxable when the asset is sold.
- Tax losses carried forward from previous years and used to reduce taxable profits.

Rollover relief

If a company disposes of a building (or other qualifying assets e.g. a ship or an aircraft) at a profit and purchases another, it can obtain what is known as '*rollover relief*' by electing to have the gain arising on the disposal deducted from the cost of the new building rather than paying tax on it:

Example 17.4 Rollover relief

Freehold premises with a cost for tax purposes of £9m are sold for £15m, producing a chargeable gain of £6m. At the same time, if the company buys new premises for £18m, it can defer payment of tax on the gain of £6m by electing to deduct the gain from the cost of the new building.

However, if the new premises are subsequently sold for, say £26m, tax would be assessed on the gain of £26m − (£18m − £6m) = £14m.

SSAP 15 does not normally require provision for deferred tax if rollover relief is available (para. 12).

FRS 19 para. 15 is more specific: 'Deferred tax should not be recognised on timing differences . . . if . . . it is more likely than not that the taxable gain will be rolled over, being charged to tax only if and when the assets into which the gain has been rolled over are sold.'

REASONS FOR 'ABNORMAL' TAX CHARGES

Even if full provision were made for deferred taxation, differences would remain between the tax charge and what might be expected bearing in mind the pre-tax profits and the normal rate of Corporation Tax. For instance, small companies pay Corporation Tax on income at a lower rate (see page 127).

Adjustments to previous years

Where tax on profits of an earlier period proves to be more or less than previously provided, FRS 3 requires that this should be included in the profit and loss account, and the effect stated if material (most companies show it by way of note; see AIR PARTNER on page 125 for example).

Permanent differences

Permanent 'differences' in tax charge, the effects of which are not offset by provisions for deferred tax, include the following items:

1. Disallowed expenses

Some items, such as the cost of entertaining customers, are charged by companies to their profit and loss account properly reducing pre-tax profits, but are not allowed as expenses by the Taxes Act in calculating taxable profits. This causes the tax charge to appear higher than 'normal'.

2. Capital gains

Tax payable on capital gains is included in the Corporation Tax charge. For example, if a company's sole taxable profit for the year arose from the £4m sale of freehold land costing £3m, and the indexation allowance was £400,000, the chargeable gain would be only £600,000.

The profit and loss account would show:

	£000
Pre-tax profit	1,000
Taxation (30% on £600,000)	180
Profit after tax	820

and the apparent rate of tax would be 18%.

3. Loans

Gains on loans are not normally subject to Corporation Tax, and losses on loans are not deductible as expenses. For example, if a company issued a loan stock at £99% and subsequently bought it in for cancellation at £95%, neither the £1% loss on issue nor the £5% gain on repurchase would be included in the calculation of the company's Corporation Tax charge. However, in 'deep discount' issues (see page 35), the 'income element' is an allowable expense.

4. Losses

Where a company makes a loss, it may carry that loss back for a limited period to recover Corporation Tax previously paid or, failing that, can carry the loss forward indefinitely to offset against future profits. However

(a) Capital losses, for example the loss on sale of fixed assets, cannot normally be offset against trading profits.

(b) Losses by UK-resident subsidiaries cannot be offset against profits elsewhere in the group unless the subsidiary is at least 75% owned by the parent company (but the provisions are complex). If the loss-making subsidiary is less than 75% owned (so that group relief is unavailable), the group's tax charge will appear abnormally high, but the losses can be carried forward within the subsidiary and, if and when it returns to profitability, subsequently matched against future profits of that subsidiary. The effect on the group's tax charge will then be reversed.

(c) The losses of a subsidiary in one country cannot be offset against the profits of subsidiaries in other countries, and this can result in an abnormally high tax charge, as THE BODY SHOP illustrated in 1998:

THE BODY SHOP *1998 accounts*

Consolidated profit and loss account 1998

	£m
Profit on ordinary activities before tax	38.0
Taxation (Note 7)	(15.2)
Profit for the financial year after tax	22.8

Note 7 Taxation	1998
	£m
The charge consists of:	
UK corporation tax	12.4
Deferred tax	2.3
Overseas tax	0.5
	15.2

The effective tax rate is higher than the standard UK corporation tax of 31% as a result of the losses of the US subsidiary in the year of approximately £11.5m which are not available for relief in the year.

Information on losses carried forward should be given either in a note on taxation or in a note on deferred taxation e.g. PILKINGTON TILE:

PILKINGTON TILE GROUP *Note to the 2000 accounts*

7. Tax on profit on ordinary activities

	2000 £000	1999 £000
Current year UK corporation tax	820	569
Less prior year over-provision	(103)	–
	717	569

The effective corporation tax rate of 21.7% is lower than the expected rate of 30% due to the utilisation of tax losses brought forward.

Tax losses within the Group, relating to continuing operations, of £1,127,000 (1999 – £3,825,815) are carried forward.

Some companies give details of when tax credits expire, e.g. BOC GROUP:

BOC GROUP *Note to the 2000 accounts*

d) Unused tax credits

. . .

On a consolidated basis, the Group has net operating loss carryforwards of £119.9m, of which £112.6m are provided for by a valuation allowance. A valuation allowance is provided when it is more likely than not that some or all of the losses will expire as follows:

Year	Net Operating loss £m
2001	4.0
2002	0.2
2003	0.7
2004	26.0

5. Overseas income

Overseas income presents special problems:

1. Overseas income of non-resident subsidiaries is not generally liable to UK taxation; it bears only foreign tax. The foreign tax may be at a higher or lower rate than UK Corporation Tax. In particular some countries, such as Ireland, give foreign companies several years of tax holidays to encourage them to set up subsidiaries there.
2. Dividends, interest or royalties remitted to the UK from certain countries, including the USA, may bear a further 'withholding tax'.
3. Overseas income of a UK-resident company is liable to UK tax whether remitted or not.
4. Double taxation relief (DTR) is given for overseas tax on income liable to UK tax, so dividends paid to the UK by overseas subsidiaries

normally bear no UK tax if the foreign tax has already been borne at a rate equal to or greater than UK Corporation Tax. If the foreign tax is lower, only the difference is payable in the UK, but in both cases this is only true for foreign taxes of an income nature (taxes of a capital nature do not qualify for relief). Example 17.5 illustrates the way in which double taxation relief is applied.

Example 17.4 Double taxation relief

A UK holding company does not trade, but has one overseas subsidiary whose profit and loss account is:

	£000
Pre-tax profits	10,000
Tax paid at 25%	2,500
	7,500
Dividends	3,000
Retentions	4,500

The UK holding company's £3,000,000 dividends are subject to 10% withholding tax (£300,000) on remittance, so the UK company actually receives £2,700,000. For UK tax purposes the dividend received by the holding company is grossed up:

	£000
Dividend from subsidiary	3,000
Associated foreign tax at 25%	1,000
Gross income from subsidiary	4,000

	£000
UK tax is: Corporation Tax 30% on £4,000,000	1,200
less DTR, which is the lesser of:	
(a) Tax paid on £2,700,000 net £1,000,000 + £300,000 = £1,300,000	
(b) UK CT liability of £1,200,000	1,200
Tax payable in the UK	0

The UK holding company's profit and loss account would show:

	£000	£000
Pre-tax profits		10,000
Taxation		
UK Corporation Tax	1,200	
less Double tax relief	1,200	
Overseas tax	2,500	
Withholding tax	300	2,800
Profit after tax		7,200

6. *Exceptional items*

Under FRS 3, exceptional items should, as explained in Chapter 16, be credited or charged in arriving at the profit or loss on ordinary activities under the statutory format headings to which they relate, and attributed to continuing or discontinued operations as appropriate.

Certain items, including provisions in respect of them, have under para. 20 of FRS 3 to be shown separately on the face of the profit and loss account after operating profit and before interest, again under the appropriate heading of continuing or discontinued operations, namely:

(a) profits or losses on the sale or termination of an operation;

(b) costs of a fundamental reorganisation or restructuring having a material effect on the nature and focus of the reporting entity's operations; and

(c) profits or losses on the disposal of fixed assets.

Relevant information regarding the effect of these items on the taxation charge and, in the case of consolidated financial statements, any minority interests should both be shown in a note to the profit and loss account. As a minimum the related tax and the minority interest should both be shown in aggregate, but if the effect of the tax and minority interests differs for the various categories of items further information should be given, where practicable, to assist users in assessing the impact of the different items on the net profit or loss attributable to shareholders.

THE EFFECTIVE TAX RATE

Effective tax rate

FRS 19 requires disclosure of a reconciliation of the current tax charge reported in the profit and loss account, with the charge which would result from applying the relevant standard rate of tax to the reported profit. This reconciliation will highlight reasons for abnormal tax charges.

W S ATKINS *Note to 2000 accounts*

8. Taxation on profit on ordinary activities

. . .

The effective Group tax charge represents 39.8% (1999: 39.8%) of profit on ordinary activities.

The variation between this rate and the UK corporation tax rate is explained as follows:

	2000	1999
	%	%
UK corporation tax rate	30.0	31.0
Pension credit	4.1	5.0
Permanent differences	4.0	1.9
Other differences	0.4	1.0
Overseas activities	0.6	0.2
Adjustments in respect of prior years	(2.2)	(0.8)
	36.9	38.3
Amortisation of goodwill	5.1	0.5
Employee benefit Trusts	(2.2)	1.0
	39.8	39.8

The reconciliation may be presented in monetary terms (see DIAGEO below) or in percentage terms (see W S ATKINS in the previous column).

DIAGEO *Note to the 2000 accounts*

9. Taxation

. . .

	2000 £000	1999 £000
Tax reconciliation		
Profit on ordinary activities before tax	1,451	1,467
Notional charge at UK corporation tax rate 30% (1999 – 30.75%)	435	451
Differences in overseas tax rates	(29)	(99)
Exceptional items	33	69
Prior period adjustments	1	41
Other items	(39)	(22)
Actual charge for taxation	401	440

The tax charge included tax relief of £71 million (1999 – £23 million) in respect of exceptional items and £4 million (1999 – nil) in respect of goodwill amortisation.

Chapter 18

PROFIT AFTER TAX, DIVIDENDS AND EARNINGS PER SHARE

PROFITS AFTER TAX

The pecking order

Minority interest, then

Any arrears of cumulative preference dividends, then
Preference dividends for the period, then
Ordinary dividends

That's the right order.
How many got it right?

After all these have been deducted, what is left is called *Retained earnings*. This is money kept in the company to help finance growth or reduce debt.

Profit after tax
The ordinary shareholders, who usually provide the bulk of a company's share capital, and are most at risk, are entitled to all the profits after tax *after* the deduction of:

- *Minority interests*
- *Arrears of cumulative preference share dividends*
- *Cu. preference dividends for the period*
- *Preference dividends for the period.*

Minority interests: As explained in detail in Chapter 20, minority interests occur when a group has one or more subsidiaries, the shares in which are only partly owned by the group.

Where the other ('minority') shareholders in the 'partially owned' subsidiary are equity shareholders they are entitled to a share in the profit or loss of *that subsidiary*; their share, called 'equity minority interests', has to be deducted in arriving at the profit attributable to the group's shareholders.

Dividends attaching to any 'non-equity minority interests' also have to be deducted (i.e. dividends on externally owned preference shares of a subsidiary).

Preference dividends and any arrears of cumulative preference dividends have to be met before any ordinary dividends can be declared.

The amount remaining after these deductions is called the *Profit attributable to ordinary shareholders*.

Profit attributable to ordinary shareholders
Ordinary dividends are paid out of this attributable profit, leaving *Retained earnings*. Retained earnings are kept in the company to help finance growth and/or reduce debt. Extracts from the accounts of the house builder BELLWAY illustrates the 'pecking order'.

BELLWAY *Profit after tax: the 'pecking order' for 2000*

	2000
Profit and loss account	£000
. . .	
Profit after tax	61,963
(1) *Minoriy interests*	(9)
Profit attributable to shareholders	61,954
Dividends	
(2) *Preference dividends*	1,900
Profit attrib. to Ord. Shareholders	60,054
(3) *Ordinary dividends*	13,546
(4) *Retained profit* for the year	46,508

133

DIVIDENDS

In deciding what profits to distribute the directors of a company should have in mind:

(a) the company's cash position (considered in Chapter 19);
(b) what is prudent;
(c) what is legally permissible.

Ideally, directors should choose the lowest of these three figures.

What is prudent

In deciding what would be prudent, directors should weigh up the cost of raising capital in various ways. Is it, for instance, better to borrow (i.e. increase the gearing) rather than ask equity shareholders to contribute more towards the net assets of the company? And, if equity shareholders are to be called upon to provide more, should they be asked to do so by means of a rights issue, in which case each shareholder has the choice of whether to take up, or sell, his rights; or should profits be 'retained', in which case the individual shareholder has no choice?

Unfortunately, the picture is confused by inflation and the present, historical cost, method of accounting. With no inflation (or an inflation accounting system recognised for tax purposes) a company would, in theory, be able to distribute its earnings and still maintain its assets in real terms. With inflation most companies need to retain a proportion of their earnings as calculated by historical cost accounting in order to maintain their assets in real terms (but more of that in Chapter 29).

Having decided how much it is necessary to retain in order to continue the existing scale of operations, and how much should be retained out of profits in order to expand the scale of operations, the directors should look at what remains.

Ideally, a company should pay a regular, but somewhat increasing, dividend. For example, from a market point of view, it is preferable to pay: 8.0p; 9.0p; 9.0p; 9.0p; 9.5p; 10.0p; rather than 8.0p; 12.0p; 10.5p; 4.0p; 10.0p; 10.0p – though both represent the same total sum in dividends over the six years – because investors who need steady income will avoid companies which are erratic dividend payers, and because a cut in dividend undermines confidence in the company's future. In other words, the directors of a company should think twice before paying a dividend this year which they may not be able to maintain, or setting a pattern of growth in the rate of dividend which could not reasonably be continued for the foreseeable future. For if they do either of these things, they are liable to disappoint shareholder expectations, to damage their market rating and to see their share price slashed if their dividend has to be cut or the rate of dividend growth cannot be sustained.

What is legally permissible

Companies are allowed to distribute only the aggregate of accumulated realised profits not previously distributed or capitalised less accumulated realised losses not previously written off in a reduction or reorganisation of capital (CA 1985, s. 263). The word 'realised' is not defined in the Act, but SSAP 2 (superseded by FRS 18) says that profits should be included in the profit and loss account 'only when realised in the form of cash or of other assets the ultimate cash realisation of which can be assessed with reasonable certainty'.

In addition, a public company may pay a dividend only if the net assets of the company after payment of the dividend are not less than the aggregate of its called-up share capital and undistributable reserves (s. 264 (1)). Undistributable reserves are defined in Section 264 (3) as:

(a) share premium account;
(b) capital redemption reserve;
(c) accumulated unrealised profits not capitalised less accumulated unrealised losses not previously written off in a capital reduction or reorganisation;
(d) any reserve which the company's Memorandum or Articles prohibit being distributed.

This requirement means that public companies now have to cover net losses (whether realised or not) from realised profits before paying a dividend.

Where the company's audit report has been qualified, the auditor must provide a statement in writing as to whether the qualification is material in deciding whether the distribution would be a breach of the Act, before any distribution can be made.

Preference dividends

As explained on page 133:

- preference shares carry a fixed rate of dividend, normally payable half-yearly;
- preference shareholders have no legal redress if the board of directors decides to recommend that no preference dividends should be paid;
- if no preference dividend is declared for an accounting period, no dividend can be declared on any other type of share for the period concerned, and the preference shareholders usually become entitled to vote at shareholders' general meetings;

- if the dividend on a cumulative preference share is not paid on time, payment is postponed rather than omitted and the preference dividend is said to be 'in arrears', and these arrears have to be paid before any other dividend can be declared. Arrears of cumulative preference dividends must be shown in a note to the accounts.

Company articles on dividend distribution

Most companies lay down their own rules for dividend distribution in their Articles by adopting Articles 102 to 108 of Table A to the Companies Act 1985 (the model set of Company Articles).

Accounting treatment

Under UK practice, any dividends the directors *recommend* should be shown:

(a) in the profit and loss account, together with any interim dividend already paid (CA 1985, Sch. 4, para. 51 (3));
(b) in the balance sheet as a liability.

In many other countries, including the USA, dividends only appear in the accounts when *approved* by the shareholders.

Dividends *paid* during the accounting period appear in a separate section of the cash flow statement.

Interim dividends

Interim dividends can be declared by the directors without reference to the shareholders, but by convention they do not normally exceed half the anticipated total for the year.

However, if the latest audited accounts disclose a 'non-distributable' position or if the level of accumulated profits has fallen significantly, interim accounts must be prepared to justify the payment of an interim dividend (CA 1985, s. 272). Interim dividends appear in the profit and loss account as a distribution, and either in the balance sheet as a liability if the company has not paid the interim dividend by the end of the accounting period or in the cash flow statement as a payment.

EARNINGS PER SHARE

Earnings per share (e.p.s.) – a key measure, but open to abuse

Earnings per share (e.p.s.) is a key measure of a company's profitability each year. It is a measure of its ability to pay dividends, and is the most widely used measure of 'growth'. But it is open to abuse.

Background

As we explained in Chapter 16, the previous rules (SSAP 6) required '*Exceptional items*' to be included in the calculation of e.p.s., and '*Extraordinary items*' to be excluded.

The definitions of these two items were open to a variety of interpretations, and led to widespread abuse: companies tended to classify unusual losses as extraordinary (excluded) and unusual profits as exceptional (included), in order to enhance their reported earnings per share.

ASB curbs 'enhancement' of e.p.s.

Action was taken to reduce the scope for creative accounting by the issue of two Financial Reporting Standards:

1. FRS 3 *Reporting financial performance* required extraordinary (as well as exceptional) items to be included in the calculation of 'Profit attributable to ordinary shareholders'. This was followed by

2. FRS 14 *Earnings per share*, requiring the total profit attributable to ordinary shareholders to be used in the calculation of *Basic e.p.s.*:

$$\frac{Profit\ attributable\ to\ ordinary\ shareholders}{Weighted\ average\ number\ of\ ordinary\ shares\ in\ issue}$$

Misleading use of the word 'basic'

What FRS 14 was actually doing was following the 'all-inclusive' concept we described on page 118.

In our view it would have been a great deal clearer to call it '*All-inclusive e.p.s.*', which is *what it is*, rather than '*Basic e.p.s.*' which, in the ordinary sense of the word 'basic', is *what it isn't*.

Company's own figures for e.p.s.

Companies are free to show their own version of earnings per share but, if they do so, they must provide a reconciliation to the 'Basic e.p.s.' figure (FRS 14, para. 74).

The ASB took the view that, if everything was included, then companies could make whatever adjustments they wished, to produce the '*Company's own e.p.s.*'.

Given the details of the adjustments, analysts would be able to judge whether the Company's own e.p.s. was a fair 'normalised' figure and, if not, to make their own adjustments.

Let's look at an example, KINGFISHER, where one or two of the adjustments are questionable:

KINGFISHER *Note on e.p.s. in the 2000 accounts*

. . . .	Earnings £millions	Per share amount pence
Basic earnings per share	419.4	30.9
Effect of exceptionals		
Aborted merger costs	3.5	0.2
Profit on disposal of properties	(6.2)	(0.4)
Basic e.p.s. before exceptionals	416.7	30.7
Acquisition goodwill amortisation	10.5	0.8
E-commerce and other new		
channels (post-tax)	18.5	1.3
Basic – adjusted e.p.s.	445.7	32.8

Although the IIMR (Institute of Investment Management and Research) approach excludes bid defence costs, as the company didn't choose to be bid for, it does not allow the costs of actions a company chooses to make, i.e. costs of a failed merger or takeover bid, to be excluded.

Similarly IIMR would not allow start-up costs like E-commerce to be excluded.

And companies do not always clearly distinguish basic, FRS 3, earnings per share from their own preferred version. Take, for instance, THE RANK GROUP (see page 137). After the deduction of minority interests [A] (*Note 24*), and preference dividends [C] and [D] (*Note 7*), Rank's profit and loss account shows three figures for 1999 e.p.s.:

[H]   19.9p   before exceptional items
[I]   (13.8p) exceptional items per share
[J]   6.1p   after exceptional items.

The basic earnings per share [J] represent actual performance, i.e. how much per share was actually available to pay ordinary dividends and provide some retained earnings to plough back into the company.

In fact Rank's 6.1p was only enough to pay about half the ordinary dividends of 12.0p, [E] plus [F], let alone anything to plough back. £46m [G] had to

be transferred from reserves to make up the short-fall on the dividends.

Had the group *not* incurred exceptional items of (13.8p) per share [I], it would have had 19.9p per share, [H], enough to pay dividends of 12.0p per share, leaving 7.9p per share of retained earnings.

Note 8 *Earnings per Ordinary share* shows the calculation of [H].

Amortisation

FRS 10 *Goodwill and intangible assets* complicates matters by allowing two methods of accounting:

(a) to retain the assets in the balance sheet at cost with an annual review for impairment; *or*
(b) amortise them over a finite period, usually a maximum of 20 years.

Some companies using method (b), particularly those with a large amount of goodwill from acquisitions on their balance sheet, have taken to showing e.p.s. both before and after amortisation, e.g. WASTE RECYCLING:

WASTE RECYCLING *Earnings per share*

Profit and loss account	1999	1998
. . .	£000	£000
Profit for the financial year	7,127	6,847
Dividends	(4,100)	(1,404)
Retained profit	3,027	5,443
Earnings per share	6.7p	13.8p
Adjusted earnings per share		
(note 9)	17.3p	13.8p

Note 9 Earnings per ordinary share

. . .

In order to show results from operating activities on a comparable basis an adjusted earnings per ordinary share has been calculated which excludes goodwill amortisation of £11,361,000 (1998 – £nil) from earnings.

Consolidated balance sheet

	1999	1998
	£000	£000
FIXED ASSETS		
Intangible assets	261,423	–
Tangible assets	129,887	52,325
. . .		

THE RANK GROUP *Group profit and loss account 1999*

Group Profit and Loss Account for the year ended 31 December 1999

	Note	*1999* Before exceptional items £m	Exceptional items £m	Total £m	*1998* Before exceptional items £m	Exceptional items £m	Total £m
. . .							
Profit (loss) on ordinary activities after tax		177	(107)	70	192	(330)	(138)
Minority interests (including non-equity interests)	[A] 24	(2)	–	(2)	(3)	–	(3)
Profit (loss) for the financial year	[B]	175	(107)	68	189	(330)	(141)
Dividends and other appropriations							
Preference	[C] and [D] 7	(21)	–	(21)	(21)	–	(21)
Ordinary	[E] and [F] 7	(93)	–	(93)	(142)	–	(142)
Transfer to (from) reserves	22	61	(107) [G]	(46)	26	(330)	(304)
Earnings (loss) per Ordinary share	8	19.9p [H]	(13.8)p [I]	6.1p [J]	22.0p	(43.2)p	(21.2)p

---

THE RANK GROUP *Extract from Note 7 to the 1999 accounts*

Note 7. Dividends

		1999 £m	1998 £m
Convertible Redeemable Preference shares			
Dividends payable for the period	[C]	19	19
Provision for redemption premium	[D]	2	2
		21	21
Ordinary shares			
Interim declared of 4.0p per share	[E]	31	43
Final proposed of 8.0p per share	[F]	62	99
		93	142

THE RANK GROUP *Extract from Note 8 to the 1999 accounts*

Note 8. Earnings per ordinary share

	1999	1998
Basic earnings (£m) [B] − ([C] + [D])	154	168
Effect of dilutions (£m)	21	21
Diluted earnings (£m)	175	189
Weighted average number of Ordinary shares (m)	773.2	765.0
Effect of dilutions	62.9	62.0
Adjusted weighted average number of Ordinary shares (m)	836.1	827.7
Earnings per share	19.9p	22.0p
Diluted earnings per share	20.9p	22.9p

Going for growth . . .

In the 4th edition of this book we gave an interesting example of a company whose pre-tax profits had *grown* by 41.9% p.a. between 1984 and 1988, but whose e.p.s. had *fallen* by 8.3% p.a. The company was MAXWELL COMMUNICATION CORPORATION, and we said: 'chairman Robert Maxwell's stated goal was to become "a global information and communications corporation before the end of the decade with annual revenues of £3–5 billion, with profits growth to match". Maxwell's sales in the period had grown from £266.5m to over £1bn, at an annual rate of 42.9% with profits growth almost to match, but this was achieved by the profligate use of paper, and earnings per share suffered accordingly.'

As subsequent events confirmed, companies which go for growth regardless of e.p.s. are best avoided. But the fact that an acquisition for paper makes e.p.s. grow at a slower rate than profits does not necessarily mean that acquisitions for paper are bad for e.p.s. It all depends on whether

Example 18.1 Acquisition for paper

	Existing company	Acquisition	Company post-acquisition
Attributable profit	800,000	200,000	1,000,000
Issued equity (shares)	8,000,000		
Vendor consideration (shares)		1,600,000	
Resulting equity (shares)			9,600,000
e.p.s.	10.0p		10.4p

In this case 1.6m shares are issued for a company bringing in £200,000 at the attributable profit level, or 12.5p for each new share, which is higher than the e.p.s. of the existing company, so the e.p.s. of the company, post-acquisition, are improved. Had the acquiring company paid more than 2m shares for the acquisition, its earnings per share would have fallen.

Example 18.2 Further acquisition

	Present company	Second acquisition	Resulting company
Attributable profits (£)	912,000	468,000	1,380,000
Issued equity (shares)	9,600,000		
Vendor consideration (shares)		2,400,000	
Resulting equity (shares)			12,000,000
e.p.s.	9.5p		11.5p

the e.p.s. are higher with the acquisition than they would have been without it (as they are in Example 18.1).

The effect of acquisitions on earnings per share
Buying earnings cheaply enables a company to boost its e.p.s. when its own earnings are static, or even falling. Suppose in Example 18.1 that the attributable profits of the company were expected to fall the following year to £912,000, despite the recently acquired business performing satisfactorily. The company finds another victim (Example 18.2).

'But,' you may say, 'how did the company in Example 18.2 manage to get the shareholders of the second acquisition to accept 2.4 million shares for attributable earnings of £468,000, which is 19.5p per share, far higher than the e.p.s. of the acquiring company?' And well may you ask – the secret is in 'market rating'.

Market rating – the PER
The measure of a company's market rating is its Price Earnings Ratio (P/E ratio, PE ratio or PER):

$$\text{Price earnings ratio} = \frac{\text{Market price per Ordinary share}}{\text{Basic earnings per share}}$$

It is normal to take the previous day's middle market price of the ordinary share divided by the earnings per share. Analysts and newspapers often take not the basic earnings per share but normalised e.p.s. (see below), so watch with care.

The PER one can expect depends mainly on four things:

- the overall level of the stock market;
- the industry in which the company operates;
- the company's record; and
- the market's view of the company's prospects.

In an average market the PER of the average company in an average sector might be around 12, with high-quality 'blue chips' like BOOTS or MARKS & SPENCER standing on a PER of around 15 and small glamour growth stocks on 20 or more, while companies in an unfashionable sector might be on a multiple of only 8.

We say more about PERs in the section 'Investment ratios' on pages 146–7.

Wonder growth by acquisition
There is nothing fundamentally wrong with improving a company's earnings per share by acquisition, and it can be beneficial all round if there is some industrial or commercial logic involved, i.e. if the acquired company's business fits in with the acquiring company's existing activities or employs common skills and technology, or if the acquirer can provide improved management and financial resources. However, the practice was open to abuse, especially in bull markets.

Enter the 'whiz-kid' (known as a 'gunslinger' on the other side of the Atlantic), who might proceed as follows:

1. Acquire control of a company that has a listing on the Stock Exchange, but little else, e.g. the DEMISED TEA COMPANY, known in the jargon as a 'shell'.
2. Reverse the shell into an unlisted company, thus giving his victim the benefit of a ready market for his shares and himself the benefit of a company with real assets.
3. Sell off some of the assets, particularly property that is ripe for development. He doesn't lose any sleep over the fact that closing a factory throws 200 people out of work, as the office block that will replace it will house twice that number of civil servants in the department recently set up to encourage investment in industry; this 'asset-stripping' process is essential to provide the cash to gain control of his next victim.
4. By now the earnings per share of the Demised Tea Company, since renamed ANGLO-TRIUMPH ASSETS, have shown remarkable growth, albeit from a very low base (it's very easy to double profits of next-to-nothing), the bull market has conveniently started and the press has noticed him.

   He projects a suitable image of dynamic young management, talking to them earnestly about the need for British industry to obtain a fair return on assets, and his photograph appears in the financial sections of the Sunday papers. The 'whiz-kid' has arrived.
5. His share price responds to press comment, putting his 'go-go' company on a PER of 15 or 20; he continues to acquire companies, but now uses shares rather than cash, thus continually boosting his e.p.s., as we have shown.
6. Following press adulation, he broadens out into TV financial panels, seminar platforms, and after-dinner speeches; the bull market is now raging. Anglo-Triumph features regularly as an 'up stock' in the price changes table in the FT as the PER climbs towards 30. Deals follow apace, and Anglo-Triumph thrusts ahead, acquiring a huge conglomeration of businesses in an ever-widening range of mainly unrelated activities – it may be shoes, or ships or sealing-wax, but it's certainly Alice in Wonderland.
7. The moment of truth. The bull market, after a final glorious wave of euphoria, tops out. Profits in Anglo-Triumph's businesses turn down as little or nothing has been done to improve their management. Asset-stripping becomes politically unacceptable, and the word 'conglomerate' is coined to describe hotch potch outfits like Anglo-Triumph.

Down goes Anglo-Triumph's share price, and with it the market rating; without a high Price Earnings Ratio the company can no longer boost profits by acquisition, and the game is up.

Whether the whole edifice of Anglo-Triumph collapses completely or it becomes just another lowly rated ex-glamour stock depends on the financial structure of the company. If it has geared up (i.e. has built up debt, on which interest has to be paid), and hasn't the cash to service the debt, the company will probably be forced into liquidation unless some sympathetic banker (possibly embarrassed by the prospect of disclosing a huge loss if the company goes under) decides to tide things over until 'hopefully' better times.

Two things, both of which are required by FRS 3, do much to prevent this happening today. They are:

(i) the publication of earnings per share; and
(ii) the subdivision of results down to operating profit level into continuing operations, acquisitions and discontinued operations, both of which have made this sort of behaviour much more transparent.

Normalised and company e.p.s.
As described on pages 118 and 136, the IIMR (which has since become UKSIP – the UK Society of Investment Professionals) developed a standard approach, focusing on the trading activities of a company, to produce *Headline earnings* and, from that figure, *Normalised earnings per share*.

This approach has been followed by the *Financial Times*, using normalised e.p.s. in calculating figures for the P/E column in their London share price pages, and is generally used in the City, though with individual variations. One or two companies also use it in their annual accounts, for example KBC ADVANCED TECHNOLOGIES:

KBC ADVANCED TECHNOLOGIES *IIMR earnings*

Profit and loss account		2000 £000	1999 £000
. . .			
Profit on ord. activities after tax		2,210	4,989
(Dividends – equity interests		(1,869)	(1,871)
Retained profit for the period		341	3,118
Earnings per share (pence)			
– basic	Note 8	4.65	10.50
– diluted		4.58	10.17
– basic on IIMR earnings		4.65	6.36

Note 8
. . .
The basic IIMR earnings per share excludes profit made on the sale of a business . . .

MITIE GROUP *Group statistical record 1995 and 1998 (extracts)*

	1998 £000	1997 £000	1996 £000	1995 £000	1994 £000	1993 £000	1992 £000	1991 £000	1990 £000
Turnover	236,293	209,425	161,149	125,183	101,732	72,994	52,276	32,699	15,594
Profit on ordinary activities before taxation	11,100	8,210	6,302	4,571	3,361	2,402	1,808	1,231	649
Earnings per share	10.3p	8.1p	6.5p	4.9p	3.4p	3.4p	3.0p	2.8p	2.37p
Dividend per share	2.5p	2.0p	1.6p	1.2p	0.9p	0.9p	0.7p	0.5p	0.25p

Earnings and Dividend per share figures have been restated to reflect the subdivision of shares in 1994 and 1997. The results of merger accounted acquisitions are reflected in full in the year of acquisition and subsequent years but only the year prior to acquisition has been restated on a comparable basis.

Most, like THE RANK GROUP (see page 137), seem to ignore the IIMR, and to prefer their own version.

As FRS 3 makes clear, basic earnings per share are only a starting point. No one number can encapsulate everything about a company's performance. It is up to the analyst to decide which, if any, of these bases provides the best view of normal earnings; or whether to make his own adjustments in calculating 'normalised' earnings. But the current position in which the scorer (accountant/auditor) adopts one set of rules (basic earnings), the commentator (analyst) another (IIMR or normalised), and the players (management) choose for themselves (company's own figures), is scarcely satisfactory.

Investigating trends

It is frequently a worthwhile exercise to set alongside one another, growth in:

(a) turnover;
(b) profit before tax;
(c) earnings per share;
(d) dividend per share.

If they are wildly different, the cause should be investigated. In the sixth edition we looked at MITIE GROUP, a relatively small cleaning and maintenance contractor, saying that it was 'taking advantage of the trend towards outsourcing such services' while at the same time expanding by making a series of small acquisitions.

We have adjusted the figures for 1990–1995 so that all are on the same basis – which has no effect on the ratios which are shown in Example 18.3.

As we said in the Sixth Edition, growth [in 1990–1995] had been spectacular:

- turnover was up almost 703% in 5 years;
- profits had almost, but not quite, kept pace (up 604%); but

- because of acquisitions for paper, e.p.s had grown only 107%;
- from a very low base (and covered nine times) dividends had increased 500%;

so shareholders certainly did not complain.

We decided to follow up the story in 1998, looking at 1995–98. As will be seen from Example 18.3, the very rapid growth in turnover has been replaced by more moderate growth (up 189% in 3 years). But there has been a consolidation: profitability before tax up 243%.

Changes in the tax system had meant that the effective rate of tax fell from 33.49% (tax of £1.531m in 1995 on profits before interest and tax (PBIT) of £4.571m) to 30.80% (tax of £3.419m in 1998 on PBIT of £11.100m) i.e. by 8% [not shown above]. There was a much greater dependence on partly owned subsidiaries: minorities as a percentage of equity shareholders' funds increased from 5.4% in 1995 to 22.0% [not shown above].

Earnings rose 110% (nearly as fast as profits before tax) and dividends kept pace (up 108%). Cover (see page 147) remained high (at about 4 times) enabling most acquisitions to be for cash. For the ninth year in succession growth in profits exceeded 30%.

The point we are making is that, however spectacular a company's growth is, the pattern (the ratios) tend to change as it matures.

Example 18.3 MITIE GROUP *Growth statistics*

	Increase 1990–95	Increase 1995–98
Turnover	7.03	1.89
Profit on ordinary activities before taxation	6.04	2.43
Earnings per share	1.07	1.10
Dividend per share	3.80	1.08

ADJUSTMENTS TO BASIC EARNINGS PER SHARE

When the number of shares in issue changes

If a company issues new ordinary shares (or redeems ordinary shares) during the year, the basic e.p.s. for that year have to be calculated using the time-weighted average number of shares in issue during the year, and those of previous years have to be adjusted to allow for any bonus element in the share issue.

FRS 14 *Earnings per share* describes in detail the method of adjustment to be used by companies for each type of issue:

1. Share split

Use the year-end figure for number of shares, and apply a factor to previous years' e.p.s. to put them on a comparable basis. For a split of 1 old share into z new shares it is $1/z$.

Example 18.4 Effect of share split on e.p.s.

On 31 March 1998 MITIE GROUP had an issued share capital of 66,428,155 ordinary shares of 10p each. In September 1998 each 10p share is split into two ordinary shares of 5p each, making the issued share capital 132,856,310 shares of 5p. The factor to be applied to previous years' earnings was $1/2$.

---

2. Scrip (bonus or capitalisation) issue

Use the year-end figure for number of shares, and apply a factor to previous years' e.p.s. to put them on a comparable basis. For a scrip issue of y shares for every x shares held, the factor is $x \div (x + y)$.

Example 18.5 Effect of scrip issue on e.p.s.

Let us suppose that UNIVERSAL plc is a company whose year ends on 31 December. At the end of 1999 the issued share capital was £4.0m, of which £1m was in $3\frac{1}{2}\%$ preference shares and £3m was the equity share capital of 12m ordinary shares of 25p each. No new shares were issued in 2000. Profits after tax and minority interests were £995,000. So the attributable profits reported in 2000 would be: £995,000 − £35,000 = £960,000 and the e.p.s.: £960,000 ÷ 12m = 8.00p. No adjustments would be required to previous years' e.p.s.

In 2001 the company made a 1-for-3 scrip issue and profits after tax and minority interests increased from £0.995m to £1.235m.

Attributable to ordinary would be: £1.235m − £35,000 = £1.200m and earnings per share for 2001 would £1.200m ÷ 16m = 7.5p which, at first sight, appear to be down on the previous year, but 2000's figure of 8p has to be adjusted by a factor of $3 \div (3 + 1)$ to make it comparable with 2001: $3/4$ of 8p = 6p.

3. Shares issued in an acquisition

Shares issued in an acquisition are assumed to have been issued at market price (even if the shares issued, the 'vendor consideration', were placed at a discount at that time). The weighted average number of shares in issue during the year is calculated and used for working out the e.p.s.:

Example 18.6 Effect of acquisition issue on e.p.s.

On 1 April 2002 Universal had in issue 16m ordinary shares of 25p each. That day it acquired another company and issued 2m new fully paid 25p ordinary shares in payment (an acquisition 'for paper').

At the year end, the profits of the new subsidiary for the period 1 April to 31 December 2002 were included in Universal's consolidated profit and loss account and the weighted average number of shares in issue during the year was calculated:

$$\frac{(16m \times 3) + (18m \times 9)}{12} = 17.5m$$

If profits at the attributable level were £1.4m that would give earnings per share for 2002 of:

£1.4m ÷ 17.5m = 8.0p.

There would be no adjustment to the e.p.s. of earlier periods.

---

4. Rights issue

A rights issue is regarded as being partly an issue at the market price and partly a scrip issue (the bonus element); the e.p.s. of previous years are adjusted by the factor appropriate to the bonus element in the same way as a scrip issue (Example 18.7).

Example 18.7 Effect of rights issue on first day of company's year on e.p.s.

Let us suppose Universal, which had in issue 18m ordinary shares of 25p each on 1 January 2003, made a rights issue on the basis of one new share for every 4 shares held at a price of 80p per share, against a market price of 100p on the last day the old shares were quoted cum-rights. The number of shares in issue would become 22.5m and the issue would have the same effect as a 1-for-5 at 100p, followed by a 1-for-24 scrip issue. The factor for adjusting the e.p.s. for previous years is thus 24/(1 + 24), which can be calculated in more complicated cases using the formula:

Theoretical ex-rights (xr) price ÷ actual cum-rights price on the last day of quotation cum-rights

where the Theoretical xr price is, in this case, 1 share at 80p plus 4 old shares at 100p each = 5 shares for 480p = 96p, and 96/100 = 24/25.

On the basis that the e.p.s. reported previously were:

2000   6.0p
2001   7.5p
2002   8.0p

comparative figures for earnings for earlier years would be:

2000   5.76p
2001   7.20p
2002   7.68p

If the profits attributable to ordinary were £1.710m in 2003, the e.p.s. for that year would be: £1.710 ÷ 22.5m = 7.6p.

If, instead of being made on the first day of the company's year (as in Example 18.7), a rights issue is made during the company's year, the calculation of the bonus element and the factor for adjusting previous years' e.p.s. is just the same but, in addition, the weighted average number of shares in issue during the year has to be calculated (see Example 18.8).

Example 18.8 Rights issue (during company's year)

If Universal (see Example 18.7) had made its 1-for-4 rights issue on 1 September 2003, then the number of shares at the beginning of the year would be adjusted by the reciprocal of the e.p.s. factor and the calculation to find the weighted average is:

$$\left[18m \times \frac{25}{24} \times \frac{8}{12}\right] + \left[22.5m \times \frac{4}{12}\right] = 20m \text{ shares}$$

which would give e.p.s. of 8.55p for the year 2003, i.e. rather than 7.6p.

Adjusting the number of shares in issue during the first 8 months of 2003 by 25/24 allows for the bonus element of the rights issue, i.e. it puts the shares in issue at the beginning of the year on the same basis as the shares in issue at the end of the year.

---

5. Share consolidations

A consolidation of shares reduces the number of ordinary shares outstanding without a reduction in resources. The number of ordinary shares outstanding before the event is adjusted for the proportionate change in the number of ordinary shares outstanding as if the event had occurred at the beginning of the earliest period reported.

But no adjustment is made to the number of ordinary shares outstanding before the event where a share consolidation is combined with a special dividend and the overall commercial effect in terms of net assets, earnings and number of shares is of a repurchase at fair value.

Example 18.9 Share consolidation

At 31 December 2003 Universal (see Example 18.8) had in issue 22.5m ordinary shares of 25p each.

It reported basic earnings per share of:

2000   5.76p
2001   7.20p
2002   7.68p
2003   8.55p

If on 1 July 2004 it performed a share consolidation, consolidating each four ordinary shares of 25p each into one ordinary share of £1 (leaving it with 5,625,000 shares of £1 each); and if profits attributable to ordinary for the 2004 were £1,968,750; earnings per share for 2004 would be £1,968,750 ÷ 5,625,000 = 35.00p and the earnings for earlier years would be adjusted to 4 times their earlier amount:

	As originally Reported	As reported in 2004
2000	5.76p	23.04p
2001	7.20p	28.80p
2002	7.68p	30.72p
2003	8.55p	34.20p

---

6. Repurchase of shares for cash

Where a company repurchases its own shares during the period this affects the weighted average number of shares outstanding, i.e. it works exactly like an issue in respect of an acquisition but in reverse.

Example 18.10 Repurchase of shares for cash

If on 30 June 2005 Universal (see Example 18.9) repurchased 4,625,000 ordinary shares out of its issued capital of 5,625,000 ordinary shares of £1 each leaving it with 1m ordinary shares of £1 each, and if profits attributable to ordinary in that year were £993,750, the weighted average number of shares in issue would be (working in months):

$$((6 \times 5,625,000) + (6 \times 1,000,000)) \div 12 = 3,312,500$$

and the e.p.s for 2005 would be £993,750 ÷ 3,312,500 = 30.0p.

Earnings of past years would not be recomputed.

Shares held by a group member

Company shares in issue that are held by a group member and are not cancelled are treated as if they were cancelled for earnings per share purposes and excluded from the calculation. Shares that are held by an employee share ownership plan (ESOP) trust and reflected in the company balance sheet as assets of the company are similarly to be treated as if they were cancelled for this purpose until such time as they vest unconditionally in the employees.

DILUTED EARNINGS PER SHARE

Causes of dilution

This is a subject that has, over the years, grown ever more complicated. It's probably best explained by starting twenty years ago, when there were three types of *potentially dilutive* securities:

1. Convertible preference shares
2. Convertible debentures, loan stock and bonds
3. Warrants.

Calculation of diluted e.p.s.

Assumptions: (a) all convertibles converted
(b) all warrants exercised.

Calculation: for each class of security in turn:

(a) *In the P&L account add* the benefit the company would derive from conversion or exercise:

1. the saving on preference dividends,
2. interest saved on convertible debt, and
3. receipt of the exercise price of the warrants.

(b) *To the number of shares in issue add*, in each case, the extra number of Ordinary shares that would be created by conversion or exercise.

(c) Calculate the diluted earnings per share:

$$\text{Diluted eps} = \frac{\textbf{Higher earnings due to (a)}}{\textbf{Higher number of shares due to (b)}}$$

Where any conversion or exercise would increase or have no effect on e.p.s. it was ignored.

And on options we took the view that any dilution was probably more than balanced by the incentive the options gave the directors and employees to improve performance.

In the second issue of the book, published in 1982, we wrote:

> '*Strictly speaking, options granted and partly paid shares issued to directors and employees under executive schemes produce potential dilution of equity earning, in the same way as warrants, but in practice they are usually sufficiently small in relation to the company's issued equity to be ignored.*'

Not any more they ain't!

Growth in share incentive schemes

Since the 1980s the use of share options and other equity-related incentives has spread a great deal. It has spread wider amongst employees by SAYE and profit-sharing schemes encouraged by generous tax concessions, and has spread thicker by more and more incentives for management.

Share greed

Although in most cases directors and senior management incentives have been reasonable in a market-driven society, the tabloid press finds that greedy management makes good copy. And there's plenty of good copy.

The worst case we have come across, let's call it SHAREGREED plc, was a small listed company, where a sheaf of options were granted to Board members with an exercise price of 25p.

When the share price subsequently fell heavily, the original options were cancelled and new options were granted with an exercise price of 5p. None were ever exercised, because the Board's greed was well matched by its incompetence.

Growth in the complexity of schemes

In an increasingly competitive world, companies have felt obliged to introduce increasingly generous and complex schemes like LTIPS, described on page 26. In doing so they have been egged on by remuneration consultants and headhunters.

Too complicated to be readily understood, these schemes haven't necessarily been in the best interest of shareholders and can backfire on the intended beneficiaries.

FRS 14 *Earnings per share*

Definitions

Basic earnings per share is a measure of past performance, calculated by dividing the net profit or loss attributable to ordinary shareholders by the weighted average number of ordinary shares outstanding during the period.

Diluted earnings per share adjusts basic e.p.s. to give effect to potential ordinary shares outstanding during the period. Only potential ordinary shares that are *dilutive* should be included.

Presentation
The basic and diluted e.p.s. should be presented, with equal prominence, on the face of the balance sheet.

Figures used in the calculation of diluted e.p.s. should be shown, with a reconciliation to the figures used for calculating basic e.p.s.

See CABLE & WIRELESS on the next page.

Further examples of dilution

As well as the potentially dilutive securities we have already described, FRS 14 gives further examples of potential dilution and how to calculate it:

CABLE & WIRELESS *extract from 2000 profit and loss account, and Note 13*

Consolidated profit and loss account

	Note	2000	1999
Basic earnings per share	13	153.6p	38.2p
Basic earnings per share before			
exceptional items and amortisation	13	19.4p	33.9p
Diluted earnings per share		150.9p	37.5p

Note 13 Earnings per share

	2000	1999
	£m	£m
Profit for the financial year attributable to ordinary shareholders	3,724	908
Interest saved on loan stock conversion for distribution	3	4
Diluted profit for the financial year attributable to shareholders	3,727	912
Weighted average number of shares in issue	2,425,134,261	2,374,463,508
Dilution effect of – share options	19,959,122	19,127,364
– convertible unsecured loan stock	24,968,987	39,947,794
Diluted weighted average number of shares	2,470,062,370	2,433,538,666

(a) share option schemes not related to performance
(b) schemes related to performance, e.g. LTIPS
(c) contingently issuable shares e.g. shares which will be issued as deferred consideration in an acquisition, providing future profit thresholds are reached.

Points to watch on incentive schemes for directors and senior management
We still take the view that the e.p.s. dilution caused by these schemes (seldom more than 1% or 2%) is usually outweighed by the improved performance they encourage, but there are a couple of points to watch:

1. Beware schemes where the interests of the scheme's beneficiaries are not in line with the interests of the shareholders e.g. generous handouts of shares depending on criteria not directly related to the share price being met.
2. Be very wary of management who move the goalposts.

STATEMENT OF TOTAL RECOGNISED GAINS AND LOSSES

The statement of total recognised gains and losses [STRGL] is a primary financial statement introduced by FRS 3. Its purpose is to highlight any items which even if they were very significant would otherwise only appear in a note to the accounts. For example, POLLY PECK took an adverse exchange rate variance of £170.3m on net investment overseas direct to reserves in 1988, a year in which it only made an operating profit of £156.9m. The exchange variance was due largely to borrowing in Deutschmarks and Swiss francs, where interest rates were low, while keeping money on deposit in very soft Turkish lira. The very high interest received on the soft currency deposits was credited to the profit and loss account, while the capital loss was taken straight to reserves, together with the increase in the sterling value of DM and SFr borrowings. This portent of disaster was missed by some analysts and by most shareholders, but would have been obvious from an STRGL.

The statement of total recognised gains and losses shows the extent to which shareholders' funds have increased or decreased from all gains and losses recognised in the period. It normally appears either immediately after the profit and loss account or after the cash flow statement.

EMI GROUP (see next page) shows it between the balance sheet and the cash flow statement.

As shown by EMI Group such statements normally begin with the profit for the financial year (or 'period').

EMI GROUP *Interim statement 1998*

Statement of total recognised gains and losses for the six months ended 30 September 1998 (unaudited)

	Notes	· £m	Six months ended 30 Sep 1998 £m	£m	Six months ended 30 Sep 1997 (restated) £m
Profit for the period:					
As reported			31.4		51.1
Prior period adjustments	9		–		(50.4)
			31.4		0.7
Currency retranslation – as reported		(32.6)		5.3	
Currency retranslation – prior period adjustments	9	–		(1.7)	
Gains (losses) on foreign currency borrowings		1.0		(0.6)	
Other recognised (losses) gains			(31.6)		3.0
Total recognised gains and losses relating to the period			(0.2)		3.7

Other items commonly found include:

- Surpluses (deficits) on the revaluation of fixed assets;
- Currency translation differences (see Chapter 23);
- Prior period adjustments.

Prior period adjustments

Material prior period items which are the result of

(a) changes in accounting policies, or
(b) the correction of fundamental errors,

are treated as 'prior period adjustments'.

It is a fundamental accounting concept that there is consistency of accounting treatment within each accounting period and from one period to the next. A change in accounting policy may therefore be made only if it can be justified on the grounds that the new policy is preferable to the one it replaces because it will give a fairer presentation of the result and of the financial position of a reporting entity (Explanation to FRS 3, para. 62).

Following a change in accounting policy, the amounts for the current and corresponding periods should be restated on the basis of the new policies. The cumulative adjustments should also be noted at the foot of the statement of total recognised gains and losses of the current period and included in the reconciliation of movements in shareholders' funds of the corresponding period in order to highlight for users the effect of the adjustments.

EMI GROUP *Note to Interim statement 1998*

9. Prior period adjustments. As explained in Note 1 Basis of preparation, FRS 9 *Associates and Joint Ventures*, FRS 10 *Goodwill and Intangible Assets* and FRS 12 *Provisions, Contingent Assets and Contingent Liabilities* were adopted with effect from 1 April 1998. In addition, the accounting treatment for our 50% holding in Jobete was changed from an associate to a subsidiary.

To reflect these changes in accounting policies and accounting treatment, the comparatives for the six months ended 30 September 1997 and the opening balances for the current reporting period have been restated as follows:

Copyrights:
. . .
Investments: associates
. . .
Provisions:
. . .

Financial statistics in historical summaries

FRS 3 does not refer to historical summaries, but where prior period adjustments are made good accounting requires that information given in such summaries be restated, and many, but not all, companies do this.

FRS 14 does have regard to such summaries. In order to give a fair comparison over the period of any historical summary presented, the basic and diluted earnings per share figures need to be restated for subsequent changes in capital not involving full consideration at fair value (i.e. bonus issues, bonus elements in other issues or repurchases, share splits and share consolidations). The resultant earnings per share figures are described as restated and under FRS 14 are to be clearly distinguished from other non-adjusted data.

Equity dividends set out in the form of pence per share are to be adjusted similarly.

Movements in shareholders' funds

FRS 3 also requires (para. 28) companies to provide a note reconciling the opening and closing totals of shareholders' funds for the period. Often this follows the Statement of total recognised gains and losses but sometimes it is found in the note on reserves.

Typically the change in shareholders' funds which it discloses represents:

(a) Transfer from profit and loss account, i.e.

    (i) profit attributable to shareholders; less
    (ii) dividends;

(b) unrealised profit (deficit) on revaluation of fixed assets (normally properties);
(c) currency translation differences;
(d) new share capital subscribed (net);
(e) goodwill on disposals written back;
(f) purchase of own shares;
(g) prior year adjustments.

INVESTMENT RATIOS

These are the ratios used by investors when deciding whether a share should be bought, sold or held. Most of them relate to the current price of the share, and therefore vary from day to day. The two most popular ones are the Price Earnings Ratio (PER), already mentioned, and the dividend yield.

The Price Earnings Ratio (PER)

$$\frac{\text{Price}}{\text{earnings ratio}} = \frac{\text{Market price per ordinary share}}{\text{Basic earnings per share}}$$

where market price = the middle market price, which is the average of the prices at which shares can be sold or bought on an investor's behalf (the market maker's bid and offer prices respectively). The analyst will normally calculate two price earnings ratios: the 'historical PER', using last year's e.p.s., and the 'prospective PER', using his estimate of e.p.s. for the current year; he may also project his earnings estimates to produce a PER based on possible earnings for the following year.

What the PER represents

One way of looking at the PER is to regard it as the number of years' earnings per share represented by the share price, i.e. x years' purchase of e.p.s., but this assumes static e.p.s., while in practice the PER reflects the market's view of the company's growth potential, the business risks involved and the dividend policy. For example, a company recovering from a break-even situation, with zero e.p.s. last year, will have a historical PER of infinity but may have a prospective PER of 12 based on expectations of modest profits for the current year, falling to 6 next year if a full recovery is achieved.

The PER of a company also depends not only on the company itself, but on the industry in which

it operates and, of course, on the level of the stock market, which tends to rise more than reported profits when the business cycle swings up and to fall more than profits in a downturn.

The Actuaries Share Indices table published in the *Financial Times* every day except Mondays also gives the PER for each industry group and sub-section, so any historical PER calculated for a company can be compared with its sector and with the market as a whole. The result of comparing it with the market as a whole (usually with the FTSE All-Share PER) is called the PER Relative:

$$\text{PER Relative} = \frac{\text{PER of Company}}{\text{PER of Market}}$$

Example 18.11 Historical and prospective PER

Suppose the fully taxed normalised e.p.s. calculated from a company's latest report and accounts, published two to three months after the year has ended, are 8.0p. The analyst is expecting profits to rise by about 27% in the current year, and for there to be a disproportionately higher charge for minorities (because one partly owned subsidiary is making a hefty contribution to the improved profits). He therefore estimates that e.p.s. will rise a little less than profits, to about 10.0p.

The current share price is 120p, so last year's e.p.s. = 8p; current year e.p.s. = 10p; historical PER = 15.0; prospective PER = 12.0.

This provides a quick indication of whether a company is highly or lowly rated, although differences in the treatment of tax by individual companies do cause some distortion here, so most analysts use e.p.s. calculated on a full tax charge to compare PERs within a sector.

In general a high historic PER compared with the industry group suggests either that the company is a leader in its sector or that the share is over-valued, while a low PER suggests a poor company or an undervalued share. In each case check to see if the prospective PER is moving back into line with the sector, as a historic PER that is out of line may be due to expectations of an above average rise in profits for the current year (in which case the historic PER will be higher than average), or to poor results being expected (which would be consistent with a low PER).

Another useful rule of thumb is to be wary when a PER goes much above 20. The company may well be a glamour stock due for a tumble or, if it is the PER of a very sound high-quality company, the market itself may be in for a fall. One exception here is the property sector, where PERs are normally very high because property companies tend to be highly geared and use most of their rental income to service their debt, leaving tiny e.p.s.; investors normally buy property company shares more for their prospects of capital appreciation than for their current earnings.

Price earnings growth factor (PEG)

The price earnings growth factor (PEG) is a yardstick introduced by Jim Slater in his very readable book *The Zulu Principle*, which is full of useful advice for the private investor. The PEG is a measure of whether a share looks overrated or underrated:

$$PEG = \frac{Price\ earnings\ ratio}{Prospective\ growth\ in\ e.p.s.}$$

Where the PER is appreciably higher than the prospective growth rate (i.e. PEG well over 1.0), the shares are likely to be expensive. Conversely a PEG of between 0.5 and 0.7 means that the prospective growth rate isn't fully reflected in the PER, and the shares look attractive.

Dividend policy and the PER

As the price of a share is influenced both by the e.p.s. and the dividend, a company's dividend policy affects the P/E ratio.

Some companies pay tiny dividends and plough back most of their profits to finance further growth. Shares in these companies may enjoy a glamour rating while everything is going well, but the rating is vulnerable to any serious setback in profits, as there is little yield to support the price.

Blue chip companies like to pay a reasonable dividend and to increase it each year to counteract the effects of inflation and reflect long-term growth; and that is what the shareholders expect,

particularly those who are retired and need income from their investments. This means that major companies usually pay out between 30% and 40% of attributable profits, retaining a substantial amount to reinvest for future growth and to avoid having to cut the dividend in lean years. For example BRITISH AIRWAYS maintained its dividend in 1991, when profits had more than halved, but the dividend was still covered.

If a company pays out much more than 50% in dividends it suggests it has gone ex-growth; it also runs a higher risk of having to cut its dividend in hard times (which tends to be very unpopular with investors) and, in times of high inflation, a company distributing a large proportion of its reported profits (calculated on a historical cost basis) will tend to lose credibility.

Dividend yield

Dividend yields are now generally based on the net amount received.

Dividend yield (%) =

$$\frac{Net\ dividend\ in\ pence\ per\ share \times 100}{Ordinary\ share\ price\ in\ pence}$$

Dividend cover

$$Cover = \frac{e.p.s.}{Net\ dividends\ per\ share}$$

Example 18.12 Calculation of dividend cover

In year 2000 Cover plc had profits attributable to ordinary of £1.240m. 20m ordinary shares of £1 each were in issue throughout the year. The company paid total ordinary dividends of 2.3p per share net.
Basic earnings per share will be £1.240m ÷ 20m = 6.2p.
Cover = 6.2 ÷ 2.3 = 2.7.

Payout ratio

The payout ratio is the reciprocal of the dividend cover. It indicates the extent to which the attributable profits are distributed to ordinary shareholders. An equally valid measure is the amount retained by the company as a percentage of the attributable profit.

Example 18.13 Calculation of payout ratio

Basic earnings per share will be £1.240m ÷ 20m = 6.2p.
Cover = 6.2 ÷ 2.3 = 2.7.
Payout ratio = 1 ÷ Cover = 1 ÷ 2.70 = 0.37 or 37%.
The payout ratio could equally well be computed:
(20m × 23p) ÷ 1.240 = 0.37 or 37%.

Chapter 19

CASH FLOW STATEMENTS

OVERVIEW OF THE CASH FLOW STATEMENT AND RELATED NOTES

 A company which runs into heavy losses often makes a recovery. But if it runs out of cash (and credit) it will rarely get a second chance.

The finance director's viewpoint
This is how the FD of a large and successful FTSE 100 company explained it to us:

- *Starting point*: You start off with a kitty of *pre-tax profit* plus *depreciation* [depreciation is added back because it has been deducted in the P & L account, but no cash is paid out]
- *Other money coming in*: *Cash* that may come in from time to time to swell the kitty, like the proceeds of disposals.
- *'No choice' expenditure*: You have to *pay tax* [though increases in deferred tax, charged to the P & L account but not paid to the Inland Revenue, will *add* to the kitty]. And you have to *pay interest* on the company's borrowings.
- *Virtually 'no choice' expenditure*: *Dividends*: although there is no legal obligation to declare a dividend, shareholders will normally expect to be paid an at least maintained one, with a modest increase if profits are up. If the company is in good health financially, any Board that cuts or passes a dividend without a very good reason does so at its peril, unless the directors have control, or are backed by a controlling shareholder.

- *What's left in the kitty is*: **What the Board is free to spend.**
    Common sense would tell you that this is the company's *Free Cash Flow (FCF)*, but there are differing opinions on the definition of FCF, which we will discuss later in this chapter.

CASH FLOW STATEMENTS

The requirements of FRS 1

FRS 1 lays down a clearly defined overall format: the cash flow statement should list cash flows for the period, classified under eight standard headings in the following order:

(a) operating activities (using either the direct or indirect method, as explained on page 152);
(b) returns on investments and servicing of finance;
(c) taxation;
(d) capital expenditure and financial investment;
(e) acquisitions and disposals;
(f) equity dividends paid;
(g) management of liquid resources;
(h) financing.

The last two headings can be shown in a single section provided a separate subtotal is given for each heading.

    Individual categories of inflows and outflows under the standard headings should be disclosed separately either in the cash flow statement or in a note to it unless they are allowed to be shown net.

ABBEYCREST *Extract from 2000 accounts*

Note 23. Reconciliation of operating profit to net cash inflow from operating activities

		Group	
		2000	1999
		£000	£000
Operating profit	[A]	**6,138**	6,042
Depreciation	[B]	**1,107**	944
Amortisation of goodwill		**6**	–
Profit on sale of tangible fixed assets		**(29)**	(34)
(Increase)/decrease in stocks		**(619)**	77
(Increase)/decrease in debtors		**(2,687)**	2,618
Increase in creditors		**2,174**	792
Net cash inflow from operating activities	[C]	**6,090**	10,439

A real example

Let's look at a real example, ABBEYCREST, a listed company whose principal activity is, as its Directors' report describes, 'the design, manufacture and distribution of gold and silver jewellery'. Not, perhaps the best sort of business to be in in a recession, but doing well at present.

Begin, as our FTSE 100 FD did, with operating profit [A], and depreciation (and amortisation) [B], which appear at the top of ABBEYCREST's Note 23 on *Reconciliation of operating profit to net cash flow from operating activities*, shown above.

The next thing to notice in Abbeycrest's reconciliation statement is that, in 2000, the *Operating profit* [A] was about the same as the *Net cash inflow from operating activities* [C], but in 1999 [C] was over 70% higher than [A], putting an extra £4 million at the disposal of the Board.

The reason was that, in 1999, the group managed to reduce its working capital by reducing the amount that customers owed (Debtors) by £2,618,000 and increasing the amount the group owed by £792,000, while keeping stock well under control.

In 2000 customers were given more credit, increasing Debtors by £2,687,000 and Stock also increased, by £619,000. This was partly counterbalanced by the group getting £2,174,000 more credit, leaving an overall increase in working capital of £1,132,000.

Watch the working capital. If it isn't kept under firm control it will gobble up the company's cash like a hungry alligator.

To move on, the *bottom line* of the reconciliation statement [C] provides the *top line* of the cash flow statement, [D]:

ABBEYCREST *Extract from 2000 accounts*

Consolidated cash flow statement

		2000	1999
		£000	£000
Net cash inflow from operating activities	[D]	**6,090**	10,439
Returns on investment and servicing of finance	[E]	**(845)**	(1,013)
Taxation	[F]	**(1,578)**	(994)
Capital expenditure and financial investment	[G]	**(2,315)**	(580)
Acquisitions and disposals	[H]	**(1,316)**	–
Equity dividends paid	[I]	**(1,236)**	(1,093)
Cash (outflow)/inflow before financing		**(1,200)**	6,759
Financing – issue of share capital	[J]	**182**	194
Decrease in debt	[K]	**(424)**	(444)
(Decrease)/increase in cash in the year	[L]	**(1,442)**	6,509

ABBEYCREST *Note to the 2000 accounts*

Note 24. Analysis of cash flows

		Group	
		2000	1999
Returns on investment and servicing of finance		**£000**	£000
Interest received		**120**	34
Interest paid		**(974)**	(1,041)
Interest element of finance lease rental payments		**(1)**	(6)
Net cash outflow for returns on investments and servicing of finance	**[E]**	**(845)**	(1,013)
Capital expenditure and financial investment			
Purchase of tangible fixed assets		**(2,420)**	(717)
Sale of tangible fixed assets		**108**	137
Increase in fixed asset investments		**(3)**	–
Net cash outflow for capital expenditure and financial investment	**[G]**	**(2,315)**	(580)
Acquisitions and disposals			
Purchase of businesses		**(2,749)**	–
Cash acquired with subsidiary undertakings		**1,433**	–
Net cash outflow for acquisitions and disposals	**[H]**	**(1,316)**	–
Financing			
Issue of ordinary share capital	**[J]**	**182**	194
Debt due within one year: repayment of secured loan	**[K]**	**(404)**	(400)
Capital element of finance lease rental payments	**[K]**	**(20)**	(44)
Net cash outflow from financing	**[M]**	**(424)**	(250)

In Abbeycrest's Cash Flow Statement the difference in the top line **[D]** between 1999 and 2000 is (in £000) 4,349 but the difference in the bottom line **[L]** is 7,951, which is 3,602 more. Analysts should ask themselves 'Why the difference?'

In Abbeycrest's case there are two principal causes:

- *Capital expenditure and financial investment* **[G]** has gone up fourfold.
- in 2000 a net 1,316 was spent on *Acquisitions and disposals* **[H]**, compared with nil in 1999.

Note 24 on *Acquisitions and disposals*, shown above, gives more details. For example, the net figure of (£000) 1,316 for *Acquisitions and disposals* comprised 2,749 spent on 'Purchase of businesses', less 1,433 of 'Cash acquired with subsidiary undertakings'.

Reconciliation of net cash flow to net debt
FRS1 requires a note reconciling the movement of cash in the period to the movement in net debt, to be shown either with (but not as part of) the cash flow statement, or in a note. Abbeycrest shows its reconciliation in a Note, shown here:

ABBEYCREST *Note to the 2000 accounts*

Note 26. Reconciliation of net cash flow to movement in net debt

		2000
		£000
Decrease in cash in the year	**[L]**	(1,442)
Cash outflow from decrease in debt and lease financing	**[M]**	424
		(1,018)
New finance leases		(113)
Loans acquired with subsidiary		(38)
		(1,169)
Net debt at beginning of year		(1,601)
Net debt at end of year		(2,770)

Reconciliation to net debt
FRS1 requires a note reconciling the movement of cash in the period to the movement in net debt, to be shown separately, either adjoining the cash flow statement, or in a Note. Abbeycrest's reconciliation, Note 25, is shown at the top of page 151.

ABBEYCREST *Note to the 2000 accounts*

Note 25. Analysis of net debt

	[R] 1 March 1999 £000	[S] Cashflow £000	[T] Acquisitions and disposals £000	[U] Non-cash changes £000	[V] **29 February 2000 £000**
Cash at bank and in hand	1,556	409	–	–	**1,965**
Overdrafts	(2,047)	(1,851)	–	–	**(3,898)**
	(491)	[L] (1,442)	–	–	**(1,933)**
Debt due after one year	(700)	4	(38)	400	**(334)**
Debt due within one year	(400)	400	–	(400)	**(400)**
Finance leases	(10)	20	–	(113)	**(103)**
	(1,110)	[M] 424	[O] (38)	[N] (113)	(837)
Net debt	[P] (1,601)	(1,018)	(38)	(113)	[Q] **(2,770)**

The changes in net debt should be analysed from the opening [R] to the closing component amounts [V], showing separately, where material, changes resulting from:

[S] The cash flows
[T] Acquisitions and disposals
[U] Other non-cash changes, and recognition of changes in market value and exchange rate movements.

Acquisitions and disposals

A note to the cash flow statement should show a summary of the effects of acquisitions and disposals of subsidiary undertakings, indicating how much of the consideration comprised cash (see TT GROUP below).

Non-cash items and restrictions on transfer

Material transactions which do not result in movements of cash of the reporting company should be disclosed in the notes to the cash flow statement if disclosure is necessary for an understanding of the underlying transactions.

TT GROUP *Note to the 1999 Cash flow statement*

Note 24. Acquisition

Prestwick Holdings plc, a manufacturer of printed circuit boards, became a subsidiary of the Group on 28 May 1999.

Assets acquired:

	Book value £million	Valuation adjust's £million	Book value and fair value £million
Tangible fixed assets	11.3	(5.4)	5.9
Stocks	4.1	(1.4)	2.7
Debtors	5.6	0.1	5.7
Net cash/(Overdrafts)	2.4	–	2.4
Total net assets	7.0	(5.6)	1.4
Goodwill			3.2
Cost of acquisition			4.6

Satisfied by:	£million
Consideration	
– Cash	0.6
– Transfer from fixed asset investments	3.8
Cash costs	0.2
	4.6

MARKS & SPENCER *Consolidated cash flow information for the year ended 31 March 2000*

Cash flow statement

		2000 £m	1999 £m
Operating activities			
Received from customers	[A]	7,989.9	7,884.1
Payment to suppliers	[B]	(5,357.1)	(5,464.2)
Payment to and on behalf of employees	[C]	(1,138.3)	(1,153.9)
Other payments		(803.8)	(793.1)
Cash flow from operating activities before exceptional item		690.7	472.9
Exceptional operating cash outflow	Note 28 (below)	(49.2)	(0.6)
Cash inflow from operating activities		641.5	472.3

. . .

Note 28. Analysis of cash flows given in the cash flow statement

	2000 £m	1999 £m
. . .		
Exceptional operating cash flows		
UK redundancy costs paid	(44.7)	(0.6)
European restructuring costs paid	(4.5)	–
Exceptional operating cash outflow	(49.2)	(0.6)

The direct and indirect methods

These are the two methods for reporting net cash flow from operating activities.

As we saw in the extract from Abbeycrest's accounts, Note 23 on page 149, the **indirect method** starts with *Operating profit* and adjusts it for depreciation and other non-cash credits and charges to get to *Net cash flow from operating activities*.

The **direct method**, on the other hand, gets to *Net cash flow from operating activities* by adding up all operating cash receipts and payments. As illustrated in the MARKS & SPENCER extract above, these include

[A] *Receipts from customers,*
[B] *Payments to suppliers* and
[C] *Payments to and on behalf of employees.*

FRS1 encourages companies to use the direct method but not many do so, because it means providing *extra* information; companies using the direct method *also* have to produce a reconciliation between *Operating profit* and *Net cash flow from operations* i.e. the same information as with the indirect method.

It is a pity that the direct method is not compulsory, as it shows the *actual size* of the cash flows in a company, giving a much better feel of the scale of operations than the indirect method's netted off figures.

Restrictions on remittability

Where restrictions prevent the transfer of cash from one part of the business or group to another, a note to the cash flow statement should specify the amounts and explain the circumstances.

CADBURY SCHWEPPES, shown below, does not specify the amounts because they have 'no material adverse impact':

CADBURY SCHWEPPES *Extract from OFR 2000*

Capital structure and resources

. . .

While there are exchange control restrictions which affect the ability of certain of the Group's subsidiaries to transfer funds to the Group, the operations affected by such restrictions are not material to the Group as a whole and the Group does not believe such restrictions have had or will have any material adverse impact on the Group as a whole or the ability of the Group to meet its cash flow requirements.

Limitations of cash flow statements

A cash flow statement is a record of historical facts. It will record expenditure upon additional plant and machinery, but can express no opinion upon whether the expenditure was necessary, or will be profitable.

Similarly it may show an expansion of stocks (or debtors), but it does not tell us whether this was due to

- poor stock or production control;
- inability to sell the finished product; or
- a deliberate act of policy, because of a feared shortage of supply, a potential price rise, or the need to build up stocks of a new model (or product) before it is launched.

Furthermore, in the case of increased debtors, it will not tell us whether it is

- the debtors who are slow to pay; or
- the credit policy which has changed; or
- the accounts department has fallen behind with invoicing; or because
- they merely represent the expansion of turnover.

It will show how new capital was raised, but not whether it was raised in the best way, nor indeed whether it really needed to be raised at all or if the need could have been avoided by better asset control.

When companies have large amounts of cash, the cash flow statement does not tell us where the cash is. Only if it is locked up in an overseas subsidiary, perhaps deposited in an obscure currency in an obscure country (like Turkish Cyprus as was the case with POLLY PECK), where it cannot be remitted to the UK, can we expect to be told – by which time it may well be too late.

Where there are large amounts of both cash and borrowings, the cash flow statement does not tell us why the company does not use the cash to reduce its debts. There may be several reasons:

1. It may be better to borrow in the US, where corporation tax is higher than in the UK, and to keep deposits in the UK.
2. The cash may not have been remitted, to avoid having to pay tax on remitting it.
3. The company may have borrowed cheaply longer-term or have favourable facilities and be 'round tripping' – borrowing at a lower rate and taking advantage of higher current interest rates to lend money back at a profit.

Borrowing facilities

Some years ago, companies used to be reluctant to disclose details of their **unused** borrowing facilities, for fear, perhaps, that if they subsequently reached the limits, they would not want to disclose 'unused facilities – Nil'.

Nowadays, FRS 13 (see Chapter 14) requires Listed Companies to disclose details e.g. LONMIN:

LONMIN *Note from the 2000 accounts*

Undrawn committed borrowing facilities

	2000 £m	1999 £m
Expiring in one year or less	12	39
Expiring in more than one year but not more than two years	80	–
Expiring in more than two years	65	58
	157	97

Although it is prudent to have plenty of financial elbow room, *it is not a good idea* for a company to have very large unused facilities in place if it has had to pay its bankers a hefty arrangement fee for setting up the facility and is paying an ongoing annual *'Commitment commission'* on the unused amount.

Take, for example, BOOTS the Chemist:

BOOTS *Extract from 2000 Financial Review*

Liquidity and funding

The company has good access to the capital markets due to its strong credit ratings from Moody's and Standard & Poor's . . .

The group has ten identical credit facilities, totalling £600,000, which mature in 2004. These facilities remained undrawn during the year, with short term needs being met from uncommitted bank lines.

. . .

It would be helpful to the shareholder to know the underlying strategy; if the £600,000 facility is part of what is known in the City as a *'War chest'* to fund acquisitions being planned, then Boots' reticence is understandable. When a takeover has been announced, a company can be more informative e.g. the Ready Mixed Concrete group RMC:

RMC *Extract from note to 1999 accounts*

Note 29. Derivatives and other financial instruments
d) Borrowing facilities

The group has undrawn, committed, borrowing facilities at 31 December 1999, including those in anticipation of the purchase of the remaining equity shares of The Rugby Group PLC . . . as follows:

	£m
Expiring in more than one year but not more than two years	50.0
Expiring in more than two years	1,347.2
Total	1,397.2

A cash flow statement may highlight a deteriorating situation, but does not tell the reader:

- just how close a company is to the limit of its facilities;
- whether it is in danger of breaching any of its borrowing covenants;
- whether the company's bankers are getting nervous, or are still confident of its recovery.

And, of course, it only shows the cash flows for the year which ended some months ago and, as we saw in the recession in the early 1990s, liquidity problems can and do arise very quickly.

Cash requirements

There are three main areas to look at in identifying cash requirements:

1. *Repayment of existing loans* due in the next year or two, including convertible loans whose conversion rights are unlikely to be exercised.
2. *Increase in working capital.* Working capital tends, in an inflationary period and/or when a business expands, to rise roughly in line with turnover. It is useful therefore to use the Working capital/Sales ratio to establish the relationship between working capital and sales.

Working capital to sales =

$$\frac{(\text{Stock} + \text{Trade debtors}) - \text{Trade creditors}}{\text{Sales}}$$

A company with a low working capital ratio should find it easier to grow than a company with a high working capital ratio.

For example ABBEYCREST, below, needed an extra £2.391 million working capital in 2000 to support the £6.634 million increase in sales **[B]**.

On top of that, another £2.934 million was needed because of the 4.187% increase **[D]** in the Working capital/Sales ratio:

ABBEYCREST *Working capital ratio*

	2000 £000	1999 £000
Stock	19,669	17,369
+ Trade debtors	11,599	8,099
− Trade creditors	(3,079)	(2,604)
= *Working capital*	28,189	22,864
YoY increase in working capital	5,325	
Sales	70,063 **[A]**	63,429
YoY increase in sales (£'000)	6,634 **[B]**	
Working capital/Sales ratio (%)	40,233	36,046 **[C]**
YoY increase in Wcap ratio (%)	4,187 **[D]**	
– due to increased sales (£'000)	2,391 **[B]** × **[C]**	
– due to increase in ratio (£'000)	2,934 **[A]** × **[D]**	
	5,325	

Compare that with TESCO:

TESCO *Working capital ratio*

	2000 £m	1999 £m
Stock	636	595
+ Trade debtors	–	–
− Trade creditors	1,248	1,100
= **Negative *Working capital***	(612)	(505)
Sales	16,995	15,814
Working capital/Sales ratio (%)	(3.6)	(3.2)

Requirements for additional working capital for expansion

Any business that can sell goods to its customers for cash *before* it has to pay for those goods, won't need any additional working capital for expansion; rather the reverse.

Conversely, companies that have to carry large amounts of stock, work in progress and finished goods at their own expense will need any additional working capital if they want to expand; for example the international mining company RIO TINTO:

RIO TINTO *Working capital ratio*

	2000 £m	1999 £m
Inventories	**959**	793
+ Accounts receivable and prepayments		
Falling due within one year	**1,041**	729
Falling due after more than one year	**392**	369
− Amounts payable and accruals	**(1,469)**	(1,087)
= Positive *Working capital*	**923**	804
Sales	**6,582**	5,747
Working capital/Sales ratio (%)	**14.0%**	14.0%

3. *Capital expenditure requirements.* This is likely to be a rough estimate, unless the company discloses details of both amounts and timing of planned Capex. Points to check:

(a) Note on capital commitments, e.g.

ABBEYCREST *Note to the 2000 accounts*

Note 28 Capital commitments
At 26 February 2000 there were commitments for capital expenditure contracted for but not provided of £303m (1999 – £260m).

(b) Cash flow statement, e.g.

ABBEYCREST *Group cash flow statement extract*

	2000 £000	1999 £000
Capital expenditure		
Payments to acquire tangible fixed assets	(1,296)	(1,032)
receipts from sale of tangible fixed assets	85	27
...		

(c) Comments in the annual report, e.g.

ABBEYCREST *Chairman's statement 2000*

The future

...

To enhance our growth potential in the UK, we are investing in new product development, sales and marketing resource and advanced IT systems. The UK distribution system now has the added benefits from the group's world class, low cost production facilities.

Our comments

A positive view about the future; the Capital expenditure figures for 1999 and 2000, above, suggest capex in 2001 is likely to be between £1.4 and £1.6 million.

Cash shortfall

If the net cash flow looks like falling short of the cash requirements we have identified, then the company may have to

a) increase its overdraft (but is it at the limit of its facilities? – we probably don't know);
b) borrow longer-term (can it do so within its borrowing limits?);
c) make a rights issue (is its share price at least 20% above par, is it at least a year and preferably two years since its last rights issue, and are market conditions suitable?);
d) acquire a more liquid and/or less highly geared company for paper (i.e. bid for another company using shares);
e) sell some assets (has it any listed investments which could be sold, or has it any activities which could be sold off without seriously affecting the business?);
f) sell and lease back some of the properties used in the business (has it any unmortgaged properties?);
g) cut back on capital expenditure that has not already been put out to contract;
h) tighten credit and stock control;
i) reduce or omit the ordinary dividend, and possibly even the preference dividend too.

If the company takes none of these steps it will run into an overtrading situation, which is likely to precipitate a cash crisis unless, as a last resort, it:

j) reduces its level of trading.

CASH FLOW – DEFINITIONS AND RATIOS

Free cash flow (FCF)

As discussed at the beginning of this chapter, common sense would suggest that *free cash flow* is 'What the Board is **free** to spend' once all obligatory and virtually obligatory payments had been made. And that was how STAGECOACH saw it in 1998, as shown in the next column.

However, in subsequent years, Stagecoach dropped the *Free Cash Flow* line from its cash flow statement. A large number of companies don't even mention FCF, while others have their 'Own brand' definitions.

CADBURY SCHWEPPES deducts *Net capital expenditure* as well as *Interest, Tax* and *Dividends* to arrive at FCF, while W. H. SMITH deducts *Dividends* after FCF.

STAGECOACH HOLDINGS *Extract from 1998 accounts*

Consolidated Cash Flow Statement	1998 £m	1997 £m
Net cash inflow from operating activities	330.4	232.7
Returns on Investment and Servicing of Finance		
Bank interest paid	(69.1)	(42.2)
Interest element of HP and lease finance	(10.9)	(8.4)
Interest received	21.9	8.1
Eurobond issue costs	(0.6)	Nil
Net cash outflow	(58.7)	(42.5)
Taxation	(47.4)	(17.5)
Free Cash Flow	**224.3**	**172.7**

But the company showing the most individuality on *free cash flow* must surely be BOOTS:

BOOTS *Extract from Financial review 2000*

Cash flow The maximization of cash flow is the key factor in value creation . . .

The following summary of cash flow demonstrates the company's ability consistently to generate a healthy **free cash flow** that is defined as **The cash flow available to all providers of capital**.

Summary of cash flows	£m 2000	£m 1999
Operating cash flows before exceptionals	773	616
Exceptional operating cash flows	(19)	(14)
Acquisitions/disposals of businesses	(3)	55
Purchase of fixed assets	(266)	(372)
Purchase of own shares	(58)	(160)
Disposal of fixed assets	93	74
Disposal of own shares	10	–
Taxation paid	(154)	(112)
Other items	–	8
Free cash flow	376	95

. . .

The following chart shows the amounts of free cash flow generated by the group for each of the last five years.

Cash generation £m

00	376.2
99	95.0
98	203.2
97	138.5
96	147.2

Authors' comments on free cash flow

On page 157 is an edited version of Boots' *Group financial record 2000* using '*common sense*' to produce bottom line values of [**f**] the free cash flow in the years 1996 to 2000.

Apart from a dip in 1997, Boots' common sense free cash flow has grown steadily, as you would expect of this prosperous 'household name' retailer.

Boots 'own brand' definition, on the other hand, produces a 53% fall in its '*Own brand*' of free cash flow in 1999, followed by a 296% rise in 2000.

Cash flow ratios

Cash flow can be given *per share*:

Cash flow per share =

(Attributable profits plus depreciation)

Number of ordinary shares in issue

The definition used by REFS (see page 224) is:

Cash flow per share =

(Cash flow from operating activities + return on investments and servicing of finance – Taxation paid)

Weighted average number of ordinary shares in issue during the period

Capex per share can then be compared with Cash flow per share. If this is done in terms of 'common sense' free cash flow, it will show how much of their '*disposable income*' the Board is spending on capital investment.

To show ABBEYCREST'S *Free Cash Flow* in 1999 and 2000, we take Abbeycrest's Consolidated cash flow statement on page 149 and rearrange it as shown on the next page. This also shows how the free cash flow was spent:

In 1999 the Board hung on to 89% of their £7.3 million FCF to improve the Group's cash position.
In 2000 the Board spent 96% of the FCF on capital expenditure and 54% on acquisitions, an overspend of 50%.

The shortfall was reduced by 7% by the issue of shares. But it at the same time it was increased by 18% by a decrease in debt.

This left a decrease in cash equal to 59% of FCF.

BOOTS *Edited extract from Group financial record 2000*

Cash flow statement	Authors' Notes	2000 £m	1999 £m	1998 £m	1997 £m	1996 £m
a Cash inflow from operating activities		753.7	601.9	605.6	515.1	536.5
b Net interest received/(Paid)		(9.8)	(24.9)	(10.5)	39.1	16.2
c Taxation		(154.4)	(112.4)	(232.8)	(174.4)	(152.7)
d = a +/− b − c	1	**589.5**	**464.6**	**362.3**	**379.8**	**400.0**
e Equity dividends paid	2	(216.3)	(207.1)	(162.8)	(169.8)	(154.4)
f = d − e	3	**373.2**	**257.5**	**199.5**	**210.0**	**245.6**

Authors' notes
1. Often called **'Gross cash flow'**
2. Excluding £400.5m special dividend paid in 1998
3. Often called **'Net cash flow'**

ABBEYCREST *Consolidated Cash Flow Statement 2000. Sequence of items rearranged*

	2000 £000	FCF	1999 £000	FCF
Net cash flow from operating activities	**6,090**		10,439	
Net interest paid	**(845)**		(1,013)	
Taxation	**(1,578)**		(994)	
Equity dividends paid	**(1,236)**		(1,093)	
Common sense free cash flow	**2,431**	**100%**	7,339	100%
Less:				
Capital expenditure and financial investment	**(2,315)**	**(96%)**	(580)	(8%)
Acquisitions and disposals	**(1,316)**	**(54%)**	–	–
Cash(outflow)/inflow before financing	**(1200)**	**(50%)**	6,759	92%
Financing – issue of shares	**182**	**7%**	194	3%
Decrease in debt	**(424)**	**(18%)**	(444)	(6%)
(Decrease)/Increase in cash in the year	**(1,442)**	**(59%)**	6,509	(89%)

'Sherlock Holmes' approach to cash flow

We call it the Sherlock Holmes approach because the cash flow statement often contains clues: clues on questions to ask, and where to look for the answers.

We will round off this chapter with examples of clues we found in ABBEYCREST's interim report for the 6 months ending 31 August 2000, shown here:

ABBEYCREST *Consolidated cash flow statement for the 6 months ended 31 August 2000*

	6 months to 31 August 2000 £000	6 months to 31 August 1999 £000	Year to 29 February 2000 £000
Net cash (outflow)/inflow from operating activities	[A] **(10,371)**	[B] (8,001)	6,090
Returns on investments and servicing of finance	**(472)**	(371)	(845)
Taxation	**(858)**	[T] (64)	[U] (1,578)
Capital expenditure and financial investment	**(1,251)**	(1,054)	(2,315)
Acquisitions and disposals	**–**	(964)	(1,316)
Equity dividends paid	**(923)**	(824)	(1,236)
Cash outflow before financing	**(13,875)**	(11,278)	(1,200)
Financing – issue of shares . . .			

Clue No. 1

[A] *Over £10 million net cash outflow from operating activities! Golly gumdrops, the company must be haemorrhaging cash. No, hang on a minute, [B] there was an £8 million outflow in H1/99. Could it be a seasonal business?*

Look back at the Directors' annual report:

ABBEYCREST *Directors' report 2000*

Principal activity

The principal activity of the group is the design, manufacture and distribution of gold and silver jewellery.

As the company manufactures, it may be building stock for Christmas. Details of changes in working capital will be in a note:

ABBEYCREST *Interim cash flow statement*

Note 1 Reconciliation of operating profit to net cash (outflow)/inflow from operating activities

...

Increase in stocks   (£000)   (10,362)

Dos the Chairman make any comment on stocks?

ABBEYCREST *Chairman's interim statement*

Review of activities

... demand began to increase in August and this combined with improved selections for the second half gave management the confidence to build stock in advance of the season.

Clue No. 2

Why was only £64,000 Taxation paid [T] in H1/99? But £1,578,000 [U] was paid in the year to February 2000.

Remember that a cash flow statement shows the amount of *tax actually paid in the period*, rather than the *tax charge for the period*, so it looks as though there was some delay in the payment of tax. Could this have been due to a dispute over tax?

We note that, in the year ended 29 February 2000, there was a prior year adjustment **[X]** that reduced the tax charge by 20%, an unusually large amount, so there may have been protracted negotiations with the Inland Revenue.

ABBEYCREST *Extract from the 2000 accounts*

	2000
	£000
Note 8 Tax on profit on ord. activities	
UK Corporation tax	**1,049**
Foreign Corporation tax	**79**
Deferred tax	**83**
Tax charge in respect of the current year	**1,211**
Adjustment in respect of prior years **[X]**	**(245)**
Total tax charge	**966**

Chapter 20

SUBSIDIARIES AND GROUP ACCOUNTS

Interests in another company

If a company, A, wishes to obtain an interest in the activities of another company, B, it may do so in three ways:

- by buying some or all of the *assets* of B;
- by buying *shares* in B;
- by *making a bid* for B.

Buying assets of company B

If company A only wishes to acquire some or all of the assets of company B, it may do so either by paying cash or by paying in shares of company A; the latter is an example of a vendor consideration issue of shares described in Chapter 18.

Example 20.1 below illustrates acquiring all the assets of a company, rather than the company itself. Note that, in the example, Company B remains an independent company.

Example 20.1 Acquisition of assets by share issue

Let us suppose that, at 31 December 1999, the balance sheets of A and B were:

	A £000	B £000
Ordinary share capital	800	80
Reserves	280	340
	1,080	420
Net assets	1,080	420

Suppose A purchases the net assets of B by the issue to company B of 600,000 £1 ordinary shares (valued at par at the time).

Company A's balance sheet at that date would become:

	£000
Ordinary share capital	1,400
Reserves	280
	1,680
Net assets (£1,080,000 + £420,000)	1,500
Goodwill (£600,000 – £420,000)	180
	1,680

Company B's balance sheet after A's purchase would show:

	£000
Ordinary share capital	80
Reserves (£340,000 + £180,000 profit on realisation of net assets)	520
	600
Investment at cost	600

Company B would not cease to exist; it would become an investment holding company.

Had A's shares been listed and had they been standing at, say, 300p at the time, A might have issued 200,000 £1 ordinary shares, and A's balance sheet after the purchase would then have been:

	£000
Ordinary share capital	1,000
Share premium account	400
Other reserves	280
	1,680
Net assets	1,500
Goodwill	180
	1,680

Buying some shares in company B

There are four possibilities:

1. If A acquires less than 3% of the equity of B, A's balance sheet would show the purchase as an investment (see Chapter 9).
2. If A acquires 3% or more of the equity of B, the purchaser would still show the purchase as an investment, but would be obliged by Section 134 of the Companies Act 1989 to declare its interest.
3. If A acquires 20% or more of the equity of B, and is allowed by B to participate in the major policy decisions of B, usually by holding a seat on B's board, then A should treat B as an associated undertaking (see Chapter 22).
4. If A acquires 30% or more of the voting rights of B, or if A in any period of 12 months adds more than 2% to an existing holding of between 30% and 50% in B, then Rules 9.1 and 9.5 of the Takeover Code oblige A to make a bid for the remainder of the equity of B at a price not less than the highest price A paid for any B shares within the preceding 12 months.

Making a takeover bid for company B

Company A may offer the shareholders of B either cash or 'paper' (i.e. shares and/or loan stock and/or warrants of A). If A has already gone over the 30% limit or has added more than 2% in 12 months to a holding of 30–50%, the offer must be in cash or be accompanied by a cash alternative. If the bid results in A acquiring 90% or more of the shares of B that it did not already own, A may force the remaining B shareholders to accept the bid using the procedure laid down in Section 428 of the Companies Act 1985.

The remainder of this chapter is concerned with cases where Company A acquires control of company B.

Two ways of accounting

There are two ways of accounting for an acquisition:

1. Acquisition accounting, and
2. Merger accounting.

The two methods are entirely different and give quite different results in the group accounts.

FRS 6 *Acquisitions and mergers*

FRS 6 restricts the use of merger accounting to those business combinations where the use of acquisition accounting would not properly reflect the true nature of the combination. Acquisition accounting is to be used for all business combinations where a party can be identified as having the role of an acquirer. Because acquisition accounting is the usual method, and by far the more common method, we assume acquisition accounting in this chapter, leaving a detailed discussion of the two methods, acquisition accounting and merger accounting, to Chapter 21.

First the reader needs to understand:

(a) what holding companies, subsidiaries and groups are;
(b) how group accounts (or consolidated accounts) work.

HOLDING COMPANIES, SUBSIDIARIES AND GROUPS

Some definitions

Under CA 1985, an undertaking is the *parent undertaking* of another undertaking (a *subsidiary undertaking*) if any of the following apply:

(i) it holds a majority of the voting rights in the undertaking;
(ii) it is a member of the undertaking and has the right to appoint or remove directors holding a majority of the voting rights at meetings of the board on all, or substantially all, matters;
(iii) it has the right to exercise a dominant influence over the undertaking:

(a) by virtue of provisions contained in the undertaking's memorandum or articles; or
(b) by virtue of a control contract in writing and of a kind authorised by the memorandum or articles and permitted by the law under which the undertaking is established;
(c) it is a member of the undertaking and controls alone, pursuant to an agreement with other shareholders, a majority of the voting rights in the undertaking;
(d) it has a participating interest in the undertaking and it actually exercises a dominant influence over the undertaking; or it and the undertaking are managed on a unified basis.

A *wholly owned subsidiary* is one in which all the share capital is held either by the holding company or by other wholly owned subsidiaries.

A *partially owned subsidiary* is one in which some of the share capital is owned outside the group. For an illustration of these terms, see Example 20.2. A parent undertaking is also often termed the *holding company*, and, as we have seen, a holding company and its subsidiaries are referred to as a *group*.

In the past, all these relationships depended on voting control, but over the years the ingenuity of companies and their financial advisors to facilitate operation overseas, or in an attempt to keep companies off balance sheet (to hide either their liabilities or true profitability or their tendency to be loss-making), or simply to avoid tax, led to numerous devices which kept companies outside the group for purposes of the consolidated accounts. The Companies Act 1985 and FRS 2 *Accounting for subsidiary undertakings* have done much to prevent this.

Group accounts

If, at the end of a financial year, a company is a parent company, group accounts have to be prepared as well as individual accounts for the parent company (CA 1985, s. 227), although small and medium-sized private groups are exempt from this (CA 1985, s. 248). Group accounts comprise:

- a consolidated balance sheet; and
- a profit and loss account dealing with the parent company and its subsidiary undertakings.

Additional information

If the matters required to be included in group or individual company accounts would not be sufficient to give a true and fair view, the Act requires that 'the necessary additional information shall be given'.

Example 20.2 Partially and wholly owned subsidiaries

H is the holding company of a group of companies, and is incorporated in Great Britain.

H holds 100,000 of the 100,000 ordinary shares of S
H holds 7,500 of the 10,000 ordinary shares of T
S holds 5,100 of the 10,000 ordinary shares of U
T holds 1,000 of the 1,000 ordinary shares of V
The H group may be depicted thus:

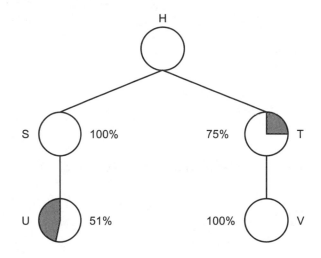

In law, the parent of a subsidiary is the parent of its subsidiary.

The H group consists of:

- H's wholly owned subsidiary S
- H's partially owned listed subsidiary T (in which there is a 25% minority)
- T's wholly owned subsidiary V (which in law is also a subsidiary of H, but colloquially a partially owned subsubsidiary of H)
- S's partially owned subsidiary U (in which there is a 49% minority).

CONSOLIDATED ACCOUNTS

The consolidated balance sheet

In simple terms a consolidated balance sheet shows all the assets and all the liabilities of all group companies whether wholly owned or partially owned. Where a partially owned subsidiary exists, its shareholders' funds are provided partly by the holding company and partly by the minority.

To illustrate the basic principles of consolidated accounts let us take the case of a holding company, H, with a partially owned subsidiary, S, and imagine that we wish to prepare the consolidated balance sheet for the H GROUP at 31 December 1998. H paid £340,000 cash for 200,000 of the 250,000 £1 ordinary shares of S on 1 January 1996.

The balance sheet of S at acquisition was:

S *Balance sheet at 1 January 1996*

	£000
Fixed assets:	
Freehold land and buildings	120
Plant and machinery	146
	266
Net current assets	169
	435
Ordinary share capital	250
Reserves	85
Ordinary shareholders' funds	335
7% Debenture	100
	435

H *and* S *Balance sheets at 31 December 1998*

	H £000	S £000
Fixed assets:		
Freehold land and buildings	150	120
Plant and machinery	250	180
	400	300
Shares in S	340	–
Net current assets	360	200
	1,100	500
Ordinary share capital	500	250
Reserves	480	150
Ordinary shareholders' funds	980	400
10% Unsecured loan stock	120	–
7% Debenture	–	100
	1,100	500

There are six steps to consolidating the two companies' balance sheets at 31 December 1998:

1. *Ascertain the goodwill* by comparing the cost to H of its investment in S with H's share of the equity shareholders' funds of S at the date of acquisition. The goodwill will be:

	£000	£000
Purchase consideration		340
Holding company's share of ordinary shareholders' funds at date of acquisition:		
4/5 of Ordinary share capital	200	
4/5 of Reserves	68	268
Goodwill		72

Note that:

(a) Any pre-acquisition profits of S which have not already been distributed will form part of that company's reserves, and are thus represented by equity shareholders' funds taken into account in computing goodwill.

(b) Any distribution by S after it is acquired by H which is made out of pre-acquisition profits (i.e. reserves existing at acquisition) must be credited not to the profit and loss account of H as income, but to the asset account 'Investment in S' as a reduction of the purchase price of that investment. The goodwill does not change.

2. *Compute the holding company's share* of the undistributed post-acquisition profits of the subsidiary.

This equals the holding company's proportion of the change in reserves since the date of acquisition:

$$\frac{200,000}{250,000} \times (£150,000 - £85,000) = £52,000$$

This, added to the holding company's own reserves, represents the reserves of the group which will appear in the consolidated balance sheet:

$$£52,000 + £480,000 = £532,000$$

3. *Compute minority interests* in the net assets of S:

$$\begin{matrix}\text{Minority} \\ \text{interests}\end{matrix} = \begin{matrix}\text{Minority} \\ \text{proportion}\end{matrix} \times \begin{matrix}\text{Equity shareholders'} \\ \text{funds of S at} \\ \text{31 December 1998}\end{matrix}$$

The minority interest in the equity shareholders' funds of S is:

$$\frac{50,000}{250,000} \times £400,000 = £80,000$$

4. *Draw up the consolidated balance sheet:*

(i) insert as share capital the share capital of the holding company;

(ii) insert the figures already computed for

- goodwill (see 1 above) and
- minority interests (see 3 above);

(iii) show as 'reserves' the total of the reserves of the holding company and the post-acquisition reserves of the subsidiary applicable to the holding company (see 2 above).

5. *Cancel out any inter-company balances*: the aim of the consolidated balance sheet is to show a true and fair view of the state of affairs of the group as a whole. Inter-company balances (where an item represents an asset of one group company and a liability of another) must be cancelled out since they do not concern outsiders. Thus, if S owes H on current account £10,000, this £10,000 will appear as an asset in H's own balance sheet, and as a liability in that of S, but it will not appear at all in the consolidated balance sheet.

6. *Consolidate*: add together like items (e.g. add freehold land and buildings of the holding company and freehold land and buildings of the subsidiary) and show the group totals in the consolidated balance sheet. Omit, in so doing, the share capital of the subsidiary, reserves, and the investment in the subsidiary, which have already been taken into account in steps 1 to 3.

It will be seen (Example 20.3 below) that only the share capital of the holding company appears in the consolidated balance sheet. The share capital of the subsidiary has disappeared, one-fifth of it becoming part of 'minority inter-

ests' while the other four-fifths (£200,000), together with H's share of S's reserves on acquisition (£68,000) and the goodwill (£72,000) balance out the removal of H's balance sheet item 'shares in S' (£340,000).

Goodwill on consolidation arising prior to 1998
For accounting periods ending before 23 December 1998 companies could choose between two significantly different accounting policies:

• to write goodwill off immediately against reserves – thus goodwill never appeared either in the balance sheet or in the profit and loss account;
• to include goodwill in the balance sheet as an intangible fixed asset – this goodwill would be amortised over a period of usually 20 years, with the amortisation charge included in the profit and loss account and reflected in the operating profit for the year.

In practice, most UK companies chose the first option of immediate write-off against reserves, to avoid their reported profits being reduced by amortisation.

When FRS 10 was introduced (see below), any goodwill *subsequently arising* had to be included in the balance sheet as an intangible fixed asset.

FRS 10 allowed companies to leave their 'old' goodwill written off against reserves rather than reinstating it on the balance sheet. In practice, most companies did *not* bring 'old' goodwill back on to the balance sheet. The effect of this may be significant where large acquisitions had taken place prior to 1988. But the Companies Act 1985 does require companies to show the cumulative amount of 'old' goodwill written off against reserves, and not reinstated, although the figure is not always easy to find in the accounts.

Goodwill on consolidation arising after 1998
Under FRS 10 *Goodwill and intangible assets* and FRS 11 *Impairment of fixed assets and goodwill*, purchased goodwill must be capitalised and either

(a) amortised over its useful economic life; or
(b) where useful economic life exceeds 20 years, or it is not amortised, its value must be reviewed annually for impairment.

Example 20.3 H GROUP *Consolidated balance sheet at 31 December 1998: Goodwill treated as a fixed asset*

	£000
Fixed assets:	
Goodwill	72
Freehold land and buildings	270
Plant and machinery	430
	772
Net current assets	560
	1,332
Ordinary share capital	500
Reserves	532
Ordinary shareholders' funds	1,032
Minority interests	80
H's 10% ULS	120
S's 7% Debenture	100
	1,332

KINGFISHER *Extract from the 1999 accounts [Edited]*

Note 1. Accounting policies (change of)

. . .

Goodwill and intangible assets

Following the introduction of FRS 10, the Group has changed its accounting policy for goodwill and intangible assets.

Intangible assets, which comprise goodwill arising on acquisitions and acquired licences and copyrights, are stated at cost less amortisation.

Prior to 31 January 1998

- Goodwill arising on all acquisitions prior to 31 January 1998 *remains eliminated against reserves.*
- This goodwill will be charged in the profit and loss account on subsequent disposal of the business to which it relates.

After 31 January 1998

- Purchased goodwill arising on acquisitions after 31 January 1998 is treated as an asset on the balance sheet.
- Where goodwill is regarded as having a limited estimated useful economic life it is amortised on a systematic basis over its life.
- Where goodwill is regarded as having an indefinite life it is not amortised. The estimated useful economic life is regarded as indefinite where goodwill is capable of continued measurement and the durability of the acquired business can be demonstrated.
- Where goodwill is not amortised, an annual impairment review will be performed and any impairment will be charged to the profit and loss account.
- All acquisitions since 31 January 1998 are considered by the directors to have an estimated useful economic life of 20 years, with the exception of BUT S.A.
- The Group's acquisition of additional shares in BUT S.A. gave rise to goodwill of £132.8m. The directors consider that BUT S.A. has a proven ability to maintain its market leadership . . . BUT S.A.'s record since 1972, when it commenced trading, has been one of consistent growth in both turnover and operating profits. Accordingly the goodwill is not amortised . . . the financial statements depart from the requirement of amortising goodwill over a finite period, as required by the Companies Act. Instead an annual impairment test is undertaken and any impairment that is identified will be charged to the profit and loss account.
- Goodwill arising on purchase of pharmacy businesses is amortised over a useful economic life of 20 years. . . .

Note 31. Reserves

The cumulative amount of goodwill written off directly to reserves in respect of undertakings still within the Group is £1,541.2m (1998: £1,541.2m).

Balance sheet as at 30 January 1999

Group	Notes	1999	£m 1998
Fixed assets			
Goodwill		264.5	–
Other intangible assets		2.8	–
Total intangible assets	13	267.3	–
Tangible assets	14	2,885.4	1,816.9

. . .

REED ELSEVIER *Annual review 1998*

Accounting policies
Goodwill and intangible assets

On the acquisition of a subsidiary, associate, joint venture or business, the purchase consideration is allocated between the underlying net tangible and intangible assets on a fair value basis, with any excess purchase consideration representing goodwill.

In accordance with the new financial reporting standard FRS 10 *Goodwill and intangible assets*, acquired goodwill and intangible assets are now capitalised and amortised systematically over their estimated useful lives up to a maximum period of 20 years. In prior years goodwill was written off directly to reserves on acquisition, whereas intangible assets were capitalised and not amortised, subject to impairment review. This new policy has been applied retrospectively and prior year figures have been restated accordingly . . .

Under transitional arrangements, any goodwill which had previously been written off to reserves could remain there, until such time as the related business is disposed of (the policy adopted by KINGFISHER).

Companies have, however, the option to reinstate as an asset old goodwill previously written off to reserves. If they do this, either all 'old goodwill' or all 'post-FRS 7 goodwill' should be reinstated. REED ELSEVIER (shown above and on the next page) reinstated all old goodwill, amortised as it would have been had the new accounting policy always applied.

REED ELSEVIER *Annual review 1998*

Note 14. Fixed assets – intangible assets . . .

Cost (£m)	Goodwill	*Intangible assets*	Total
At 1 January 1998 as originally reported	–	2,751	2,751
Prior year adjustment (adoption of FRS 10)	1,980	–	1,980
At 1 January 1998 as restated	1,980	2,751	4,731
Acquisitions	866	362	1,228
Transfer from investments in joint ventures	82	68	150
Disposals of businesses	(113)	(220)	(333)
Exchange translation differences	12	12	24
At 31 December 1998	2,827	2,973	5,800
Accumulated amortisation and depreciation			
At 1 January 1998 as originally reported	–	250	250
Prior year adjustment (adoption of FRS 10)	909	900	1,809
At 1 January 1998 as restated	909	1,150	2,059
Transfer from investments in joint ventures	7	5	12
Disposals of businesses	(71)	(130)	(201)
Amortisation of goodwill and intangible assets	157	166	323
Exchange translation differences	6	3	9
At 31 December 1998	1,008	1,194	2,202
Net book amount			
At 1 January 1998 as restated	1,071	1,601	2,672
At 31 December 1998	1,819	1,779	3,598

As can be seen the effect on the balance sheet is significant. But so is that on profits:

REED ELSEVIER *Extract from combined profit and loss statement for the year ended 31 December 1998*

£m	1998 *Before exceptional items and amortisation*	*Exceptional items and amortisation*	Total
Gross profit	2,099	–	2,099
Net operating expenses before exceptional items and amortisation . . .	(1,304)	–	(1,304)
Exceptional items . . .	–	(79)	(79)
Amortisation of goodwill and intangible assets	–	(323)	(323)
Operating profit before joint ventures	795	(402)	393

As a consequence, few companies reinstated pre-FRS 10 goodwill. As a result, UK GAAP remain out of step with US GAAP (see Chapter 30); and ratios based on either earnings (which are after *some* amortisation of goodwill) or net asset values (which may include all goodwill (amortised) or some goodwill (and the cut off date will vary from company to company) or no goodwill (if it is all prior to FRS 10)) are distorted.

The consolidated profit and loss account

Consolidated profit and loss accounts follow the same pattern as described for single companies at the beginning of Chapter 16, except that if the group contains partially owned subsidiaries, the minority interests in the profits of those subsidiaries have to be deducted at the after-tax level. Continuing with our example (see page 161) of H owning four-fifths of the £250,000 ordinary share capital of S, let us suppose that at the beginning of 1997, S issued 30,000 £1 7% preference shares to a third party as part payment for a fixed asset, and that the pre-tax profits and tax charges of H and S for that year were as shown here:

	H	S	Total
	£	£	£
Profit before tax	72,000	51,200	123,200
Corporation Tax at 25%	18,000	12,800	30,800
Profit after tax	54,000	38,400	92,400

The combined pre-tax profit, tax and profit after tax will be shown in the group's consolidated profit and loss account.

Calculation of minority interests
The minority interests in the profits after tax of S will then be computed as follows:

	S	Minority interests
	£	£
Profit before tax	51,200	
less Corporation Tax	12,800	
Profit after tax	38,400	
less Preference dividends	2,100	2,100
Attributable to ordinary shareholders	36,300 × ¹/₅ = 7,260	
Minority interests total		9,360

It is this sum of £9,360 which will be deducted as 'minority interests' from the profit after tax in the consolidated profit and loss account.

Appropriations of the subsidiary
Suppose, for instance, that S proposed a single ordinary dividend of 4p for 1997. Then the profit attributable to S's ordinary shareholders would be appropriated as follows:

	Total	Minorities	H
Attributable	36,300	7,260	29,040
Proposed dividend of 4.0p per share	10,000	2,000	8,000
Retentions	26,300	5,260	21,040

H's share of the proposed dividend (£8,000) would also appear, as dividends receivable, in the holding company's accounts, and the two figures would cancel out on consolidation. The dividends payable to minority shareholders (£2,000) would be charged (behind the scenes) against the minority interests deducted on consolidation, and the minorities' share of the retentions (£9,360 – £2,100 preference dividends – £2,000 ordinary dividends = £5,260)

added to the consolidated balance sheet item 'minority interests'.

The group profit and loss account
Suppose H Group declared dividends of £25,000 for the year. The group profit and loss account would then show:

	£
Profit before tax	123,200
Taxation	(30,800)
Profit after tax	92,400
Minority interests	(9,360)
	83,040
Dividends	(25,000)
Retentions	58,040

Retained profit
The group's retained profit of £58,040 would be carried forward partly in the holding company's accounts:

	£
H's profit after tax	54,000
H's dividends from S	8,000
less Dividends paid by H	25,000
	37,000

The remainder, £21,040 (see column opposite), would be carried forward in S's accounts, being H's share of S's retentions.

Some companies show where the retained profits of the group are being carried forward either in the profit and loss account or in a note to the accounts.

Unrealised profits on stocks
It frequently happens that one group company supplies another company within the group with goods in the ordinary course of trade; indeed, this sort of trading link may often be at the very heart of the existence of the group in the first place. But where one group company has made a profit on the supply of goods to another group company and those goods, or some of them, remain in stock at the end of the accounting year, a problem arises and, although nothing can normally be gleaned from the accounts, the procedure for consolidation is designed to prevent a group's profits being artificially inflated by sales within the group.

Parent company's own balance sheet
Subsidiaries are normally shown in the parent company's own balance sheet at cost less any amounts

written off, but some companies show them at their underlying net asset value, i.e. they use the equity method of accounting (see pages 175–6), which includes the investment at cost plus the parent company's share of the post-acquisition retained profits and reserves.

Parent company's own profit and loss account

Under Section 230 (3) of the Companies Act 1985, the parent company's profit and loss account may be omitted from the consolidated accounts providing the parent company's balance sheet shows the parent company's profit or loss for the year, as is shown by TT GROUP below. In practice one seldom if ever sees the parent company's own profit and loss account.

TT GROUP *Extract from note 21 to the 1998 accounts*

In accordance with the exemption allowed by Section 230 of the Companies Act 1985, the Company has not presented its own profit and loss account. Of the profit available for appropriation, the sum of £24.4m (1997 – £19.3m) has been dealt with in the financial statements of the Company.

Accounting periods and dates

The financial statements of all subsidiary undertakings to be used in preparing the consolidated financial statements should, wherever practicable, be prepared to the same financial year end and for the same accounting period as those of the parent

undertaking of the group (FRS 2, para. 42).

Where the financial year of a subsidiary undertaking differs from that of the parent of the group, interim financial statements should be prepared to the date of the parent's year end. If it is not practicable to use such interim financial statements, the financial statements of the subsidiary for its last financial year should be used, providing that year ended not more than three months before the relevant year end of the parent undertaking of the group.

Further statutory requirements

Emoluments of directors

Directors' emoluments and other details required by the Companies Act 1985 only have to be shown in respect of directors of the parent company, but all their remuneration from the group has to be included (e.g. fees they receive for being directors of subsidiaries).

These requirements have to be met by each subsidiary in its own accounts, which are not normally published but do have to be filed at Companies House.

Information on subsidiaries

The Companies Act 1985 requires a company to disclose the following for each of its subsidiaries:

*   the subsidiary's name;
*   if incorporated outside Great Britain, the country of incorporation;
*   if unincorporated, the address of its principal place of business.

Chapter 21

ACQUISITIONS AND MERGERS

INTRODUCTION

As we explained in Chapter 20, in the UK there are two methods of accounting for acquisitions (or business combinations):

1. Acquisition accounting, and
2. Merger accounting.

The rules for both methods are set out in FRS 6 *Acquisitions and mergers*, which restricts the use of merger accounting to rare situations (see page 172).

Acquisition accounting should be used for the majority of business combinations where a party can be identified as having the role of an acquirer.

ACQUISITION ACCOUNTING

In Chapter 20 we also considered the principles of acquisition accounting. We look now at some of the detailed requirements of financial reporting standards.

Year of acquisition or disposal
In acquisition accounting, when a subsidiary is acquired (or disposed of) during the accounting period, the results of the subsidiary are included from the effective date of acquisition (or to the effective date of disposal), e.g. RMC GROUP:

RMC GROUP *Extract from accounting policies 1999*

Group accounts
The Group accounts comprise the audited accounts of the parent company and all its subsidiary undertakings made up to 31st December . . .

Where subsidiary undertakings, joint ventures and associated undertakings are acquired or disposed of during the year, the Group profit and loss account reflects their results from the date of acquisition or to the date of disposal.

Purchased goodwill
FRS 10 defines purchased goodwill as the *difference* between

(a) the cost of the business that has been acquired, and
(b) the fair value of its identifiable assets less liabilities.

Purchased goodwill is sometimes described as *'Goodwill on consolidation'*.

Determining fair values
FRS 7, *Fair values in acquisition accounting*, contains detailed rules for arriving at the cost of the business, as well as the fair value of the assets and liabilities.

Fair value rules

The fair value rules are:

- ***Tangible fixed asset***:
  - (a) market value, if assets similar in type and condition are bought and sold on a open market; or
  - (b) depreciated replacement cost, reflecting the acquired business's normal buying process and the sources of supply and prices available to it. The fair value should not exceed the asset's recoverable amount.
- ***Intangible fixed asset*** recognised in the accounts: replacement cost, normally its estimated market value.
- ***Stocks***, including commodity stocks:
  - (a) where trading is on a market in which the acquired business participates as both a buyer and a seller – current market prices.
  - (b) other stocks, and work in progress: – should be valued at the lower of replacement cost and net realisable value.
- ***Quoted investments***: market price, adjusted if necessary for unusual price fluctuations or for the size of the holdings.

The fair values of monetary assets and liabilities (including provisions) should take into account the amounts expected to be received or paid, and their timing and, if significant, be discounted to present value.

Special rules apply to businesses held exclusively with a view to resale.

Assets at the date of acquisition

The identifiable assets less liabilities of the acquired business (affecting the consequent goodwill calculation) should be those that existed at the date of acquisition, and should *not* reflect

- (a) increases or decreases in asset values/liabilities resulting from the acquirer's intentions or future actions;
- (b) impairments or other changes resulting from events subsequent to the acquisition;
- (c) provisions for future operating losses or re-organisation costs to be incurred as a result of the acquisition (even if these were reflected in the purchase price).

The message from FRS 7 is clear – the effects of the above should be reflected in the group's operating profit/loss for the period after acquisition.

Provisional fair values

If possible, the identification and valuation of assets and liabilities should be completed by the date on which the accounts relating to the year of acquisition are approved by the directors.

Where this is not possible, *provisional* valuations should be made. If necessary, these should be amended in the accounts of the following year with a corresponding adjustment to goodwill.

For years after that, any adjustment should be dealt with as a revaluation adjustment unless it relates to the correction of a fundamental error.

Subsequent disposals

The relevant date of disposal of a subsidiary is the date when the former parent relinquishes control.

The group's gain or loss on disposal is calculated by comparing the carrying amount of the net assets, including any related goodwill not previously written off through the profit and loss account, with any proceeds received.

Pre-FRS 10 goodwill that has been written off direct to reserves *must* be included.

Disclosure requirements

The disclosure requirements for business combinations accounted for as acquisitions are listed in paras. 23–35 of FRS 6 *Acquisitions and mergers*.

If the acquisition is a '*substantial acquisition*', there are further disclosure requirements (FRS 6 paras. 36–37).

Substantial acquisitions

For *listed* companies a '*substantial acquisition*' is a Class 1 or Super Class 1 transaction (see page 221). For *other* companies it is, broadly, where the net assets or operating profits of the acquired company exceed 15% of those of the acquirer.

Example of a substantial acquisition

For example, in 1999 WASTE RECYCLING made two major acquisitions from the Kelda group (formerly Yorkshire Water), which tripled Waste's turnover.

A note to Waste's accounts on the larger of the two acquisitions, shown opposite, illustrates the main disclosures for a substantial acquisition:

[A] A summarised profit and loss account of the acquired company from the beginning of its financial year to the date of acquisition.

[B] The post-acquisition results of the acquired company should be disclosed separately, where they have a major impact.

[C] The profit after tax and minorities for the acquired company's previous financial year.

[D] A table of book values and fair value adjustments, analysed as shown opposite.

[E] Where fair values can only be determined on a provisional basis at the end of the accounting period, this should be stated, and the reasons should be given.

[F] The amount of '*Purchased goodwill*' arising (in Waste's case £158.6 million).

[G] Details of the consideration given, including any deferred or contingent consideration (none in Waste's case).

[H] Waste will have to disclose and explain any subsequent material adjustments.

Post balance sheet events

Where a material acquisition or disposal takes place shortly after the balance sheet date, it will be a post balance sheet event requiring disclosure under SSAP 17 *Accounting for post balance sheet events*. For example the cement company BLUE CIRCLE:

BLUE CIRCLE *Note 29 to the 2000 accounts*

[Replacing BLUE CIRCLE 1998 example]
Note 29 Post balance sheet events
On 8 January 2001, it was announced that Blue Circle and Lafarge had agreed the terms on which Lafarge SA ... proposes to acquire Blue Circle Industries plc.

A circular setting out details of the proposed acquisition was sent to shareholders on 24 January 2001 and the acquisition was approved at shareholders meetings on 19 February 2001.

Shareholders will receive 495 pence for each Blue Circle share. The acquisition is subject to various conditions, including regulatory clearance from competition authorities in the US, Canada and the European Union.
...

WASTE RECYCLING *Extract from note to the financial statements, year ended 31 December 1999*

Note 28 Acquisitions

(a) Yorkshire Environmental Global Waste Management (YEGWM)

On 29 January 1999 the Company acquired the business of YEGWM for a total consideration of £181,278,000. Additionally, acquisition expenses of £1,601,000 were incurred. The results of YEGWM were as follows:

	[B] Date of acquisition to 31 December 1999 £000	**[A]** 1 January 1999 to date of acquisition £000
Turnover	59,962	6,535
Cost of sales	(44,743)	(5,540)
Administrative expenses	(3,751)	(706)
Operating profit	11,468	289
Taxation		(98)
Profit after taxation		191
Minority interests		(59)
Retained profit		132

[C] The profit after taxation for the preceding financial year ended 31 December 1998 was £4,709,000.

The following table analyses the book value of the major categories of assets and liabilities acquired:

[D]

	Book value at date of acquisition £000	*Accounting policy alignment* £000	*Revaluation adjustments* £000	**[E]** *Provisional fair value of net assets* £000
Tangible fixed assets	48,372	(2,336)	(5,403)[1]	40,633
Debtors	11,147	–	(131)[2]	11,016
Cash balances	8,217	–	–	8,217
Creditors and accruals	(11,810)	–	(1,465)[3]	(13,275)
Borrowings	(10,850)	–	–	(10,850)
Deferred taxation	2,594	(2,709)	–	(115)
Provisions	(13,452)	2,616	–	(10,836)
Minority interests	(553)	–	–	(553)
Net assets acquired	33,665	(2,429)	(6,999)	24,237
[F] Goodwill				158,642
Consideration				182,879

Satisfied by

[G] Shares	181,278
Acquisition costs	1,601
	182,879

[1] This adjustment represents a revision of the book values of landfill sites to reflect market royalty rates and the permanent impairment of the values of certain other fixed assets.

[2] Additional bad debt provision.

[3] Additional corporation tax provision and accruals for additional liabilities identified.

[H] ... The provisional fair values represent the Directors' current estimates of the net assets acquired. However, in accordance with FRS7, the values may be revised as further information becomes available.

MERGER ACCOUNTING

Introduction

With the introduction of FRS 6 *Acquisitions and Mergers*, the use of merger accounting has become quite rare. The FRS restricts its use to business combinations where, by meeting strict criteria (see box in the next column), the two companies concerned can demonstrate that the combination is a genuine merger, not a takeover by one of the other, e.g. BP's merger with AMOCO, illustrated on the next page.

The mechanics of merger accounting

Under merger accounting, aptly called *'pooling of interests'* in the United States, the following occur:

1. The assets and liabilities of both companies are incorporated into the group accounts at book value. They are not required to be adjusted to fair value on consolidation, though appropriate adjustments are made to achieve uniformity of accounting policies.
2. The pre-acquisition reserves of the merging companies are not capitalised, but are available to the enlarged group.
3. The shares issued as consideration are recorded at their nominal value (so there is no share premium, and no goodwill arises on consolidation).
4. If the total nominal value of the shares issued is more than the total value of the shares of the merged company, the difference is deducted from group reserves. If the total value is less, the shortfall becomes a non-distributable reserve. The merger expenses are not included as part of this adjustment, but charged through the profit and loss account.
5. At the subsequent year end, the consolidated profit and loss account takes in the turnover, costs and profits of all merging companies for a full year.

Profits in the year of merger

The consolidated profit and loss account should include the profits (or losses) of all merged entities for the entire period, i.e. without adjustment for that part of the period prior to the merger. Corresponding amounts should be presented as if the companies had been combined throughout the previous period.

FRS 6 extends the requirements of the Companies Act 1985 somewhat. In particular, it requires:

MERGER ACCOUNTING
Criteria

Under FRS 6, a business combination should be accounted for using merger accounting *if, and only if*:

(a) the use of merger accounting is not prohibited by the Companies Act 1985; and
(b) the combination meets certain criteria:

  (i) no party to the combination is portrayed as either acquirer or acquired;
  (ii) all parties to the combination participate in establishing the management structure for the combined entity and in selecting the management personnel, and such decisions are made on the basis of a consensus;
  (iii) the relative sizes of the combining entities are not so disparate that one party effectively dominates the combined entity merely by virtue of its relative size;
  (iv) the consideration must be all or virtually all equity;
  (v) no equity shareholder of any of the combining entities must retain any material interest in only one part of the combined entity.

---

1. An analysis of the principal components of the current year's profit and loss account and statements of recognised gains and losses into:

  (i) amounts relating to the merged entity for the period after the merger; and
  (ii) for each party to the merger, amounts relating to the period up to the merger.

2. An analysis between the parties to the merger of the principal components of the profit and loss account and statements of total recognised gains and losses for the previous financial year.
3. The composition and fair value of the consideration given by the issuing company and its subsidiary undertakings.
4. The nature and amount of significant accounting adjustments made to the net assets of any party to the merger to achieve consistency of accounting policies.
5. A statement of the adjustments to consolidated reserves resulting from the merger.

BP AMOCO *Brief extract from 1988 accounts*

Note 45 Merger accounting

The financial statements have been prepared using the merger method of accounting in relation to the merger of BP and Amoco.

Under merger accounting the results and cash flows of BP and Amoco are combined from the beginning of the financial period in which the merger occurred . . .

The merger became effective on 31 December 1998. Income statements for each company for the year ended 31 December 1998 are presented below, together with their respective balance sheets at 31 December 1998.

Income statement		$ million
	Amoco	*BP*
	UK GAAP	
Historical cost profit	1,582	4,314
Interest expense	473	580
Profit before taxation	1,109	3,734
Taxation . . .		

Balance sheet		
Fixed assets		
Intangible assets	735	2,302
Tangible assets	23,345	31,120
Investments . . .		

Statement of total recognised gains and losses		
Profit for the year	732	2,528
Currency translation differences	30	25
Total recognized gains and losses	762	2,553

The actual note is more than three pages long, giving ample information on the merger.

Comparison of accounting methods

Finally in this chapter, Example 21.1 below shows the balance sheet of a business combination produced firstly by merger accounting and secondly by acquisition accounting.

Example 21.1 Business combination – a comparison of merger accounting and acquisition accounting

Before the combination

At 31 December 2000 the balance sheets of companies A and B were:

	A	*B*
	£000	£000
Ordinary share capital	800	80
Reserves	280	340
	1,080	420
Net assets	1,080	420

Company A combined with Company B

Company A issues 200,000 new A £1 ordinary shares (standing at 300p each, a premium of 200p above par value) in exchange for the entire share capital of B.

In acquisition accounting, the fair value of the net assets of B is assessed as £480,000, compared with the book value of £420,000, an increase (*uplift*) of £60,000. In merger accounting there is no fair value adjustment.

After the businesses had combined

The consolidated balance sheet of A Group (A + B) would appear, under the two different methods of accounting, as:

	Merger		**Acquisition**	
	Note	£000	Note	£000
Ordinary £1 shares	1	1,000	1	1,000
Share premium account		–	2	400
Distributable reserves	3	500	4	280
		1,500		1,680
Net assets (excl. goodwill)	5	1,500	6	1,560
Goodwill			7	120
		1,500		1,680

Notes:

1. Company A's original £800,000 share capital plus the £200,000 shares A issued.
2. The premium of 200p per share on the 200,000 shares Company A issued.
3. Computed as follows:

	£000
distributable reserves of A	280
distributable reserves of B	340
	620

less the excess of the nominal value of the shares issued (£200,000) over the nominal value of the shares in B (£80,000) — (120)

500

4. Distributable reserves = reserves of Company A (£280,000), plus the increase in Company B's reserves since acquisition (£Nil), as the acquisition has only just taken place).
5. Net assets of Company A (£1,080,000) plus net assets of Company B (£420,000).
6. Under acquisition accounting, the net assets of B were taken at fair value of £480,000, rather than at book value of £420,000.
7. Goodwill is the amount by which the cost of the investment (£600,000) exceeds the fair value of the net assets acquired (£480,000).

Chapter 22

ASSOCIATES, JOINT VENTURES AND RELATED PARTIES

INTRODUCTION

Companies Act definitions

The Companies Act 1985 includes the terms: a *participating interest in an undertaking*, and an *associated undertaking*.

Undertakings include partnerships and unincorporated associations carrying on a trade or business as well as companies.

An *interest* includes convertible securities and options as well as shares.

A *participating interest* is an interest held by the investing group or company on a long-term basis to secure a contribution to its activities by the exercise of control or influence. A holding by group companies of 20% or more of the shares of an undertaking is presumed to be a participating interest unless the contrary is shown.

An *associated undertaking* is an undertaking (other than a subsidiary or a joint venture) in which the investing group or company has a participating interest and over whose operating and financial policy it exercises a *significant* influence.

Accounting standards

FRS9 *Associates and joint ventures* contains the rules on accounting for associates and joint ventures.

It recognises five types of interest:

1. A subsidiary (which we considered in Chapters 20 and 21; see also FRS 2);
2. a joint arrangement that is not an entity;
3. a joint venture;
4. an associate;
5. a simple investment (which we considered in Chapters 9 and 12).

This chapter deals with 2, 3 and 4.

Joint arrangement that is not an entity

Where two or more entities, e.g. companies, participate in an arrangement to carry on part of their trade, that arrangement falls under this heading unless it carries on a trade or business of its own.

A joint arrangement will not be an entity if it is no more than a cost- or risk-sharing means of carrying out a process in the participants' trades or businesses – for example a joint marketing or distribution network or a shared production facility.

A joint arrangement carrying out a single project (as, for example, occurs in the construction industry) tends to fall under this head, but the nature of such a joint arrangement may change over time – for example, a pipeline operated as a joint arrangement that initially provided a service only directly to the participants may develop into a pipeline business providing services to others.

Each party to a joint arrangement that is not an entity should account for its own share of the assets, liabilities and cash flows in the joint arrangement, measured according to the terms of that arrangement.

Joint venture

Where the investor holds a long-term interest and shares control under a contractual arrangement that arrangement is referred to as a joint venture.

The joint venture agreement can override the rights normally conferred by ownership interests with the effect that:

- acting together, the venturers can control the venture and there are procedures for such joint action;
- each venturer has (implicitly or explicitly) a veto over strategic policy decisions.

DIAGEO *Extract from 2000 accounts*

Consolidated profit and loss account

			Year ended 30 June 2000			Year ended 30 June 1999		
		Notes	Before goodwill and exceptional items £ million	Goodwill and exceptional items £ million	Total £ million	Before goodwill and exceptional items £ million	Goodwill and exceptional items £ million	Total £ million
Turnover	[A]	2	11,870	–	11,870	11,795	–	11,795
Operating costs		4	(9,890)	(198)	(10,088)	(9,892)	(386)	(10,278)
Operating profit		2	1,980	(198)	1,782	1,903	(386)	1,517
Share of profits of associates	[B]	6	198	(3)	195	188	(8)	180
Trading profit	[C]		2,178	(201)	1,977	2,091	(394)	1,697
Disposal of fixed assets			–	5	5	–	(10)	(10)
Exceptional items	[D]	7	–	(168)	(168)	–	104	104
Interest payable (net)	[E]	8	(363)	–	(363)	(324)	–	(324)
Pre-tax profit			1,815	(364)	1,451	1,767	(300)	1,467
Tax	[F]	9	(476)	75	(401)	(463)	23	(440)
Profit after tax			1,339	(289)	1,050	1,304	(277)	1,027

Note 6 Associates

		2000 £ million	1999 £ million
Share of operating profit before exceptional items	[B]	198	188
Share of interest payable (net)	[E]	(3)	(3)
Share of exceptional items	[D]	(3)	(8)
Share of taxation	[F]	(72)	(72)
Equity minority interests		(2)	(2)
Dividends received by the group	[G]	(64)	(58)
Share of profits retained by associates	[H]	54	45

. . .

Consolidated statement of total recognised gains and losses

		Year ended 30 June 2000 £ million	Year ended 30 June 1999 £ million
Profit for the year – group		858	837
Profit for the year – associates	[I]	118	105
		976	942

Exchange adjustments . . .

Consolidated balance sheet

			30 June 2000 £ million	30 June 1999 £ million
		Notes		
Fixed assets				
Intangible assets			5,289	5,188
Tangible assets			3,078	3,178
Investments	[J]	14	1,496	1,354
			9,863	9,720

Current assets . . .

ASSOCIATES

Definition

Where the investor holds a *participating interest* and exercises *significant influence* the entity is an *associate*. This covers cases where the investor

- has a *long-term interest* and
- is actively involved, and influential, in the direction of its investee through its participation in policy decisions covering the aspects of policy relevant to the investor, including decisions on strategic issues such as

  (a) the expansion or contraction of the business, participation in other entities or changes in products, markets and activities of its investee;
  (b) determining the balance between dividend and reinvestment.

The investor should include its associates in its consolidated financial statements using what is called *the equity method* of accounting.

The equity method

Under the equity method:

1. **Turnover does *not* include the turnover of associates.**

See [A] in the DIAGEO consolidated profit and loss account opposite.

Where a group wishes to give an indication of the relative size of associates, it may give the associates' turnover in a note, or include it in an overall figure, provided the group's share of its associates' turnover is clearly distinguished.

For example, RIO TINTO includes its share of associates' (and joint ventures') turnover in *Gross turnover*, and then deducts them both to arrive at *Consolidated turnover*:

RIO TINTO *Extract from 1999 accounts*

Profit and loss account	1999 £m	1998 £m
Gross turnover (including share of joint ventures and associates)	**5,747**	5,562
Share of joint ventures' turnover	**(931)**	(902)
Share of associates' turnover	**(373)**	(370)
Consolidated turnover	**4,443**	4,290

. . .

---

2. The group's share of its associates' operating results should be included immediately after group operating profit, [B] opposite.
3. Any amortisation or write-down of goodwill arising in associates should then be charged [DIAGEO had none].
4. The group's share of any exceptional items [D] should be shown separately. DIAGEO does so in a note:

DIAGEO *Extract from note to 2000 accounts*

Note 7 Exceptional items

. . .

Associates The £3 million associate exceptional charge is in respect of reorganization costs at Ice Cream Partners (1999 – £8 million in respect of East African Breweries Limited).

---

5. Below the level of trading profit [C], the group's share of the relevant amount for associates should be included within the amounts for the group, but may be shown separately in the notes: Exceptional items [D] and Note 7 (above); Interest payable [E] and Note 8 (not shown); Taxation [F] and Note 9 (not shown).

   DIAGEO also shows details in *Note 6 Associates*, opposite, together with *Dividends received by the Group* [G] and *Share of profits retained by associates* [H].

    A group's share of associates'profits is only available to the group when it is paid out by the associates as dividends.

6. The group's share of the gains and losses of its associates should be included in the *Consolidated statement of total recognised gains and losses*, and should be shown separately under each heading, if material. See [I] opposite.

   Note that [I] = [G] + [H].

7. In the *Consolidated balance sheet* the group's share of the net assets of its associates should be included, and separately disclosed. Diageo has included it in *Investments* [J] opposite, giving details in Note 14, shown on page 177.

DIAGEO *Extract from 2000 accounts*

Note 14 Fixed assets – Investments

	Investment in associates £ million	Total £ million
Cost		
At 30 June 1999	1,114	1,440
Exchange adjustments	(14)	(12)
Additions	80	222
Share of retained profits	54	54
Disposals	(1)	(128)
At 30 June 2000	1,233	1,576
Provisions/amortisation		
At 30 June 1999	1	86
Amortisation of own shares	–	16
Created	2	2
Disposals	–	(24)
At 30 June 2000	3	80
Net book value		
At 30 June 2000	1,230	1,496
At 30 June 1999	1,113	1,354

8. The *cash flow statement* should include cash flows between the group and its associates, **[K]** and **[L]**:

DIAGEO *Extract from 2000 accounts*

Consolidated cash flow statement

		2000 £m	1999 £m
Net cash inflow from operating activities		2,043	1,966
Dividends received from associates	**[K]**	64	58
. . .			
Free cash flow		864	373
Purchase of subsidiaries		(151)	(380)
Sale of subsidiaries and businesses		638	330
Sale of associates	**[L]**	–	171
. . .			

9. Goodwill arising on the group's acquisition of its associates, less any amortisation or write-down, should be included in the carrying amount for associates but should be disclosed separately.

Interest held on a long-term basis

For an interest to be an associate the investor must have a long-term interest, i.e. the interest must be held other than exclusively with a view to subsequent resale. An interest held exclusively with a view to subsequent resale is:

(a) an interest for which a purchaser has been identified or is being sought, and which is reasonably expected to be disposed of within approximately one year of its date of acquisition; or

(b) an interest that was acquired as a result of the enforcement of a security, unless the interest has become part of the continuing activities of the group or the holder acts as if it intends the interest to become so.

Significant influence

For an investment to be an associate, its investor must exercise (not simply *be in a position to exercise*) significant influence over the investee's operating and financial policies. The investor needs an agreement or understanding, formal or informal, with its associate to provide the basis for its significant influence. An investor exercising significant influence will be directly involved in the operating and financial policies of its associate rather than passively awaiting the outcome of its investee's policies.

Active involvement in the operating and financial policies of an associate requires inter alia that *the investor should have a voice in decisions on strategic issues* such as determining the balance between dividend and reinvestment.

The investor's involvement in its associate is usually achieved through nomination to the board of directors (or its equivalent) but may result from any arrangement that allows the investor to participate effectively in policy-making decisions.

It is unlikely that an investor can exercise significant influence unless it has a substantial basis of voting power. A holding of 20 per cent or more of the voting rights in another entity *suggests, but does not ensure*, that the investor exercises significant influence over that entity (FRS 9, para. 16).

JOINT VENTURES

Definition

Where the investor holds a long-term interest and shares control under a contractual arrangement that arrangement is referred to as a *joint venture*.

The joint venture agreement can override the rights normally conferred by ownership interests with the effect that:

- acting together, the venturers can control the venture and there are procedures for such joint action;
- each venturer has (implicitly or explicitly) a veto over strategic policy decisions.

There is usually a procedure for settling disputes between venturers and, possibly, for terminating the joint venture.

The venturer should use the *gross equity method* to account for the joint venture.

Gross equity method

Under what is termed the gross equity method, all the amounts included under the equity method (see page 175) have to be shown and, in addition:

(a) *in the consolidated profit and loss account*, the venturer's share of their operating profit, **[A]** in the GREAT UNIVERSAL STORES (GUS) illustration below, distinguished from that of the group, and

(b) *on the face of the group balance sheet*, the venturer's share of the gross assets, **[B]** in the GUS illustration below, and the gross liabilities **[C]** of its joint ventures.

Had it not been for the requirement to use the gross equity method, GUS would have shown the investment in BL Universal in 2000 as £129.4m (1999 £110.2m) **[D]** rather than spelling out the very substantial gross assets and liabilities involved.

This was often the case where there was a joint venture between the owners of land and builders/developers.

Where the venturer conducts a major part of its business through joint ventures, it may show fuller information provided all amounts are distinguished from those of the group (see Note 15 on the next page).

GREAT UNIVERSAL STORES *Extracts from the 2000 accounts*

Consolidated profit and loss account

	Notes	2000 £m	1999 £m
Operating profit – continuing operations		420.7	538.0
Share of operating profit of BL Universal PLC (Joint venture)	**[A]**	**33.9**	**31.9**
Share of operating profit of associated undertakings		11.3	22.1
Profit on sale of fixed asset investments		11.0	–
Trading profit		477.0	592.0

. . .

Group balance sheet

	Notes	2000 £m	2000 £m	1999 £m	1999 £m
Fixed assets					
Goodwill			1,437.6		1,503.5
Other intangible assets			139.1		123.4
Tangible assets			834.7		799.0
Investment in joint venture					
Share of gross assets	**[B]**	**535.0**		**526.9**	
Share of gross liabilities	**[C]**	**(405.6)**		**(416.7)**	
	[D]	**129.4**		**110.2**	
Loans to joint venture		**81.5**		**138.8**	
			210.9		**249.0**

. . .

GREAT UNIVERSAL STORES *Extract from a note to the 2000 accounts*

Note 15 Investment in joint venture

	Shares £m	Loans £m	Total £m
Cost or valuation			
At 1 April 1999	110.2	138.8	249.0
Share of profit after taxation	4.9	–	4.9
Share of revaluation of investment properties	14.3	–	14.3
Repayment of loans	–	(57.3)	(57.3)
At 31 March 2000	129.4	81.5	210.9

The Group holds 50% of the ordinary share capital of BL Universal PLC. The Group's share of cumulative retained profits at 31 March 2000 is £12.1m (1999 £7.2m) and its share of turnover for the year, excluded from Group turnover, is £30.9m (1999 £29.5m).

The consolidated balance sheet of BL Universal PLC is as follows:

	2000 £m	1999 £m
Fixed assets	1,043.7	1,046.8
Current assets	26.3	30.8
Creditors – amounts falling due within one year	(90.5)	(80.1)
Creditors – amounts falling due after more than one year	(720.6)	(777.0)
Equity shareholders funds	258.9	220.5
Attributable to the Group	129.4	110.2

Proportional consolidation

It has been a long-standing practice in certain industries (e.g. oil exploration, engineering and construction) to account for certain types of joint venture using proportional consolidation; and this is recognised by the Companies Act. Proportional consolidation involves adding the investor's share of the joint venture to each line of the consolidated profit and loss account and balance sheet. This is not the same as consolidation of, say, a minority interest in a subsidiary, where what is added line by line is the whole of the subsidiary's figure (the minority interest being taken out separately).

IAS 31 (International Accounting Standard 31) *Financial reporting of interests in joint ventures* does not recommend the use of the equity method, on the grounds that proportional consolidation better reflects the substance and economic reality of a venturer's interest in a jointly-controlled entity. The

ASB believes that it can be misleading to represent each venturer's joint control of a joint venture – which allows it to direct the operating and financial policies of the joint venture only with the consent of the other venturers – as being in substance equivalent to its having sole control of its share of each of that entity's assets, liabilities and cash flows. FRS 9 abolishes proportional consolidation, but the accounting treatment for joint arrangements which are not an entity is, arithmetically, virtually identical to proportional consolidation.

Joint ventures are often a means of sharing risks where the risks are particularly high. The amounts involved can be considerable, and the effects of failure – spectacular.

RELATED PARTIES

ASB warning

To quote the Press Notice released by the Accounting Standards Board on the publication of FRED 8 (subsequently superseded by FRS 8, *Related party disclosures*):

> **'Related party transactions have been a feature of a number of financial scandals in recent years, many of which have had in common *the dominance of the company by a powerful chief executive* who was also involved with the related party.'**

The italics are ours. Analysts should be particularly wary of companies where the posts of chairman and of chief executive are held by one person.

Disclosure rules

Schedule 5 of the Companies Act 1985 contains requirements for the disclosure of related undertakings, and Chapters 11 and 12 of the UK Listing Authority's *Listing Rules* define related party transactions and lay down requirements on disclosure.

FRS 8 *Related party disclosures* extends the definition of related parties and increases the disclosure requirement.

It requires a company to disclose all material transactions with related parties, i.e. parties having a relationship (control or influence) that affects the independence of either the reporting entity or the other party and could have a significant effect on the financial position and operating results of the reporting entity. There are a number of exceptions, e.g. pension contributions paid to a pension fund.

Ultimate controlling party

Regardless of whether or not there have been transactions during the year, financial statements must disclose the name of the company's ultimate controlling party. For companies within widely-held public groups, this will be the holding company.

For all other companies, the directors must look beyond the corporate structure to name the controlling interests. There may even be cases where the ultimate controlling party cannot be identified: if so, that fact must be disclosed.

Who is a related party?

The definition of related parties in the FRS is widely drawn. It includes, in addition to the more obvious relationships, such as ultimate and intermediate parent undertakings, subsidiaries and fellow subsidiaries, associates and joint ventures, directors of the reporting entity, pension funds, key management,

members of the close family of any party in this list, and partnerships, companies, trusts and other entities in which any individual in the list or his close family has a controlling interest. Entities managed by the reporting entity under management contracts come within the definition of related parties. 'Close family' includes family members, or members of the same household, 'who may be expected to influence or be influenced . . . '. This clearly includes adult children as well as minors and **would have made the late Robert Maxwell's children related parties**.

Subject to certain exemptions, transactions with related parties have to be disclosed even if no consideration passes.

Related parties are considered in two groups:

- those that are deemed to be related; and
- those where a related party relationship is presumed.

The existence of '*deemed*' related party relationships cannot be rebutted; all material transactions with directors, group members, associates and joint ventures must normally be disclosed.

The existence of a '*presumed*' relationship can be rebutted (and transactions need not therefore be disclosed) if it can be demonstrated that the relevant party does not exercise significant influence over the entity's financial and operating policies.

Disclosures

Not only are related parties potentially numerous, the required disclosures are also lengthy:

(a) names of the transacting related parties;
(b) description of the relationship and the transactions;
(c) amounts involved;
(d) balances with the related parties at the balance sheet date, including provisions made and amounts written off such balances; and
(e) any other elements necessary for an understanding of the financial statements.

Just how useful disclosures about related parties are to the average investor remains to be seen:

1. They are often extremely complicated;
2. Their significance is difficult to assess;
3. Nevertheless, they largely remove the excuse 'if only I had known, I would not have bought into the company'.

Consider, for example, TARSUS GROUP, the consolidated profit and loss account of which is shown on the next page. Start by trying to decide what happened to the group in 1997–98. We will comment and then gradually add further information.

TARSUS GROUP *Consolidated profit and loss account for 1998*

Consolidated profit and loss account for the year ended 31 December 1998

	Notes [A]	Before Exceptional Items £000	Exceptional Items £000	1998 12 months Total £000	1997 8 months Total £000
TURNOVER – acquisitions		4,784	–	4,784	–
– discontinued operations	[B]	702	–	702	563
		5,486	–	5,486	563
Operating costs		(4,562)	(402)	(4,964)	(539)
OPERATING PROFIT – acquisitions		1,008	(402)	606	–
– discontinued operations		(84)	–	(84)	24
		924	(402)	522	24
Goodwill amortisation		(180)	–	(180)	–
		744	(402)	342	24
Loss on disposal of discontinued operation . . .		–	(3,404)	(3,404)	–
Profit/(loss) on ordinary activities before interest . . .		744	(3,806)	(3,062)	24

The first thing that strikes one is that 1997 represented an eight-month accounting period [A]. There is always a reason for an odd length period.

The second thing is that turnover in 1997 consisted entirely of discontinued activities [B]; this means that the entire nature of the business changed completely between 1997 and 1998.

We looked at the directors' report for clues.

TARSUS GROUP *Extract from the directors' report 1998*

Principal activities etc

The principal activity of the Group since 25 June 1998 has been the ownership, organisation and management of exhibitions, conferences, related trade publications and new media.

Prior to 25 June 1998 the Group was principally engaged in design, publishing, marketing and computer related activities. These businesses were sold on 25 June 1998 to Glowdawn Ltd, a company controlled by Philip O'Donnell, a director of the company.

Since 25 June 1998 the Group has developed new and existing events and publications and has acquired business media companies with growth potential.

The related party mention led us to:

TARSUS GROUP *Extract from the directors' report 1998*

Close company status

The company is a close company within the meaning of the Income and Corporation Taxes Act 1988. There has been no change in this respect since the end of the financial year.

And that in turn led us to:

TARSUS GROUP *Extract from the directors' report 1998*

Substantial shareholdings

At 24 February 1999 the Company had been notified of the following discloseable interests in its issued ordinary share capital pursuant to section 198 Companies Act 1985:

	Number of Ordinary Shares	Percentage
N D Buch	6,229,171	26.7
C A Smith	5,000,000	21.4
P O'Donnell	3,828,159	16.4

We studied the note on related party transactions.

TARSUS GROUP *Note 23 to the 1998 accounts*

23. Related party transactions
During the year the Group disposed of the subsidiary BBB Design Ltd to Glowdawn Ltd, a company controlled by P. O'Donnell, a director of the Company. The consideration was £346,000 satisfied in cash. An adjustment may be made to the consideration depending upon the outcome of certain litigation claims as referred to in note . . .

The Company acquired the Labelex Group of companies in June 1998. One of the Labelex vendors was C. Smith, a director of the Company. The initial combined consideration paid was £4.3m and an estimated deferred consideration of £850,000 in respect of the results for the two years ended 31 December 1998. A further deferred consideration payment may be made in 2000 based on the results of Tarsus Publishing Ltd for the year ended 31 December 1999 capped at £250,000. Lease agreements were entered into, at the time of the Labelex acquisition, between Tarsus Exhibitions Ltd, the Labelex Ltd Retirement and Death Benefit Scheme (C. Smith's pension fund) and C. Smith, for the property situated at 129–131 Southlands Road, Bromley. The term of the lease is for five years with an option to break after three years for a combined annual rental of £34,000.

An acquisition search agreement was entered into between the Company and Mayfield Media Strategies Ltd, a company controlled by S. Monnington, a director of the Company. Under the agreement Mayfield Media Strategies Ltd is entitled to receive fees for acquisition search work and further fees for successful acquisitions introduced. The fees paid under this agreement to S. Monnington in 1998 amounted to £33,510.

The fees paid to N. D. Buch (£12,500), S. A. Monnington (£20,000) and B. T. R. Scruby (£3,750) as Directors of the Company are paid to companies controlled by these Directors namely . . .

We are not criticising these accounts. Far from it: they provide a model of modern disclosure, leaving the individual investor to decide whether this is the right group for him.

The note on acquisitions is lengthy, so we reproduce only part of it below. We do so for two reasons: firstly it shows just how much information is available on related party transactions; and secondly it demonstrates how acquisition accounting works including:

(i) the calculation of goodwill in a case where the net assets are negative;
(ii) the accounting adjustments made on an acquisition; and
(iii) a business purchase satisfied by a complex structure of consideration including deferred terms.

TARSUS GROUP *Extract from note 4 to the 1998 accounts*

4. Acquisitions
The Group made three acquisitions during the year for a total consideration of £7,761,000, of which £1,216,000 is deferred. These acquisitions resulted in goodwill of £9,413,000 before amortisation. From the date of acquisition to 31 December 1998 the acquisitions contributed £4,784,000 to turnover and £1,008,000 to operating profit before interest, goodwill amortisation, exceptional items and taxation.

All of these purchases have been accounted for as acquisitions. The fair value of the Group's identifiable assets and liabilities at the acquisition date (including goodwill) were:

Labelex Group

	Book value £000	Consistency of accounting [X] policies £000	Other £000	Total £000
Net liabilities acquired				
Goodwill	175	–	(975)	
Tangible fixed assets	226	(36)	–	190
Cash	1,500	–	–	1,500
Debtors	2,702	–	28	2,730
Creditors	(5,501)	(20)	(20)	(5,541)
Provisions	–	–	(485)	(485)
Negative net assets **[Y]**	(898)	(28)	(680)	(1,606)
Goodwill on acquisition				7,247
				5,641
Satisfied by: Cash				1,450
Shares allotted				2,500
Deferred purchase consideration				1,100
Costs of acquisition				591
				5,641

Chapter 23

FOREIGN EXCHANGE

INTRODUCTION

Floating exchange rates bring both accounting problems and operating problems. This chapter will deal first with the accounting problems, and then look at what companies do to mitigate the adverse effects that currency fluctuations may have on their operations.

ACCOUNTING PROBLEMS

The main problem

The main accounting problem is the rate (or rates) of exchange to be used in translating the accounts of foreign subsidiaries, associates and branches, which are kept in foreign currencies, into sterling when producing the consolidated accounts of a group.

The choice lies between:

(a) the *closing rate*: the spot rate of exchange at the balance sheet date;
(b) the *average rate* of exchange during the period; and
(c) the *historical rate*: the spot rate of exchange at the date of the transaction.

Various methods of translation use different combinations of these rates.

The UK accounting standard

SSAP 20 *Foreign currency translation* is concerned with:

(a) *individual companies* which enter directly into business transactions denominated in foreign currencies, and
(b) *groups* which conduct foreign operations through subsidiaries, associated undertakings or branches whose operations are based in a country other than that of the investing company, and whose accounting records are maintained in a currency other than that of the investing company.

Individual companies

When a company enters into transactions denominated in a foreign currency (i.e. a currency other than that in which the company's accounts are kept), SSAP 20 requires that they should normally be translated at the rate ruling at the date of each transaction, i.e. at the spot rate.

In the accounts of the individual company:

(a) *Non-monetary assets*, e.g. plant and machinery, will already be carried in the accounts in the company's reporting currency, having been translated at the time of acquisition.
(b) *Foreign equity investments*, being non-monetary assets, are normally shown at the rate of exchange ruling at the time the investment was made but, where financed by foreign currency borrowings, they may be translated at the closing rate. Any exchange differences on the investments are then taken to reserves, where the exchange differences on the foreign borrowings may be offset against them (SSAP 20, para. 51).

(c) *Monetary assets and liabilities denominated in foreign currencies* should be translated at the closing rate.

(d) All *exchange differences*, except those in (b) above, should be reported as part of the profit or loss for the year, e.g. differences arising from variations in exchange rates between the dates of invoicing in a foreign currency and the dates of payment. It is comparatively rare for such differences to be 'material' and nothing is normally disclosed.

Example 23.1 illustrates the treatment of four simple transactions involving foreign currency.

Example 23.1 Treatment of foreign transactions by an individual company

ABLE is a UK company whose accounting year ends on 31 December. During the year, Able:

		Rate of exchange
(i)	Purchases hock from a West German company, Weinburger GmbH, on 31 October for DM40,000	£1 = DM3.20
	Pays Weinburger GmbH on 30 November	£1 = DM3.04
	Goods remain in stock at 31 December	
(ii)	Sells cider to Pomme et cie, a French company, for FFr105,000.	£1 = FFr10.50
	Debt remains unpaid at 31 December	
(iii)	Borrows on long-term loan from a Swiss bank SFr750,000 on 1 April	£1 = SFr3.0
(iv)	Purchases plant and machinery from a US company for $480,000 on 15 August	£1 = US$1.50
	Pays on 30 September	£1 = US$1.60

On 31 December exchange rates are:

£1 = DM2.95
£1 = FFr10.00
£1 = SFr2.50
£1 = US$1.55

The company maintains its bank account in sterling and buys or sells foreign exchange as needed on the spot market.

Under SSAP 20 the transactions of Able will be treated as follows:

(i) The purchase will be recorded at the rate ruling on 31 October, £1 = DM3.20. The hock will appear in stock at a book cost of £12,500 and the eventual cost of sales will also be £12,500. When the account is paid, the rate has fallen to £1 = DM3.04, so it is necessary to pay £13,158 to buy the necessary currency.

An exchange loss of £658 (£13,158 − £12,500) will be charged to the profit and loss account for the year.

(ii) The sale is translated at the rate ruling at the date of the transaction, £1 = FFr10.50, giving £10,000. At the end of the year, the debtor is a monetary item and translated at the closing rate, £1 = FFr10.00 = £10,500.

The resulting exchange gain of £500 (£10,500 − £10,000) will be credited to the profit and loss account for the year.

(iii) The loan will initially be translated at the transaction rate of £1 = SFr3.00, i.e. as £250,000. At the year end the loan will be translated at the closing rate £1 = SFr2.50, i.e. as £300,000.

The exchange loss of £50,000 (£300,000 − £250,000) may be treated as 'financing' and *may be* disclosed separately as part of 'other interest receivable/payable and similar income/expense'.

(iv) The fixed asset will be translated at the transaction rate of £1 = $1.50, i.e. as £320,000. The asset will continue to appear at this cost unless it is revalued. Depreciation will be charged on £320,000. Payment for the machine will take (at £1 = $1.60) £300,000.

The gain of £20,000 (£320,000 − £300,000) will be credited to the profit and loss account for the year and will appear separately if considered material.

In Able's statement of accounting policies, the treatment of these purchases and sales would be explained in a note similar to that in ML LABORATORIES' accounts, illustrated below.

ML LABORATORIES *Extract from accounting policies 2000*

Foreign currency translation
Foreign currency transactions are translated into sterling at the rate prevailing at the date of the transaction. Assets and liabilities held at the year end are translated into sterling at the rate prevailing at the balance sheet date. The resulting exchange differences are dealt with in the profit and loss account.

Group accounts
Where a company has foreign subsidiaries, associates, joint ventures or branches, the '*closing rate net investment method*' is normally used in translating local currency financial statements. Under this method:

(a) *Balance sheet* items should be translated into the currency of the holding company at the 'closing rate' (the spot rate on the balance sheet date). Where this year's closing rate differs from the previous year's closing rate, the differences arising from the retranslation of the opening *net investment* at this year's closing rate should be taken to reserves and will appear in both the Statement of recognised gains and losses and the Movements in shareholders' funds (see pages 144–6).

The *net investment* is the holding company's proportion of the subsidiary or associates' share capital and reserves. Long-term indebtedness between members of the group should be treated as part of the net investment. The translation process is illustrated in Example 23.2.

(b) *Profit and loss account* items should be translated using either the average rate for the accounting period or the closing rate and the method chosen should be applied consistently.

Any difference between translation at the average rate and the closing rate should be taken to reserves.

The rate used can make a considerable difference to the reported profit; for example, if a West German subsidiary made a profit of DM27m during a year in which the rate of exchange fell from DM3.10 = £1 at the beginning of the year to DM2.70 = £1 at the end of the year, averaging DM3.00 = £1 because most of the fall occurred in the last three months, on an average basis the group accounts would include West German profits of £9m; on a closing rate basis they would include £10m.

If the closing rate method is used, no difference will arise between the profit or loss in sterling terms used for profit and loss account purposes, and the result of translation for balance sheet purposes. If the average rate is used there will be a difference, which should be recorded as a movement on reserves. The method used should be stated in the accounts. The advantage of using the average rate is that the translated results correspond more nearly to those given by management accounts prepared (say) on a monthly basis. Indeed, to reflect those results even better, GRAND METROPOLITAN used to say it employed the *weighted* average rate of exchange (on the basis that it takes account of seasonal fluctuations in profitability).

GRAND METROPOLITAN *Accounting policies 1995*

Foreign Currencies

. . .

Profits and losses of overseas subsidiaries and associates are translated into sterling at weighted average rates of exchange during the year other than material exceptional items which are translated at the rate on the date of the transaction. The adjustment to financial year end rates is taken to reserves.

Example 23.2 Translation of an overseas subsidiary's accounts

On 31 December 2000, Injection Moulders PLC acquired a small foreign manufacturing company, Ruritanian Plastics, to expand its operations into Ruritania, and paid asset value, 60m Ruritanian dollars (R$), for it. At the time the exchange rate was R$10 = £1, so the sterling cost was £6m.

During the first year of operation as a subsidiary Ruritanian Plastics made a profit after tax of R$10m, and the R$ fell to R$12.5 = £1. Ruritanian Plastics' actual and translated balance sheets for 2000 (R$10 = £1) and 2001 (R$12.5 = £1) were:

Year ended 31 December	2000		2001	
	R$m	£000	R$m	£000
Fixed assets	100	10,000	100	8,000
Current assets	20	2,000	32	2,560
	120	12,000	132	10,560
5 year State loan	50	5,000	50	4,000
Current liabilities	10	1,000	12	960
	60	6,000	62	4,960
Shareholders' funds	60	6,000	70	5,600

The difference between the opening net equity of R$60m translated at R$10 = £1 (the closing rate in the 2000 accounts) and at R$12.5 = £1 (the 2001 closing rate) is £6m − £4.8m = £1.2m, which would be taken from group reserves at 31 December 2001 as an exchange translation difference.

The profit of R$10m (represented in the absence of any capital input or dividends by the difference between opening and closing shareholders' funds) has been translated in the group accounts at the closing rate of R$12.5 = £1 to produce £0.8m.

The fall in sterling terms in the net equity of Ruritanian Plastics from £6m to £5.6m is made up of the exchange translation loss of £1.2m less the £0.8m profit for 2001, i.e. £0.4m.

(c) *Foreign exchange borrowings*: where borrowings have been used to finance equity investment in foreign subsidiaries or associates, differences arising on their translation (at the closing rate) due to currency movements during the period may be offset against differences arising from the retranslation of the opening net investment, as is explained by PIC INTERNATIONAL (see below).

PIC INTERNATIONAL *Extract from accounting policies 2000*

(h) Foreign currencies

The results of overseas subsidiaries are translated into sterling at average exchange rates and assets and liabilities are translated at the rates on 30 June. Exchange differences which arise from the translation of the net assets and results of overseas subsidiaries at rates different from the average rate during the year and the rate used at 30 June in the prior year are dealt with through reserves.

Differences arising on the translation of foreign currency borrowings which hedge group equity investments in foreign enterprises are taken directly to reserves to the extent of corresponding exchange differences on translation of the related net investment. The tax on those exchange differences which are taken directly to reserves is also recorded as a direct movement on reserves.

. . .

Hyperinflation

Urgent Issues Task Force (UITF) Abstract 9 is concerned with accounting for operations in hyperinflationary economies. The Abstract requires adjustments to be made when incorporating operations in hyperinflationary economies into consolidated accounts where the distortions caused by hyperinflation are such as to affect the true and fair view given by the accounts. In any event, adjustments are required where the cumulative inflation rate over three years is approaching or exceeds 100% (a level widely accepted internationally as an appropriate criterion). The Abstract discusses acceptable methods of handling the problem, one of which is to translate the results of operations in hyperinflationary economies using a relatively stable currency as the functional currency.

One group which operates in countries suffering very high rates of inflation, even hyperinflation, is LONMIN (formerly LONRHO) (see p. 188).

Where restrictions prevent the transfer of cash from one part of the business or group to another, a note to the cash flow statement should specify the amounts involved and explain the circumstances (see page 151).

The temporal method

Where, and only where, the trade of a subsidiary is a direct extension of the trade of a holding company,

e.g. a subsidiary acting purely as a selling agency in a foreign country, the temporal method of translation should be used in consolidation:

(a) all transactions should be translated at the rate ruling on the transaction date or at an average rate for a period if this is not materially different;
(b) non-monetary assets should not normally be retranslated at the balance sheet date;
(c) monetary assets and liabilities should be retranslated at the closing rate; and
(d) all exchange gains and losses should be taken to the profit and loss account as part of the profit and loss from ordinary activities.

Current UK practice

A growing number of companies use the average rate rather than the closing rate in translating overseas profits, and state which method is used in their accounting policies.

Mitigating the effect of currency fluctuations

Exchange rate movements are difficult to predict.

 Beware of companies that trade in currency futures, unless they have in-house expertise, tight controls, and a deep pocket.

Remember BARINGS, a merchant bank with an impeccable reputation, brought down by failure of management to control a rogue trader in Singapore.

Recent fluctuations

Between 1996 and 1999 the US dollar fluctuated between a low of about US $1.50/£1 and highs of up to $1.72/£1; see Example 23.3. The Deutschmark weakened steadily against sterling from 1995 to 1998, losing almost 40% between the beginning of 1996 and the beginning of 1998, but pulled back subsequently (see Example 23.4).

The rise in the Yen has been even more marked. It gained about 25% between August 1998 and January 1999 (see Example 23.5).

The way in which companies have sought to protect themselves against the effect of these and other currency fluctuations, both on their earnings and on their balance sheets, is explained in Chapter 14.

Although selling currency forward does protect the sterling value of future foreign income, doing so can have adverse effects if the foreign currency then strengthens rather than weakens. For example, if a UK motor manufacturer covers the US dollar forward, when its European competitors do not, and the US dollar strengthens, they will have scope for cutting their prices in the United States, while UK manufacturers will not.

Example 23.3 US$/£ exchange rate

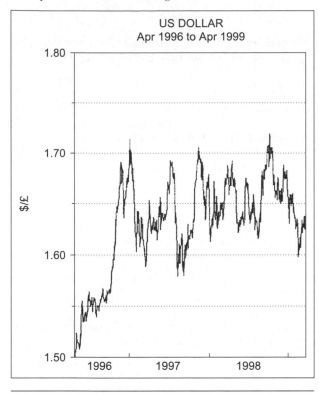

Example 23.4 The DM/£ exchange rate

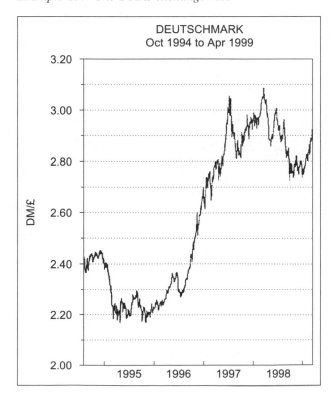

Example 23.5 The Yen/£ exchange rate

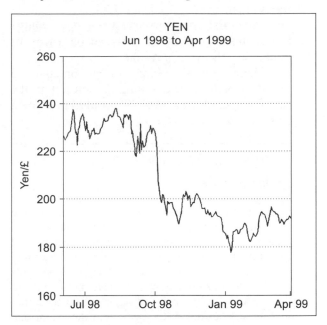

Protecting the balance sheet can be done in a variety of ways, the most obvious one being to borrow in the foreign currency. If the foreign subsidiary does the borrowing, the net equity investment in the subsidiary will be reduced. If the parent company borrows in the foreign currency and switches it into sterling, it will have a gain (or loss) to offset against any loss (or gain) on translating the net equity investment of the foreign subsidiary. If interest rates in sterling are higher than those in the foreign currency the parent company will also make a profit on the differential.

What the analyst should study

As has been seen, information about foreign currency tends to be scattered around in reports and accounts. A suggested sequence for the analyst to follow is:

1. *Accounting policies on foreign currencies*
    Check that, as required by SSAP 20, differences on unmatched foreign borrowings are dealt with in the P & L account and not taken direct to reserves. Before SSAP 20, some companies borrowed in a hard currency, e.g. Deutschmarks or Swiss francs, to reduce their cost of borrowing for investment in the UK. The lower interest rates (broadly reflecting the lower expectations of inflation) increased the companies' profits and, when the foreign currency inevitably strengthened, they debited the increase in the sterling value of their borrowings direct to reserves. This method of enhancing the profits was short-sighted and often very costly. For example the WEIR Group managed to lose £3.6m on a DM denominated loan originally worth £6.3m, and the loss would have been even

greater if the company hadn't arranged early repayment.

Note also if there has been any change in accounting policy, as this can be a way of enhancing the year's results.

There seems nothing strange or changed about LONMIN's accounting policies, but the rate changes during 1997–98 could have given more cause for worry.

LONMIN *Accounting policies 1998*

Exchange rates

Foreign currency assets and liabilities and the results for the year are translated into sterling at the rates ruling at 30 September. Exchange differences arising from the retranslation of the opening net investment in overseas companies are disclosed as movements on reserves. Exchange adjustments relating to borrowings which have been used to finance or provide a hedge against foreign equity investments are taken to reserves to the extent that they are matched by exchange movements on those investments. All other adjustments due to fluctuations arising in the normal course of trade are included in profit before taxation. The principal sterling exchange rates used to translate foreign currency assets and liabilities and the results for the year are:

	1998	1997
South Africa rand	9.9171	7.5160
United States dollar	1.7025	1.6058
Zimbabwe dollar	54.0550	20.2411

But information is not always all in one place even in accounting policies.

LONMIN *Extract from the statement of accounting policies 1998*

Consolidation of Group companies

. . .

Results of subsidiaries and associates operating in hyper-inflationary economics are adjusted to reflect current price levels in those countries concerned.

---

2. *Note analysing operating profit*
   It is here that differences arising from variations in exchange rates between the dates of invoicing in a foreign currency and the dates of payment, and on monetary items, should be (but are not always) shown where material. Most companies, including LONMIN, show nothing.

3. *Statement of recognised gains and losses and Movements in shareholders' funds*
   Check whether the adjustments for currency fluctuations are material in relation to (i) the profit for the financial year and (ii) the transfer (from profit and loss account) to reserves.

LONMIN *Statement of total consolidated recognised gains and losses 1998*

Statement of total consolidated recognised gains and losses for the year ended 30 September

	1998 £m	1997 £m
Profit for the year – Group	30	139
– Associates	9	3
Dilution of the Group's interest in Ashanti	1	22
Unrealised net surplus on revaluation of assets		66
Exchange adjustments – Group	(116)	(46)
– Associates	(7)	(3)
Total recognised (losses)/gains relating to the year	(83)	181

£123m (in total) against a total profit for the year of £39m is certainly material!

LONMIN *Reconciliation of movement in equity interests*

Reconciliation of movement in equity interests for the year ended 30 September

	1998 £m	1997 £m
Total recognised (losses)/gains relating to the year	(83)	181
Dividends	(27)	(41)
Shares issued in lieu of cash dividends	5	9
Shares issued		3
Share buyback	(196)	
Demerger of Lonrho Africa	(221)	
Net surplus/(goodwill) on acquisition of subsidiaries and associates	8	(9)
Net goodwill on acquisition of subsidiaries by Ashanti	(19)	(37)
Share buyback in Ashanti	(4)	
Net (surplus)/goodwill realised on sale of subsidiaries	(56)	75
Movement of the Group's interest in Dulker Mining	(2)	
Other items	(3)	(5)
Net (reduction)/increase in equity interests in the year	(598)	176
Equity interests at 1 October	975	799
Equity interests at 30 September	377	975

In May 1998 shareholders received shares in Lonrho Africa following its demerger.

The £123m of exchange adjustments, incorporated in the figure for Total recognised (losses)/gains relating to the year (£83m), is certainly also material in relation to, say, closing equity interests of £377m.

4. *If the exchange adjustments thus found are large*
Look for further information elsewhere. Wherever a balance sheet or cash flow statement note explains the change in an accounting item over the year, e.g. fixed assets, provisions or cash, if foreign currency is involved there may be a 'Currency translation difference'. It is here that depositing money in a soft depreciating currency (as POLLY PECK did) or borrowing (at a low rate of interest) in appreciating currency (as WEIR, mentioned above, did) would come to light.

5. *The reconciliation of group operating profit to net cash flow from operations*
The reconciliation of group operating profit to net cash flow from operations does not usually show any exchange translation differences, but it may. This is likely to happen where a group translates 'profits, losses and cash flows' from overseas subsidiaries at average rate rather than closing rate (as TT GROUP did in its 1998 accounts).

TT GROUP *Extract from reconciliation of group operating profit to net cash flow from operations*

	1998 £m	1997 £m
. . .		
Exchange translation differences	(1.7)	(2.1)
. . .		

---

6. *Again, if the figures seem significant . . .*
Look for comments in the Financial Review, if there is one, or in the chairman's statement or possibly in the directors' report, or even elsewhere in the notes. Where exchange rates have a significant effect, further information may include tables of exchange rates.

7. *Study the note on contingent liabilities*
Most companies did not in the past consider the potential liability in relation to swaps. But the note on contingent liabilities may today provide interesting information.

8. *Study any note on derivative financial instruments*
FRS 13 *Derivatives and other financial instruments* (see page 89) calls for a good deal of information on the use being made of derivatives and similar financial instruments. BP AMOCO included more than a page on the matter in its 1998 accounts.

9. *Look for any indication of significant exchange rate changes having an effect on profitability*
Look also for any indication of the risks/costs/benefits of using financial instruments.

Activities on a global scale inevitably involve many types of risk. Few companies spell this out quite so clearly or at such length as BP AMOCO. Their annual report for 2000 illustrates the complexity of the subject (the italics are ours).

BP AMOCO *Extracts from the financial review 2000*

Financial risk management
The group co-ordinates certain key activities on a *global basis* in order to optimise its financial position and performance. These include the *management of the currency*, maturity and interest rate profile of borrowing, cash . . .

Market risk
Market risks include the possibility that *changes in currency exchange rates,* interest rates or oil and gas prices will adversely affect the value of the group's financial assets, liabilities or future cash flows . . .

Currency exchange rates
Fluctuations in exchange rates can have significant effects on the group's reported profit. The effects of most exchange rate fluctuations are subsumed within business operating results through changing cost competitiveness, lags in market adjustment to movement in rates, and conversion differences accounted for on specific transactions. For this reason *the total effect of exchange rate fluctuations is not identifiable separately in the group's reported profit.* The main underlying economic currency of the group's cash flows is the US dollar and the group's borrowings are predominantly in US dollars. *Our foreign exchange management policy is to minimise economic and material transactional exposures arising from currency movements against the US dollar.* The group co-ordinates the handling of foreign exchange risks centrally, by netting off naturally occurring opposite exposures whenever possible, to reduce the risks, and then dealing with any material residual foreign exchange risks.

Interest rates
. . .
The group is exposed predominantly to US dollar LIBOR (London Inter-Bank Offer Rate) interest rates as *borrowings are mainly denominated in, or are swapped into, US dollars.*

BP AMOCO *Extract from notes to the 2000 accounts*

26. Derivative financial instruments
The following table shows the trading income arising from derivatives and other financial instruments. For oil price contract trading, this also includes income or losses arising on trading of derivative commodity instruments and physical oil trades, representing the net result of the oil-trading portfolio.

	2000 Net gain (loss)	$m 1999 Net gain
Interest rate trading	1	–
Foreign exchange trading	52	23

. . . . .

10. Consider the state of any overseas economies
Probably equally if not more important for the profitability of foreign operations than a weak exchange rate is the state of the economy in the foreign countries concerned. If the weak exchange rate reflects a weak economy, then adverse trading conditions may be more damaging for profits than translation.

LONMIN *Extract from chief operating officer's review 1998*

Factors which have had a significant impact on the trading environment included the ever deepening Asian financial crisis, the devaluation of the Rand, the increase in interest rates to unprecedented levels and the abnormally warm 1998 winter in South Africa, which resulted in poor inland sales.

Remedial steps taken in the face of these developments include:

- actively seeking alternative markets in order to limit our exposure to the Far East
- using the export capacity of the Group to the full so as to maximise the benefits of the weaker exchange rate and so benefit from the higher margins on export sales
- focusing inland sales on a higher value, more stable customer base
- continuously pursuing cost saving and productivity measures
- curtailing cash outflows, working capital requirements and capital expenditure in order to reduce net borrowings and minimise financing costs.

. . .

Chapter 24

HISTORICAL SUMMARIES, RATIOS AND TRENDS

HISTORICAL SUMMARIES

Variations in form and content

In 1964 the Chairman of the Stock Exchange wrote to the chairmen of all listed companies asking for various items of information to be included in their reports and accounts. One of the items which 'might be included' was 'Tables of relevant comparative figures for the past ten years'.

Apart from this request, listed companies are under no obligation to provide any form of historical summary: there is no FRS or SSAP, and no uniformity of content, layout, or period covered.

The majority of companies give a five-year summary; most of the remainder show ten years, although a few choose a different period, usually for a specific reason; e.g. LONRHO's 'Financial Record' for many years went right back to 1961, the year their then chief executive, Tiny Rowland, joined the company. Renamed LONMIN, the group now shows only five years.

Because there is, as yet, no standard on historical summaries, the content varies enormously. BULGIN, for example, show only five basic items in their 'Group five year record', illustrated below. (Readers may recall BULGIN from Chapter 5, and will note the pain of 1997 and marked improvement in profits, earnings and dividends in 1998.) Many companies give much more information than this. GLAXOWELLCOME, for instance, devotes three pages to its five-year record, as well as six pages of quarterly trends for the most recent year. Some companies include information of particular relevance to their type of business; e.g. TESCO, in their five-year record (see overleaf), show the number of stores, sales area opened during the year and total sales area, and a number of other statistics which provide the reader with growth ratios some of which are not available from the accounts. BP is among a number of oil companies giving useful statistics.

BULGIN *Extract from report and accounts 2000*

Group Five Year Record	2000	1999	1998	1997	1996
Turnover – continuing operations	**13,373**	12,058	13,514	12,757	14,271
– discontinued operations	**1,039**	4,740	5,982	6,398	6,002
	14,412	16,798	19,496	19,155	20,273
Profit/(loss) before taxation	**665**	(271)	586	100	901
Shareholders' net assets	**4,518**	4,218	4,760	4,774	4,906
Earnings/(loss) per share – basic	**1.06p**	(0.71p)	1.21p	0.05p	2.01p
– diluted	**1.05p**	(0.71p)	1.20p	0.04p	1.94p
Dividends per share	**0.41p**	1.25p	1.25p	0.50p	0.45p

Including adjustment for the compensatory scrip issue at enfranchisement

---

Have a look at TESCO's five-year record below. Do you think that *Turnover per employee* and *Profit per Employee* have grown satisfactorily between 1996 and 2000?

TESCO *Extracts from five-year record*

		1996	1997	1998[1]	1999	2000
•••						
Operating margin[2]	**[A]**					
UK		6.2%	5.8%	5.8%	5.8%	5.9%
Rest of Europe		2.1%	1.8%	2.5%	4.1%	3.7%
Asia		–	–	–	(1.3)%	(0.2)%
Total Group		6.0%	5.6%	5.5%	5.6%	5.5%
•••						
Return on shareholders' funds[6]	**[B]**	20.4%	20.1%	21.3%	21.3%	20.9%
Return on capital employed[7]	**[B]**	16.9%	17.1%	18.7%	17.2%	16.1%
Net assets per share[8]	**[B]**	56p	60p	59p	65p	70p
UK Retail profitability	**[C]**					
Turnover per employee[9]		143,359	146,326	149,799	151,138	156,427
Profit per employee[9]		8,841	8,478	8,755	8,771	9,160
Wages per employee[9]		13,948	14,222	15,079	15,271	15,600
UK Retail statistics						
Market share in food and drink shops[12]		13.4%	14.2%	14.8%	15.4%	15.5%
Number of stores		545	568	618	639	659
Total sales area – 000 sq ft[11]		13,397	14,036	15,215	15,975	16,895
Average store size (sales area – sq ft)[13]		25,600	26,300	26,600	26,654	27,720
Full-time equivalent employees[14]		80,650	89,649	99,941	104,772	108,409
•••						

Tesco's Notes to above summary
1. 53 week period
2. Operating margin is based on turnover exclusive of VAT

6. Underlying profit divided by weighted average shareholders' funds
7. Operating profit divided by average capital employed
8. Based on number of shares at year end
9. Based on turnover exclusive of VAT; operating profit and total staff costs per full-time equivalent employee
10. Based on weighted average sales area and turnover inclusive of VAT, excluding property development
11. Store sizes excludes lobby and restaurant areas
12. Based on Tesco food, grocery, non-food and drink sales and Institute of Grocery Distribution/Office for National Statistics data for the year to the previous December
13. Average store sizes exclude Metro and Express stores
14. Based on average number of full-time equivalent employees in the UK

OUR COMMENTS ON TESCO's FIVE-YEAR RECORD 1996–2000

[A] UK fairly steady. Rest of Europe improving. Asia likely to be profitable in 2001
[B] All unreliable, due to *Immediate write-off* of goodwill prior to FRS 10, and *not* reinstated
[C] UK retail productivity, adjusted for inflation. In £ of 1996

	1996	1997	1998[1]	1999	2000
RPI in February	150.9	155.0	160.3	163.7	167.5
Factor to divide by each year	1.000	1.027	1.062	1.085	1.110
Turnover per employee	143,359	142,479	141,054	139,298	140,925
Profit per employee	8,841	8,255	8,244	8,084	8,252
Wages per employee	13,948	13,848	14,199	14,075	14,054
Weekly sales per sq ft	18.31	18.96	19.28	19.40	19.31

BP includes statistics on refinery throughput, crude oil and natural gas reserves, capital expenditure and acquisition in five pages of historical information, and is among companies which now provide historical cash flow data.

There is a growing tendency for companies either to omit the normal table of historical information altogether in favour of often colourful diagrams of a few salient items. TAY HOMES, in its annual report for 2000, devoted half a page to presenting six items of basic information in six clever little blue-washed diagrams in a way that didn't immediately draw attention to the large losses made in the previous year, nor to nil dividends in 1999 and 2000.

The majority of listed companies manage to show between 25 and 35 items in a single-page five-year record.

A few companies, like WATERMARK, provide no historical information at all.

No FRS planned

A Financial Reporting Standard would be welcome on historical summaries, but because they fall outside the statutory accounts, there appear to be no plans for one.

The main difficulty facing the shareholder or analyst who tries to interpret a five- or ten-year summary is lack of consistency. We will consider this under five heads:

1. inflation;
2. changes in accounting standards;
3. accounting changes made by the company;
4. changes in the business environment;
5. changes in the composition of the group.

Inflation

It used to be reasonable to regard a pound sterling today as the same as a pound last year and a pound next year. Inflation has made this concept of a stable currency (referred to in the US as the *uniform dollar concept*) seriously misleading.

To read a ten-year record as though currency were stable is to obtain a false picture, and would be just as misleading as the company chairman who makes much of 'yet another year of record profits' when they have advanced a mere 2% compared with a 3% or 4% rate of inflation.

We show, in the TESCO example on page 192, how, by adjusting by the RPI, the effects of inflation can be stripped out.

Changes in accounting standards

The first of the Accounting Standards Board's standards, FRS 1 *Cash flow statements*, was published in September 1991. We are now up to FRS 19 *Accounting policies*, and there is hardly an area

of company accounts that hasn't been affected by one or more of these standards.

Take, for instance, goodwill. FRS 10 *Goodwill and intangible assets* requires goodwill arising in accounts periods ending after 23 December 1998 to be capitalised and amortised (see page 48). This change has affected most groups, since most had previously chosen to account for goodwill by *immediate write-off against reserves*, which was (absurdly) the **officially preferred method** before FRS 10.

Companies may, under FRS 10, choose to reinstate goodwill previously written off as though it had been capitalised and amortised throughout. In this case a five- or ten-year summary could, and probably would, show comparable figures throughout. But the ASB 'does not require reinstatement', and the large majority of listed companies have not done so.

For example TESCO:

TESCO *Extracts from 2000 accounts*

Note on accounting policies

Goodwill

Goodwill arising from transactions entered into after 1 March 1998 is capitalised under the heading 'Intangible assets' and amortised on a straight line basis over its useful economic life, up to a maximum of 20 years.

All goodwill entered into prior to 1 March 1998 has been written off to reserves.

Note 11 Intangible fixed assets

	2000 £m	1999 £m
Net carrying value At 26 February 2000	136	112

Note 24 Reserves

. . .

The cumulative goodwill written off against the reserves of the Group as at 26 February 2000 amounted to £718m (1999 – £718m).

Prior to FRS 10, Return on Capital Employed (ROCE) and similar ratios were often considerably inflated in acquisitive companies by *immediate write-off* of goodwill. And these ratios will continue to be inflated in the Historical Summaries of companies like Tesco (with £718m written off against reserves) for many years to come.

Accounting changes made by the company

Accounting changes made by the company can make a significant difference to reported profits.

Take, for example, ML LABORATORIES' change of accounting policy on Research and Development from capitalisation and subsequent amortisation to write off as incurred (page 46), or THORNTONS, the Derbyshire-based chocolate manufacturer and retailer, which changed the expected useful life of its shop-fits to reflect an operational change of policy:

THORNTONS *Finance director's review 2000*

Accounting standards and policy changes

. . .

Our change in strategic emphasis will result in a slower shop-opening programme and fewer shop refits, which means that capital investments already made will last longer.

We have, therefore, revised the depreciation policy on fixtures and fittings from four to five years. The net impact on profit is a gain of almost £2 million this year, and we expect a net gain of £1 million next.

Almost £2 million was a significant amount in a year when pre-tax profit halved from £11 million to £5.5 million and the company, under new management, was wisely cutting back on capital expenditure.

Changes in the business environment

Changes may be imposed on the company: for example, changes in the rate and/or method of taxation, as was the case with the reduction of ACT in the 1990s and its subsequent abolition.

Changes in the composition of the group

Where a group either grows other than internally or deliberately gets rid of activities, year on year comparability is bound to be affected. The changes can be carried out in several ways:

1. Acquisitions
2. Disposals
3. Termination of a specific activity

Acquisitions

FRS 3 *Reporting financial performance* requires profit and loss account figures down to the operating profit level to be split *inter alia* into (a) continuing activities and (b) acquisitions.

Few companies do this in any five- or ten-year summary, simply lumping the figures together as con-

tinuing activities. You can safely assume that data represent total sales from all activities including new activities developed internally and acquisitions and that the operating profits include such activities. We discuss the rules on new acquisitions on page 168.

Continuing and discontinued operations

As explained on page 119, FRS 3 requires the subdivision in the profit and loss account of results down to operating profit level into continuing operations, acquisitions and discontinued operations.

It also requires separate disclosure, after operating profit and before interest, of:

- profits or losses on the sale or termination of an operation;
- costs of a fundamental reorganisation or restructuring having a material effect on the nature and focus of the reporting entity's operations; and
- profits or losses on the disposal of fixed assets.

The FRS does not mention five- or ten-year summaries, which therefore do not *have* to do this.

Most but not all do divide turnover and operating profit into those from continuing operations and those from discontinued operations. Most do not show profits or losses on the disposal of fixed assets.

In a simple case (like that of BENSONS CRISPS on the next page) one has little difficulty seeing what happened and when. In 1994, the entire business was unprofitable at the operating profit level; and operations with a turnover of £5.501m discontinued in that year are said to have lost £880,000.

In more complex cases (such as ALLDAYS) on page 196 it may be difficult to tell whether there has been one disposal or several over a period of years.

ALLDAYS' turnover figures (see p. 195) would be consistent with there having been just one discontinuance of activities (in 1998). The analysis of operating profit makes it clear that there was an earlier discontinuance; and that the figures for 1996 and earlier represent both sets of activities since discontinued.

Just as there is little consistency in *what* is disclosed in a historical summary, there is no one order of *columns* which may, as in the ALLDAYS example, run in reverse chronological order from left to right (showing the most recent figures first), or may run in the other direction (as with BRUNEL HOLDINGS).

BENSONS CRISPS *Extract from five-year record 1998*

Summarised profit and loss accounts

	1998 £000	1997 £000	1996 £000	1995 £000	1994 £000
Turnover					
Continuing operations	38,011	34,514	32,797	31,184	30,182
Discontinued operation	–	–	–	–	5,501
	38,011	34,514	32,797	31,184	35,683
Operating profit/(loss)					
Continuing operations	3,332	2,875	2,544	928	(2,690)
Discontinued operation	–	–	–	–	(880)
	3,332	2,875	2,544	928	(3,570)

. . .

ALLDAYS *Extract from five-year record 1998*

Five year record

	1998 £000	1997 £000	1996 £000	1995 £000	1994 £000
Turnover:					
Continuing operations	493,826	455,801	410,427	378,925	348,894
Discontinued operations	203,832	181,705	166,175	118,911	91,676
Total turnover	697,658	637,506	576,602	497,836	440,570
Operating profit before exceptional items:					
Continuing operations					
Alldays:	14,720	19,492	15,064	12,086	7,949
Trademarket	590	1,518	1,650	1,602	1,940
Total – continuing operations	15,310	21,010	16,714	13,688	9,889
Discontinued operations					
W&P Foodservice	3,434	4,582	4,031	3,389	2,281
Wholesaling activity	–	–	2,754	3,261	3,840
Other	–	–	427	427	427
Total – discontinued operations	3,434	4,582	7,212	7,077	6,548
Total operating profit before exceptional items	18,744	25,592	23,926	20,765	16,437

BRUNEL HOLDINGS *Extract from 2000 report and accounts*

Five Year Record	1996	1997	1998	1999	2000
Turnover (£m)					
Continuing operations	73.3	77.2	77.3	65.5	72.0
Discontinued operations	115.0	65.0	22.4	6.6	–
Total	188.3	142.2	99.7	72.1	72.0
Operating profit (£m)					
Continuing operations	4.6	5.3	2.9	(6.9)	0.4
Discontinued operations	2.4	2.1	–	(0.5)	–
Total	7.0	7.4	2.9	(7.4)	0.4

Brunel has seen a gradual whittling away of operations but, after years of painful restructuring, the group may now possibly be out of the wood. In the words of the present chairman, appointed a little over two years ago:

BRUNEL HOLDINGS *Extract from Chairman's 2000 statement*

Prospects
Today, Brunel is a more tightly controlled, more disciplined and more focused Group. We view the next twelve months with a sense of quiet optimism.

ALLDAYS, on the other hand, has run into deep trouble:

ALLDAYS *Extract from Directors' 2000 report*

Results and dividends
The consolidated profit and loss account, set out on page 16, shows a retained loss after interest, tax and exceptional charges of £65,276,000 (1999: loss of £90,659,000). [and, surprise surprise] The directors do not recommend the payment of a dividend (1999: nil).

Alldays no longer includes a Five Year Record in its annual report and accounts.

When a company omits or reduces the information that it provided last year, always ask yourself

'Why?'

If you can find no good reason, treat it as a warning signal.

The first time we came across this was many years ago, but it's a good example nevertheless (if you live long enough, you will have seen it all before):

BURMAH OIL *Details of ship chartering*

	£ million
1971	
Tanker in-charters	204
Tanker out-charters	127

1972
Tanker in-charters had been lumped in with other contractual commitments in a total of £470 million, and the note went on to say that 'a substantial part of these commitments is already matched by tanker out-charters and other long term arrangements'.

1973/74
When the tanker charter market subsequently collapsed, Burmah's unmatched in-charter commitments ran up huge losses for the company and it had to be rescued by the Bank of England.

This was a classic example of a rogue trader bringing a company down. The person running Burmah's tanker chartering at the time was, we vaguely recall, a gentleman called Culukundis who, after the disaster, didn't feel he'd done anything wrong.

But to get back to Alldays, there was a good reason for omitting the Five Year Review. A new chairman and a new chief executive had been appointed towards the end of 1999, and five of the 'old guard' directors had since left. We presume the new team wanted to disassociate themselves from the (very murky) past.

RATIOS

The key to using ratios is selectivity, not saturation.

Choice of ratios
With the profit and loss account, balance sheet and cash flow statement each containing a minimum of 10 to 20 items, the scope for comparing one item with another is enormous, so it is important to be selective, both to limit the calculations required and, more importantly, to make the presentation of the selected ratios simple and readily understandable. No decision-maker wants a jungle of figures, so the ratios chosen should be the key ones, logically grouped.

Ratios can conveniently be divided into

- *operating ratios*, which are concerned with how the company is trading, and take no account of how the company is financed;
- *financial ratios*, which measure the financial structure of the company and show how it relates to the trading activities;
- *investment ratios*, which relate the number of ordinary shares and their market price to the profits, dividends and assets of the company.

MAIN RATIOS

Indexed by type

Operating ratios	*Page*
Operational gearing	43–4
Profit margin	120–1
Return on capital employed (ROCE)	121–2*
Working capital ratios	97
Financial ratios	
Cash flow per share	156
Financial gearing; Leverage effect	43*
Interest cover	43
Liquidity: Current and Quick ratios	98–9
Investment ratios	
Dividend yield	147
Earnings per share (e.p.s.)	135–44
Price/Earnings ratio (P/E or PER)	146–7

* Unreliable

Some companies include a table of key ratios in their report and accounts, and a few, like UNILEVER, below, explain their definitions. This sort of table can be useful for looking at trends within the company concerned but, if you have the time and want to make inter-company comparisons, it may be preferable to work out your own ratios by a standard method.

In describing these ratios we give what we regard as the most useful and practical definition of each component.

Although there is an increasing trend towards standardisation, individual analysts do not always agree on definitions, while companies do not all define ratio components in the same way.

Why capital-based ratios are unreliable

Ratios like ROCE, Debt/Equity and Return on shareholders' funds have been distorted by inflation, which has made Historical Cost (HC) values increasingly irrelevant. As David Tweedie (until recently the chairman of the ASB) pointed out, to show a building at its HC of £20m when the bank had taken it as security for a £60m loan is clearly neither true nor fair.

And, more importantly in companies with an acquisitive history, the *immediate write-off* method of accounting for purchased goodwill has made millions and millions of pounds of shareholders' money simply disappear from the balance sheet, reducing shareholders' funds and thus increasing the return on them.

As UNILEVER pointed out in a note to its Five year record, shown below, 'Return on shareholders' equity is substantially influenced' by the Group's policy, prior to 1998, of *immediate write-off*, and 'Return on capital employed and net gearing are also influenced but to a lesser extent.'

Earnings per share

Here we are spoilt for choice. You can have basic e.p.s., IIMR e.p.s. (UKSIP now, I suppose), and any 'Own Brand' e.p.s. a company or broking house likes to define. Of course David Tweedie was right to make it all-inclusive – so it couldn't easily be fudged.

But it's a shame that the ASB decided to call it '*Basic*', which it isn't, rather than '*All-inclusive*', which it is. A serious and misleading misuse of the English language. Too many accountants and not enough Arts graduates, we suppose. If you aren't sure, ask yourself 'Is my "basic" salary all-inclusive?' We doubt it except, possibly, in a roaring bear market.

How e.p.s. can be 'smoothed' a little

In the years BT (Before Tweedie) there was a great deal of scope for fudging the figures. Now there is

---

UNILEVER *Extract from Five year record*

	Note	1995	1996	1997	1998	% **1999**
Key ratios						
Return on shareholders' equity	1	26.4	29.4	48.3	24.5	**42.7**
Return on capital employed	1	14.2	15.2	27.6	16.0	**22.3**
Operating margin		8.0	8.6	8.0	10.9	**10.5**
Net profit margin	2	4.7	4.8	11.2	7.3	**6.8**
Net interest cover (times)		10.1	11.6	65.6	–	**319.0**
Net gearing	1	24.0	23.5	–	–	–

Notes [**of particular interest**]

1. Return on shareholders' equity is substantially influenced by the Group's policy, prior to 1998, of writing off purchased goodwill in the year of acquisition as a movement in profit retained. Return on capital employed and net gearing are also influenced but to a lesser extent.
2. Net profit margin includes the profit on sale of the speciality chemicals businesses in 1997.

much less, but still some. To help e.p.s. up/(down) a company can:

1. Decrease (increase) various provisions, for bad debt etc.
2. Be slack (strict) on writing down old or surplus stock.
3. Put intangible assets on the balance sheet, but don't depreciate, do annual reviews instead.
4. When reviewing annually, be optimistic (pessimistic) about the value of each intangible.
5. Extend (shorten) '*useful lives*' to reduce (increase) the depreciation charge.
6. Defer (accelerate) bringing home profits from overseas to reduce (increase) tax on remission.

Now some of these measures may be taken in good faith e.g. THORNTONS, as a matter of policy, increasing the number of years between retail outlet refurbishments from 4 to 5 (see page 194). And it's always a good idea to be rather more 'prudent' in good years, but the analyst and investor should watch out for signs of profit enhancement, which may include:

1. Plausible rather than reasonable reasons for a change in accounting policies or practices.
2. Threats of being taken over, a galvanising reason for reporting, or forecasting the best profits you can.
3. Reporting profits only a whisker above last year's results. The company may have strained every muscle to avoid a fall in profits, particularly if it has an unbroken record. Using up all the company's 'spare fat' in one year makes it more likely that the company will fall out of bed the following year if trading conditions don't improve.

Two modern ratios
Before we move on from ratios we would like to consider two relatively new ones:

1. *Fixed charges cover*;
2. *Total return to shareholders.*

Older hands will remember the way property development companies went down like ninepins in 1989–90, when the UK property market virtually dried up.

Those that survived, as at least one shrewd property analyst had predicted, were the ones that had sufficient rental income to cover their fixed costs until times got better.

Whether this experience gave W.H. SMITH the idea we do not know, but we like the ratio they have come up with:

Fixed charges cover
Other companies may use the ratio internally, but this is the only company we have spotted publishing it in their annual report and accounts:

W. H. SMITH *Extract from 2000 accounts*

Note 11 Fixed charges cover

	2000 £m	1999 £m
Interest income	(6)	(14)
Operating lease rentals	154	141
Property taxes	32	30
Other property costs	11	9
Total fixed charges	191	166
Profit before tax	140	134
Profit before tax and fixed charges	331	300
Fixed charges cover	**1.7x**	**1.8x**

Fixed charges cover is calculated by dividing profit before tax and fixed charges by total fixed charges

and W.H. Smith also includes the fixed charge cover in its Five Year Summary.

Total return to shareholders
This has become popular in more recent years for use as a criterion for extra remuneration to directors and senior managers, for example BOOTS:

BOOTS *Extract from 2000 report*

Financial review
. . .

Shareholder return In our opinion the best overall measure of group performance is total return to shareholders. This measure has been successfully utilised within the group for over ten years. We monitor our performance on a rolling five year basis against ten peer companies . . .

Shareholders returns of The Boots Company compared with peer companies
Returns are calculated using average listed share prices over the three months to 31st March.

Five years to 31st March 2000	%
1 Smith Kline Beecham	246.8
2 Kingfisher	176.4
3 Tesco	145.0
4 Alliance UniChem	71.3
5 Smith & Nephew	39.3
6 Boots	**33.6**
7 Reckitt Benckiser	9.9
8 W.H. Smith	(1.1)
9 J. Sainsbury	(15.2)
10 GUS	(16.0)
11 Marks & Spencer	(20.8)

Long term bonuses for the executive directors and other senior management are also tied to a total shareholder return measured on a rolling four year basis.

Although this is a good way of comparing companies it is hardly original; the concept of total return has been central to UK portfolio performance measurement since 1971 or earlier. And it is too historic to be of any great value to the analyst.

What we naively don't understand is why bonuses should be handed out during a bear market, when the share price and shareholders are taking a thrashing.

We are highly distrustful of incentive schemes which do not align the interests of directors and senior management with the interests of shareholders.

TRENDS

It is frequently a worthwhile, even profitable, exercise to set alongside one another, growth in:

(a) turnover;
(b) profit before tax;
(c) earnings per share;
(d) dividend per share.

If they are wildly different, the cause should be investigated. In the sixth edition we looked at MITIE GROUP, a relatively small cleaning and maintenance contractor, saying that it was 'taking advantage of the trend towards out-sourcing such services' while at the same time expanding by making a series of small acquisitions.

As is shown in the first extract below, from Mitie's 1995 group statistical record, growth between 1990 and 1995 was spectacular:

- turnover was up almost 703% in 5 years;
- pre-tax profit (up 604%) had nearly kept pace; but
- because of acquisitions for paper (issuing new Mitie shares to the vendor, rather than paying cash), e.p.s. had only grown 165%;
- from a very low base, and nine times covered, dividends had increased 500%, which must have pleased the long-term shareholders.

Taking a subsequent period, 1996 to 2000, shown in the second extract below:

- the growth in turnover had slowed down a little, but still an impressive increase of 115% in four years;
- profit before tax, up 205%, grew almost twice as fast as sales;
- the increase in e.p.s. of 153% was quite a lot less than the rise in pre-tax profit, due to acquisitions for paper;
- dividends grew by 150%, roughly in line with e.p.s.;
- dividend cover had remained at around 4 × throughout the five years. The low payout ratio of around 25% left 75% invested in the group to help finance Mitie's continued growth.

In other words the group was exhibiting ratios typical of a highly profitable, but more mature group.

Common size statement
Another ways of looking at these figures is to draw up a *Common size statement*. All the earliest year's values are rebased at 100 and each subsequent year's value for each item is divided by the increase in the Retail Price Index (RPI).

MITIE GROUP *Extract from Group statistical record 1995 (extract)*

	1995 £000	1994 £000	1993 £000	1992 £000	1991 £000	1990 £000	Increase 1990–1995
Turnover	125,183	101,732	72,994	52,276	32,699	15,594	702.8%
Profit on ordinary activities before taxation	4,571	3,361	2,402	1,808	1,231	649	604.3%
. . .							
Earnings per share	12.2p	8.5p	6.6p	5.8p	5.5p	4.6p	165.2%
Dividend per share	3.0p	2.25p	1.75p	1.375p	1.0p	0.5p	500.0%

Earnings and Dividend per share figures have been re-stated to reflect the sub-division of shares referred to in Note
. . .
   The results of merger accounted acquisitions are reflected in full in the year of acquisition and subsequent years but only the year prior to acquisition has been re-stated on a comparable basis.

MITIE GROUP *Extract from Group statistical record*

	2000 £000	1999 £000	1998 £000	1997 £000	1996 £000	Increase 1996–2000
Turnover	346,514	264,455	236,293	209,425	161,149	115.0%
Profit on ordinary activities before taxation	19,240	14,508	11,110	8,210	6,302	205.3%
. . .						
Earnings per share	8.1p	6.5p	5.1p	4.0p	3.2p	153.1%
Dividend per share	2.0p	1.6p	1.2p	1.0p	0.8p	150.0%

Earnings and Dividend per share figures have been re-stated to reflect the sub-division of shares in 1997 and 1998 . . .

MITIE GROUP *Common size statement 1996–2000 and Average annual growth*

	2000	1999	1998	1997	1996	Average growth p.a.
Turnover	215.0	164.4	146.6	130.0	100.0	21.1%
Profit on ordinary activities before tax	305.3	230.2	176.2	130.3	100.0	32.2%
. . .						
Earnings per share	253.1	203.1	159.4	115.0	100.0	26.1%
Dividend per share	250.0	200.0	150.0	125.0	100.0	25.8%

Chapter 25

CHAIRMAN'S STATEMENT, OPERATING AND FINANCIAL REVIEWS AND DIRECTORS' REPORT

In this chapter we look at what can be learned from those parts of the report of a company which are not strictly part of the accounts. The directors' report has long been part of the reporting system and is required by the Companies Act 1985. The other documents covered in this chapter, for example, the chairman's statement, the operating (or operational) review, and the financial review, are relatively new and not required by the Companies Act.

Sequence of study of a report and accounts
It is difficult to lay down a set of rules as to the best order in which to study a report and accounts, and each individual will – indeed should – develop his or her own method. The important thing is not to miss information regardless of where it is presented.

One stockbroker tells us he always goes straight to the directors' holdings to see if they are reducing their holdings! – indeed, one co-author maintains on file details of all directors' share transactions in their own company and spends a few minutes each week studying them.

That the directors have sharply reduced their holdings in the company certainly tends to be a warning sign – but it is unwise for a director (or any other investor) to have too many eggs in one basket – so reductions are not necessarily a warning signal – an individual director may have special, personal, financial needs at a particular time.

Similarly, an increase in directors' holdings tends to be encouraging particularly where a company's shares seem undervalued or under pressure, but directors can and do get it wrong, personally as well as commercially, pouring good money after bad even when it is their own.

Major own-share activity on the part of one or more directors does, however, focus attention: something seems to be happening. One needs to find out what.

It is certainly helpful to start by glancing at the chairman's statement and the directors' report simply to see whether anything has occurred which would invalidate a straightforward comparison between one year and another. If, for instance, a major acquisition took place early in the year under review, almost all operating and financial ratios are likely to have been affected. This does not mean that the ratios are useless: simply that the analyst must bear in mind that change in composition every time he compares one ratio with another.

Having then studied the accounts (a process we will discuss in detail in Chapter 31) and having examined any segmental analysis of turnover and pre-tax profits between classes of business and any geographical analysis of turnover and trading results outside the United Kingdom, the reader will have a good idea of how the company has fared in the past year, but little idea why (except in the context of happening to know that it was a good, average or bad year for the industry or industries in which the company operates), and little idea of how the company is likely to do in the current year and beyond. It is to the chairman's statement and the operating review, if there is one, that we should look for this information.

The chairman's statement
Companies are not required to publish a chairman's statement, but listed companies invariably do. In the case of companies which believe in keeping shareholders well informed, the chairman's statement will usually contain comment on:

(a) overall trading conditions during the period, current climate and general outlook;

(b) the performance achieved by each activity, current trading and future prospects;

(c) items of special interest (e.g. closures and new ventures);

(d) changes in the board;

(e) company strategy and plans for the future.

Study the chairman's statement, not only for what it says, but also for what it does not, where one is left to read between the lines. We find it's useful to read through the whole statement highlighting with a marking pen key phrases and points of interest as we go, before getting down to any detailed analysis.

Review of operations

A growing number of companies produce, sometimes instead of a Chairman's Statement but more commonly in addition to one, either a Chief Executive's Review or an Operational Review. BTP has all three.

Where these documents exist, and even the more enlightened and/or investment hungry smaller companies publish them too, they provide a vital part of the information package, often avoiding the stilted form and language of the directors' report and shedding additional light on information in the accounts.

Typically, where one or more of these documents exist in addition to a Chairman's Statement, that document is devoted largely to overall performance, plans and strategy, while the detailed review of operations, usually division by division, is left to the Chief Executive's Review and/or Operational Review. It is here that one learns in detail what the various parts of the group do, where, and how, the group's various markets are shaping, and where the focus of management attention lies. Statistics and graphs often present useful information on this and on trends over the years.

Financial Review

The Accounting Standards Board's Best Practice Statement, *Operating and Financial Review*, recommends listed companies to provide supplementary information in the form of an Operating and Financial Review (OFR).

Additionally the DTI's current Company Law Review proposes a statutory requirement for listed companies to include an OFR in the full annual report.

The Operating review (or Review of operations) was referred to above.

The main purpose of the Financial Review part of an OFR is to explain the accounts and to shed light on financial performance and strategy:

- Why did interest payable rise (or fall) so much year on year?
- What exactly do the exceptional items represent?
- Why does the effective tax rate differ from the rate of UK corporation tax?
- Where does the group keep its main cash reserves – the UK? If not, why there?
- What has happened to gearing, and why?
- What was the capital expenditure during the year actually used for? How much more is needed to complete the group's plans, and where is it coming from? (Is it in place?)
- How was (is) the group affected by exchange rates and interest rates?
- Risk management, with comment on:

  (a) treasury risk management;
  (b) liquidity risk;
  (c) finance and interest rate risk;
  (d) currency risk;
  (e) commodity risk;
  (f) credit risk.

- Which recent accounting standards have been adopted for the first time in the accounts?

Where a financial review is included, it should be regarded by analysts as being, to all intents and purposes, part of the accounts; and studied as such.

Environmental reports

In recent years there has been a growth in environmental reporting in the UK. More and more companies now include information on environmental issues in their annual reports and accounts and there are now over 50 dedicated environmental reports available.

The scope of environmental matters covered is wide; perhaps 20 separate issues are discussed. Some of these are obvious and covered by most of the reports, e.g. waste, emissions, use of natural resources, energy usage and recycling. Others, like the decommissioning of oil rigs, are problems specific to particular industry groups.

Until such time as environmental reporting has matured to the stage where there is a substantial amount of historical information and a free flow of information on environmental matters, the usefulness of any information to shareholders and analysts is limited. Nevertheless, environmental issues cannot be ignored. The costs of a major environmental disaster or of decommissioning could mortally wound all but the largest groups.

Legal claims, particularly in the US, may run back many years; may be covered by insurance or uncovered; and the courts seem unpredictable, not to say wild, in their assessment of damages. Any note on contingent liabilities in this area needs to be studied with care (see page 103).

Example 25.1 Estimating current year profits: POLYGON HOLDINGS PLC

Activity	Industrial climate	Chairman's remarks	Previous year £m	Reported year £m	Estimate of current year £m
Building	Continued recession	'Further decline inevitable'	1.0	0.8	0.5–0.6
Paper	Cyclical upturn	'Marked improvement'	2.2	1.8	2.4–2.8
Bookmaking	One of the UK's few growth industries	'Continued progress'	1.0	1.2	1.4–1.5
Plastic extrusions	Demand flat	'Market share increasing but lower margins'	0.6	0.75	0.6–0.8
Interest charges	Rates down 2%	'Improvement in liquidity likely'	−0.8	−1.0	−0.8
		Pre-tax total	4.0	3.55	4.1–4.9

Estimating current year profits

A rough estimate of profits for the current year can be constructed (for each activity which is separately reported on) by quantifying the chairman's comments (and those by the chief executive and finance director in related reports – for simplicity we will refer to the chairman), bearing in mind prevailing conditions and prospects for the industry concerned; for example, POLYGON HOLDINGS PLC (Example 25.1 above).

The chairman may also give an overall indication, e.g. Polygon Holdings' turnover in the first three months of the current year has been 22% higher than the same period last year, the paper division's order-book is now four months, compared with one month last year, and, despite constant pressure on margins and the increasing ineptitude of government, the outlook for the group is encouraging. 'Outlook encouraging' sounds to us like a 20–25% increase in pre-tax profits, i.e. to £4.3–£4.5m, pointing to the middle of the range we constructed division by division.

Other points to bear in mind in making a profits estimate are these:

1. Loss-makers discontinued will not only eliminate the loss but should, in addition, improve liquidity (and thus reduce interest charges, assuming there is an overdraft). But have all terminal losses been provided for?
2. What is the chairman's previous record? Has he been accurate, cautious, unduly optimistic – erratic? Have past assurances of better times ahead remained unfulfilled?
3. Remember, too, that one of the chairman's most important jobs is to maintain general confidence in the company, so he is likely to concentrate on the good points and only touch briefly or remain silent on the weaker aspects of the company. Here it is a good idea to jot down questions one would like the answer to, even if the analyst or shareholder is unlikely to have the opportunity of putting them to the company, because it focuses the mind and helps to establish what the chairman hasn't revealed and whether any unexplained area is likely to be significant. Good questions to ask oneself are (i) 'What are the company's main problems?' and (ii) 'What is being done about them?'
4. Beware of vague statements, such as:

   (a) 'Turnover in the first ten weeks of the current year has exceeded the corresponding figure for last year.' It could be 1% ahead in value because inflation more than covered the 4% drop which occurred in volume.
   (b) 'Unforeseen difficulties have occurred in . . . and a provision of £1.3m has been made.' Unless there is some indication of the likely overall cost of overcoming these difficulties, or of abandoning the activity altogether, the company should be assumed to have an open-ended loss-maker on its hands.

Longer-term prospects

The chairman of a company should be continually looking to the future and, unless he and his board have good sound ideas on where the future growth in profits is likely to come from, and are steering the company in that direction, then above-average profits growth is unlikely. Although there must, of course, be some restrictions on what a chairman discloses about plans for the future, because of competition, he will usually include some indication of where he thinks the company is going in his annual statement.

A good past growth record is clearly encouraging (a no-growth company is likely to stay a no-growth company unless the management or the management's attitude changes), but what indications are there of future growth? Possibilities to look for are the following:

1. ***Better margins on existing business***. This is an unreliable source of growth unless the company has *either*

   (a) some very strong competitive advantage, such as patents or lucrative long-term contracts, or
   (b) spent large sums of money building up brand images and carving out market share, and is now beginning to reap the benefits, and even then the profits growth will only last until the patents expire, the long-term contracts run out or the brand images tarnish.

2. ***Further expansion of existing activities within the United Kingdom***. Is there any scope for this, or is the company in a position like BOOTS or W.H. SMITH, with a store in every town of any size, or like PILKINGTON, with 90% of the UK glass market?

3. ***Diversification within the United Kingdom***. This was BOOTS' answer to its saturation problem with chemist shops: it widened the range of goods sold to include records and tapes, hi-fi, cameras, binoculars, even sandwiches. BOOTS was using its retailing expertise in wider product ranges, rather than going into some totally unrelated activity, and there does need to be some logic in diversifications or they can come very badly unstuck.

4. ***Acquisition within the United Kingdom***. Has the company got a successful record of acquisitions, or would this method of growth be new to it (and therefore more risky)? This was part of W.H. SMITH's solution for further growth: in 1986 it took over the recorded music chain OUR PRICE, with 130 outlets, added 40 music outlets it already had and by 1990, with further acquisitions, built the chain up to around 300 outlets.

5. ***Exports***. Is the product suitable for export, or would transport costs make competitiveness overseas unlikely or impossible (e.g. bricks)? Does the company export already, is it a significant amount, and is it growing? The chairman may report that 'exports are 80% up on last year', but if this is an increase from 0.1% to 0.18% of turnover, it is hardly thrilling, and one should be wary of the chairman whose efforts to paint a rosy picture involve misleading statements like that, which should in honesty be qualified by some phrase like 'albeit from a very low base'.

6. ***Are there opportunities for overseas growth*** like W.H. SMITH's acquisition of the US news and gifts chain ELSON, specialising in shops in hotels and airports, or PILKINGTON putting down float-glass plants overseas, either on its own or in joint ventures, or by licensing the process to foreign glass manufacturers? There are, however, a good many hazards in opening up operations abroad, apart from the initial expense: different business ethics and practices, language, law, accounting and tax systems, and so on. For manufacturing abroad, cost levels and exchange rates may change over time, so that what today looks a good investment may prove otherwise in years to come if the cost of living rises faster in that country than elsewhere.

7. ***Is the company spending money on, and attaching importance to, developing new products?*** This is particularly important for pharmaceutical companies; GLAXOWELLCOME, for instance, in 1998 reported £1,163m spent on research and development, representing 14.6% of the group's turnover.

   Although any manufacturing company that isn't developing new products is almost certainly going downhill, it is also bad news if the chairman is always eulogising about new products that never come to anything: the company's track record on product development should be checked.

8. ***Is the company ploughing profits back?*** Profits in most industries cannot expand beyond a given point unless the asset base (needed to support the trading needed to generate the profits) is also expanded. There is a limit to gearing up, while acquisitions and rights issues don't necessarily enhance e.p.s.: only steady ploughback gives scope for steady growth in e.p.s.

In the context of future growth, it is also worth checking press cuttings for stories on the company, which often contain glimpses of the company's thoughts on the future (many people use the FT McCarthy press cutting service).

Information on the quality of management

Returning to the business of assessing the strength of the management, perhaps the most encouraging facet is when the chairman admits to a mistake or to being caught wrong-footed, and reports what is being or has been done about it. A classic example comes from the 'rag trade': the chairman's statement for WEARWELL in 1976, a year in which trading results had fallen from £1m profit to £28,000 loss on turnover down from £7.1m to £6.2m and with over £^{1}/$_2$m in terminal losses, contained the following comments:

WEARWELL *Extracts from chairman's report 1976*

... in 1973 we operated what was basically a cash and carry operation. [In 1974 and 1975 the company made two acquisitions for cash and we] found ourselves in the business of building up stock and financing customers for considerable periods ... sales not as buoyant as expected ... liquidity difficulties in the opening weeks of 1976 instituted immediate measures, namely:

1. Closure of the mail order supply business which has required the financing of substantial stocks.
2. Cutting out much of the credit business with chain stores.
3. The waiver by directors of a substantial part of their salary entitlement together with a waiver of between 94.0% and 99.9% of their total entitlement to the interim dividend.
4. Strenuous efforts were made to liquidate stocks.

... your company operates now only in the cash and carry type business which is where your management has proved its expertise.

Wearwell's drastic action paid off. The company just managed to get out of the red in 1977, and from then on pre-tax profits grew steadily; five years later the chairman, Asil Nadir (of POLLY PECK fame, the group which Wearwell subsequently joined) was able to report pre-tax profits in excess of £4m.

Wearwell's shareholders had a bumpy ride: from an Offer for Sale price of 30p (adjusted for subsequent scrip and rights issues) in July 1973 they saw the ordinary share price fall to a low of 8p in November 1976, and received no dividends at all in 1977 and 1978. But if they got out in time (i.e. before Polly Peck bit the dust) they were amply rewarded: in 1984 Wearwell merged with Polly Peck, whose chairman was also Mr Asil Nadir. The deal gave Wearwell shareholders 53 Polly Peck shares for every 100 Wearwell, valuing Wearwell's ordinary shares at 164p each: twenty times the 1976 level.

In contrast, the chairman of a housebuilding company reported proudly in 1974 that 'notwithstanding all these problems [the three-day week, the shortage of mortgage funds, rising interest rates and increases in building costs] your company increased its turnover to a new record level'. The turnover had risen from £25.4m to almost £44m on an equity base of less than £2m net of goodwill and after writing £8.7m off the value of the land bank, by then in the books at a mere £24.4m plus £23.4m work in progress. Apart from the feeling that the chairman was steering his company straight for the eye of a financial typhoon, and his failure to even mention the year's pre-tax loss of £6.3m in his statement, there were a number of fairly conspicuous danger signals scattered around the report:

(a) the notice of the AGM included a resolution to appoint a top London firm of accountants to be joint auditors with the existing provincial firm of auditors;
(b) the directors' report contained a little paragraph on 'financial arrangements', which revealed that the group's bankers had agreed to 'roll up' interest on group borrowings.

But perhaps the most telling fact was an omission: the group's habit of including a historical summary (which in the previous year's accounts had shown a seven-year progression in pre-tax profits from £142,000 to over £7m) had been discontinued! The fall into loss was too painful to face. Liquidation followed quite shortly afterwards.

THE DIRECTORS' REPORT

Contents

The contents of the directors' report fall broadly into three categories:

- *Information required by law* – the statutory requirements – a mass of information some of which is obvious from the accounts anyway, some of which is of comparatively little interest to the analyst (but appears to have been motivated by political considerations, e.g. contributions for political purposes), but some of which may be of vital interest and importance to anyone interpreting the accounts, e.g. the review of the year and likely future developments.

- *Information required by the UK Listing Authority*, which we described in Chapter 4, some of which overlaps the statutory requirements.

- *Voluntary information* – additional information and commentary which the company wants to include: this is usually concerned with the events of the past year, current trading and future plans and prospects.

Voluntary information is, these days, normally contained mainly or wholly in the chairman's statement or the operating review or similar reports, leaving the directors' report to be largely a catalogue of compulsory details. But if there is no chairman's statement and, as we said earlier, there is no compulsion for a chairman to report separately from the board of directors, any voluntary information will be included in the directors' report.

Statutory requirements

Under the Companies Act, a directors' report must give the following information:

(i) a fair review of the development of the business during the year, together with an indication of likely future developments and of research and development activities;
(ii) the names of the directors and details of their interests (shareholdings);
(iii) details of company's own shares acquired by the company during the year;
(iv) important events affecting the company which have occurred since the end of the year; see also post balance sheet events, page 209;
(v) details of political or charitable contributions, if over £200 in the year.

During a recent slump, it was suggested that some companies, often leading companies, were bringing problems to their suppliers by delaying payment. As a consequence directors of public companies and their large subsidiaries are required to give details of policies for the payment of suppliers in the following year.

Such statements often refer to the CBI's Prompt Payment Code but tend to be bland and of little use to the analyst. SAFEWAY doesn't and its note is slightly more interesting than most.

SAFEWAY *Extract from the 1998 directors' report*

Suppliers' Payment Policy
A strategic objective of the group is to have mutually beneficial long-term relationships with our suppliers and we seek to settle, in advance, the terms of payment with suppliers and abide by those terms. The average number of days credit taken by the group for trade purchases at 28 March 1998 was 46 days (1997 – 43 days), whereas the average during the year was 39 days (1997 38 days).

This makes the point, and it is worth remembering: figures (e.g. bank balances and ratios) at balance sheet date are not necessarily typical of those the rest of the year.

An analyst would certainly find more revealing a report by a junior member of the accounts department of a food company whose products are on every supermarket's shelves that instructions are frequently given by the managing director to 'call for a copy invoice – that will keep them happy for another couple of weeks'.

Control of the company

It is always worth checking whether a company is a 'bid prospect'. If an acquisition-minded company has a substantial holding, this can explain why the company's shares are looking overrated or expensive in comparison with other similar companies.

On the other hand, if the company is under the control of its directors or if the directors' interests are substantial although not controlling, the dividend policy is likely to be conservative. In addition, growth will probably be limited to ploughing back profits, because directors or the controlling shareholders are unlikely to be in a position to take up their entitlement in a rights issue, and because acquisitions for paper would dilute their control.

However, if the principal director shareholder is nearing retirement, with no obvious successor (check list of shareholders for family names of the next generation, and remember that new issue prospectuses give directors' ages), then an agreed bid could well be in store.

The board of directors

This is, perhaps, an opportune time to discuss the board. Although many companies are built up primarily through the efforts of a single person, a one-man band is a potentially dangerous situation. He's going to present a succession problem in due course, and what would happen if he had a heart attack tomorrow? And, if he's egocentric, he may surround himself with yes-men and come an awful cropper with 'his' company, as Tomkins illustrates (see p. 207).

Investors prefer a top management *team*: it is, for example, preferable not to combine the posts of chairman and managing director, and to have a separate finance director, and to have at least five board members. We were (and probably, today, the market would be) unhappy with the statement of one chairman/MD: 'Apart from overall control of the Group's affairs, I shall have particular responsibility for financial control, and investigating possible acquisitions by the company.'

Non-executive directors

We have long liked the inclusion of a few non-executive directors. This is now a requirement of the Combined Code on Corporate Governance – one which most companies accept though a few loudly proclaim their disagreement.

Non-executive directors are valuable provided, and only provided, they:

(a) are of a healthily independent disposition;
(b) devote sufficient time to the company to have a good grasp of its affairs (i.e. to know what's going on);

FINANCIAL TIMES *Extract from LEX column, 1 July 2000*

Tomkins

Tomkins is, belatedly, doing some sensible things: improving corporate governance, buying back its unloved shares and – when it actually happens – selling Ranks Hovis McDougall. What a shame the conglomerate did not do all this three or four years ago. Greg Hutchings is finally giving up his dual role as chairman and chief executive. Bringing in a non-executive chairman and putting some heavyweight outsiders on the board is good news. The company will start listening to its shareholders now. Though, with the stubborn Mr Hutchings continuing as chief executive, more than a few investors will continue to give Tomkins a wide berth.

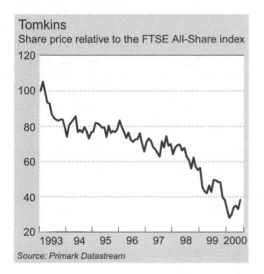

Tomkins
Share price relative to the FTSE All-Share index

Source: Primark Datastream

Selling RHM is long overdue. It was a disastrous acquisition. Tomkins shares have underperformed the market by 60 per cent since it acquired the food group in 1992. . . .

It is very hard to see this phoenix rising from the flames.

(c) are prepared to make a stand/resign if they disagree on important issues; and

(d) bring relevant experience to the boardroom.

Even so, history suggests that non-executive directors provide little protection from a dominant chairman/chief executive.

Where a company has been in difficulties or has become complacent, the effects of a change in the top management should be followed closely. It often marks the beginning of an upturn in a company's fortunes; for example the appointment of Eugene Anderson as chief executive of JOHNSON MATTHEY after a disastrous foray into banking and the appointment of Derek Birkin as chief executive of RTZ after several years of little or no real growth in e.p.s.

It is well worth checking on the track record of new management and, if you can, going to the AGM to meet them.

Internal controls and looking to the future

Terms which often figure in accounts, directors' reports and chairmen's statements are: estimates, forecasts and budgets. Not only do business decisions depend upon estimates, forecasts and budgets, so do interim statements and annual accounts. The future cannot be foretold with certainty, but managers have to try.

But it is not just the future that has to be estimated. Some information about the past (e.g. a detailed breakdown of a competitor's local sales; or a detailed analysis of a potential acquisition's cost and revenue structure) may not be available at all. Even where information about the past was potentially available, it may not have been collected. Or it may have been collected, e.g. as part of a computerised sales system, but never analysed.

In all such cases resort is frequently had to estimation. Sometimes this may be based on a limited sample; often it is largely or entirely unsupported.

Management can be criticised:

- for not using information which was obtainable;
- for failing to undertake research;
- for conducting it sloppily; or
- for drawing incorrect or unwise conclusions.

TERMINOLOGY

Estimates, forecasts and budgets

An **estimate** is a judgement (i.e. an opinion) as to the amount, or quantity, of something, e.g. sales, expenses or profit, often, but not necessarily, made before the event. It is of necessity approximate. The accuracy of an estimate depends upon (i) the skill of the estimator; and (ii) the accuracy with which the facts upon which it is based are known or can be forecast.

A **forecast** is simply a prediction. But the term **profit forecast** has a special meaning. A profit forecast is a formal statement drawn up in connection with a bid (see Chapter 28).

A **budget** is a formal **plan**, i.e. a statement of intentions. Most companies budget as a regular annual exercise; but where one or more factors change significantly, a **revised budget** is prepared. More usually, a system of continually **reforecasting** the current year is employed. This terminology is clearer: the budget remains the budget; the forecast represents current expectations.

It is often necessary to look forward, i.e. to make forecasts, e.g. when acquiring new plant, entering a new line of business, or expanding in a particular direction. It is fair to criticise managers if they have clearly been over-optimistic, or have failed to do their homework. But it is wrong to criticise managers for *trying* to forecast the future.

No manager can expect, or be expected, to be right 100% of the time.

A budget is a formal plan. Logically, it too needs to be based on forecasts: indeed, on a mutually consistent group of forecasts and plans. Too often, in an attempt to meet market expectations, budgets are imposed from above without proper regard to consistency.

Combined Code on Corporate Governance

Another factor influencing reports and accounts is the Combined Code on Corporate Governance (see Chapter 26).

Statements published in compliance with that Code are supposedly designed to shed light on internal controls and systems, and refer to the forecasting, budgeting, reporting and control structure which lies behind the annual accounts and has a marked influence upon them.

Consider GEORGE WIMPEY.

GEORGE WIMPEY – *Extract from Corporate Governance 2000*

. . .

Internal Control

The Board is responsible for the Group's system of internal control and for reviewing its effectiveness. The system can only manage rather than eliminate risk and can only provide reasonable and not absolute assurance against material mis-statement or loss.

The Board has reviewed in detail the areas of major risk that the Group faces in its operations. It has noted and is satisfied with the current control mechanisms and reporting lines that have been in place throughout the year.

In order to ensure that the system of internal control becomes embedded in the operations of the Company and forms part of its culture, each division of the Group has identified similar major risks to its activities and introduced effective controls. These procedures are reviewed by Internal Audit who discuss their findings with the Audit Committee. Any issues raised are subsequently discussed by the Board.

In addition to the major risk review process, the Group operates under an established internal control framework, which can be described under three headings:

Financial and Operating Reporting – there is a comprehensive budgeting system with an annual budget approved by the Board. Forecasts are prepared three times a year. Monthly actual performance of each business unit is reviewed by divisional management and subsequently reported to the Board against both budget and forecast. Particular emphasis is placed on cash flow as well as profit and loss and balance sheet reporting, and on key operating issues.

Business Unit Controls – controls and procedures, including information systems controls, are detailed in procedure manuals and other written instructions. Compliance with these procedures is reviewed by the Company's internal auditors and management at divisional level.

Land Purchase and Investment Appraisal – the Group has clearly defined guidelines for purchase of land and for capital expenditure. These include annual budgets, detailed appraisal and review procedures, levels of authority and due diligence requirements. In addition to financial aspects, a detailed environmental appraisal of land due to be acquired is carried out before purchase.

In following these procedures the Board has reviewed the effectiveness of the group's system of internal controls . . .

That looks like a good system. But in the recent past (if not still today) many organisations:

(i) reported to management cumulative, year-to-date, 'actuals' and compared these with the budget to date (thus failing to focus specifically on the results of each individual month or quarter);

(ii) tried to hold to the budget even when it was patently outdated (i.e. no longer achievable);

(iii) failed to reforecast the expected annual results;

(iv) lacked a continuous inventory system;

(v) often prepared no balance sheet at the end of the month or quarter (and, if they did, fell back upon estimates, budgets and forecasts rather than used 'hard' accounting data);

(vi) failed even to consider cash flows in the succeeding period.

We are not convinced that the Combined Code has done much to prevent this.

Under the Combined Code of Best Practice directors are also called upon to report that the business is a going concern. We cover this in Chapter 26.

POST BALANCE SHEET EVENTS

It might be thought that, since a company's report and accounts reflect the state of affairs at the balance sheet date, events arising after that date would be excluded, but this is not entirely the case: post balance sheet events (events occurring between the balance sheet date and the date the accounts are approved by the board) should be reflected or disclosed if they are important.

SSAP 17 *Accounting for post balance sheet events* distinguishes between two types of post balance sheet event: (i) Adjusting events; (ii) Non-adjusting events.

Adjusting events
Adjusting events are post balance sheet events which provide additional evidence of conditions existing at the balance sheet date. The accounts should be adjusted accordingly, but separate disclosure is not normally required.

Typical adjusting events include:

- the subsequent determination of the purchase price of a fixed asset purchased or sold before the year end;
- a property valuation which provides evidence of an impairment in value;
- receipt of the financial statements or other information regarding an unlisted company which provides evidence of a permanent diminution of value of a long-term investment;
- the receipt of evidence that the previous estimate of accrued profit on a long-term contract was materially inaccurate.

Where any subsequent events indicate that the 'going concern' concept should not have been applied to the company or to a material part of it, the accounts should also be adjusted accordingly.

Non-adjusting events
Non-adjusting events are post balance sheet events which concern conditions which did not exist at the balance sheet date. The events should be disclosed together, if practicable, with an estimate of the financial effect, e.g. MEDEVA:

MEDEVA *Note 27 to 1998 accounts*

27. Post balance sheet events

...

On 4 February 1999 Medeva signed an agreement to dispose of the Group's Swiss manufacturing operations to RSP Pharma AG ('RSP'), a company owned by the local management team. Details of this transaction are set out in the Operating and Financial Review on page . . .

Although SSAP 17 calls for the disclosure of post balance sheet events in the financial statements,

(i) there is normally no 'pointer' to any such note in the accounts, i.e. it is 'stand alone', so it is necessary to read the notes in their entirety and not rely on references to them elsewhere in the accounts;
(ii) non-adjusting events tend also to be mentioned or further detail given in the Chairman's Statement, Financial Review or Review of Operations. For example MEDEVA told more about the RSP deal in its Operating and Financial Review.

MEDEVA *Extract from the operating and financial review 1998*

On 5 February 1999 the conditional disposal of the Swiss manufacturing operations to RSP Pharma AG ('RSP'), a company owned by the local management team, was announced. The transaction is expected to be effective by 23 April 1999. The assets being disposed of consist of the manufacturing facility and products and certain development projects. In 1998 these assets generated sales of £6.7m (1997: £5.9m) and an operating loss of £0.2m (1997: loss £0.3m). These assets are being sold to RSP at their net asset value of £3.9m and thus no gain or loss will be generated on this disposal. Medeva will receive an initial payment of £1.7m, with the balance payable over a maximum period of 12 years, depending on the profitability of RSP. As part of the deal Medeva will also retain the rights to earn royalties on certain products RSP plan to develop, mainly Purepa, a concentrated, modified fish oil product. Medeva has also entered into an agreement to acquire a 20% investment in RSP at a cost of £0.7m.

Window dressing
One method of improving the appearance of a company's accounts was to borrow short-term money, perhaps just overnight, in order to bump up liquidity at the balance sheet date, a trick that was particularly popular amongst fringe bankers in the early 1970s.

SSAP 17 endeavours to preclude this and similar types of cosmetic operation by requiring the disclosure of 'the reversal or maturity after the year end of transactions entered into before the year end, the substance of which was primarily to alter the appearance of the company's balance sheet'.

This requirement does not prevent this type of window dressing, but it certainly discourages auditors from being party to deliberate deception.

Chapter 26

CORPORATE GOVERNANCE AND THE AUDITORS' REPORT

CORPORATE GOVERNANCE

Background

Corporate governance, the system by which companies are managed and controlled, has existed since the creation of the first company.

However, it was the publication of the Cadbury Committee's Code of Best Practice in 1992 that focused particular attention on it. Interest was reinforced by a series of incompetencies and scandals which had made it clear that assumptions on the part of investors of the competence and honesty of boards of directors were, in some cases, misplaced.

The Cadbury Committee Report was followed in 1994 by the Greenbury Committee Report on directors' remuneration. Shortly after this, the Hampel Committee published a report recommending that directors should review the effectiveness of all internal controls, financial and otherwise. Subsequent guidance on internal controls was published in September 1999 in the Turnbull Report.

The Stock Exchange (and subsequently the UK Listing Authority, the Financial Services Authority) incorporated the recommendations of the above reports within the Listing Rules.

The Combined Code

The UK Listing Authority's Combined Code contains 14 principles of good governance and 45 code provisions which are applicable to listed companies. It is in four parts:

- A – Directors
- B – Directors' remuneration
- C – Relations with shareholders
- D – Accountability and audit.

The directors are required in their report to state how the principles of the code have been applied. But the required information, which we will not list in detail, may be found almost anywhere in the report and accounts.

ROYALBLUE *Extract from Corporate Governance Statement 2000*

Compliance with the Combined Code

Royal**blue** is committed to high standards of corporate governance. During the period under review the Board of directors has complied with the provisions set out in Section 1 of the combined Code as annexed to the Listing Rules of the UK Listing Authority with the exception of the following items:

- The Audit Committee comprises two independent non-executive directors whilst the Combined Code requires there to be three. The directors believe that two are adequate at this stage of the company's development.
- The Combined Code requires there to be a senior non-executive director, other than the chairman, to whom the Board may express concerns. The Board considers this unnecessary at present because of its small size and that it would be divisive as the Chairman of the Board is non-executive.

Much of the information required is of background interest only and does not assist one in interpreting the accounts proper. For example:

ROYALBLUE *Extract from Corporate Governance Statement 2000*

The Board
The company is controlled through the Board which at 31 December 2000 comprises three executive and three non-executive directors, two of which are independent. Their profiles are set out on page 17. The Board meets formally on a regular basis to review trading performance and forecasts, to review strategy and policy and report to shareholders. The Board is responsible for the Group's system of corporate governance. Operational control is delegated by the Board to the executive directors. A procedure exists to allow directors to seek independent legal advice in respect of their duties at the company's expense where the circumstances are appropriate. All directors have access to the Company Secretary for his advice and services. Directors are required to seek election by shareholders at the first opportunity after their appointment and to seek re-election every third year thereafter. The following committees deal with specific aspects of the Group's affairs.

[Audit Committee . . .
Remuneration Committee . . .
Nominations Committee . . .]

One gains some reassurance from descriptions of internal controls, while at the same time recalling banks, merchant banks, local authorities and major listed companies which firmly believed that they had appropriate controls in place only to find, to their cost, that they had not worked.

ROYALBLUE *Extract from Corporate Governance Statement 2000*

Internal control
The Board is ultimately responsible for the Group's system of internal control and for reviewing its effectiveness. However, such a system is designed to manage rather than eliminate the risk of failure to achieve business objectives, and can provide only reasonable and not absolute assurance against material misstatement or loss.

The Combined Code requires that directors review the effectiveness of the Group's system of internal controls, including those of an operational and compliance nature, as well as internal financial controls.

The Board is of the view that there is an ongoing process for identifying, evaluating and managing the Group's significant risks and that this has been in place for the period under review and up to the date of approval of the Annual Report. The Board's agenda includes a regular item for consideration of risk and control, and any actions that may be considered necessary, and it receives reports thereon from the executive directors.

Management are responsible for the identification and evaluation of significant risks applicable to their areas of business together with the design and operation of suitable internal controls. These risks are assessed on a continual basis and may be associated with a variety of internal or external sources including competition, control breakdowns, disruption in information systems, natural catastrophe and regulatory requirements. A process of control assessment and reporting is established and defined in the Group's Quality Management System. This system is independently audited to ISO 9001 on a regular basis.

A comprehensive budgetary process is completed once a year and is reviewed and approved by the Board. Re-forecasts are prepared on a monthly basis throughout the year. The operating results are reported monthly to the Board and compared to the budget and re-forecasts as appropriate. The company reports to its shareholders twice a year.

An internal audit function has been in operation from 1999. The Board focuses the activity of the internal Audit function on those areas where they consider there to be the greatest risk.

Investors expect, indeed are entitled to expect, the directors of companies in which they invest to conduct the companies' affairs properly, efficiently and honestly. Cadbury was set up because some boards failed to meet those expectations. What the reports the Combined Code requires tell investors, if anything, is less important than what they tell directors. By focusing their attention on their own performance and methods of working, and compelling them to state in writing their procedures, directors cannot avoid being made conscious of what is expected of them.

Going concern
As explained in Chapter 2, FRS 18 *Accounting policies* requires a company to prepare its financial statements on a going concern basis unless

- the company is being liquidated or has ceased trading, or
- the directors have no realistic alternative but to liquidate the company or to cease trading.

Under the Listing Rules the report must include a statement by the directors that the company is a going concern. The statement normally appears in the report on corporate governance where there is one, or in the directors' report if there is not, but it can be in the financial review or statement of directors' responsibilities.

That the company is a going concern is of obvious importance to all who deal with it; but any suggestion that it might not be could result in its early demise. Once again what matters is that the directors should give thought to the morrow. The statement tends to be a simple formal statement. ROYALBLUE is more explicit than most:

ROYALBLUE *Extract from Corporate Governance Statement 2000*

Going concern

Having reviewed the future plans and projections for the business, the directors believe that the company and its subsidiary undertakings have adequate resources to continue in operational existence for the foreseeable future. For this reason, they continue to adopt the going concern basis in preparing the financial statements.

Auditors' review

In addition to their audit of a listed company's financial statements, auditors are required by the Code to review the directors' statements concerning the company's compliance with the Combined Code.

LATTICE GROUP *Extract from the auditors' report 2000*

Respective responsibilities of Directors and Auditors

The Directors' responsibilities for preparing the Annual Report and the financial statements in accordance with applicable United Kingdom law and accounting standards are set out in the Statement of Directors' responsibilities.

Our responsibility is to audit the financial statements in accordance with relevant legal and regulatory requirements, United Kingdom Auditing Standards issued by the Auditing Practices Board and the Listing Rules of the Financial Services Authority.

We report to you our opinion as to whether the financial statements give a true and fair view and are properly prepared in accordance with the United Kingdom Companies Act 1985. We also report to you if, in our opinion, the Directors' report is not consistent with the financial statements, if the Company has not kept proper accounting records, if we have not received all the information and explanations we require for our audit, or if information specified by law or the Listing Rules regarding Directors' remuneration and transactions is not disclosed.

We read the other information contained in the Annual Report and consider the implications for our report if we become aware of any apparent misstatements or material inconsistencies with the financial statements.

We review whether the corporate governance statement reflects the Company's compliance with the seven provisions of the Combined Code specified for our review by the Listing Rules, and we report if it does not. We are not required to consider whether the Board's statements on internal control cover all risks and controls, or to form an opinion on the effectiveness of the Company's or Group's corporate governance procedures or its risk and control procedures.

Remuneration Report

The Listing Rules require listed companies to include a report to the shareholders by the board of directors.

This report must deal with:

* company policy
* remuneration of each director analysed between salary, fees, benefits in kind, bonuses and compensation for loss of office (with total amount for the previous year), presented in tabular form
* share option information for each director
* details of long-term incentive schemes
* details of service contracts with a notice period exceeding one year
* company policy on granting of options or share award schemes
* pension benefits for each director
* arrangements for non-executive directors.

The resultant report tends to be long and detailed – that of CADBURY SCHWEPPES in its 1998 report running to 10 pages. Typically the report details:

* composition of the Remuneration Committee
* remuneration policy
* annual incentive awards
* share option schemes
* long-term incentive plan
* retirement benefits
* share schemes
* service agreements
* external appointments policy
* non-executive directors
* directors' emoluments.

There is an obvious overlap with information required in the directors' report. This tends to be overcome by a cross reference in the directors' report. The information provided is often interesting, but it is doubtful if it sheds much light on the accounts and their interpretation. One paragraph of CADBURY SCHWEPPES' report does perhaps deserve comment:

CADBURY SCHWEPPES *Extract from the 1998 report*

Report on Directors' Remuneration . . .
Executive directors – outside appointments

The Company recognises the benefits to the individual and to the Company of involvement by Executive Directors of the Company as Non-Executive Directors in companies not associated with the Company. Subject to certain conditions, each Executive Director is permitted to accept an appointment as a Non-Executive Director in another company. The Executive Director is permitted to retain any fees paid for such service. Unless otherwise determined by the Board, Executive Directors may not accept more than one such Non-Executive Directorship.

When, in other groups, one reads that the chief executive, X, is president of the Institute of . . . , a member of the . . . Committee, and of the Council of . . . , and a non-executive director of A, B and C, one does somehow wonder about his time commit-ments, or even his commitment to the group. On the other hand, the man or woman who joins a group at 20 and never works anywhere else can scarcely be said to have the breadth of experience necessary to direct a public company.

THE AUDITORS' REPORT

Appointment of auditors

Every company is required to appoint at each annual general meeting an auditor or auditors to hold office from the conclusion of that meeting until the conclusion of the next AGM.

Auditors' access to information

Under the Companies Act 1985 it is an offence for a director or company secretary to give false or misleading information to auditors, and auditors of holding companies have the right to obtain information about subsidiary companies which they themselves do not audit.

The auditor has a right of access at all times to the books and accounts and vouchers of the company and to require from the officers of the company such information and explanations as he thinks necessary for the performance of his duty. He has the right to attend any general meeting, and to be heard thereat on any part of the business of the meeting which concerns him as auditor.

Scope of the report

The auditors are required to report to the members (i.e. to the shareholders) whether in their opinion the profit and loss account and the balance sheet, and any group accounts, have been properly prepared in accordance with the Companies Act and all relevant accounting standards, and give a true and fair view of the profit and state of affairs of the company or group.

If they are of the opinion that proper accounting records have not been kept, or that the accounts are not in agreement with the books, or if they are unable to obtain all the information and explanations necessary for their audit, they must state the fact in their report; i.e. they must qualify their report.

The Auditing Practices Board (APB)

The APB was formed to develop auditing practice in the United Kingdom and the Republic of Ireland.

The APB's most important role is to establish and publish statements of the principles and procedures with which auditors are expected to comply.

The pronouncements of the APB fall into three principal categories:

1. Statements of Auditing Standards (SASs)
2. Practice notes
3. Bulletins.

Auditors who do not comply with Auditing Standards when performing company or other audits in Great Britain make themselves liable to regulatory action by the recognised supervisory body (RSB) with whom they are registered. Practice notes and Bulletins are persuasive rather than prescriptive. However, they indicate what is regarded as good practice.

Statement of Auditing Standards 600

Statement of Auditing Standards 600 (SAS 600), *Auditors' reports on financial statements*, requires that auditors' reports on financial statements contain:

* a title identifying the person or persons to whom the report is addressed;
* an introductory paragraph identifying the financial statements audited;
* separate sections, appropriately headed, dealing with

    (a) respective responsibilities of directors (or equivalent persons) and auditors;
    (b) the basis of the auditors' opinion;
    (c) the auditors' opinion on the financial statements;

* the manuscript or printed signature of the auditors; and
* the date of the auditors' report.

Responsibilities of directors and auditors

SAS 600 requires auditors to distinguish between their responsibilities and those of the directors. This is usually achieved by including:

* a statement of directors' responsibilities, either as a separate statement or as part of the directors' report (see example below) and
* a statement of respective responsibilities within the audit report (see example above).

LATTICE GROUP *Extract from the director's report 2000*

Statement of Directors' responsibilities for preparing the financial statements

The Directors are required by the Companies Act 1985 to prepare financial statements for each financial year which give a true and fair view of the state of affairs of the Company and of the Group as at the end of the financial year and of the profit and loss of the Group for the financial years.

The Directors consider that in preparing the financial statements detailed in the following sections, the Company has used appropriate accounting policies, consistently applied and supported by reasonable and prudent judgements and estimates and all applicable accounting standards have been followed: Principal accounting policies, Accounts, Notes to the accounts and Operating and financial review.

The Company has complied with UK disclosure requirements in this report in order to present a consistent picture to all shareholders.

The Directors have responsibility for ensuring that the Company keeps accounting records which disclose with reasonable accuracy the financial position of the Company and of the Group and which enables them to ensure that the financial statements comply with the Companies Act 1985.

The Directors have general responsibility for taking such steps as are reasonably open to them to safeguard the assets of the Group and to prevent and to detect fraud and other irregularities.

The Directors, having prepared the financial statements, have requested the Auditors to take whatever steps and to undertake whatever inspections they consider to be appropriate for the purposes of enabling them to give their audit report.

The Directors confirm that the Audit Committee continues to review the adequacy of the system of internal financial controls adopted by the Group.

Auditors' report

The content of the auditors' report is determined by the Companies Act 1985 and various requirements of the Auditing Practices Board. Following APB guidance in January 2001, UK company audit reports should refer to United Kingdom law, accounting standards and auditing standards. An example of wording follows:

LATTICE GROUP *Extract from the annual report for 2000*

Independent Auditors' report to the members of Lattice Group plc

We have audited the financial statements which comprise the profit and loss account, the balance sheet, the cash flow statement, the statement of total recognised gains and losses and the related notes which have been prepared under the historical cost convention (as modified by the revaluation of certain fixed assets) and the accounting policies set out under 'Principal accounting policies'.

Respective responsibilities of Directors and Auditors
[see reproduced extract on page 212]

Basis of audit opinion

We conducted our audit in accordance with auditing standards issued by the United Kingdom Auditing Practices Board. An audit includes examination, on a test basis, of evidence relevant to the amounts and disclosures in the financial statements. It also includes an assessment of the significant estimates and judgements made by the Directors in the preparation of the financial statements, and of whether the accounting policies are appropriate to the Company's circumstances, consistently applied and adequately disclosed.

We planned and performed our audit so as to obtain all the information and explanations which we considered necessary in order to provide us with sufficient evidence to give reasonable assurance that the financial statements are free from material misstatement, whether caused by fraud or other irregularity or error. In forming our opinion we also evaluated the overall adequacy of the presentation of information in the financial statements.

Opinion

In our opinion the financial statements give a true and fair view of the state of affairs of the Company and the Group at 31 December 2000 and the profit and cash flows of the Group for the year then ended and have been properly prepared in accordance with the United Kingdom Companies Act 1985.

PricewaterhouseCoopers   27 February 2001
Chartered Accountants and Registered Auditors
1 Embankment Place
London WC2N 6RH

The auditors' opinion

An auditors' report 'should contain a clear expression of opinion on the financial statements' (SAS 600.5).

That opinion may be unqualified (as was the report to shareholders of LATTICE GROUP illustrated above) or qualified.

A *qualified* opinion is issued when either

(a) there is a limitation on the scope of the auditors' examination; or
(b) the auditor disagrees with the treatment or disclosure of a matter in the financial statements.

Example 26.1 A qualified opinion where there is limitation of scope

... However, the evidence available to us was limited because £... of the company's turnover comprises cash sales, over which there was no system of control on which we could rely for the purposes of our audit. There were no other satisfactory audit procedures that we could adopt to confirm that cash sales were properly recorded.

In respect alone of the limitation of our work relating to cash sales, we have not obtained all the information necessary for the purposes of our audit; and we were unable to determine whether proper accounting records had been maintained.

Example 26.2 A qualified opinion where there is disagreement

Qualified opinion arising from disagreement about accounting treatment

Included in the debtors shown on the balance sheet is an amount of £y due from a company which has ceased trading. XYZ plc has no security for this debt. In our opinion the company is unlikely to receive any payment and a provision of £y should have been made, reducing the profit before tax and net assets by that amount.

Except for the absence of this provision ... give a true and fair view ...

Adverse opinion

An adverse opinion is issued when the effect of disagreement is so material or pervasive that the auditors conclude that the financial statements are seriously misleading, i.e. that they did not give a true and fair view.

Example 26.3 An adverse opinion

Adverse opinion

As more fully explained in Note ... no provision has been made for losses expected to arise on certain long-term contracts currently in progress, as the directors consider that such losses should be off-set against amounts receivable on other long-term contracts. In our opinion, provision should be made for foreseeable losses on individual contracts as required by SSAP 9. If losses had been so recognised, the effect would have been to reduce the profit before and after tax for the year ... and the contract work in progress at 31 December 19 .. by £x.

In view of the effect of the failure to provide for the losses, in our opinion the financial statements do not give a true and fair view ...

Disclaimer of opinion

A disclaimer of opinion is expressed when the possible effect of a limitation on scope is so material or pervasive that the auditors have been unable to obtain sufficient evidence to support, and accordingly are unable to express, an opinion on the financial statements.

Example 26.4 An adverse opinion with disclaimer

... However, the evidence available to us was limited because we were appointed auditors on ... and in consequence we were unable to carry out auditing procedures necessary to obtain adequate assurance regarding the quantities and condition of stock and work in progress appearing in the balance sheet at £z. Any adjustment to this figure would have a consequential effect on the profit for the year.

Disclaimer on view given by financial statements

Because of the possible effect of the limitation in evidence available to us, we are unable to form an opinion as to whether the financial statements give a true and fair view ...

Fundamental uncertainty

Where an inherent uncertainty exists which in the auditors' opinion is fundamental and is adequately accounted for and disclosed in the accounts, auditors include an explanatory paragraph in their report, making it clear that their opinion is not qualified. Such opinions are comparatively rare, so we look back for an example (see below) to REGALIAN PROPERTIES' 1994 accounts. This is emphasis: the auditors are simply drawing attention to something already fully covered in the accounts.

REGALIAN PROPERTIES *1994 Accounts: an unqualified opinion with fundamental uncertainty*

Fundamental uncertainty

In forming our opinion, we have considered the adequacy of the disclosures made in the accounts concerning the carrying value of the Group's investment in its associated undertaking. Uncertainty exists as to whether the Group's associated undertaking will be able to develop with financial success a site at Bishopsbridge, Paddington. In view of this we are unable to determine whether any further write down of the Group's investment in that undertaking is required.

Details of the circumstances relating to this fundamental uncertainty are described in note 14. Our opinion is not qualified in respect of the above matter.

But the degree of uncertainty about the outcome of a future event and its potential impact on the view given by the financial statements may be very great. In such a case a disclaimer of opinion is appropriate.

Going concern assumption

The Combined Code calls upon directors to report that the business is a going concern. Take HUNTER-PRINT GROUP: in 1993 the group suffered its fifth consecutive year of loss-making. In 1992, there had been a capital reduction scheme.

HUNTERPRINT GROUP *Extract from financial review 1993*

Going concern

The directors have considered the adequacy of the group's banking facilities and cashflow forecasts as outlined in Note 1 to the financial statements and have concluded that the preparation of financial statements on the going concern basis is appropriate.

The auditors have also concluded that it is appropriate to draw up the financial statements on the going concern basis and accordingly have issued an unqualified audit opinion. However, under the circumstances of the group's funding, and in accordance with Auditing Standards, the auditors have included reference to going concern in their report, under the heading of 'fundamental uncertainty'.

HUNTERPRINT GROUP *Extract from Notes to the 1993 accounts*

1. Group funding

The group's bankers have recently confirmed their agreement to extend the group's loan and overdraft facilities which remain payable on demand, through to 30 September 1994. The group meets its day to day working capital requirements through its overdraft facility, which at the year end was substantially utilised.

The nature of the group's business is such that there can be considerable variations in the timing of cash inflows and continued tight financial management is required for the group to remain within its available facilities. The directors have prepared projected cashflow forecasts covering the period through to September 1995. On the basis of:

- this cashflow information;
- the confirmed availability of borrowing facilities through to 30 September 1994; and
- the group's demonstrated ability to control its cash requirements tightly,

the directors consider it appropriate to prepare financial statements on the going concern basis.

But they were proved wrong. The ordinary shares, which stood at around 25p in June 1994, fell sharply in the second half of 1994, and shareholders received about 2p a share when the group was taken over by a major Canadian printer.

Chapter 27

INTERIM REPORTS

UK Listing Rules

The rules reflect the European Union Directive on Interim Reports, which requires each listed company to prepare a report on its activities and profit and loss for the first six months of each financial year.

The rules also require that the report *either* be sent to shareholders *or* be inserted in at least one national newspaper, not less than 3 months after the end of the period (Chapter 12 para. 50).

INTERIM REPORTS

ASB Statement of Best Practice

This statement is intended for voluntary use.

It suggests that Interim Reports should be drawn up employing the same principles and practices as those used for annual reporting.

They should *include*:

(a) a narrative commentary;
(b) summarised profit and loss account;
(c) balance sheet;
(d) cash flow statement;
(e) a statement of total recognised gains and losses, where relevant.

And should *provide* details of:

(a) acquisitions and discontinued operations
(b) segmental information
(c) exceptional items
(d) comparative figures for the corresponding interim period and for the previous full financial year.

Companies are encouraged to make their interim reports available with 60 days of the interim period end.

Auditors' review

One of the recommendations of the Cadbury Report on Corporate Governance was that interim reports should be reviewed by the Company's auditors.

The review process, which is **'best practice' rather than mandatory**, is described in a Bulletin *Review of Interim Financial Information*, issued by the Auditing Practices Board.

Many smaller companies and some larger ones, e.g. the hotel group HILTON (Market capitalisation £3.5 billion), don't have their interim reports reviewed, and it is open to debate as to whether the benefits of a review justify the costs.

In those companies where the auditor *has* reviewed the interim information, his report will appear in the company's interim report. The prescribed format of the report is, in some people's views, both long winded and pedantic. For example, the Review report by the auditors to the Ready Mix Concrete Group RMC takes up more than half a page of A4, and gets its own page. Here is an abridged version:

RMC *Extract from Review report by the auditors*

Introduction

We have been instructed by the Company to review the financial information set out on pages 6 to 11 and we have read the other information contained in the 2000 Interim Statement for any apparent misstatements or material inconsistencies with the financial information.

Directors' responsibilities

The 2000 Interim Statement . . . is the responsibility of, and has been approved by the Directors. The Listing Rules of the FSA, require that the accounting policies and presentation applied to the interim figures should be consistent with those applied in preparing the preceding annual accounts except where any changes, and the reasons for them, are disclosed.

Review work performed

We conducted our review in accordance with the guidance contained in Bulletin 1999/4 issued by the Auditing Practices Board.

A review consists principally of making enquiries of Group management and applying analytical procedures. . . . A review excludes audit procedures such as . . . It is substantially less in scope than an audit . . . and therefore provides a lower level of assurance than an audit. Accordingly we do not express an audit opinion . . .

Review conclusion

On the basis of our review we are not aware of any material modifications that should be made to the financial information as presented for the six months ended 30 June 2000.

Chartered Accountants
London
6 September 2000

With so many disclaimers in the report, the boards of some companies may decide that an auditors' review is hardly worth the candle.

Accounting policies

The ASB Statement expects interim reports to be prepared on the basis of accounting policies used in the previous annual accounts. Where there has been any change, this should be spelt out, e.g. PEARSON:

PEARSON *Note to the 'Interim Results' 1999*

4. Basis of preparation

The interim results for the six months to 30 June 1999 have been prepared in accordance with the accounting policies set out in the 1998 Annual Report, except that FRS 12 'Provisions, Contingent Liabilities and Contingent Assets' has been adopted.

Major transactions

Although not specifically mentioned, it is clearly desirable that interim statements should report other major transactions such as the redemption or conversion of shares or the purchase of a company's own shares and their subsequent cancellation e.g.

DIAGEO *Note to the interim statement 1999*

8. Repurchase of shares

In July 1998, 3m B shares were redeemed at a cost of £15m. On 1 August 1998, the company converted the remaining B shares into 12m ordinary shares at a price of 725 pence per share. In October 1998, the company purchased, and subsequently cancelled, 10.5m ordinary shares at an average price of 555 pence per share for an aggregate consideration of £59m.

Exceptional items

As explained earlier, interim statements are not audited, and in the past, when they were not reviewed either, it is possible that the stringent look which is given to the balance sheet at the end of the year, and the consequent making of adequate provisions, did not occur at the half-year. It perhaps still does not, and this tends to mean that adverse exceptional items are somewhat more likely to be included in the second half of a year than in the first half. But where they are found in the first half year figures they may be material as is demonstrated by DIAGEO:

DIAGEO *Note to the interim statement 1999*

2. Exceptional items

	Six months ended 31 Dec 1998 £m	Six months ended 31 Dec 1997 £m
Charged to:		
Operating profit		
Merger integration costs	(156)	(44)
Haagen-Dazs plant closure	(35)	–
Foodservice integration costs	(7)	–
Agreement with LVMH	–	(250)
	(198)	(294)

Half year on half year comparisons

It is obvious that a careful item by item comparison of this year's interim figures (H1/Year2) with last year's interim figures (H1/Year 1) will help with assessing how the company is doing. It should also prompt questions about the cause of any sudden jump.

But it is rather less obvious that the same comparison should be made of H2/Year 2 with H2/Year 1, because companies hardly ever publish their second half figures.

 H2 = (Full year − H1)

Second half figures have to be calculated, but the effort can be very worthwhile, revealing information that might otherwise be overlooked.

For example, LOCKER GROUP, where the Chairman's statement in the annual report to 31 March 2000 did not mention that the Group had plunged into loss in the second half, but this is easily deduced:

LOCKER GROUP *Second half results*

Operating profit reported

	£000
Six months to 30 September 1999	1,758
Year ended 31 March 2000	482
Operating loss in second half, deduced	**(1,276)**

Seasonal businesses

According to the ASB 'Fluctuating revenues of seasonal businesses are generally understood by the marketplace and it is appropriate to report them as they arise'. What, in the past, may have been less well known, is the effect on the balance sheet and cash flow statement (which traditionally were not disclosed) e.g. THORNTONS:

THORNTONS *Half yearly fluctuations due to seasonality*

	Reported		Deduced
	H1 1999 28 weeks to 9 January 1999 £000	Full year 1999 52 weeks to 26 June 1999 £000	H2 1999 24 weeks to 26 June 1999 £000
Consolidated profit and loss account			
Turnover	87,760	141,267	53,507
H1 and H2 adjusted to 26 weeks	81,491		57,966
Operating profit	13,172	13,085	(87)
Margin	15.0%	9.2%	Zilch
Consolidated balance sheet			
Cash at bank and in hand	5,140	2,941	
Bank loans (etc.) due within one year	(3,204)	(11,100)	
Consolidated cash flow statement			
Cash inflow from operating activities	24,505	29,693	5,188

H2 and H1 compared
Operating profit in H2 was about £13.2m lower than H1. The knock-on effect in the balance sheet was a fall of about £2.2m in cash, while short-term loans and overdraft increased by about £7.9m.
H1's Christmas sales dominate, in spite of H2's Easter eggs.

Company strategy
The Chairman, in his Statement in the 1999 annual report, said 'we plan to radically revitalise our ranges for the Easter and Spring season'.

Chapter 28

OTHER SOURCES OF INFORMATION

Keep your eyes open!

Investors and analysts should recognise that the annual report and accounts of a company represent only a part, albeit a key part, of the total information available to them, and they should not neglect other sources. For convenience the other sources can be divided into:

(a) information the company provides;
(b) external information.

INFORMATION PROVIDED BY THE COMPANY

The main sources of information from the company itself, apart from the annual report and accounts, are:

(a) half-yearly (and in a few cases quarterly) reports, considered in Chapter 27;
(b) prospectuses;
(c) circulars;
(d) form 20-F (if listed in the US);
(e) company newsletters and magazines;
(f) catalogues and sales information literature;
(g) annual meetings;
(h) company visits.

Prospectuses and listing particulars

When a company offers shares or debentures for sale to the general public it is obliged in law to issue a prospectus.

When a company 'goes public' – that is, when its shares gain a listing on the Stock Exchange (see Chapter 4) – its prospectus has to include all the information required for listing (see the UK Listing Authority's *Listing Rules*, Chapter 6: 'Contents of Listing Particulars'), and so the prospectus is about the most comprehensive document a company ever produces about itself. The normal layout used is as follows:

1. Details of the offer, share capital and indebtedness.
2. Details of the company's directors, secretary, auditors, financial advisers, solicitors, bankers and stockbrokers.
3. Description of the company, giving:

   • an introduction and a brief history;
   • a comprehensive description of its business;
   • information on the management and staff;
   • details of the company's premises;
   • the use to be made of the proceeds of the issue (where any new shares are being issued);
   • the earnings record, with a forecast for the current year's profits and intended dividends;
   • the company's plans and prospects for the future.

4. The accountants' report, containing a table of the last three years' profit and loss accounts and cash flow statements and the latest balance sheet.
5. Various statutory and general information on share capital and options, on the Articles of Association, on subsidiary and associated companies, directors' interests and service agreements, taxation clearances, material contracts, and any pending litigation.

On other occasions of shares being offered to the general public either directly, as in a secondary offer for sale of existing shares already listed, or indirectly, as in a rights issue of new shares of a company whose existing securities are already listed, much less information is required; nevertheless, the prospectus of a secondary offer or the circular letter to shareholders produced for a rights issue can be a useful source of up-to-date information on a company.

Circulars on acquisitions and disposals

Chapter 10 of the Purple Book divides transactions into classes, as shown in Example 28.1 below.

When a listed company makes a Class 1 transaction (i.e. equivalent to 25% or more of the existing company), shareholders have to be sent a circular giving full details; alternatively, if the company is making a takeover bid, they can be sent a copy of the offer document, provided the offer document includes all the information required for circulars on acquisitions (as contained in Chapter 10 of the Purple Book). In either case the information provides the analyst with useful details of any

major additions to or realisations of the company's assets.

Where there is a Class 1 transaction or reverse takeover, it must be subject to shareholders' approval, and the acquiring company will normally be treated as a new applicant for listing.

Circulars also have to be sent to shareholders for transactions with related parties (those involving a director or substantial shareholder, past or present); these can be of considerable interest if the transactions are large and/or if there is any question of sharp practice, but the majority are fairly mundane, produced mainly to ensure that shareholders' interests are scrupulously protected (see Chapter 11 of the Purple Book).

Documents issued in a contested bid

When the management of a company defends a bid, it has to make the best possible case for the company's continued independence and, in doing so, it will often be rather more forthcoming about the company's future plans and prospects than it normally is in the annual report. Analysts should therefore find it worth reading any documents that a company has

---

Example 28.1 Criteria for classification of transactions

Class	Size of acquisition or disposal (A)	Ratios in relation to acquiring or disposing company (B)	UKLA requirements
	Gross assets (i.e. fixed assets plus current assets)	to listed company's gross assets	
	Pre-tax profits	to listed company's pre-tax profit	
	Turnover	to listed company's turnover	
	Consideration given or received	to listed company's market capitalisation	
Class 1		Transaction is Class 1 if any of the five ratios (A)/(B) is 25% or over	Company must inform the Company Announcements Office (CAO) and send circular to shareholders. Shareholders' approval required.
Class 2	as above	Class 2 if any ratio is 5% or more but none is 25% or more	Company must notify CAO
Class 3	as above	Class 3 if all ratios less than 5%	Company must notify CAO if listing is being sought for securities in consideration
Reverse takeover	as above	Reverse takeover is acquisition by a listed company of a business, an unlisted company or assets where any percentage is 100% or more or which would result in a fundamental change in the business or in a change in board or voting control of the listed company	On announcement of a reverse takeover, suspend listing, prepare Class 1 Circular, obtain prior approval of shareholders and (where company wishes to be listed) prepare listing particulars as if new applicant.

A fifth ratio applies to acquisitions only – namely the gross capital of the company or business being acquired (widely defined to include consideration given plus shares and debt security not being acquired plus all other non-current liabilities plus any net current liabilities) divided by the market capitalisation of the listed company.

issued in successfully contesting a bid. It is also interesting to see whether a company subsequently lives up to any rosy picture it may have painted of its future at the time of the bid.

The detail provided often far exceeds that in published accounts. ENTERPRISE OIL's offer to purchase/prospectus in respect of LASMO in April 1994 ran to 259 pages.

Related party transactions

Where transactions involve, or involve an associate of, a director, past director, substantial shareholder or past substantial shareholder, the Stock Exchange should be consulted beforehand. A circular to shareholders and their consent in general meeting is required unless the transaction is 'small' (all ratios less than 0.25%). See page 180 regarding FRS 8 *Related party disclosures*.

Company newsletters and magazines

An increasing number of companies now produce a house magazine or newsletter for employees, and many produce a 'report to employees' summarising the company's results for the year, often presenting the information in charts or diagrams.

These publications can be very helpful in giving the analyst (as well as the employee) a better feel for the company, and they may contain information that is not included in the accounts.

Companies producing an annual newsletter or report to employees may also send copies to shareholders to ensure that information given to employees is also made available to the shareholders, but where newsletters are published more frequently or where a large group has several subsidiaries, each of which has its own separate newsletter, they are unlikely to be distributed to investors. If the analyst can lay his hands on them he may gain a better insight into the various activities of the company and pick up facts that are not generally available.

Company websites

A growing number of companies have websites and these can be useful sources of recent news and may provide information not available, or not easily available, elsewhere e.g. the text of press releases, preliminary announcements, new product details etc. Some sites are more obviously investor-orientated than others; and many larger groups are currently conspicuous by their absence, but a number offer a free newsletter, or provide their employee newsletter on Internet request. Others offer a free company news service via the Internet.

Form 20-F

This is the annual report that UK and other 'foreign' companies have to file with the Securities and Exchange Commission (SEC) if their shares are listed in the United States. Most companies supply copies to shareholders on request. BP used to offer to do so in their annual report but their accounts now include Form 20-F information.

Companies which are listed in the US normally provide additional information in their accounts on the differences between their accounts, following UK GAAP, and similar accounts prepared under US GAAP. The differences can be quite startling, as shown in Chapter 30.

Catalogues and sales information literature

The shareholder or analyst who really wants to know a company should study its catalogues and sales literature for evidence of pricing policy, marketing ability, and changes in product range, quality or design.

Failure to adapt to changing circumstances is an early sign of sleepy management. Innovation may be essential if the company is to keep moving – but not every management is capable of thinking up new ideas and of putting them into practice. Promotional literature on new products can sometimes indicate the potential for success.

Annual General Meeting

When all is going well, annual meetings tend to be sparsely attended. This is a pity, because they provide an opportunity for investors and analysts to seek and obtain further information about the company.

The routine business of an AGM is:

(a) to receive the report and accounts;
(b) to declare a dividend;
(c) to elect directors;
(d) to appoint auditors;
(e) to transact any other ordinary business.

The chairman will often take the opportunity to make a statement on current trading and/or to amplify the statement he made in the annual report. This is usually done before the routine business, sometimes to pre-empt hostile questions.

Any ordinary shareholder may attend the AGM and speak. Normally his best opportunity to obtain information is upon the motion considering the accounts. If the information he seeks is reasonable (e.g. not of a confidential nature or likely to be of more value to the competition than to members) and he does not obtain a satisfactory answer, he should press the point and state publicly his dissatisfaction. He may find he has more support than he expects.

Generally, directors are prepared to answer all reasonable questions when times are good, but become guarded when the situation is unsatisfactory. If this occurs, the individual shareholder may find that he can obtain the information during informal discussion after the meeting.

Company visits

Companies differ widely in their attitude to company visits by analysts and/or shareholders. Most major companies welcome the interest of both and arrange from time to time group visits at which plans and prospects are discussed in depth, and those interested are able to seek further information.

When making a visit ask yourself:

- Is there any evidence of cut-back, of falling sales and growing stocks or of maintenance delayed to save cash?
- Is the workforce contented – or are labour relations uneasy?
- Do they look efficient – or is there a general atmosphere of chaos?
- Do people appear forthcoming, or are they hiding something?
- Do management appear enthusiastic? . . . the sort of people you could trust?

It is also worth asking management whether it is experiencing any difficulties. Good management is usually prepared to talk about the problems facing the company, and to explain the action being taken to overcome them. But companies have to be careful not to provide those visiting with price-sensitive information which has not first been released to the market.

Always ask about the competition

The replies will help to show whether the management has a practical and realistic attitude to the business environment in which it operates, and may well provide useful information about other companies in the industry. We well remember on one company visit, in reply to a question about a competitor, the chairman simply remarked 'that company is structured for disaster'. It did indeed go bust a year later.

EXTERNAL INFORMATION

There is a vast range of external information useful to the analyst who wishes to make a study in depth of a particular company, group or industrial sector.

We list sources which we personally find useful and, where we find it helpful, their website.

The Registrar of Companies

The Registration Department of the Department of Trade and Industry has offices at Companies House, 55–71 City Road, London EC1Y 1BB, at Crown Way, Cardiff CF4 3UZ (Information Centre Tel 0870 33 33 636) and in Birmingham, Leeds, Manchester, Edinburgh and Glasgow.

Rules for filing accounts
Section 244 of the Companies Act 1985 requires a company to lay its annual report and accounts before its members in general meeting and to deliver them to the Registrar within certain time limits fixed by reference to its accounting year end. The limit for a UK public company is seven months, which can be extended by three months if the company has interests outside the United Kingdom.

The UK Listing Authority requires listed companies to issue an annual report and accounts within six months of the end of the financial year being reported on (The Purple Book, Chapter 12, para. 42), but this may be extended for companies with significant overseas interests.

Other information to be filed
Companies are also required to file with the Registrar:

(a) copies of their Memorandum and Articles of Association, and details of any changes;
(b) the address of the registered office, and the place at which the company's registers are kept, if not at the registered office;
(c) details of the company's share capital and debentures;
(d) details of each mortgage and charge on the assets of the company;
(e) a list of the directors and secretary and any changes.

In addition, Section 363 of the Companies Act 1985 requires a company to file an *annual return*, which contains a summary of (b) to (e) above and a list of past and present members. Every third year the list must be a complete list of persons holding shares or stock in the company; in the intervening years only changes need be given, but in each year the return must show anyone whose name has appeared on the register as holding shares or stock in the company at any time since the last return. It is therefore possible to find out if anyone has been a registered shareholder at any time, however short the period of ownership, although nominee names may hide the beneficial owner.

Microfiche records

Companies House holds the public records of more than one million companies. Members of the public making a standard search of a company record are provided with a microfiche copy of information held.

Companies House Direct

Companies House Direct provides on-line information direct to your PC and is a fast, accurate and inexpensive way of obtaining up-to-date information from Companies House.

Available to subscribers, it brings the Companies House database directly to one's personal computer. It gives direct access to the names and addresses of company directors and secretaries, with their appointments history since 1991; lists of documents filed by companies; dates of accounts and annual returns filed, and details of disqualified directors since 1986. You can also select images of accounts (registered since March 1995) for on-line viewing, printing or downloading to your PC. Microfiche ordering facilities are provided, including the option to order up to 20 microfiches at a time.

Counter staff at any of the offices can answer any general enquiries about Companies House Direct. For more specific queries and for demonstration and subscription details, contact the Companies House Direct Help Desk (0845 757 3991).

Analysing a group

Most group accounts contain a general breakdown of their activities, but much more detail can sometimes be obtained by examining the accounts which each subsidiary and associated company has to file at Companies House.

Further information

Companies House publishes a large number of helpful information leaflets on its services and on company law and practice. A good starting point is CHN32 *Products and services information and price list* (free from any of their offices) – *http://www.companieshouse.gov.uk/*

Newspapers and journals

The *Financial Times*, daily, and the *Investors Chronicle*, weekly, are required reading for any investor or analyst who wants to keep abreast of the market and of news about individual companies.

There are numerous journals, newsletters and tip sheets which vary greatly in quality but which may point one in the direction of a company worth investigating further.

H S Financial Publishing

H S Financial Publishing Ltd (phone 020 7278 7769, website www.hsfinancial.com), Arnold House, 36–41 Hollywell Lane, London EC2A 3SF is one of the leading suppliers of business information and investment data on UK registered quoted companies. A team of analysts collect, collate and analyse data from primary sources to maintain the Hemmington Scott Corporate Information Database. From this database a number of equity products are generated.

Jointly devised by Jim Slater and Hemmington Scott Publishing, REFS (Really Essential Financial Statistics) draws upon his experience as a successful private investor, putting together all the key statistics and ratios needed by investors seeking growth and value.

As the Body Shop illustration on the next page shows, in a single source one can find:

- individual brokers' estimates from over 50 contributing research houses plus the consensus estimate;
- detailed five-year financials plus two years' estimates;
- listing of all directors and their shareholdings;
- company contact details;
- activities;
- concise coverage of events, announcements and changes affecting the company in the last 12 months;
- all the usual key performance statistics and value indicators and many more, such as:
    - Price earnings growth rate
    - Price to book value
    - Price to cash flow
    - Price to sales
    - Price to research
    - Net cash per share.

Definitions of all the ratios and terms used in REFS are supplied and are available from their website which also provides enlightening information on Jim Slater's investment philosophy and strategy – *www.companyrefs.com*

BODY SHOP INTERNATIONAL (THE)

	SEDOL:	108313		PRICE (NMS 3) 28-MAR-02	96.5p
	EPIC:	BOS	BLMBG: BOS		

PRICE (p) — 5p Ords vs FTSE All-Share vs norm eps

	98	99	00	01	02
HIGH	146	139	134	127	117
LOW	67	83	87	72	87
AVE PER	9.7x	11.3x	9.8x	12.7x	12.0x

RELATIVE	%
1M	+2.9
3M	−13.5
6M	+5.8
1Y	+39.6
Beta rel	1.31

ACTIVITIES ANALYSIS (01AR)

		T/O	Pr
Skin & haircare products	%	100	100
UK	%	40	40
Americas	%	32	21
Europe & Middle East	%	17	16
Asia Pacific	%	12	24

			m	s
market cap		£196m		
position		442nd		
index		FTSE SmallCap		
norm eps (pr)		11.3p		
turnover (01AR)		£374m		
pretax (01AR)		£12.8m		
DY (pr)	%	5.91	◉	◉
PER (pr)	x	8.55	◉	◉
PEG	f	na	⊕	⊕
GR (pr)	%	17.6	⊖	⊖
ROCE	%	13.9	⊖	⊖
MARGIN	%	5.48	⊖	⊖
GEAR	%	39.6	⊖	⊖
PBV	x	1.69	⊖	⊖
PTBV	x	2.33	⊖	⊖
PCF	x	32.3	⊖	⊖
PSR	x	0.49	⊖	⊖
PRR	x	27.4	⊖	◉
nav ps (01AR)		57.2p		
net cash ps (01AR)		na		

SECTOR: General Retailers. **ACTIVITIES:** Development and sale of skin and hair care products.

DIRS: A D P Bellamy (ch), P Saunders (ceo), A S N Murray (fd), J M J Keenan*, R de Waal*, Irene Miller*, T G Roddick*, Anita L Roddick OBE*. **HEAD & REG OFF:** Watersmead, Littlehampton, West Sussex, BN17 6LS. Tel: (01903) 731500. Fax: (01903) 726250. **REGISTRAR:** Lloyds TSB Registrars, Worthing. Tel: (0870) 600 3964

BROKERS: Hoare Govett Ltd. **AUDITORS:** BDO Stoy Hayward.

INTERIM: (2-Oct-01) 1/2 yr to 01 Sep 01. T/O £167m (£160m). Pre tax profit £2.60m (£6.80m). EPS 1.00p (2.50p). Int div 1.90p (1.90p).

OUTLOOK: (1-May-01) AR: ce - "We are reporting a pre-tax profit £25.0m...this is below our expectations and we are disappointed with the outcome...we did not deliver on the implementation of our strategy". (17-Sep-01) Ann: "The Board now anticipates full year profit to be broadly in line with last year". (2-Oct-01) Int: ch - "...our outcome for the full year is highly reliant on trading during the Christmas period, but our profit outcome remains unchanged...broadly in line with last year". (17-Jan-02) Ann: ceo - "Group turnover for the first ten months of the year was 3.00% higher than in the comparable period last year. Although retail sales generally reached expecations, wholesale sales were lower year on year".

NEWSFLOW: (16-Jul-01) Ann: The company announces today that conditional agreement has been reached to purchase BSI USA Inc, the holding company of Bellamy Retail Group, for the consideration of approximately £7.90m. (9-Aug-01) Ann: The company announces that the resolution of the acquisition of BSI USA Inc, was duly passed. Completion is expected to be on the 11 August 2001. (17-Sep-01) Ann: The Board is not in discussions with any third party regarding a potential offer for the company, but will be considering whether it is appropriate to take any of these approaches forward. (2-Oct-01) Int: The company announce that following our recent announcement concerning expressions of interest from third parties exploring the possibility of acquiring The Body Shop, the board now confirms that it has reviewed these approaches and that preliminary discussions are taking place with a number of interested parties. (12-Feb-02) Ann: Patrick Gournay has resigned as Chief Executive Officer and leaves the board with immediate effect. (12-Feb-02) Ann: Peter Saunders has been appointed as Chief Executive Officer with immediate effect. (12-Feb-02) Ann: The board has terminated all offer discussions for the company as they were unlikely to result in proposals that fairly reflect the inherent value of the company.

SHARE CAPITAL, HOLDINGS, DEALINGS

203m 5p Ords (Maj 50.0%, Dirs 29.9% [d]).

I B McGlinn	%	23.5	
Fidelity Intl Ltd	%	6.38	1 +
Schroder Inv Mgmt Ltd	%	5.03	2 −
WE Fin & Servs - dup	%	4.78	
A S N Murray (fd)	k	20.0	
J M J Keenan*	k	45.0	2 +
R de Waal* - dup	%	5.00	
Irene Miller*	k	120	2 +
T G Roddick* - dup	%	12.5	
A Roddick OBE* - dup	%	12.4	

year ended 28 Feb		1997	1998	1999	2000	2001	2002E	2003E
turnover	£m	271	293	304	330	374		
depreciation	£m	11.5	12.0	12.7	13.4	14.0		
int paid (net)	£m	0.20	0.10	0.10	1.50	4.40		
FRS3 pretax	£m	31.7	38.0	3.40	28.8	12.8		
norm pretax	£m	38.6	38.3	26.5	32.5	16.1	27.5	31.7
turnover ps	£	1.41	1.52	1.58	1.73	1.96		
op margin	%	14.3	13.1	8.76	10.3	5.48		
ROCE	%	26.6	25.9	21.2	27.1	13.9		
ROE	%	17.1	17.6	15.9	18.1	10.5		
FRS3 eps	p	9.20	11.7	−2.40	9.60	4.90		
norm eps	p	11.7	11.9	9.62	11.5	6.62	9.60	11.3
norm eps growth	%	+16.4	+1.72	−18.8	+20.0	−42.6	+45.0	+17.7
tax rate	%	44	40	235	36	27	31	29
norm per	x					14.6	10.1	8.54
provisional peg	f							
cash flow ps	p	19.0	12.8	18.8	10.6	2.99		
capex ps	p	3.70	5.80	4.69	6.07	7.51		
dividend ps	p	4.70	5.60	5.70	5.70	5.70	5.70	5.70
dps growth	%	+38.2	+19.2	+1.79	-	-		
dividend yield	%					5.91	5.91	5.91
dividend cover	x	2.48	2.12	1.69	2.02	1.16	1.68	1.98
shrholders funds	£m	130	130	114	121	122		
net borrowings	£m	−25.2	−6.80	−5.10	17.8	48.2		
net curr assets	£m	67.9	53.9	30.3	19.4	14.7		
ntav ps	p	67.2	61.7	52.2	46.3	41.4		

		2002 ESTIMATES			**2003 ESTIMATES**		
Broker	Date	Rec	Pretax £m	Eps p	Dps p	Pretax £m	Eps p	Dps p
ING Barings Charterhouse	15-Feb-02	SELL −	27.4	10.1	5.70	29.4	10.8	5.70
Seymour Pierce Ltd	19-Feb-02	BOW +	27.5	9.60	5.70	32.0	11.3	5.70
ABN AMRO	4-Mar-02	HOLD	24.0 −	8.76 −	5.70	31.5 −	11.3 −	6.10
Consensus			27.5	9.60	5.70	31.7	11.3	5.70
1M change			−0.00	−0.25	-	+1.03	+0.24	-
3M change			+0.00	−0.27	-	+1.16	+0.26	-

GEARING, COVER (01AR)

		Incl	Excl
intangibles			
net gearing	%	39.6	54.8
cash	%	11.3	15.6
gross gearing	%	50.9	70.3
under 5 yrs	%	50.5	69.8
under 1 yr	%	48.2	66.6
quick ratio	r		0.65
current ratio	r		1.14
interest cover	x		4.35

KEY DATES

next AR year end	28-Feb-02
fin xd (3.80p)	5-Jun-00
int xd (1.90p)	4-Dec-00
year end	3-Mar-01
annual report	1-May-01
prelim results	2-May-01
fin xd (3.80p)	6-Jun-01
agm	21-Jun-01
int results	2-Oct-01
int xd (1.90p)	5-Dec-01

ON THE INTERNET

A number of City institutions and services have web pages; and a great deal of helpful information is readily available free. The number of sites grows daily but among the more useful at the time of writing are:

Accounting standards and financial reporting

Accountancy, the journal of the Institute of Chartered Accountants in England and Wales, which provides, on its UK edition pages, a progress update on new and forthcoming UK standards, and on its overseas edition pages, international standards – *http://www.accountancymag.co.uk.*

The Accounting Standards Board website is – *http://www.asb.org.uk/*

For those interested in standards internationally, the home page of the US Financial Accounting Standards Board is – *http://www.rutgers.edu:80/Accounting/raw/fasb/*

City and general news

The *Financial Times* provides news, prices, and an excellent information service. You can obtain the current annual/interim report of any company annotated with ♣ in the newspaper or the London Share Price Service by phoning 020-8391-6000, or ordering through the Internet *http://ft.ar.wilink.com.* Reports will be posted the next working day subject to availability. An instant snapshot of key financial and fundamental information on more than 11,000 listed companies world-wide is available, free. There is also a useful glossary and set of ratio definitions – *http://www.financialtimes.co.uk.*

Chapter 29

INFLATION ACCOUNTING

INTRODUCTION

Some people, some of the time, think that company accounts should make allowance for the effects of inflation, while others think it's too difficult: 'don't let's bother'. The latter tend to predominate unless the rate of inflation is high.

In the 1970s and early 1980s, when inflation in the UK was running in double figures, efforts were made to introduce inflation accounting, but the accountancy profession was split between two methods: Current Purchasing Power (CPP), which simply adjusts figures for the rise in the Retail Price Index (RPI), and Current Cost Accounting (CCA), which allows for changes in relative prices.

Because both these methods have been tried and abandoned, there is a temptation to treat the subject as irrelevant. This attitude is like the ostrich burying its head in the sand: even a single figure rate of inflation has an insidious effect on reported profits. For example, if a company reports steady earnings per share in a period when inflation is running at

3% per annum, and the reported e.p.s. are adjusted for inflation, the result is:

Year	0	5	10	25
Reported e.p.s.	10p	10p	10p	10p
E.p.s. in constant £s	10p	8.58p	7.37p	4.67

This adjustment only allows for the effect of inflation on reported e.p.s. If inflation was allowed for in the accounts themselves, i.e. in calculating the e.p.s., then the earnings per share by Year 10 or Year 25 would probably be much less for the majority of companies.

If the Chancellor fails to keep the lid on inflation, or some future government resorts to Harold Wilson's old trick of promising the earth, and paying for it by printing money, then the whole subject will be back at the top of the agenda.

We first examine the shortcomings of historical cost accounts in some detail, and then give a brief history and description of CPP and CCA.

THE SHORTCOMINGS OF HISTORICAL COST ACCOUNTING

In attempting to present a true and fair view of a company's affairs, accounting systems have two principal enemies: inflation and subjective judgement.

Historical cost (HC) accounting

In a time of stable prices, the historical cost system works well. What an asset cost is seldom in dispute, and although the directors have to assess the expected useful lives of fixed assets, and their

likely disposal values, there is limited scope for subjective judgement. Furthermore, the quality of historical cost accounts has steadily improved over the years, largely thanks to the efforts of the ASC; and, more recently, the ASB have considerably reduced the number of options available.

Though problems do still remain, few other than accounting theorists would seriously suggest that historical cost be abandoned as the basis of accounting in a period of zero inflation.

HC accounting and inflation

In a period of substantial price rises (which, for simplicity, we will term 'inflation'), historical cost accounting has five main weaknesses:

1. *Depreciation is inadequate for the replacement of fixed assets.*

   Historical cost accounting seeks to write off the cost of fixed assets over their effective lives. It does not set out to provide a fund from which the fixed assets can be replaced at the end of their lives. Nevertheless, in a period of stable prices, sufficient cash could be set aside over the life of an asset to replace it at its original cost. In times of inflation, insufficient is provided in this way to enable the business to replace its assets. For example, where an asset is written off on a straight line basis over ten years, the total provisions for depreciation as a percentage of cost (in constant pounds) are:

Inflation rate	*Depreciation as % of cost*
5%	79.1%
10%	64.4%
15%	53.8%

2. *Cost of sales is understated.*

   In historical cost accounts, stock consumed and sold is charged against sales at its original cost, rather than at the cost of replacing it. But, in order to retain the same stock level, the company has to finance the difference entirely out of profits after tax. This is perhaps most easily understood if we add a few figures. Assume that the company has in stock items which cost £4,000. It sells them for £6,000, incurring overheads of £1,600, and replaces them at a cost of £4,400. Corporation tax is payable at, say, 30%.

   HC accounts will say that the company has made a profit of £400 (£6,000 – £4,000 – £1,600) on which it will pay corporation tax of £120, leaving a net profit after tax of £280. But out of this the company has to meet the additional cost of replacement (£400), so it will be left with minus £120.

3. *Need for increase in other working capital not recognised.*

   In most companies, debtors are greater than creditors, so, on an unchanged volume of business, 'debtors minus creditors' increases with inflation, requiring extra money to be provided for working capital. Historical cost accounts fail to recognise that this extra working capital is necessary to maintain the operating capacity of a business and that it has to be provided (again out of after tax profits) for the business to remain a going concern.

4. *Borrowing benefits are not shown.*

   Borrowings are shown in monetary terms, and if nothing is repaid, and nothing further is borrowed, borrowings appear stable. This is a distortion of the picture, because a gain has been made at the expense of the lender (since in real terms the value of the loan has declined): some people feel that this gain ought to be reflected in the accounts.

5. *Year-on-year figures are not comparable.*

   In addition to being overstated due to

   (a) inadequate provision for depreciation,
   (b) understated cost of sales, and
   (c) no provision for increase in other working capital,

   profits are stated in terms of money which has itself declined in value. Similarly, sales and dividends are not comparable with those of other years, because they are expressed in pounds of different purchasing power.

Although inflation has moderated, it has not disappeared; and memories are short. Before studying Examples 29.1 and 29.2, try this test: sketch out approximately the trend in year-on-year inflation:

- between 1982 and 1998;
- between 1997 and 1999.

If your estimates bear any real resemblance to the graphs below, we shall be surprised.

Example 29.1 Sixteen years of inflation

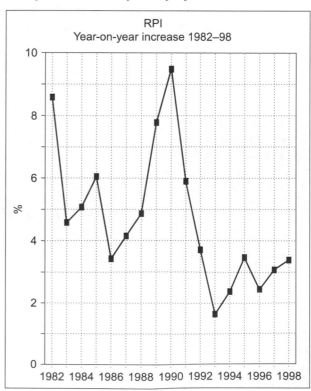

Example 29.2 A downward trend? But can it be sustained? That is always the question.

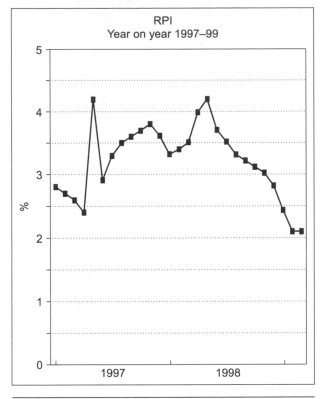

RPI
Year on year 1997–99

So how good is the average investor or analyst likely to be at stripping out inflation accurately off the top of his head?

Key point

The reporting of profits in inflated pounds gives a far too rosy impression of growth in profitability:

- This lulls both managers and shareholders into thinking that their company is doing much better than it really is;
- It encourages unions and employees to expect wage increases that are unmatched by real (as opposed to reported) profit growth; and
- It encourages government measures that are harmful to the long-term prosperity of companies, e.g. price controls or excess profits tax made on a completely false impression of profitability.

It is somewhat difficult, without making proper adjustment, even in times of modest inflation, to estimate profits, earnings and dividends, and their trend in real terms, as is shown below by building and construction group JOHN LAING.

JOHN LAING *Five year review 1998*

	1998	1997*	1996	1995	1994
Turnover £m	1,606.6	1,461.4	1,254.9	1,206.4	1,171.7
Profit before taxation £m	20.1	32.2	24.5	20.1	23.8
Profit attributable to shareholders £m	15.5	26.1	18.7	14.8	17.9
Shareholders' funds £m	219.0	214.3	198.5	192.3	185.4
Cash net of borrowings £m	43.8	19.7	64.6	53.1	65.1
Profit before taxation as % of – turnover %	1.3	2.2	2.0	1.7	2.0
– shareholders' funds %	9.2	15.0	12.3	10.5	12.8
Earnings per share pence	14.0	25.7	17.7	13.5	17.0
Dividends per share pence	10.75	10.50	9.50	9.00	9.00
Dividend cover times	1.3	2.4	1.9	1.5	1.9

*Restated to comply with Financial Reporting Standard 9, *Associates and joint ventures* (see Accounting Policies).

Looking at these figures in terms of year-on-year percentage change we get:

JOHN LAING *Year on year percentage change: actual prices*

	1998/ 1997	1997*/ 1996	1996/ 1995	1995/ 1994
Turnover	9.9	16.5	4.0	3.0
Profit before taxation	(37.6)	31.4	21.9	(15.5)
Profit attributable to shareholders	(40.6)	39.6	26.4	(17.3)
Shareholders' funds	2.2	8.0	3.2	3.7
Cash net of borrowings	122.3	(69.5)	21.7	(18.4)
Profit before taxation as % of – turnover %	(40.9)	10.0	17.6	(15.0)
– shareholders' funds %	(38.7)	22.0	17.1	(18.0)
Earnings per share	(45.5)	45.2	31.1	(20.6)
Dividends per share	2.4	10.5	5.6	0.0

To allow for inflation it is necessary to restate these figures at the price levels ruling at a particular point in time. Two obvious points are 1994 (the beginning of the five years) or 1998 (the end). We have chosen to convert everything to 1994 prices, using the average index for each year:

Example 29.3 Computation of adjustment factor to convert to 1994 prices

	1998	1997	1996	1995	1994
Average RPI for year	162.9	157.5	152.7	149.1	144.1
Factor to bring to average 1994 prices*	0.885	0.915	0.944	0.966	1.000

* Index for 1994/Index for current year

JOHN LAING *Five year summary 1998: adjusted for inflation to 1994 prices using factors in Figure 29.3*

	1998	1997	1996	1995	1994
Turnover £m	1,421.8	1,337.2	1,184.6	1,165.4	1,171.7
Profit before taxation £m	17.8	29.5	23.1	19.4	23.8
Profit attributable to shareholders £m	13.7	23.9	17.7	14.3	17.9
Shareholders' funds £m	193.8	196.1	187.4	185.8	185.4
Cash net of borrowings £m	38.8	18.0	61.0	51.3	65.1
Profit before taxation as % of – turnover %	1.3	2.2	2	1.7	2
– shareholders' funds %	9.2	15	12.3	10.5	12.8
Earnings per share pence	12.4	23.5	16.7	13.0	17.0
Dividends per share pence	9.5	9.6	9.0	8.7	9.0

JOHN LAING *Year on year percentage change: at 1994 prices*

	1998/ 1997	1997*/ 1996	1996/ 1995	1995/ 1994
Turnover	6.3	12.9	1.6	(0.5)
Profit before taxation	(39.7)	27.7	19.1	(18.5)
Profit attributable to shareholders	(42.7)	35.0	23.8	(20.1)
Shareholders' funds	(1.2)	4.6	0.9	0.2
Cash net of borrowings	115.5	(70.5)	18.9	(21.2)
Profit before taxation as % of – turnover %	(40.9)	10.0	17.6	(15.0)
– shareholders' funds %	(38.7)	22.0	17.1	(18.0)
Earnings per share pence	(47.2)	40.7	28.5	(23.5)
Dividends per share pence	(1.0)	6.7	3.4	(3.3)

Not only do the adjusted figures look less promising, the year-on-year change looks much less happy. We see, for instance, that in real terms :

- shareholders' funds fell in 1998 and grew very little in either 1995 or 1996;
- dividends failed to keep pace in two years out of four.

But unlike many companies, JOHN LAING made no attempt to hide this (see opposite column).

Now we are not suggesting that all this was due to inflation; cost over-runs are often due to inefficiency and JOHN LAING clearly blame management. But fixed price contracts, and contracts with limited price protection, do present problems in a period of rising prices – and not merely to on site management.

JOHN LAING *Extract from the chairman's statement 1998*

Although 1998 did not meet the Board's expectations, this was entirely due to the Millennium Stadium project in Cardiff and the consequent acceleration of the reorganisation in our Construction activities. Profit before taxation was £20.1m in comparison with the £32.2m achieved in the previous year. The Board is, as indicated in October, recommending a maintained final dividend of 7.0 pence (1997 – 7.0 pence) making a total of 10.75 pence (1997 – 10.5 pence) for the year.

This disappointing result includes a provision of £26.1m on the Millennium Stadium due to costs exceeding the guaranteed maximum price quoted to the client. There is still much work to be done but we believe that the provision is sufficient to complete the contract. . . .

A comprehensive programme of reorganisation is being accelerated within our Construction activities, for which a charge of £5.1m is included in the results, and which involves new management appointments.

The staggering impact of inflation

Before going on to discuss how inflation accounting developed, it is worth looking in more detail at the impact that even quite modest rates of inflation have on the value of money if they persist for several years.

Example 29.4 Effect of inflation on the value of £1

Annual rate of inflation	After 5 years	After 10 years	After 20 years
2$\frac{1}{2}$%	88.3p	78.1p	61.0p
5%	78.3p	61.3p	37.6p
7$\frac{1}{2}$%	69.6p	48.5p	29.5p
10%	62.0p	38.5p	14.8p
15%	49.7p	24.7p	6.1p
20%	40.1p	16.1p	2.6p

Between 1960 and 1996 inflation averaged a touch over 7.2% compound; but it was extremely variable in rate (from a low of 1.3% p.a. to a peak of over 25%); and it was throughout that period very difficult to predict what the rate of inflation would be a year later.

It wasn't always like this. Prior to the Second World War prices had changed surprisingly little in a hundred years. By 1940, prices were a shade over twice their 1840 level.

But, as Example 29.5 shows, the effect of inflation on the value of money since 1940 and, in particular, since 1970, has been staggering.

The effect of inflation on the investor in fixed interest stocks

Anyone who bought £100 of Government, irredeemable, 3$\frac{1}{2}$% War Loan when it stood at par in the 1940s by 1996 saw it standing at about 45, which reflected interest rates and inflationary expectations at that time. If one adjusted the original £100 by the subsequent movement in the RPI (which was about 24 times its 1940 level), and expressed £100

Example 29.5 The RPI at 5-year intervals (1915 = 100)

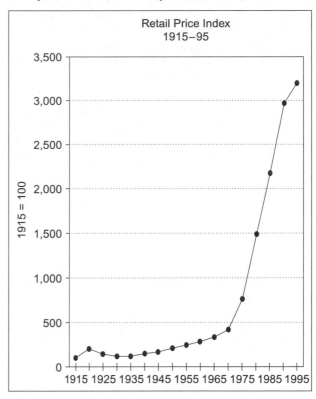

in 1996 pounds, one got about £2,400. In real terms the investor had lost over 98% of his capital: horrifying! Since then, interest rates have fallen and inflationary expectations are much less.

The years 1996 to 1999 have seen a gain in real terms on stocks like War Loan – but nothing will ever make up for the inroads of 60 years' inflation.

In 1940 the RPI was 6.6 (taking 1987 = 100) and that in March 1999 was 164.1, which represents an increase of 2386%.

Appendix 3 provides tables showing the effect of inflation in the United Kingdom on the Retail Price Index.

THE DEVELOPMENT OF INFLATION ACCOUNTING SYSTEMS

Current purchasing power accounting (CPP)

An Exposure Draft, ED 8 – *Accounting for changes in the purchasing power of money* – was issued in 1973 recommending that companies adopt what came to be known as current purchasing power accounting (CPP). The main features of ED 8 were that, in addition to HC accounts, listed companies would show a *supplementary statement* in terms of the value of the pound at the end of the period being reported on, and that the RPI should be used in making the adjustments.

CPP accounting was concerned solely with removing the distorting effects of changes in the general purchasing power of money on accounts prepared in accordance with established practice (i.e. on a historical cost basis). It did not deal with changes in the *relative* values of non-monetary items such as raw materials of various types (which can and do occur in the absence of inflation).

CPP accounts were criticised on a number of grounds. Among these were the following:

- Shareholders were faced with a choice between two sets of figures which frequently gave very different results. Both could not be correct.
- CPP accounting enhanced the profits of companies which were heavily borrowed, particularly those showing low profits on a historical cost basis, and could even turn a loss into a profit. This was because assets on which perhaps little or no profit was being made (e.g. land held for use and not for resale) were shown by CPP to be increasing in value in line with inflation (i.e. maintaining their real value), while money borrowed to acquire them was treated as declining in real value. The more heavily borrowed the company, the more the profits became boosted by CPP:

GRAND METROPOLITAN *Extracts from 1974 accounts*

	£000
Ordinary shareholders' funds	429,436
less Goodwill	295,361
OSF net of goodwill	134,075
10% CULS 1991/96	121,114
Other loan capital	281,219
Bank overdrafts and short-term borrowings	130,396
Total debt	532,729
Earnings per share (historical)	7.3p
Earnings per share (CPP basis)	35.2p

- The Retail Price Index is not a true index of general purchasing power: it may quite badly represent the effects of inflation upon some groups of individuals, and it is not *designed* to reflect the effects of inflation on companies.

In spite of being adopted by quite a large number of public companies, CPP accounting was overtaken by the appointment of the Sandilands Committee, which was set up by government in 1974 under the chairmanship of Mr (later Sir) Francis Sandilands.

Current cost accounting (CCA)
The Sandilands Report
The Sandilands Committee reported to the Chancellor of the Exchequer and the Secretary for Trade in June 1975: the Committee rejected the proposals contained in PSSAP 7 (a provisional SSAP on CPP, which had been issued as a follow-up to ED 8 pending the Sandilands findings), and recommended instead the development of a system to be known as current cost accounting (CCA), in which:

- no adjustment is made for inflation (i.e. for changes in the purchasing power of money);
- assets and liabilities are shown in the balance sheet at their 'value to the business'; unfortunately, this can be very much a matter of subjective judgement;
- 'operating profit' is struck after charging the value to the business of assets consumed during the period, thus excluding holding gains from profit and showing them separately.

The Sandilands report also recommended that current cost accounting should become the basic published accounts of companies 'as soon as practicable'.

Opposition
In response to the Sandilands recommendations there followed much debate and a special committee, which produced an Exposure Draft (ED 18) in November 1976. ED 18 met with considerable opposition – the members of the Institute of Chartered Accountants in England and Wales actually voted at an extraordinary general meeting that current cost accounting should not be made compulsory – so a new committee was appointed, leading to the eventual publication of a Standard on CCA (SSAP 16) in March 1980.

SSAP 16
SSAP 16 required larger companies to produce a separate current cost P & L account and balance sheet, to recognise two basic concepts, that:

- The profitability of a company should be assessed after deducting the amount of money it needs in order to stand still in real terms.
- The assets of a company should be shown at their value to the business.

The SSAP 16 system of CCA calculates the profit of a business by making adjustments to the HC profit and loss account.

Three *operating adjustments* are made to the HC trading profit to allow for the impact of price changes:

1. The *depreciation adjustment*.
2. The *cost of sales adjustment*.
3. The *monetary working capital adjustment*.

A fourth adjustment, the *gearing adjustment*, is then made to allow for the proportion of assets financed by borrowings.

Specific price indices are used in CCA in calculating the operating adjustments, to reflect relative price changes and, for a time, the Government Statistical Service produced a special book annually, *Price Index Numbers for Current Cost Accounting* containing a myriad of industry-specific and asset-specific indices, updating it by a monthly supplement.

But, in spite of the enormous effort put into developing CCA, the system had major shortcomings:

•   It was very complicated: even the Accounting Standards Committee's step-by-step guide *CCA the Easy Way* ran to 145 pages of A4.

•   There was much scope for discretion, so that similar companies produced wildly different figures for individual adjustments.
•   The figures produced each year were not comparable with figures for the previous year.
•   The system was irrelevant for tax purposes.

Attempts were made to modify the system (by ED 35), but CCA failed to gain sufficient acceptance to become the basis of published accounts of companies, as Sandilands had recommended. When inflation eased, SSAP 16 was gradually abandoned.

SSAP 16 was suspended in June 1985, and formally withdrawn in April 1988.

THREE VALLEYS WATER PLC *Extracts from the Regulatory Accounts*

Current cost profit & loss account for total business
for the year ended 31 March 2000

	Note	2000 £000	1999 £000
Turnover	2	148,381	139,882
Current cost operating costs		(98,951)	(99,481)
Other operating income/(costs)		151	(88)
Working capital adjustment		686	407
Current cost operating profit	4	50,267	40,720
Other income		1,408	1,358
Net interest payable		(8,228)	(9,620)
Financing adjustment		3,709	2,949
Current cost profit before taxation		47,156	35,407

1   Statement of accounting policies

Basis of current cost accounting
These accounts have been prepared in accordance with relevant Regulatory Accounting Guidelines (RAGs).

The current cost accounts have been prepared for the Appointed Business of the Company in accordance with guidance issued by the Director General of Water Services for modified real terms financial statements for regulation in the water industry. They measure profitability on the basis of real financial capital maintenance, in the context of assets which are valued at their current cost value to the business, with the exception of certain assets acquired prior to 31 March 1990, the effective commencement of the new regulatory system . . .

Real financial capital maintenance adjustments
These adjustments are made to historical cost profit in order to arrive at profit after maintenance of financial capital in real terms:

Depreciation adjustment – this is the difference between depreciation based on the current cost value of assets in these accounts and depreciation charged in arriving at historical cost profit.

Working capital adjustment – this is calculated by applying the change in the RPI over the year to the opening total trade debtors and stock less trade creditors.

Financing adjustment – this is calculated by applying the change in the RPI over the year to the opening balance of net finance, which comprises all monetary assets and liabilities in the balance sheet apart from those included in working capital.

Disposal of fixed asset adjustment – per RAG. 01 – this is calculated by applying the difference between the net book value of the current cost and the net book value of the historical cost of disposed assets, to the profit from disposal of fixed assets as shown in the historical cost accounts . . .

WHAT ARE WE TRYING TO ACHIEVE?

The nub of the matter is whether we are trying to achieve:

- a system that allows for the general effect of inflation, or
- what the Sandilands Committee was asked to produce, a system to 'allow for changes (including relative changes) in costs and prices'.

Measuring inflation

The Sandilands Committee took the view that inflation was 'not a phenomenon capable of independent and objective measurement' and, in line with government thinking at the time, rejected the concept of using the Retail Price Index (RPI) to index accounts. As the RPI has since been used satisfactorily by government to index personal tax allowances, for Index-linked gilt-edged securities and SAYE schemes and, most recently, for the indexation of acquisition cost in CGT calculations, the Sandilands view is scarcely tenable. The RPI *is* the generally accepted measure of inflation in the United Kingdom.

What we believe inflation accounts should achieve

Let us consider the problem under five heads:

1. If the cost of a fixed asset is written off in pounds of falling value, the provision for depreciation is inadequate. In order that the total amount written off over the useful life of a fixed asset should be its cost (less residual value) expressed in *pounds at the date of purchase*, each annual depreciation charge needs to be adjusted by the movement in the RPI since the asset was acquired. Fixed assets should therefore appear in the balance sheet at cost less accumulated depreciation, adjusted for inflation into balance sheet date pounds.
2. In calculating the cost of goods sold, the opening stock should be adjusted for the RPI movement during the year so as to eliminate stock profits due to general inflation; and profits so computed should provide the basis for taxation.

3. The amount of additional working capital required by a company due to the effects of inflation should be deducted in calculating distributable profits.
4. The benefit of inflation in reducing the real value of borrowings and the adverse effect of inflation on holdings of cash should be taken into account.
5. Figures for previous years should be adjusted to balance sheet date pounds, so that like can be compared with like, a point well recognised by the Central Statistical Office (imagine how misleading their financial statistics would be if they weren't expressed in constant pounds).

Because inflation accounting would allow for the general effect of inflation but not for any relative change in price levels, inflation accounts would, in a long period of zero inflation, produce the same figures as historical cost accounts. But there is nothing wrong with that.

The future

Until the purpose of inflation accounting is agreed no system of inflation accounting is likely to be introduced.

Consequently, HC accounts will continue:

(i) to lull many managers and shareholders into thinking that their companies are doing better (sometimes considerably better) than they really are, and
(ii) to encourage unions and employees to seek wage increases that are not justified by real (as opposed to reported) profits.

Furthermore, unless the system so developed produces accounts acceptable to the Inland Revenue for tax purposes and which become the *only* accounts a company produces, there will continue to be a problem. The production of *two* sets of accounts will always pose the question 'Which one is to be believed?'

Chapter 30

INTERNATIONAL ACCOUNTING COMPARISONS

INTRODUCTION

Hot potato

When, in 1979, this book was first published, the idea of global accounting standards was *pie in the sky*. About ten years ago it moved on to the *wish list*, and now it's got onto the *job list*.

Why has it suddenly become a *hot potato*?

Well, it's been warming up for several years, but we haven't been paying attention. We've been too busy coping with the fusillade of Financial Reporting Standards – 1 to 19 – not to mention FRS 1 (Revised), UITF Abstracts and the ASB Statement of Principles.

Progress in the last ten years

On the UK domestic front, the ASB has corrected a number of serious weaknesses in the UK rules, bringing the UK much closer to US and international practice.

These corrections included:

- replacing the old '*Sources and application of funds statement*' with the much more useful and easy to understand '*Cash flow statement*';
- removing the ludicrous 'preferred method' of dealing with purchased goodwill, *immediate write-off straight to reserves*, that made a complete nonsense of **ROCE** (**R**eturn **O**n Capital Employed). See our article 'Big black hole of British accounting' in the May 1994 edition of *The Professional Investor*.

On the world scene, global business is demanding global accounting standards.

In Europe, in June 2000, the European Commission announced that companies within the EU would have to use IASs from 2005 onwards in order to list on EU markets.

Most recently, at the beginning of 2001, Sir David Tweedie, the 'Tiger Woods' of the Accountancy profession, moved from the chairmanship of the ASB to the chairmanship of the IASB.

This chapter

This chapter is divided into two parts. Firstly a comparison of UK GAAP (**G**enerally **A**ccepted **A**ccounting **P**ractices) with US GAAP, which we have divided into:

1. **Narrowing differences** – where UK GAAP is getting closer to US GAAP
2. **Significant differences**
3. **Less significant differences**.

Secondly, on **global harmonisation**, we look at International Accounting Standards (IASs), comparing UK GAAP with IASs, and drawing up a table giving examples of comparisons: **UK GAAP v US GAAP v IASs**.

We have also added BPs Glossary of UK and US terms as an Appendix to the book.

UK v US GAAP DIFFERENCES

Introduction

Shareholders resident in the UK are accustomed to UK GAAP, whilst those in the US are used to US GAAP. Clearly it is unsatisfactory for two major accounting countries to account for key items in different ways – both cannot be right, hence the crying need for global harmonisation, further referred to below.

This section will consider individual areas where differences currently exist, and conclude with an example of a UK / US GAAP reconciliation.

Narrowing differences

December 1997 marked an important turning-point in the attempt to narrow accounting differences between UK GAAP and US GAAP. This was when the Accounting Standards Board published FRS 10 on goodwill and intangible assets. This Standard requires purchased goodwill to be included on the balance sheet.

FRS 10 prohibits the former practice of allowing companies to write goodwill off against reserves at the date of acquisition. However, FRS 10 does not insist that pre-1998 goodwill is reinstated on the balance sheet and this will result in significant differences between UK GAAP and US GAAP profits and assets for some time to come (see below).

Examples of other areas where some progress has been made in narrowing the differences are:

- Impairment of fixed assets (for example, due to technological obsolescence, fall in demand for the product or physical damage).
- Deferred tax – FRS 19 brings the UK closer to international practice by requiring companies to provide deferred tax in full (but note the Standard only becomes compulsory for year ends on or after 23 January 2002 and differences will remain, for example the option in FRS 19 to discount deferred tax balances).

On retirement benefits, the new Standard FRS 17 (which may be phased in over a three-year period) brings the UK closer to international practice. Differences remain in the treatment of actuarial gains and losses. The ASB's hope is that, now they have developed an innovative new standard, international practice may take the full principles of FRS 17 on board.

UK GAAP AND US GAAP

Significant differences

Examples of significant differences are:

1. Pre-1998 goodwill
2. Pre-FRS 19 deferred tax
3. Proposed dividends
4. Pre-FRS 17 pension costs
5. Restructuring costs
6. Tangible fixed assets
7. Foreign exchange
8. Exceptional items
9. Acceptances
10. Sale and leaseback
11. Fixed asset investments
12. Discontinued operations
13. Cash flow statements
14. Stocks

---

1. Pre-1998 goodwill

Under UK GAAP prior to FRS 10, goodwill arising on the acquisition of a subsidiary was charged against reserves in the year in which the subsidiary was acquired. Under US GAAP, prior to new rules issued in July 2001, such goodwill is capitalised and is amortised through the profit and loss account over its estimated useful life, not exceeding 40 years. FRS 10 (see pages 163–5) changed things, but does not remove past differences, as BASS explains:

BASS *Extract from notes to the 2000 accounts*

Note 40 Intangible fixed assets

Intangible fixed assets
Goodwill and separately identifiable intangible fixed assets arising on the acquisition of subsidiaries and associates are capitalised and amortised over their estimated useful lives. Goodwill arising on acquisitions prior to 30 September 1998 was eliminated against reserves. Under US GAAP, all intangible fixed assets would be capitalised and amortised to the income statement over their estimated useful lives, not exceeding 40 years.

---

2. Pre-FRS 19 deferred tax

Under UK GAAP, SSAP 15 requires that no provision is made for deferred taxation if there is reasonable evidence that such deferred taxation will not be payable in the foreseeable future.

Under US GAAP, deferred taxation is provided for on all differences between the book and tax bases of assets and liabilities. For example:

BASS *Extract from notes to the 2000 accounts*

Deferred tax

The Group provides for deferred taxation using the liability method only where, in the opinion of the directors, it is probable that the tax liability will crystallise within the foreseeable future.

Under US GAAP, deferred taxation would be computed on all differences between the tax bases and book values of assets and liabilities which will result in taxable or tax deductible amounts arising in future years. Deferred taxation assets under US GAAP would be recognised only to the extent that it is more likely than not that they would be realised.

---

3. Proposed dividends

Under UK GAAP, final ordinary dividends are provided in the financial statements on the basis of the recommendation by the Directors which requires subsequent approval by the shareholders to become a legal obligation of the Company. Under US GAAP, dividends are only provided when the legal obligation to pay arises, e.g. BARCLAYS:

BARCLAYS *Extract from notes to the 1999 accounts*

Note 61 Differences between UK and US accounting principles

Dividend payable
UK GAAP
Dividends declared after the period end are recorded in the period to which they relate.
US GAAP
Dividends are recorded in the period in which they are declared.

---

4. Pre-FRS 17 pension costs

Under UK GAAP (SSAP 24) the costs of providing pension benefits may be calculated by the use of any recognised actuarial method which is appropriate and whose assumptions reflect the long-term nature of the assets and liabilities involved. Under US GAAP, the costs of providing these benefits are calculated using the projected unit credit method and a discount rate (being the rate of interest at which pension liabilities could be effectively settled) which affects current market rates. e.g. BASS:

BASS *Extract from the notes to the 2000 accounts*

Note 40 Pension costs

The Group provides for the cost of retirement benefits based upon consistent percentages of employees' pensionable pay as recommended by independent qualified actuaries.

Under US GAAP, the projected benefit obligation (pension liability) in respect of the Group's two principal pension plans would be matched against the fair value of the plans' assets and would be adjusted to reflect any unrecognised obligations or assets in determining the pension cost or credit for the year.

---

5. Restructuring costs

Under UK GAAP provisions are made for restructuring costs once a detailed formal plan is in place and valid expectations have been raised in those affected that the restructuring will be carried out. US GAAP requires a number of specific criteria to be met before such costs can be recognised as an expense. Among these is the requirement that all the significant actions arising from a restructuring and their completion dates must be identified by the balance sheet date. For example BARCLAYS:

BARCLAYS *Extract from notes to the 1999 accounts*

Note 61 Differences between UK and US accounting principles

Restructuring of business provisions
UK GAAP
In accordance with FRS 3, provisions have been made for any direct costs and net future operating losses arising from a business that management is committed to terminate.
US GAAP
The application of Emerging Issues Task Force (EITF) 94-3 has created recognition timing differences in respect of certain of the termination provisions.

EITF 94-3 sets out specific conditions which must be met to enable liabilities relating to involuntary terminations to be recognised in the period management approve the termination plan . . .

---

6. Tangible fixed assets

Under UK GAAP, fixed assets and, in particular, properties may be restated on the basis of appraised values in financial statements prepared in all other respects in accordance with the historical cost convention. Such restatements are not permitted under US GAAP.

BARCLAYS *Extract from note to the 1999 accounts*

Note 61 Differences between UK and US accounting principles

Revaluation of property
UK GAAP
Property is carried either at original cost or at subsequent valuation less related depreciation (as described in Accounting policies), calculated on the revalued amount where applicable. Revaluation surpluses are taken directly to shareholders' funds, while deficits below cost, less any related depreciation, are included in attributable profit.
US GAAP
Revaluations of property are not permitted in the accounts, under US GAAP. As a result, when a property is disposed of, a greater profit or lower loss is generally recorded under US GAAP than under UK GAAP.

7. Foreign exchange
Under UK GAAP unrealised gains and losses on foreign currency transactions to hedge anticipated, but not firmly committed, foreign currency transactions may be deferred and accounted for at the same time as the anticipated transactions. Under US GAAP such deferral is not permitted except in certain defined circumstances. For example:

CADBURY SCHWEPPES *Extract from notes to the 2000 accounts*

Note 31 (d) Foreign currency hedges
Under US GAAP, hedging of foreign currency transactions is only allowable for transactions which are firm commitments. Some of the Group's foreign currency hedge forecast or budgeted transactions which do not meet the definition of firm commitment; gains or losses on these contracts cannot be deferred but must be recognised in net income.

Under UK GAAP, these gains or losses can be deferred until the hedge transaction actually occurs.

8. Exceptional items
Although the UK and the US have grown much closer in recent years in accounting for exceptional items, important differences of presentation remain. For example:

BP AMOCO *Extract from note 45 to the 1998 accounts*

(e) Exceptional items
Under UK GAAP, certain exceptional items should be shown separately on the face of the income statement after operating profit. Under US GAAP these items would be classified as operating income or expenses.

For 1998 there were profits on the sale of businesses of $8m ($117m) and on the sale of fixed assets of $312m ($495m) and merger expenses of $119m.

9. Acceptances and similar transactions
Treatment under US GAAP is different from the treatment under UK GAAP, as BARCLAYS notes:

BARCLAYS *Extract from notes to the 1999 accounts*

Note 61 Differences between UK and US accounting principles

Acceptances
UK GAAP
Acceptances are not recorded in the balance sheet.
US GAAP
Acceptances and the related customer liabilities are recorded within the balance sheet.

In its accounts according to UK GAAP, BARCLAYS recorded acceptances and endorsements as a contingent liability of £1,530m. Under US GAAP they would both be an asset (i.e. the customers' obligations) and a liability (the bank's obligation).

10. Sale and leaseback
Under UK GAAP, any profit or loss on the sale and operating leaseback of fixed assets can generally be taken to profit immediately. US GAAP requires any gain or loss to be deferred over the contract lease period.

BP AMOCO *Extract from 1998 accounts*

Note 45 (g) Sale and leaseback
The sale and leaseback of the Amoco building in Chicago is treated as a sale for UK GAAP whereas for US GAAP it is treated as a financing transaction. The effect of this adjustment is to increase exceptional items and profit for the year by $211m. Net assets are increased by $211m.

11. Fixed asset investments
Under UK GAAP, fixed asset investments are held in the balance sheet at cost less any impairment in value. Under US GAAP, fixed asset investments are recorded at market value.

12. Discontinued operations
Under UK GAAP a loss or gain on discontinuance of operations appears in the profit and loss account between 'total group operating profit including associates' and 'Profit on ordinary activities before taxation'.

Under US GAAP, any gain on discontinued operations is shown below 'Profit for the financial year'.

13. Cash flow statements

There are significant differences between UK and US GAAP, and these are further referred to later in the UK GAAP / US GAAP / IAS comparison.

REUTERS explains the principal differences:

REUTERS GROUP *Extract from 2000 accounts*

Cash flow statement

The cash flow statement set out on pages 47–49 [not reproduced] has been prepared in conformity with UK FRS 1 (Revised) *Cash flow statements*.

The principal differences between this statement and cash flow statements presented in accordance with US FAS 95 are as follows

1. Under UK GAAP, net cash flow from operating activities is determined before considering cash flows from (a) returns on investment and servicing of finance and (b) taxes paid.

    Under US GAAP net cash flow from operating activities is determined after these items.
2. Under UK GAAP, capital expenditure is classified separately, while under US GAAP it is described as an investing activity.
3. Under UK GAAP dividends paid are classified separately, while under US GAAP dividends paid are classified as financing activities.
4. Under UK GAAP movements in short-term investments are not included in cash but classified as management of liquid resources.

    Under US GAAP short term investments with a maturity of three months or less at the date of acquisition are included in cash.
5. Under UK GAAP movements in bank overdrafts are classified as movements in cash, while under US GAAP they are classified as a financing activity.

---

14. Stocks

Even something as simple as stock can be treated differently under the two GAAPs. Consider, for instance, the difference that the choice of GAAP made to the figures for AMOCO at the time it was merged with BP.

BP AMOCO *Extract from 1998 accounts*

Note 45 (b) Stock accounting

Amoco carried stocks at the lower of current market values or cost. Cost is determined under the last-in, first-out (LIFO) method for the majority of stocks of crude oil, petroleum products and chemical products . . .

BP carried stocks at the lower of cost or net realisable value. Cost is determined using the first-in, first-out (FIFO) method. . . .

As a result of this adjustment [to Amoco's accounts] . . . there are stockholding losses of \$415m; profit for the year is reduced by \$408m. The carrying value of stock is increased by \$549m.

UK GAAP AND US GAAP

Less significant differences

Examples of less significant differences are:

15. Capitalised interest
16. Equity accounting

---

15. Capitalised interest

Traditionally, British companies have under UK GAAP been allowed in certain circumstances to capitalise interest but have not been required to.

ICI *Extract from the 2000 accounts*

Capitalisation of interest

There is no requirement in the UK to capitalise interest and the Group does not capitalise interest in its Group financial statements. Under US GAAP, SFAS No. 34, 'Capitalization of Interest Cost', requires interest incurred as part of the cost of constructing fixed assets to be capitalised and amortised over the life of the asset.

---

16. Equity accounting

Although the differences in GAAP have no overall effect on either profit for the year or net assets, the detailed figures for equity accounted investments look rather different.

RECONCILIATION OF UK GAAP TO US GAAP

UK companies reporting on both UK and US GAAP provide a reconciliation between the two. For example CADBURY SCHWEPPES:

CADBURY SCHWEPPES *Extracts from the 2000 accounts*

Effects on profit of differences between UK and US generally accepted accounting principles

	2000 £m	1999 £m	1998 £m
Profit for the Financial Year from continuing operations, net of tax (per UK GAAP)	**496**	642	348
US GAAP adjustments:			
Amortisation of goodwill and trademarks	**(102)**	(89)	(87)
Restructuring costs	**9**	–	–
Depreciation of capitalised interests	**3**	(6)	(6)
Pension costs	**7**	3	14
Exceptional item/Disposal gain adjustment	**(22)**	23	(7)
Timing of recognition of foreign currency hedges	**2**	(3)	4
SAYE/LTIP	**(9)**	–	–
Other items	**(5)**	–	–
Taxation on above adjustments	**–**	2	1
Deferred taxation	**4**	22	(10)
Profit for the Financial Year from continuing operations, net of tax, as adjusted for US GAAP	**383**	594	257

Cumulative effect on Shareholders' Funds of differences between UK and US generally accepted accounting principles

	2000 £m	1999 £m	1998 £m
Shareholders' Funds per UK GAAP	**2,633**	2,240	1,843
US GAAP adjustments:			
Goodwill and intangibles	**896**	1,011	1,063
Pension costs	**(33)**	(31)	(30)
Interest capitalisation	**12**	9	15
Property revaluations	**(62)**	(58)	(62)
Dividends	**146**	141	135
Other items	**2**	(4)	–
Taxation on above adjustments	**(4)**	(2)	(5)
Deferred taxation	**(51)**	(54)	(77)
Employee Trust	**(153)**	(88)	–
Shareholders' Funds as adjusted for US GAAP	**3,386**	3,164	2,882

TOWARDS GLOBAL ACCOUNTING STANDARDS

International accounting standards (IASs) – moving forward

Harmonisation of accounts has been on the international reporting agenda for many years. Progress in this area should yield many benefits:

- Savings for companies with cross-border listings as a result of only having to produce one set of accounts
- Improved comparability of performance of companies for investors
- Speedier reporting of results.

IAS 2005

In June 2000, the European Commission announced that companies within the EU would have to use IASs in order to list on EU markets.

This requirement would become effective in 2005.

IASB has responded rapidly to the above deadline. In August 2001 it announced its agenda of technical projects. Exposure drafts of the new-style International Financial Reporting Standards (IFRSs) are likely to commence in the first half of 2002 with definitive standards starting to emerge during 2003.

Differences between UK GAAP and IASs

In January 2001, the Institute of Chartered Accountants in England and Wales published '*The Convergence Handbook*', which makes a detailed comparison between UK GAAP and International Accounting Standards, and makes recommendations for changes to standards to bring the two sets of rules closer together.

The handbook divides the differences into four categories:

- Current UK GAAP items not permitted by IASs
- Current UK GAAP optional treatments not permitted by IASs

- IAS requirements which are more extensive than current UK GAAP
- IAS requirements which would give more flexibility to UK companies than UK GAAP.

UK GAAP, US GAAP and IAS differences

As at January 2002, there are significant differences in the three sets of Generally Accepted Accounting Principles.

The table below gives some examples which illustrate the obstacles to be overcome in arriving at global harmonisation of standards.

Topic	UK GAAP	US GAAP	IASs
Dividends proposed	• Liability recognised when directors propose dividend	• Liability recognised *only* when legal obligation to pay arises	• Liability recognised *only* when legal obligation to pay arises
Cash flow statements *Definition of cash flow*	• Cash	• Cash and cash equivalents	• Cash and cash equivalents
Main headings	• Operating activities • Dividends from joint ventures and associates • Returns on investment and servicing of finance • Taxation • Capital expenditure and financial investments • Acquisitions and disposals • Equity dividends paid • Management of liquid resources • Financing	• Operating activities • Investing activities • Financing activities	• Operating activities • Investing activities • Financing activities
Capital expenditure	• Own heading	• Subdivision of financing activities	• Subdivision of investing activities
Equity dividends paid	• Own heading	• Subdivision of financing activities	• Subdivision of operating activities *or* financing activities
Short-term investments	• Part of 'management of liquid resources'	• Part of 'cash and cash equivalents' if maturity at purchase of 3 months or less	• Part of 'cash and cash equivalents' if maturity at purchase of 3 months or less
Deferred tax	*2001 and earlier (SSAP 15)* • Partial provision *2002 onwards (FRS 19)* • Full provision based on timing differences • Option to discount liability to present value • Deferred tax not provided on revaluations	• Full provision based on temporary differences (wider-ranging than just timing differences) • No option to discount	• Full provision based on timing differences (wider-ranging than just timing differences) • No option to discount

Chapter 31

PUTTING IT ALL TOGETHER

INTRODUCTION: THE BODY SHOP

THE BODY SHOP was chosen as our company example for the previous (7th) edition of this book because it had, for a long time, been a spectacular success. Then, as euphoria took over from common sense, profits faltered and the share price tumbled.

In this edition, we will also look at how the company fared since July 1998, when Gordon Roddick (Chairman) and his wife, founder Anita Roddick (Chief Executive), became co-chairmen, appointing an externally recruited Chief Executive, Patrick Gournay.

Finally we review the prospects for THE BODY SHOP since February 2002, when the Roddicks stepped down from Co-Chairmen to Non-Executive Directors, and Patrick Gournay resigned.

ANITA RODDICK IN CHARGE

Controlling shareholders

THE BODY SHOP was started from scratch by Anita Roddick, whose enormous panache enabled her, by 1998, to become the UK's only truly world-wide retailer, with 1,663 outlets in 47 countries. The share price has behaved spectacularly, reflecting investor sentiment: euphoria followed, after two profit warnings in four months, by disenchantment. See the share price graph on page 245.

We are told that at the time Anita formed the company her flatmate had a friend, a Littlehampton garage owner, who put in £4,000 for a 50% stake. He is still the principal shareholder.

THE BODY SHOP *Extracts: 1998 report and accounts*

Directors' report
Substantial shareholdings
At 12 May 1998 the Company had been notified of the following interests of 3% or more in its ordinary shares (excluding Directors' share interests which are disclosed in Note 6 to the Accounts): Mr I.B. McGlinn had a beneficial interest in 45,666,768 ordinary shares, amounting to 23.5%; Prudential Corporation had an interest in 6,911,146 ordinary shares, amounting to 3.6%; and . . .

Note to the accounts
Directors' share interests
The beneficial interests of directors in the ordinary shares of the Company are shown below as at the beginning of the year and at the end of the year.

	At 28 Feb 1998	At 2 Mar 1987
A.L. Roddick OBE	24,010,456	24,010,456
T.G. Roddick	24,226,680	24,226,680

[The other 9 directors hold 29,085 shares between them, with options on 5,028,365 shares.]

From this we deduced that:

1. Mr McGlinn had done well with his £4,000 investment – we didn't know whether he had done any profit taking, but his stake at the financial year end was worth £55m (1997: £106m).
2. Between them Anita Roddick, her husband Gordon Roddick and Mr McGlinn held around 48.5% of the equity. In practice this amounted to control, assuming the Roddicks still had Mr McGlinn's support, in spite of the value of his holding declining by £51m during the previous financial year. We checked the 1997 accounts and his holding was unchanged.

Ground rules
Let's start with a couple of ground rules:

1. Always make a list of questions you would like to ask, firstly to make clear to yourself what you do know and what you don't about the company, and secondly because you may get a chance to ask them. Here's our first question:

Q1. Have the Roddicks still got Mr McGlinn's support?

2. Always make a note too of anything you notice, and may want to follow up later, but haven't got the time to do so now.

In checking Mr McGlinn's holding at the end of FY 1997 (FY = Financial Year), we noticed that the 1997 report and accounts felt a lot thinner than 1998.

To be precise, it was 40 pages compared with about 68 pages in 1998. We say 'about' because page numbering in 1998 didn't start until page 25.

The 1998 report – a 'new look'
The reason for the increased thickness was the inclusion, as the first 20 pages, of a series of large illustrations of varying relevance:

Unnumbered
Page	*Contents*
1	A message from Anita Roddick, which began 'Another year – and if anyone has managed to sort out the difference between stress and enthusiasm, they haven't told me. But at least we are now in a very interesting place, a place where the competition won't easily follow.' [*Our reaction:* 'She's in overdrive this year!']
2	Colour photo of a marijuana plant.
3	A tube of cream labelled '*Hemp Hand Protector* Dry to very dry skin 100ml'.
4 & 5	*Aromatherapy.* Top half of a 'port quarter' view of a naked lady, arms outstretchcd.
6 & 7	*Bergamot* a small and inedibly bitter fruit.
8 & 9	Double spread photo of a Body Shop.
10 & 11	The Body Shop Direct at home shopping.
12 & 13	Human rights.
14 & 15	Our model children's home in Romania.
16 & 17	*The Big Issue* magazine about the homeless, set up in the UK by Gordon Roddick in 1992.
18 & 19	*Self-esteem.* Photo of a very fat Barbie-type doll, lying on a sofa. Caption: 'The dawn of a new consciousness in the beauty business: Love your body – just the way it is.'
And, eventually	The Chairman's statement, printed on tomato red paper:

THE BODY SHOP *Extract from chairman's statement 1998*

We have recently carried out a comprehensive strategic review of all of our activities which has highlighted the need for some fundamental changes in order to develop the business going forward . . . The proposed joint venture in the USA and the senior management changes . . . signal the first stages of a plan that will define the future of The Body Shop.

[*Our first reaction:* Are they in trouble?]
Let's have a quick look at earnings per share and cash flow.

THE BODY SHOP *Extract from the 1998 accounts*
Profit and loss account
	1998	1997
Eps including exceptional item	11.8p	9.2p
Eps excluding exceptional item	11.8p	11.4p

Note 3 on Operating expenses
Administrative expenses – exceptional item £6.5m

This was a provision against the amounts advanced and facilities extended to the former head franchisee in France prior to the acquisition of the French business [by The Body Shop] in November 1997.

Cash flow statement	1998	1997
Not cash inflow from operating activities	41.5	51.7

[We also noticed a £20.3m Loan Repayment]

Group balance sheet
	1998 £m	1997 £m
Current assets		
Cash at bank and in hand	29.6	47.1

Nothing obvious to worry about there, though we did notice the tax charge was rather high; something to which we will return.

Before we continue we would like to make one important point:

Hype – a warning signal

In our experience, when a company's report and accounts are hyped, it raises questions. Excessive hype or a marked increase in hype (as in the case of THE BODY SHOP) are often a strong warning signal.

Take, for example, SPRING RAM's 1991 report and accounts, which was plastered with colour photographs or drawings of sporting events: stylised drawing of relay race runners crossing the line on the front cover and, inside, mountaineers reaching a peak, with snow covered mountain tops in the background – white water rafting – show jumping – boat race – cycle track racing – boxing – bobsleighing – polo – sky diving. You name it, they had it, and all to reinforce the chairman's message:

SPRING RAM *Extracts from preface and chairman's statement*

Successful enterprises must employ able motivated and effective people in order to progress profitably.

When those people operate as focused teams, not only within the company but in partnership with suppliers, with advisers and with customers, then synergistic benefits are quite remarkable. This synergy at Spring Ram multiplies rather than merely adds value and produces impressive results.

Profitable growth will continue to be a major cornerstone in Spring Ram's future strategy and will be achieved through teamwork.

Operating profit slipped the following year from £32.9m to £18.7m, and into a £33.2m operating loss in 1993.

Now we are not suggesting that The Body Shop is in any way comparable to Spring Ram (where the combined chairman/chief executive was expanding the bathroom and kitchen manufacture in the teeth of a looming recession), but we do get a bit anxious when management begins to believe its own PR.

So, back to square one.

Assumptions about our readers
For this chapter we will assume you are working from home, with no ready access to a business library, a stockbroker's office or other financial institution.

Getting a first feel
One book we always have to hand at home and in the office is the *Hemscott Company Guide*. Each UK Listed and AIM company gets a one-sixth of a page entry, or a larger entry for companies prepared to pay for the extra space. For further details, see page 224.

On p. 245 we show the 1989 and 1998 entries for The Body Shop.

They present quite a record:

	1984 £m	1998 £m	*Compound growth per annum*
Turnover	4.91	293	34%
Pre-tax profit	1.04	38	29%
Earnings per share	1.50p	11.8p	16%
Dividend per share	0.18p	5.60p	26%

Three points to make before we move on:

1. Notice how the payout ratio (d.p.s./e.p.s.) has gone from 12% in 1984 to 47% in 1998. A high retention rate (i.e. very low payout ratio) is a good sign in a small company: retentions help to fuel expansion.
2. Calculations based on e.p.s. and d.p.s. growth can't be relied on unless you have details of rights and scrip issues.
3. The Guide entry gives the telephone number of the Registrars, Lloyds, Worthing. We can phone them for a copy of the latest report and accounts, and any subsequent interim report.

While we wait for the report and accounts – and Lloyds are particularly good at posting them promptly – let us look at The Body Shop's share price graph (see Example 31.1, next page).

We also like to look at a Lin/Log graph of sales growth. If a company's turnover goes up by a given percentage year after year, a Lin/Log graph will show a straight line. On a linear scale, the growth will appear to be exponential.

We show The Body Shop's turnover since 1984 both ways:

- on a linear scaled graph (Example 31.2);
- as a Lin/Log graph (Example 31.3);

which make it very clear why we prefer a Lin/Log presentation.

Historical background from the *Investors Chronicle*
Unless you've kept them year by year, it's not easy to lay your hands on the last 5 or 10 years' reports and accounts of any company. With or without them, a good place to get some history is the *Investors Chronicle*, which we take and keep

BODY SHOP INTERNATIONAL PLC (THE)

ACTIVITIES Produces and sells natural skin and hair care products.
STATUS: Full. FT LIST: Drapery & stores.

HEAD & REG OFF: Hawthorn Road, Wick, Littlehampton, West Sussex BN17 7LR Tel: (0903) 717107. Tlx: 877055 Fax: (0903) 726250. REGISTRARS: Lloyds, Worthing Tel: (0903) 726250

ANNCMNTS: Int – mid Nov Final – mid Jun, AGM late Jul.

GEARING: 15.7 (8 10%). ROCE: 39.3% (83.5%).
NOTES: Period to Feb 89, 517 days (17 months)

year ended 30 September		1984	1985	1986	1987	1989
turnover	£m	4.91	9.36	17.4	28.5	73.0
pre tax profit	£m	1.04	1.93	3.45	6.00	15.2
retained profit	£m	0.41	0.87	1.76	3.13	7.11
earn per share	p	1.50	2.55	5,15	9.30	20.4
div per share	p	0.18	0.38	1.50	1.50	3.38
intangibles	£m	–	–	–	–	–
fixed assets	£m	0.61	0.68	1.74	4.09	15.6
fixed investments	£m	0.03	–	–	–	–
stocks	£m	0.87	2.20	4.23	4.61	15.7
debtors	£m	1.32	1.95	3.13	5.67	8.98
cash, securities	£m	0.25	0.01	1.06	0.83	0.20
creditors short	£m	1.93	1.89	6.47	5.34	16.2
creditors long	£m	0.32	0.26	0.23	0.12	0.24
prefs, minorities	£m	–	–	0.02	0.16	0.52
ord cap. reserves	£m	0.81	1.68	3.45	6.59	23.5

Extracts from the Hambro Company Guide (above for 1989; below for 1998)

BODY SHOP INTERNATIONAL PLC (THE)

ACTIVITIES: Produces and sells naturally based skin and hair care products and related items STATUS: Full INDEX: FTSE Small Cap. SECTOR: Retailers, general

HEAD & REG OFF: Watersmead, Littlehampton, West Sussex BN17 6LS Tel: (01903) 731500 Fax: (01903) 726250 REGISTRARS: Lloyds, Worthing. Tel: (01903) 502 541

ANNCMNTS: Int – late Oct, Final – mid May, AGM mid Jun

INTERIM: (29 Oct 97) 1/2 yr to 30 Aug 97. T/O £123m (£117m) Pre tax profit £12.3m (£11.8m). EPS: 3.80p (3.60p) int div 1.80p (1.50p). NOTES: Figures from 28 Feb 92 in accordance with FRS 3.

year ended 25 February		1994	1995	1996	1997	1998
turnover	£m	195	220	257	271	293
pre tax profit	£m	29.7	33.5	32.7	31.7	38.0
norm earn per share	p	10.3	11.8	10.0	11.7	12.0
FRS 3 earn per share	p	10.3	11.5	9.80	9.30	11.8
div per share	p	2.00	2.40	3.40	4.70	5.60
intangibles	£m	3.70	2.20	0.70	–	–
fixed assets	£m	67.9	73.6	78.2	74.9	78.4
fixed investments	£m	0	0.50	0.50	0.50	2.00
stocks	£m	34.6	38.6	37.6	34.5	47.7
debtors	£m	37.2	44.3	44.0	45.0	47.0
cash, securities	£m	24.9	29.0	30.1	47.1	29.6
creditors short	£m	35.6	51.2	49.1	59.0	70.4
creditors long	£m	35.8	26.6	19.4	13.2	4.00
prefs, minorities	£m	–	–	–	–	–
ord capital, reserves	£m	96.9	111	123	130	130

Example 31.1 The Body Shop: A bumpy ride! But a potential recovery situation?

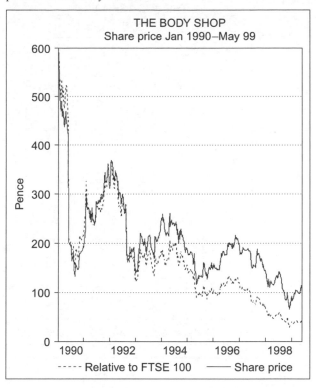

Example 31.2 Body Shop's ever-increasing turnover on a linear scale

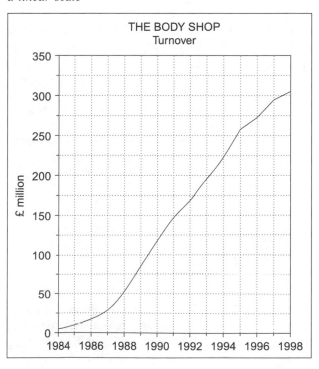

Example 31.3 The same turnover as a Lin/Log graph

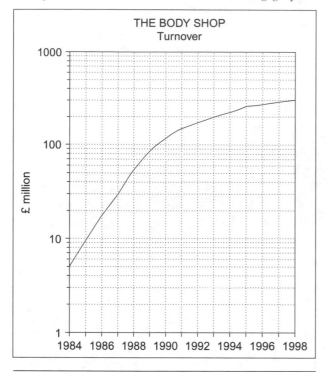

THE BODY SHOP
Turnover

for six or seven years. Below are some of the more interesting extracts from the *Investors Chronicle* (*IC*) together with our comments and questions (**Q2** etc.).

THE BODY SHOP *Extracts from the Investors Chronicle and the questions they raise*

> *IC 15/01/93*
>
> [After profits warning] At 158p . . . less than half what they were a year ago, when they were trading at 350p. . . . while discount competition nibbles at volumes in some of its low cost standard items, like bubble baths, Body Shop is slow to expand its presence in other areas, such as cosmetics.
>
> Questions about the group's management and financial controls have never disappeared. There has been concern that the marketing and buying functions have minds of their own. And there have been worries as to whether Body Shop is wise to be tying up so much working capital by making its own bottles.

In Chapter 15 we looked at Body Shop's working capital (see pages 97–8) and noticed an alarming jump in stocks in 1998. We may be on to something there, so another question for our list:

Q2. Are stock levels a problem and, if so, what is the company doing about it?

After we'd finished reading the *IC* cuttings, we phoned the company and asked to speak to Angela Bawtree, Head of Investor Relations – we had spotted her name in a couple of the *IC* articles. Introducing ourselves as prospective investors – quite true; we are always on the qui vive for interesting investments – we asked her some of our questions.

On stocks, Angela told us:

- Bottle making had been sold to PLYSU a couple of years ago.
- Stocks were receiving the attention of the new Chief Executive, with a target to cut by 20%.
- EPOS (Electronic Point of Sale) was being put in more stores, to improve stock control.

> *IC 14/05/93*
>
> Body Shop has just come through the most difficult year in its remarkable history. Two profits warnings in four months left investors bruised and brought to an end the company's long romance with the market . . . its first ever fall in full-year profits . . . Thanks to aggressive overseas expansion, Body Shop now generates only about half of sales and profits in the UK.
>
> *IC 28/05/93*
>
> . . . the group has more enthusiasm and commitment than most of its competitors.
>
> *IC 22/10/93*
>
> Competition is intensifying, particularly from BOOTS.

Q3. How is morale standing up in adversity?
Q4. Are margins being squeezed? Let's do an analysis.
Q5. Is there any independent market research data on UK market shares in the sector?
Q6. And in the US?
Q7. How serious is BOOTS as a competitor?
Q8. How much of a premium are Body Shop customers prepared to pay?

> *IC 15/07/94*
>
> For the first time since March 1988 two Body Shop International founders sold a sizeable stake in the company. A week ago MD Anita Roddick and chairman Gordon Roddick sold 3.5m shares at 240p, taking their joint holding down two percentage points to 25.4%. The shares fell just 3p to 240p.
>
> In 1988 the MD and Mr McGlinn sold 5% of the equity as part of a placing of shares to raise £9.6m to build a new warehouse. The shares fell 8 per cent immediately after the cash call.
>
> News that the £8.4m raised this time will be used to fund several philanthropic ventures including a Healthcare Foundation project and a film, is apparently more acceptable to the markets. [We think the writer here may be jumping to conclusions.

If the 1988 placing was done at say, a 10% discount, a fall of 8% could easily have been due to market makers marking the price down to discourage placees from making a quick turn.]

IC 26/08/94
BODY SHOP CRITICS MAKE A VICE OUT OF A VIRTUE. The cuddly image of Anita and Gordon's retail empire has taken a series of knocks. However insubstantial the allegations the loss of goodwill can't avoid hammering the value of the company. . . . The US Federal Trade Commission is understood to have requested information concerning a dispute between the company and disgruntled franchisees.

Q9. How have turnover and profits in the US been affected? We need a segmental analysis.

IC 02/09/94
Just why Body Shop is panicking over its green image may become apparent in a critical report to be published in the US . . . Mr Entine's report is expected to call Body Shop to account . . . over the terms under which the company operates its 'Trade, Not Aid' links with developing countries [and] the use of non-renewable resources. Body Shop has expended more effort on discrediting the author than on rebutting his charges. Mr Entine, an award winner several times over for TV documentaries, has been engaged in 'a single-minded campaign of vilification against the Body Shop', according to this week's communiqué from Chairman Gordon Roddick.

. . . Instead of improving its lot, the Body Shop has come over as an overbearing tyrant.

Q10. Who handles the company's PR now?

The Body Shop has already said that it will soon appoint two non-executive directors. The latest flap highlights the need for an independent boardroom voice in a company which is no stranger to the charges of autocratic management.

Q11. How many non-executive directors (NEDs) are there on the Board now?
Q12. Who are they? and
Q13. Are the Roddicks likely to listen to them?

IC 21/10/94
Competition is hotting up with US chain Bath and Body Works launching in the UK.

Q14. How has Bath and Body Works fared in the UK since launch?

Body Shop's head of investor relations told us that Bath and Body Works still have only five UK stores.

IC 27/10/95
Last time's £1.5m operating profit evaporated into a £2.4m loss and concerns are growing about Body Shop's US strategy. It now has 262 US shops, up from 199, a large proportion company owned rather than franchised out. It's thus responsible for a large chunk of US sales, whereas the strength of franchising . . . only has to worry about manufacturing the product.

Q15. How many shops are there now, and what proportion are franchised in each geographical area?

IC 03/11/95
It's official: Anita and Gordon Roddick have discussed taking Body Shop International private, but said this week that they had no plans formally to propose such a move 'in the near future, if at all'. There is no love lost between Anita and the City gents she has so often accused of 'short-termism'.

IC 10/05/96
Anita and Gordon Roddick abandoned their attempts to buy back the 75% of Body Shop they don't already own, fearing that the burden of debt would restrict expansion opportunities. Chairman Gordon Roddick said he would prefer to maximise returns to shareholders in the longer term than offer them cash today.

IC 08/11/96
First the good news: Body Shop is doing well in Asia. Now the bad news: Body Shop is still losing money in the US. The loss was £3.4m – £1m more than last time. The recently appointed head of US operations, Steen Kanter, has plenty of retailing experience. He spent 22 years with Swedish retailer IKEA and was chief executive with US houseware retailer Lechters. [Leading retail analyst] John Richards regards the US problem as insoluble: 'the point is that they are trying to be a retailer, but they are not.'

IC 16/05/97
Body Shop . . . shocked the market by making a £6.5m provision to cover loans made to its French franchisee.

Q16. What's happening in France now?

The company told us they needed to take it under their direct control to sort it out, and may perhaps refranchise it later.

IC 31/10/97

Only 261 of 1530 stores in 47 countries are directly owned. The downside is that franchised stores need hefty handouts when profits fail.

Q17. What *are* the normal terms of contracts with franchisees?

IC 31/10/97

An old concept called the Green Room, where customers could pay for beauty treatments and massages, has been revamped as The Doorway. It has been rolled out in five stores so far and will be expanding in the second half.

Q18. Not a very inspiring name. How is it going?

IC 23/01/98 [in a leading article on the woes of Laura Ashley and The Body Shop]
One [Ann Iverson] played the City to the letter, pocketing £3m in two years. The other [Anita Roddick] has railed against such excess, lambasting the City and admitting 'finance bores the pants off me.'

Q19. What are Gordon and Anita's salaries?

We subsequently checked the Notes to the 1998 accounts, and what we found is shown at the foot of this page.

IC 23/01/98 [in a leading article on the woes of Laura Ashley and The Body Shop] continued
. . . Body Shop's added Asian flu to its woes in the US and its mature UK market.

. . .

'Companies with entrenched family shareholdings tend not to be so responsive to the market', says one institutional shareholder in both companies. 'They tend to wait until there in a crisis before they start reacting.'

. . .

Gordon Roddick said: 'We are taking a conservative view with regard to trade in South East Asia.' That translates as: our big growth market, worth over a third of operating profits, has just collapsed.

. . .

Neither is there any sign of a pick-up in the US. Despite buying back many of its franchised stores to improve operational controls – it now owns 203 of its 291 US shops – Body Shop is still heading for the same-again losses. Mr Roddick complains of 'aggressive discounting' by copycat US competitors, such as Garden Botanica.

One problem is that US consumers do not rate Body Shop as a premium brand. 'It's a completely different market to the UK,' says Matthew Siebert, retail analyst at the company's house broker ABN Amro Hoare Govett. 'The consumer is much more price-driven.'

IC 12/02/98
US HEADACHE AS BOSS QUITS. This week's sudden resignation of Steen Kanter, head of US Operations, has rekindled speculation over Body Shop's strategy for the US.

[Leading retail analyst] John Richards said; 'To move heavily into direct retail (owning the stores) was both high risk and a mistake. Especially in the US, which is the most difficult retail market in the world.'

Top management
Our first meeting. We first met Anita and her husband at a Body Shop AGM in the eighties. It was held in their warehouse at Littlehampton on a Friday afternoon.

After the formal proceedings, tea was laid out on a long double line of trestle tables down the centre of the warehouse, and Anita came round with a smile and a tray of sticky buns. A really friendly person and a wonderful personality, unspoilt by her meteoric success. We thought she was terrific, but didn't buy any shares, because they were on an astronomical P/E.

Our second meeting. Two or three years later, in 1991, we went again to the AGM, this time held at the Beach Hotel, Marine Parade, Worthing.

We felt short changed! Anita Roddick wasn't even there, but a taped message from her was played at the start of the proceedings. The gist of her message was that she was out scouring the world for new products. But the message we got was that she didn't care about shareholders, and why should she? She effectively had control:

THE BODY SHOP *Extract from the 1998 accounts*

6. Directors: Total Directors' emoluments

Name	Position	SALARY 1998 £000	SALARY 1997 £000	BENEFITS 1998 £000	BENEFITS 1997 £000
A.L. Roddick OBE	Chief Executive	140	135	22	12
T.G. Roddick	Chairman	140	135	22	14
S.A. Rose	Managing	250	240	–	1

The Remuneration Committee recommended that the salary of both A.L. Roddick and T.G. Roddick should be at a rate of £300,000 per annum, but the Roddicks have chosen to be remunerated at the rate set out in the table above.

THE BODY SHOP *Note to the 1991 accounts*

25. Close company
The close company provisions of the Taxes Act 1988 applied to the Company at 28 February 1991 [the year end] and have continued to apply since that date.

Hadn't anyone told her that it is bad manners for an MD to duck her own AGM deliberately? We also noted that there were no non-executive directors, but we struck up a conversation with one of the executive directors, who told us that she had been with Body Shop's PR agents, but that Anita had brought her on to the Board full time. We groaned inwardly. Any GCSE business studies student knows that PR people are in the flattery business.

Key point

It is the duty of non-executive directors (NEDs) to tell management what management *needs* to hear, not what management *wants* to hear, and to do this effectively they should be completely independent (see page 206).

Including as an NED anyone connected with the company's solicitors, auditor, financial adviser, stockbroker or PR agency is not to be recommended. It is too cosy, and tends to preclude any criticism of the professional adviser concerned.

Dominant personality

To understand a company dominated by a *star*, you need to understand that star. Anita's picture appeared on the cover of the *Investors Chronicle* of 22 December 1989, to accompany a lead story 'Secrets of Body Shop's success' and a few quotes from that two-pager may help the reader understand Anita and, hence, the company and some of the investment community's reservations:

INVESTORS CHRONICLE *Extracts from an article on The Body Shop, 22 December 1989*

Body Shop is that great contradiction, caring capitalism. Roddick admits that it is 'very much a benign dictatorship'.

In 1984, when Greens were still too weird to take, Body Shop came to the market, with 7 of its own shops and 92 franchises . . . Valued at £4.75m, a prospective rating of 25 times was thought demanding . . . Less than six years on, and the Body Shop share price stands at more than 520p . . . now valued at over £440m.

Awards have been showered on her like acid rain: Business Woman of the Year (1985), Company of the Year (1987), Order of the British Empire (1988), Communicator of the Year (1988), Retailer of the Year (1989), United Nations 'Global 500' award, for her work in the rainforests (1989).

On the business side, Body Shop is essentially a franchising and wholesaling operation. This has helped to keep down capital and staff needs.

The Body Shop ethos includes a determination to cut out hype, packaging and (wherever possible) company cars. Using natural products, it aims to promote health rather than glamour ('Our concept of beauty is Mother Teresa, not some bimbo' is a throwaway line from the past). However, the priority is the company. 'I'm not responsible for those people who come in for monetary gain.' The company's holistic view places the interests of shareholders a poor fourth, behind those of the staff, the community and the planet. 'Nobody asks the shareholders what they think,' Roddick once said. 'So far they can only be grateful.'

But not any more they can't. At the financial year end February 1998 the share price (over 500p in 1990) stood at 120.5p, compared with 192.5p at the end of February 1997. The fall of 37% during the year appeared to be of no consequence to the Chief Executive: the inside front cover of the 1998 report and accounts showed a personable young man saying to Anita 'what's a nice girl like you doing in a place like this', and Anita's reply 'I own it'. This attitude, and the reminder that one is involved with a close company, tends to jar both shareholders and the market. And in 1998 her one-pager on page one ended: 'We're doing it our way, which demands a huge amount of reflection, dialogue and consideration. To me, that feels like the only way to run a socially responsive company, especially one that is on course for the future.' This is not the thing to do if your profits have just fallen out of bed and your share price is down to 20% of its all time high.

Now we are not against 'socially responsive' companies, though some potential investors are, and reject THE BODY SHOP for two reasons: they don't want *their* money, shareholders' money, spent on someone else's good causes; and they prefer managers who manage rather than become involved in countless good works. Others welcome this 'kind faced capitalism'.

That kind face is understandable in view of Anita's background:

THE BODY SHOP *Extract from 1997 Directors Report*

Board of Directors
Anita L. Roddick OBE (Age 54) Chief Executive
Anita Roddick is responsible for the Company's style and image. She opened the first branch of The Body Shop in Brighton in 1976. Before opening a restaurant and hotel with her husband Gordon in 1970, Anita was a member of staff in the Women's Rights Department of the International Labour Organisation based at the United Nations in Geneva.

But it inevitably has its effect on the share price.

ANITA AS CO-CHAIRMAN

In May 1998 the Roddicks finally acknowledged that they needed a more professional top management, and appointed a CEO from outside the Group:

THE BODY SHOP *Press release 12 May 1998*

The Body Shop International is pleased to announce the appointment of Patrick Gournay as Chief Executive Officer with effect from 14 July 1998. From the same date Anita Roddick will share the role of Co-Chair with Gordon Roddick . . .

Patrick Gournay joins the Company from Groupe Danone, where he is currently Executive Vice President of Danone's North and South American Division . . . He has spent the past 26 years with Groupe Danone, the multi-product food group headquartered in Paris with sales of £8 billion.

Gordon Roddick, Chairman of The Body Shop, said: *'We are delighted that Patrick has accepted this key role. His leadership . . . will help shape the future of our business in a new era of success and innovation. His energy, enthusiasm and good sense of humour will go down well in The Body Shop.'*

Mr Gournay's initial interview for the job was, to put it mildly, unusual. As the Press reported:

SUNDAY TELEGRAPH *City Profile, 31 January 1999 'Body Shop's Mr Makeover'*

When Patrick Gournay first met Anita Roddick last year, she took him to her Oxford Street store and booked him in for a massage. Hardly your every day interviewing technique, but this is Body Shop after all . . .

'Then we looked at the store and she told me her thoughts on what needed to be done. And that was it – then she left.'

A strange sort of interview, and the massage made us feel uneasy. Was it intended to demean Patrick? *Was Anita, wittingly or unwittingly, showing that she intended to continue in her dominant role?*

To continue our quote:

SUNDAY TELEGRAPH *31 January 1999*

Last week Gournay went public on probably the most radical reshape Body Shop has seen since Roddick founded the business in 1974. Manufacturing operations in Littlehampton, employing 550 people, will be sold; franchising operations will be reappraised; a new structure will organise the business into four regions – UK, Europe, American and Asia . . .

Although the new CEO was doing his best to make THE BODY SHOP more commercial, the missionary influence of Anita Roddick was still overwhelming, as the 1999 Report made clear:

THE BODY SHOP *Extract from 1999 report*

MISSION STATEMENT
OUR REASON FOR BEING

* To dedicate our business to the pursuit of social and environmental change . . .

TRADING CHARTER

. . .

OUR TRADING PRINCIPLES REFLECT OUR CORE VALUES

WE AIM TO ENSURE that human and civil rights, as set out in the Universal Declaration of Human Rights, are respected throughout our business activities. We will establish a framework based on this declaration . . .

Results in the Patrick Gournay years

As the Summary Profit and Loss accounts on the next page show, there was a great deal of activity, considerable expense, but not much improvement to show for Exceptional and Restructuring costs [C] totalling £36 million.

In fact no improvement at all, rather the reverse.

[A] Although Turnover had gone up by an encouraging average of 8.5% per annum, this was due entirely to new openings; like for like sales remained flat.

[B] Operating expenses before exceptional costs increased by 40.7%, compared with an increase in turnover of 27.6% during the period.

[D] Operating profit declined from £38.1 million to £29.4 million.

[E] Interest payable (net) increased during the period from £0.1 million to £4.4 million helping the company run into a Retained loss [G] for 2001, after a maintained Dividend [F].

The maintained dividend was probably just as well, for less than a month after the 2001 preliminary announcement the company was approached by the Mexican vitamins retailer Groupe Omnilife. The offer was rumoured to be as much as 180p, and the shares spiked to 126p. But a formal bid never emerged, and the shares fell to 74p.

THE BODY SHOP *Consolidated profit and loss account, 1998–2001*

Consolidated profit and loss account

	Comment	2001 £m	2000 £m	1999 £m	1998 £m
Turnover	[A]	374.1	330.1	303.7	293.1
Cost of sales		(149.0)	(130.9)	(127.7)	(115.9)
Gross profit		225.1	199.2	176.0	177.2
Operating expenses before exceptional costs	[B]	(195.7)	(166.2)	(151.4)	(139.1)
Operating profit before exceptional costs		29.4	33.0	24.6	38.1
Exceptional costs	[C]	(11.2)	–	(4.5)	–
Operating profit	[D]	18.2	33.0	20.1	38.1
Restructuring costs	[C]	(1.0)	(2.7)	(16.6)	–
		17.2	30.3	3.5	38.1
Interest payable (net)	[E]	(4.4)	(1.5)	(0.1)	(0.1)
Profit on ordinary activities before taxation		12.8	28.8	3.4	38.0
Taxation on profit on ordinary activities		(3.5)	(10.4)	(8.0)	(15.2)
(Loss)/profit for the financial year		9.3	18.4	(4.6)	22.8
Equity minority interests		0.2	–	–	–
Dividends paid and proposed	[F]	(10.9)	(10.9)	(10.9)	(10.8)
Retained profit (loss)	[G]	(1.4)	7.5	(15.5)	12.0

. . .

Too much, too quickly?

One of Patrick Gournay's early moves was to sell off the manufacturing operation at the two Littlehampton factories ($^1/_3$ of product was already outsourced), and introduce a mass of new products at the expense of some old favourites. As Maggie Urry reported in an article contrasting the troubled Body Shop and the rejuvenated Laura Ashley:

FINANCIAL TIMES *13 January 2001*

Body Shop issued a profits warning as its new product strategy hit problems . . . Patrick Gournay admitted a strategy of stepping up new product development had been poorly executed and had failed to generate the expected sales gains, while customers hankered for old products that had been discontinued . . .

'We paid the price in margin and inventory' – Higher stock levels had cost the group £3 million – lower than expected UK sales cost £4 million – Wholesale sales to franchisees in Europe and Asia cost £3–£3.5 million.

Neglect of the franchisees

In earlier years The Body Shop had relied on franchisees to provide capital for expansion, and enthusiasm for the products. But then the balance changed in favour of concentrating on opening more, larger, company owned stores, and buying in franchisees who didn't want to expand.

In the year to February 1997 there were 1,282 franchised outlets accounting for 65% of sales, with 209 company owned outlets accounting for 35%. By 2002 the mix had virtually reversed, with 507 company owned stores accounting for 63% of sales.

The disregard for franchisees was illustrated by a group of German and Dutch franchisees turning up for the 2000 AGM to bewail the discontinuation of well established and very popular lines such as the Peppermint Foot Cream. Sales had suffered, and good customers had been lost.

The United States

The US had been a thorn in The Body Shop's side from the outset. Looking back over the 1990s:

251

THE BODY SHOP *Extracts from segmental analyses*

		USA		Group
Year	Turnover	Operating profit	Operating margin	Operating margin
	£m	£m	%	%
1990	5.8	(1.9)	(33.2)	20.0
1991	13.3	(0.6)	(4.7)	19.0
1992	23.4	1.5	6.4	18.9
1993	37.8	2.1	5.5	14.4
1994	50.4	6.2	12.3	15.4
1995	58.8	4.9	8.3	15.7
1996	70.8	(1.3)	(1.8)	13.1
1997	73.1	(3.0)	(4.1)	11.8
1998	78.0	(1.7)	(2.2)	13.0
1999*	97.8	0.8	0.8	6.6

* The Americas, as opposed to USA

But interestingly, between 1990 and 1998 the segmental analysis showed 'USA' and 'Americas (excluding USA)' separately. In 1999 they were reported together as 'Americas'.

We look below at 1998 as reported, separately, and at what the figures would have been had they been reported together:

THE BODY SHOP *Extracts from segmental analyses*

As reported, separately

		USA		Group
Year	Turnover	Operating profit	Operating margin	Operating margin
	£m	£m	%	%
1998	78.0	(1.7)	(2.2)	13.0

Americas (excluding USA)

				Group
Year	Turnover	Operating profit	Operating margin	Operating margin
	£m	£m	%	%
1998	12.8	3.4	26.5	13.0

If they had been reported together

		Americas		Group
Year	Turnover	Operating profit	Operating margin	Operating margin
	£m	£m	%	%
1998	90.8	1.7	1.9	13.0

Our immediate reaction to the combining of 'USA' and 'Americas (excluding USA)', with their very different margins, was 'naughty naughty!'

Key point

Always be highly suspicious when a company reports *less* information than it did last year. Ask yourself: is there a good reason, or is this a cover-up?

Q20. In the 1999 segmental analysis, why are 'USA and Americas (excluding USA)' now reported together?

The reason may be the current reorganisation into four new regional businesses, which Patrick Gournay describes later in his report: UK, The Americas, Europe & Middle East and Asia Pacific.

But management in the United States was changing. The company had entered into a joint venture with Adrian Bellamy, one of the executive directors:

THE BODY SHOP *Extract from 1999 Directors' Report*

Board of Directors
Adrian Bellamy (Age 57) Executive Director
... appointed to the Board on 6 January 1997 as Executive Director. On 19 June 1998, Adrian entered into a joint venture arrangement with the Company which granted him management rights over the US subsidiary and an option to acquire up to a 51% interest in the US business between the years 2000 and 2002, subject to the achievement of performance targets.

And progress was being made:

THE BODY SHOP *Extract from the CEO's 1999 review*

In the USA, a number of actions have been taken under the management of Adrian Bellamy following the joint venture arrangement which took effect last June.

These include reorganisation of the central office and the creation of a product and marketing team now located in San Francisco, 28 store buy-backs from franchisees, the closure of 11 under-performing stores, the closure of three warehouses to consolidate the distribution system, a reduction in inventory levels of over 30%, the transfer of bottle filling to a third party and the closure of our filling plant. In the USA, we are close to achieving our targeted mix of stores for that market, with some three quarters of the stores now company-owned.

Recent progress in the United States
Continuing the record:

THE BODY SHOP *Extracts from segmental analyses*

		Americas		Group
Year	Turnover	Operating profit	Operating margin	Operating margin
	£m	£m	%	%
1999	97.8	0.8	0.8	6.6
2000	99.5	6.5	6.5	10.0
2001	118.5	14.3	12.0	4.5

In August 1991, Mr Bellamy's links with the retailer tightened as The Body Shop bought out his share of the joint venture for a mixture of cash and shares, and appointed him to a two-year consultancy to oversee the US business and spread his expertise more generally around the group.

The contrast with the ailing UK was stark, so it was hardly surprising that when, in February 2002, the Roddicks decided to step down as co-chairmen and Patrick Gournay left, Bellamy got the top job.

ANITA STEPS DOWN?

There are two questions to answer:

Q21. Can Mr Bellamy repeat his success in the US throughout the entire Company?
Q22. Will Anita let him?

Adrian Bellamy's track record
As the FT reported the day after the announcement of Bellamy's appointment to Executive Chairman:

FINANCIAL TIMES *13 February 2002*

Body Shop's US management team moves in
. . . [Mr Bellamy's] expertise draws on his experience as a non-executive director of a number of companies, including Reckitt Benckiser, Gucci and Gap . . .

Yesterday Mr Bellamy highlighted ways in which performance in North America had been improved.

Some of them are straightforward in retailing terms, emphasising what an unconventional company Body Shop had become in some respects as it expanded under its founders Anita and Gordon Roddick.

'We've been able to simplify and rationalise our supply chain and we have implemented fast a new IT structure that gives us enormous capacity to remain in stock of our most wanted items' Mr Bellamy said.

The successful introduction of new ranges has been critical in increasing sales. . . . The new elements have also helped the group move slightly upmarket in the US.

A delicate issue is how to make commercial sense of the group's strong association with ethical issues such as protecting the environment and defending human rights.

Mr Bellamy is adamant that he and Mr Saunders [the CEO in the US, who is to replace Mr Gournay as CEO of the company] will go 'hand in hand with Gordon and Anita in terms of the values programme'.

But it is hard to escape the conclusion that some campaigns are part of its heritage rather than part of its future.

Anita still irrepressible
The Daily Telegraph's **City comment** showed that Anita had no intention of taking her non-executive role at other than 'full throttle':

DAILY TELEGRAPH *13 February 2002*

'Body Shop holders must be utterly thrilled to add to the public good'
Anita Roddick says she is 'thrilled' that the Body Shop has called off its takeover talks [other predators had shown interest after the Mexican approach came to nothing].

'I'm very, very happy' she gushes in a Hello-style interview with her spin doctor's website: 'This is going to be a springboard for some really exciting times.'

So exciting, in fact, that she's taking a back seat . . . This is 'just what the company needs,' while 'being now a non-exec is going to be more fun for me because you can be much more of a tyrant, challenging, asking and being a consultant.'

Well, that's a point of view. Unfortunately Mrs Roddick was too tyrannical to talk to journalists yesterday, because the website really answers every question that matters. Those that don't include why she decided that her chief executive Patrick Gournay had finally reached his sell-by date. Four years ago Mrs Roddick banged on about the wonders of the former Danone chief exec. She chose him to run the Body Shop because he was a delightful conversationalist, wasn't dictatorial and, most of all, she liked the way he treated his wife.

Conclusion
We think Adrian Bellamy should be capable of turning the whole company round; but will Anita let him do so without undue interference?

The big bear point is that Anita and her husband, with the support of their original backer, Mr McGlinn, still have a majority holding.

The next AGM should be a good time to gauge whether Mr Bellamy is being allowed to exercise his undoubted skills unfettered. If he is, then the shares will be a very interesting 'BUY FOR RECOVERY'.

Chapter 32

FUTURE DEVELOPMENTS IN ACCOUNTING

INTRODUCTION

This chapter is divided into seven parts:

1. Introduction
2. Overview
3. Financial Reporting Standards coming into force.

   - FRS 17 *Retirement benefits*
   - FRS 19 *Deferred tax*

4. FRED 22 *Statement of financial performance*
5. The Accounting Standards Board's work list:

   - Business combinations
   - Derivatives and other financial instruments

   - Revenue recognition
   - Shorter financial statements for share-holders
   - Leasing
   - Share-based payment
   - Operating and financial review

6. Any other business

   - *Historical summaries*
   - *Ratios*

7. Looking back and looking forward

OVERVIEW

The Accounting Standards Board

Over the past ten years the ASB has done a great deal to make accounts more informative and to close loopholes.

When the Board was set up, following the wise recommendations of the Dearing Report, there were more holes in the UK accounting rules than in a sieve. Now the rules are like a bucket with a few holes: leaks here and there, but generally holding water.

We also have in place a sound reporting framework, the **Statement of Principles**, within which to continue building.

In the past it was sometimes suggested that ASB was going too far, too fast. But if earlier standards regimes had an overwhelming fault it was that progress was slowed to the pace of the slowest – and that in some areas, like fundamental principles of accounting and accounting theory, not only was nothing achieved, nothing much was even attempted.

The degree to which ASB pronouncements, despite the speed of change, have met with acceptance, among the accounting and auditing professions, the City and private investors, is quite remarkable. Indeed, there is little to suggest any degree of overkill on the part of financial reporting standards (although not all would agree with this).

But the overall position of company reporting is less satisfactory for two reasons: firstly there are too many rule makers and secondly, following on from the first, too much corporate governance.

Too many rulemakers

In the 1950s and 1960s company accounts only had to comply with the Companies Act 1948 and, for listed companies, the Stock Exchange's *Listing Rules* as well.

Now we have *European Directives* as well as company law, while the Listing Rules have fallen into the maw of the Financial Services Authority.

The ASB has been a huge improvement on its predecessor, the Accounting Standards Committee, but, in political knee jerk reaction, we have had Cadbury on corporate governance, Greenbury on directors' remuneration and Hampel, who was asked to sweep up after the other two. He, poor chap, was criticised in some quarters for not adding any further complications to speak of.

Rather more low profile is the Auditing Practices Board to provide support to fee-dependent auditors being unduly leaned upon by their more aggressive clients. The threat of investigation by the Financial Reporting Review Panel is a valuable deterrent, but he who pays the piper still largely calls the tune.

Company law

In our 7th edition we commented:

> *Company law is in a mess . . . Company legislation is long overdue not just for consolidation, but for a fundamental rethink . . .*

We are pleased to note that the Department of Trade and Industry has launched a fundamental review of company law. A consultation document issued in March 2000

> *. . . favoured the delegation to an appropriate standard-setting body such as the ASB of all the rules and standards on the form and content of company accounts . . .*

The Steering Group made its final recommendations to the DTI in June 2001 but as at 30 April 2002 there are no further developments.

Too much Corporate Governance

In the 50s, the annual report and accounts of a major listed company like MARKS & SPENCER consisted of four pages (quarto pages, smaller than A4).

We are not suggesting going back to that, but the amount of verbiage these days is, in some companies, quite dreadful. For instance do we really need the many pages of additional information required by the Combined Code (14 pages in BARCLAYS' 1999 Report) – 14 pages of *Corporate Governance*, a large part of which is what David Tweedie calls 'Boiler-plating' – standard forms of words. As one City veteran commented:

> 'All the rules on earth won't stop the Maxwells of this world. All these rules do is add to the costs of the honest.'

And who reads them anyway?

FINANCIAL REPORTING STANDARDS COMING INTO FORCE

New standards

Two new Standards which will be particularly important during 2002 and 2003 are FRS 17 *Retirement benefits* (see Chapter 16) and FRS 19 *Deferred tax* (see Chapter 17).

Readers of accounts should look at annual reports for clues as to the likely impact of these new rules once they have to be implemented. The gas distributors LATTICE GROUP is a good example of a company which gave useful information in its 2000 accounts.

FRS 17 *Retirement benefits*

Financial journalists are already commenting on the likely impact of FRS 17 on company accounts, even though the standard's full implications will not be felt by all companies until years ending after 23 June 2003.

For example, *The Times* of 18 April 2001 quoted Bacon & Woodrow, the actuarial consultant,

who said that FRS 17 would 'introduce significantly greater volatility into both balances and profit and loss accounts . . .', a theme also highlighted by Lattice Group.

LATTICE GROUP *Extract from 2000 accounts*

Note 1 New accounting standards
. . . This Standard [FRS 17] will have a significant impact on the Group's financial results and position, as indicated in Note 24, . . . notably by increasing the volatility of these results in line with changes in actuarial assumptions and short-term fluctuations in fund assets . . .

Note 24 Pensions and post-retirement benefits
. . . Some preliminary work has been done to estimate the financial impact of FRS 17 . . . It has been estimated that the surplus of the Scheme, using a corporate bond discount rate of 5.4%, would be in the range of £1.2bn to £1.4bn . . .

FRS 19 *Deferred tax*

Companies with large amounts of deferred tax unprovided in the balance sheet will find that FRS 19 has a significant impact. Earnings per share will be reduced once tax charges reflect the full impact of deferred tax.

Balance sheet gearing will increase once provisions have reflected the full impact of FRS 19. LATTICE GROUP gives an early indication of the Standard's likely impact.

Companies currently providing deferred tax in full will not be significantly affected by the introduction of FRS 19.

LATTICE GROUP *Extracts from 2000 accounts*

Note 1 New accounting standards

... This Standard [FRS 19] will have a significant impact on the Group's financial results and position as indicated in Note 19 ...

Note 19 Provisions for liabilities and charges

Deferred corporation tax.... unprovided potential deferred tax liabilities for 2000 of £1.27 billion ...

If full provision were made on an undiscounted basis for deferred taxation, the total provision required at 31 December 2000 would be approximately £1,200 million (on a discounted basis, approximately £650 million) ...

FRED 22 *STATEMENT OF FINANCIAL PERFORMANCE*

Introduction

FRS 3 *Reporting financial performance*, which introduced a new primary statement, STRGL (*Statement of Total Recognised Gains and Losses*), has been under review for some time.

In June 1999, the ASB published a Discussion Paper '*Reporting financial performance: proposals for change*' and this was followed, in December 2000, by FRED 22.

FRED 22's proposal

FRED 22 proposes replacing both the P & L account *and* STRGL with a single performance statement, the *Statement of Financial Performance (SoFP)*, which would be divided into three sections:

* Operating
* Financial and treasury
* Other gains and losses.

The first two sections would be comparable to the profit and loss account in terms of items included:

Operating would include turnover, cost of sales, operating expenses, resulting in a figure for Operating profit or Operating loss.

Financing and treasury would include interest on debt and income from investing surplus funds.

Other gains and losses would include items currently included in STRGL, for example revaluation gains and losses, and foreign currency translation adjustments.

Five years of exceptionals

A particularly interesting proposal is for companies to publish a five-year table disclosing all exceptional items dealt with over that period. This is hardly likely to be welcomed by some companies but will be a part of the accounts that analysts will look at hard, not just in relation to the performance statement but also to earnings per share disclosures.

THE ACCOUNTING STANDARDS BOARD'S WORK LIST

Projects in hand

The ASB projects in hand include:

* Business combinations
* Derivatives and other financial instruments
* Revenue recognition
* Shorter financial statements for shareholders
* Leasing
* Share-based payment
* Operating and financial review

In addition to the above, the ASB announced in April 2002 that it proposed issuing a number of Financial Reporting Exposure Drafts (FRED 23

to FRED 30 inclusive) – these are listed in Appendix 1.

Business combinations

In December 1998 the ASB published a Discussion Paper '*Business combinations*'. This was, in effect, a Position Paper it had prepared for the international group known as the G4+1 – a group which includes accounting standard-setters for five countries: the UK, Australia, Canada, New Zealand and the USA; with the former International Accounting Standards Committee (IASC) as an observer.

The Paper's main recommendation is that only one method of accounting for business combinations should be used: acquisition accounting. Merger accounting should be banned. The ASB has not itself debated the Position Paper, but international harmonisation would provide an excellent excuse for getting rid of what to many seems a rather uncomfortable anomaly: that provided five criteria are met, merger accounting has to be used, which gives an entirely different balance sheet and results, not just in the first year but permanently.

The idea is that a standard will in time supersede FRS 6 *Acquisitions and mergers*.

Derivatives and other financial instruments

Financial instruments can rapidly transform the risk profile of a group in a way that is not made apparent under present reporting practices. For example, a derivative, acquired for nil cost (and so not recognised in the balance sheet) can be used to convert a dollar floating rate liability into a sterling fixed rate one. Or a derivative may be used to 'hedge' the risk that sales expected to occur next year in a foreign currency may be worth less when converted into sterling because sterling may strengthen in the meantime. In both cases, the value of the derivative can change very significantly so that it represents a substantial asset or liability by the year end. This probably will not be apparent to the reader under present accounting standards.

In some cases derivatives and other financial instruments have been used unwisely, exposing entities (not just companies but local authorities) to potentially large losses. Under the present system of reporting, such gains and losses are often not reported as they arrive, but are deferred until realised. This gives rise to the abuse of 'cherry picking' (in a bad year selling instruments with an otherwise unrealised gain so as to boost reported profits).

These concerns and proposals to meet them were set out in a Discussion Paper issued in July 1996. That Paper proposed that a standard on disclosure should be developed as fast as possible, disclosure being a relatively uncontentious area. The result was FRS 13 *Derivatives and other financial instruments*.

That left the more difficult question of how financial instruments should be measured (i.e. cost or fair value) and whether hedge accounting should be used. The 1996 Discussion Paper proposed that the best approach would be for all financial instruments – both derivatives and non-derivatives and both assets and liabilities – to be measured at fair value.

A further Consultation Paper, *Financial Instruments and Similar Items*, was published by the ASB in December 2000. This Paper was developed by an international 'Joint Working Group'.

The Paper's main proposals are:

- All financial instruments should be measured at fair value (ideally market value)
- Financial liabilities, for example debt, should be shown in the balance sheet at fair value, compared with existing practice which shows these at cost or redemption value
- All gains and losses arising on changes in the fair value of financial instruments would be recognised immediately in the profit and loss account
- No hedge accounting techniques would be allowed if the hedging instrument was a financial instrument.

Revenue recognition

That there is urgent need to develop a standard on this topic is hardly in doubt. In July 2001, the Lex column of the *Financial Times* said:

> '... If you want to defraud investors by fiddling your company accounts, there are few better places to start than the field of revenue recognition ...'

ASB recognises the need for a coherent framework that can be used to address revenue recognition issues in different contexts, for example, the software and media sectors. The starting point for this was the publication by ASB in July 2001 of the Discussion Paper entitled '*Revenue recognition*'.

Shorter financial statements for shareholders

In February 2000, ASB published a Discussion Paper, *Year-end Financial Reports: Improving Communication*, which looked at ways that ensured all shareholders received information that was relevant to their needs.

The Paper proposed that companies should normally send shareholders financial statements shorter than those presently sent. Companies would have some flexibility on form and content, but minimum requirements would be specified.

The ASB has passed on responses received to the DTI so that these can be considered in the DTI's Company Law Review.

Leasing

The ASB and other standard-setters regard present leasing standards as deficient because they omit material assets and liabilities arising from operating lease contracts. Furthermore, the 'all or nothing' approach of SSAP 21 to capitalisation of leased assets does not, the ASB believes, adequately reflect modern complex transactions.

A paper *Accounting for leases: A new approach – recognition by lessees of assets and liabilities arising under lease contracts* was prepared by the G4+1 and published in 1996. The suggestion was that new standards should be developed removing the distinction between finance leases and operating leases. All material rights and obligations arising under lease contracts would then be capitalised.

Share-based payment

This Discussion Paper looks at the accounting treatment of transactions where companies purchase goods or services from suppliers and employees and the consideration is in the form of shares or share options.

The Paper proposes that transactions involving share-based payment should be measured at the fair value of the shares or share options. An estimate of the transaction amount should be spread over the period of performance. Where this period extended over several years, adjustments would be required for subsequent changes in the market value of the shares or share options.

Operating and financial review (OFR)

We discussed OFRs in Chapter 25. The ASB is considering a limited amendment to its Best Practice Statement. This will extend OFRs by encouraging companies to provide further information on resources, particularly intangibles, which will affect future profitability but which under existing conventions are either not recorded in the accounts at all, or are shown only at cost. An example of this is given by REUTERS GROUP:

REUTERS *Extract from Annual Report 2000*

Operating and financial review

. . .

4. Shareholder value

Reuters aims to grow its value and outperform its peers. Reuters believes that its mix of assets, some of which are unique to the company, will help to meet this aim. These assets, some of which are not included in the consolidated balance sheet, include:

- Reuters independence
- Goodwill attached to the Reuters name
- Software and other intellectual property
- Global databases of financial and other information
- An integrated global organisation . . .
- The market value of investments held at cost . . .

A postscript – the DTI's Company Law Review is proposing that OFRs should be mandatory for all PLCs with a turnover exceeding £50m and private companies with a turnover exceeding £500m.

ANY OTHER BUSINESS

Historical summaries

As discussed in Chapter 24, the title and contents of a company's historical summary is left entirely to the discretion of the company or its graphic design agency. Summaries range from very detailed and comprehensive four- or five-pagers to a few colourful dinky-pooh diagrams embellishing the main body of the report, or nothing at all.

We raised the matter in an interview with the then plain Mr David Tweedie, who said it was low priority, and would be dealt with after the ASB had sorted out the Annual Accounts.

Is it time to add it to the ASB's work list?

Ratios

Some FRSs give definitions of ratios, earnings per share for example, though we would prefer '*basic*' to be called what it actually is: '*all inclusive e.p.s.*'.

In other areas, cash flow for instance, the FRSs make no mention of ratios and, as a result, confusion continues to reign amongst the compilers of annual reports and accounts. '*Free cash flow,*' as the Red Queen said, 'means what I want it to mean. No more, and no less.'

Would the Accounting Standards Board consider it within their remit to include definitions of key ratios in the appropriate FRSs?

LOOKING BACK AND LOOKING FORWARD

Looking back

As we discussed at the beginning of this chapter, ten years ago or so the accountancy profession, and auditors in particular, had fallen into disarray, if not into widespread disrepute. The rot may have started some years earlier with the 'Great Inflation Accounting Fiasco', which we discussed in Chapter 29.

But the real crunch came when the economy turned down in 1989/1990 and a string of listed companies, including some household names, went bust. They failed with little or no warning, because the auditors had helped the companies paper over the cracks.

Towards the end of 1990, just as the ASB was being set up, an article which we wrote in the *FT* highlighted the main problems:

FINANCIAL TIMES *Summary of an article in the 'Accountancy Column' on 1 November 1990*

Five reasons not to trust company figures

1. The present accounting rules can and do make nonsense of some figures. For example, the preferred method of dealing with purchased goodwill, writing it off immediately against reserves . . . distorts any calculation of 'return on capital employed' and similar ratios.
2. The present rules give companies far too much flexibility. For example, two completely different methods allowed in accounting for acquisitions. . . .
3. We are wary of taking company accounts at face value because of the enormous influence that seemingly quite small changes in accounting policies can make to reported results.
4. The seemingly endless ingenuity of some financial advisers in devising new ways of 'helping' clients . . . new financial instruments are hawked around the City by deal-oriented banks intent on generating substantial fees for themselves, with scant regard for their clients' long-term interests.
5. Auditors, in spite of the charade of being appointed by the shareholders at the AGM, are effectively in the pay of the directors. So when directors want to take maximum advantage of accounting rules and loopholes to enhance reported profits, auditors may be tempted to let them do so [or, in truth, actively help them to do so] . . .

The new and much more powerful Accounting Standards Board is now in a position to make sweeping improvements to our crumbling accounting standards.

The present

It has taken ten years, but in that time the ASB has certainly made some huge improvements.

Referring to the five points we listed in our FT article:

1. Immediately writing off purchased goodwill is no longer allowed. But, alas, companies were not obliged to reinstate all purchased goodwill previously written off against reserves. Only a handful did. So for most companies measures like ROCE will remain suspect, and in some cases downright misleading for another ten to fifteen years.
2. Merger accounting can now only be used for combinations meeting strict criteria and, with the influence of Europe, may be banned altogether.
3. A new Financial Reporting Standard, FRS 18 *Accounting policies*, was published in December

2000. As well as updating the basic '*Fundamental Accounting Concepts*', the FRS sets out the objectives and constraints to be considered when selecting and changing accounting policies. This won't stop 'creative' companies from trying it on, but should make it more difficult, and easier to spot.
4. We referred to derivatives and other financial instruments on page 257.
5. Auditors are now in a stronger position to resist top management who want to bend the rules. They can keep accounts reasonably 'true and fair' by pointing out that anything a bit 'iffy' runs the risk of being drawn to the attention of the Financial Reporting Review Panel.

Jobbing backwards for a minute to 1990. When a company that had managed to turn a £4 million loss into a £6 million profit by some Joint Venture subterfuge subsequently went belly up, we phoned up their auditors – a provincial office of one of the 'Big Six'.

The partner concerned pointed out that the £10 million profit on the half interest sale to a VC partner was clearly spelt out in Note 23, so he, the auditor, was in the clear. And he then added 'you should have seen what they *tried* to get away with.'

But back to today:

International Accounting Standards Committee
For many years the IASC didn't have much clout or much credibility (we've noticed that the two tend to go together).

The IASC was a splendid organisation if you like travelling, but a bit low on achievement.

Now that's all changed with the recent revamping of the IASC to become the International Accounting Standards *Board* (IASB), and the announcement by the European Commission that it proposes to make International Accounting Standards mandatory by 2005 for all companies with listings on European Stock Exchanges.

The ASB's priority is now to work with the IASB and other national standard-setters in seeking improvements in international standards and achieving convergence on global standards. Future standards adopted in the UK are likely to be based on the new style International Financial Reporting Standards (IFRSs).

Looking forward
Whether we like it or not, we have to live on the same planet as some very aggressive and not always entirely scrupulous top management (that's often how they got where they did).

It's also true that we will always have equally, perhaps even more aggressive 'financial advisers' who invariably put their own interests well ahead of the interests of their clients.

The question is this:

'Will Auditors in future uphold Accounting Standards and stand up to bullying management – including the Cap'n Bobs of this World (alias that canny Scot "Robert McSwell")?'

Sir David Tweedie, until the end of 2000 the Chairman of the Accounting Standards Board, is reported to have strong views on the matter:

FINANCIAL TIMES *Extract from an article by Michael Peel, Accountancy correspondent, published on 8 December 2000*

Auditors told to avoid 'smart Alec' approach

Sir David Tweedie, who steps down from the ASB this month after 10 years in office, warned auditors yesterday against returning to the 'smart Alec' approach which bedevilled the profession in the 1980s, saying that auditors could face a rule-making clampdown if they failed to exercise their judgment.

'**The profession has got to decide which way it has to go**', he said. '**If you won't obey the spirit [of the law] you get a rule book**.'

We don't know whether the arrival of Sir David Tweedie as chairman of the IASC has anything to do with it being upgraded to become the IASB, or with the European Commission taking the new body more seriously. An interesting coincidence.

We wish Sir David well in his new endeavours. *If Tweedie comes, can change be far behind?*

APPENDICES

APPENDIX 1 – CURRENT FINANCIAL REPORTING STANDARDS AND EXPOSURE DRAFTS

The following Standards, UITF Abstracts and Exposure Drafts were current in May 2002:

Date of Issue

Standards

ASB	Foreword to accounting standards	Jun 1993
FRS 1	Cash flow statements (revised Oct 1996)	Sep 1991
FRS 2	Accounting for subsidiary undertakings	Jul 1992
FRS 3	Reporting financial performance (amended Jun 1993 regarding insurance companies)	Oct 1992
FRS 4	Capital instruments	Dec 1993
FRS 5	Reporting the substance of transactions (amended re insurance broking transactions Dec 1994 and regarding private finance initiative and similar contracts Sep 1998)	Apr 1994
FRS 6	Acquisitions and mergers (amended Nov 1997 and Dec 1998)	Sep 1994
FRS 7	Fair values in acquisition accounting	Sep 1994
FRS 8	Related party disclosures	Oct 1995
FRS 9	Associates and joint ventures	Nov 1997
FRS 10	Goodwill and intangible assets	Dec 1997
FRS 11	Impairment of fixed assets and goodwill	Jul 1998
FRS 12	Provisions, contingent liabilities and contingent assets	Sep 1998
FRS 13	Derivatives and other financial instruments	Sep 1998
FRS 14	Earnings per share	Oct 1998
FRS 15	Tangible fixed assets	Feb 1999
FRS 16	Current tax	Dec 1999
FRS 17	Retirement benefits	Dec 2000
FRS 18	Accounting policies	Dec 2000
FRS 19	Deferred tax	Dec 2000
FRSSE	Financial reporting standard for smaller entities (effective Jun 2002)	Dec 2001

Urgent Issues Task Force (UITF)

ASB	Foreword to UITF Abstracts	Feb 1994
Abstract No.:		
4	Presentation of long-term debtors in current assets	Jul 1992
5	Transfers from current assets to fixed assets	Jul 1992
6	Accounting for post-retirement benefits other than pensions[1]	Nov 1992
7	True and fair view override disclosures	Dec 1992
9	Accounting for operations in hyper-inflationary economies	Jun 1993
10	Disclosure of directors' share options	Sep 1994
11	Capital instruments: issuer call options	Sep 1994
12	Lessee accounting for reverse premiums and similar incentives[2]	Dec 1994
13	Accounting for ESOP trusts	Jun 1995
14	Disclosure of changes in accounting policy	Nov 1995
15	Disclosure of substantial acquisitions (revised Feb 1999)	Jan 1996

17	Employee share schemes (revised Oct 2000)	May 1997
18	Pension costs following the 1997 tax changes in respect of dividend income[3]	May 1997
19	Tax on gains and losses that hedge an investment in a foreign enterprise	Feb 1998
21	Accounting issues arising from the proposed introduction of the euro	Mar 1998
22	Accounting for acquisition of a Lloyd's business	Jun 1998
23	Application of the transitional rules in FRS 15	May 2000
24	Accounting for start-up costs	Jun 2000
25	National Insurance contributions on share option gains	Jul 2000
26	Barter transactions for advertising	Nov 2000
27	Revisions to estimates of the useful economic life of goodwill and intangible assets	Dec 2000
28	Operating lease incentives	Feb 2001
29	Website development costs	Feb 2001
30	Date of award to employees of shares or rights to shares	Mar 2001
31	Exchanges of businesses or other non-monetary assets for an interest in a subsidiary, joint venture or associate	Oct 2001
32	Employee benefit trusts and other intermediate payment arrangements	Dec 2001
33	Obligations in capital instruments	Feb 2002

Notes
1   Superseded by FRS 17
2   Superseded by UITF 28
3   Superseded by FRS 17

Exposure Drafts

FRED 22	Revision of FRS 3, Reporting financial performance	Dec 2000
FRED 23	Financial instruments: Hedge accounting	May 2002
FRED 24	The effects of foreign exchange rates; Financial reporting in hyperinflationary economies	May 2002
FRED 25	Related party disclosures	May 2002
FRED 26	Earnings per share	May 2002
FRED 27	Events after the balance sheet date	May 2002
FRED 28	Inventories; Construction and service contracts	May 2002
FRED 29	Property plant and equipment	May 2002

Discussion Papers

The role of valuation in financial reporting	Mar 1993
Derivatives and other financial instruments	Jul 1996
Business combinations	Dec 1998
Leases – implementation of a new approach	Dec 1999
Share-based payment	Jul 2000
Financial instruments and similar items	Dec 2000
Revenue recognition	Jul 2001

Non-mandatory statements

Operating and financial review	Jul 1993
Interim reports	Sep 1997
Preliminary announcements	Jul 1998

ASB Statement of Principles

Statement of principles for financial reporting	Dec 1999

Accounting Standards Committee

The following standards issued by the ASC continue in force:

SSAP 2	Disclosure of accounting policies[1]	Nov 1971
SSAP 4	Accounting for government grants (revised Jul 1990)	Apr 1974
SSAP 5	Accounting for value added tax	Apr 1974
SSAP 9	Stocks and long-term contracts (Part 6 added Aug 1980, revised Sep 1988)	May 1975
SSAP 13	Accounting for research and development (revised Jan 1989)	Dec 1977
SSAP 15	Accounting for deferred tax (revised May 1985, amended Dec 1992)[2]	Oct 1978
SSAP 17	Accounting for post balance sheet events	Aug 1980
SSAP 19	Accounting for investment properties (amended Jul 1994)	Nov 1981
SSAP 20	Foreign currency translation	Apr 1983
SSAP 21	Accounting for leases and hire purchase contracts (amended Feb 1997)	Aug 1984
SSAP 24	Accounting for pension costs[3]	May 1988
SSAP 25	Segmental reporting	Jun 1990

Notes
1   Superseded by FRS 18
2   Superseded by FRS 19
3   Superseded by FRS 17

APPENDIX 2 – PRESENT VALUE

£1 received in a year's time is worth less than £1 received today, because £1 available today could be invested to earn interest for the next 12 months. If £1 now could be invested at a rate of interest i (expressed as a decimal), it would be worth £$(1 + i)$ in a year's time. If the £$(1 + i)$ at the end of the year was left invested, it would be worth:
£$(1 + i) \times (1 + i) =$ £$(1 + i)^2$ at the end of the second year, and £$(1 + i)^3$ at the end of the third year, and so on; in other words, it would earn compound interest at the rate of i per annum.

Present value is like compound interest in reverse: the value of £1 received in a year's time is worth £1 ÷ $(1 + i)$ now, and £1 in two years' time is worth £1 ÷ $(1 + i)^2$ now, and so on. For example, if i (known as the discount rate) is 10% p.a., then the present value of £1 received in a year's time is £1 ÷ $(1 + 0.10) =$ £0.9091. Similarly the present value of receiving £1 in two years' time is:
£1 ÷ $(1 + 0.10)^2 =$ £0.8264
and £1 in three years' time is:
£1 ÷ $(1.10)^3 =$ £0.7513,
and £1 in n years' time is £1 ÷ $(1.10)^n$.

Tables *of present values* are available for various rates of interest and periods of years. The table below is a very simplified and abbreviated version.

Present value tables refer to the value of 1, rather than the value of £1, because they can be used for any currency: the 1 may be $1, €1, DM1, 1 peseta or 1 of any other currency you care to name.

The present value concept (which is also the basis of discounted cash flow, DCF) can be applied to any streams of future income and to repayments of cap-ital. For example, £20 nominal of 5% loan stock redeemable in three years would be worth the interest payments of £1 at the end of each year plus the £20 in three years' time, all discounted at 10% per annum, to give a present value of:

$$\frac{£1}{(1.1)^1} + \frac{£1}{(1.1)^2} + \frac{£1}{(1.1)^3} + \frac{£20}{(1.1)^3}$$

$$= £(0.909 + 0.826 + 0.751 + 15.026) = £17.512$$

The calculation of the present value of a steady stream of income can be assisted by the use of annuity tables, an annuity of 1 for n years simply being an annual payment of 1 for n years; such a table is set out below.

In our previous example, the present value of £1 per annum for three years, discounted at 10%, could have been obtained from the annuity table: three years at 10% = 2.487.

In practice, interest on fixed-interest securities is usually paid half-yearly in arrears (i.e. at the end of each half-year), and so the half-yearly discount rate, which is the square root $(1 + i)$, is used to discount each half-yearly interest payment. For example, £100 of 5% Loan Stock with three years to redemption, discounted at 10% per annum, would have a present value of:

$$\frac{250}{(\sqrt{1.10})} + \frac{250}{(\sqrt{1.10})^2} + \ldots + \frac{250}{(\sqrt{1.10})^6} + \frac{10}{(1.10)^3}$$

$$= 2.3837 + 2.2728 + \ldots + 1.8784 + 75.1315$$
$$= £87.8734.$$

Annuity table: present value of 1 in n years' time

n	1%	2%	3%	4%	5%	10%	15%
1	0.990	0.980	0.971	0.962	0.952	0.909	0.870
2	0.980	0.961	0.943	0.925	0.907	0.826	0.756
3	0.971	0.942	0.915	0.889	0.864	0.751	0.658
4	0.961	0.924	0.889	0.855	0.822	0.683	0.572
5	0.951	0.906	0.863	0.822	0.784	0.621	0.497
10	0.905	0.820	0.744	0.676	0.614	0.386	0.247
20	0.820	0.673	0.554	0.456	0.377	0.149	0.061

Annuity table: present value of an annuity of 1 for n years

Rate of interest (the discount rate)

n	1%	2%	3%	4%	5%	10%	15%
1	0.990	0.980	0.971	0.962	0.952	0.909	0.870
2	1.970	1.942	1.913	1.886	1.860	1.736	1.626
3	2.941	2.884	2.829	2.775	2.723	2.487	2.283
4	3.902	3.808	3.717	3.630	3.546	3.170	2.855
5	4.853	4.713	4.580	4.452	4.329	3.791	3.352
10	9.471	8.983	8.530	8.111	7.722	6.145	5.019
15	13.865	12.849	11.938	11.118	10.380	7.606	5.847

APPENDIX 3 – RETAIL PRICE INDICES SINCE 1950

The Retail Price Index (RPI) as published in the Government Statistical Service's *Monthly Digest of Statistics*.

Space has been left for the reader to insert RPIs month by month in the future as they are announced in the press.

Accountancy, the monthly journal of the Institute of Chartered Accountants in England and Wales, publishes each year a long-range table, currently from 1915 (the latest in April 2002 issue) and the *Investors Chronicle* includes figures for the last three months under Economic Indicators.

Year	Jan	Feb	Mar	Apr	May	Jun	Jul	Aug	Sep	Oct	Nov	Dec	Average for year
1950	8.3	8.3	8.3	8.3	8.4	8.3	8.3	8.3	8.3	8.4	8.5	8.5	8.40
1955	10.7	10.7	10.7	10.8	10.7	11.0	11.0	10.9	11.0	11.1	11.3	11.3	10.90
1960	12.4	12.4	12.3	12.4	12.4	12.5	12.5	12.4	12.4	12.5	12.6	12.6	12.50
1965	14.5	14.5	14.5	14.8	14.9	14.9	14.9	14.9	14.9	14.9	15.0	15.1	14.80
1970	17.9	18.0	18.1	18.4	18.4	18.5	18.6	18.6	18.7	18.9	19.0	19.2	18.50
1975	30.4	30.9	31.5	32.7	34.1	34.8	35.1	35.3	35.6	36.1	36.6	37.0	34.20
1976	37.5	38.0	38.2	38.9	39.3	39.5	39.6	40.2	40.7	41.4	42.0	42.6	39.80
1977	43.7	44.1	44.6	45.7	46.1	46.5	46.6	46.8	47.1	47.3	47.5	47.8	46.10
1978	48.0	48.3	48.6	49.3	49.6	50.0	50.2	50.5	50.7	51.0	51.3	51.8	50.00
1979	52.5	53.0	53.4	54.3	54.7	55.7	58.1	58.5	59.1	59.7	60.3	60.7	56.70
1980	62.2	63.1	63.9	66.1	66.7	67.4	67.9	68.1	68.5	68.9	69.5	69.9	66.80
1981	70.3	70.9	72.0	74.1	74.6	75.0	75.3	75.9	76.3	77.0	77.8	78.3	74.80
1982	78.7	78.8	79.4	81.0	81.6	81.9	81.9	81.9	81.9	82.3	82.7	82.5	81.20
1983	82.6	83.0	83.1	84.3	84.6	84.8	85.3	85.7	86.1	86.4	86.7	86.9	84.90
1984	86.8	87.2	87.5	88.6	89.0	89.2	89.1	89.9	90.1	90.7	91.0	90.9	89.20
1985	91.2	91.9	92.8	94.8	95.2	95.4	95.2	95.5	95.5	95.6	95.9	96.1	94.60
1986	96.2	96.6	96.7	97.6	97.9	97.8	97.5	97.9	98.3	98.5	99.3	99.6	97.80
1987	100.0	100.4	100.6	101.8	101.9	101.9	101.8	102.1	102.4	102.9	103.4	103.3	101.90
1988	103.3	103.7	104.1	105.8	106.2	106.6	106.7	107.9	108.4	109.5	110.0	110.3	106.90
1989	111.0	111.8	112.3	114.3	115.0	115.4	115.5	115.8	116.6	117.5	118.5	118.8	115.20
1990	119.5	120.2	121.4	125.1	126.2	126.7	126.8	128.2	129.3	130.3	130.0	129.9	126.10
1991	130.2	130.9	131.4	133.1	133.5	134.1	133.8	134.1	134.6	135.1	135.6	135.7	133.50
1992	135.6	136.3	136.7	138.8	139.3	139.3	138.8	138.9	139.4	139.9	139.7	139.2	138.50
1993	137.9	138.8	139.3	140.6	141.1	141.0	140.7	141.3	141.9	141.8	141.6	141.9	140.70
1994	141.3	142.1	142.5	144.2	144.7	144.7	144.0	144.7	145.0	145.2	145.3	146.0	144.10
1995	146.0	146.9	147.5	149.0	149.6	149.8	149.1	149.9	150.6	149.8	149.8	150.7	149.10
1996	150.2	150.9	151.5	152.6	152.9	153.0	152.4	153.1	153.8	153.8	153.9	154.4	152.70
1997	154.4	155.0	155.4	156.3	156.9	157.5	157.5	158.5	159.3	159.5	159.6	160.0	157.50
1998	159.5	160.3	160.8	162.6	163.5	163.4	163.0	163.7	164.4	164.5	164.4	164.4	162.90
1999	163.4	163.7	164.1	165.2	165.6	165.6	165.1	165.5	166.2	166.5	166.7	167.3	165.40
2000	166.6	167.5	168.4	170.1	170.7	171.1	170.5	170.5	171.7	171.6	172.1	172.2	170.25
2001	171.1	172.0	172.2	173.1	174.2	174.4	173.3	174.0	174.6	174.3	173.6	173.4	173.35
2002	173.3												

APPENDIX 4 – PROBLEMS AND SOLUTIONS

Problem 1.1

Elcho (Mossdale) Ltd is a small company manufacturing a simple safety device. Chairman and managing director, Mr Charles Farnesbarn, is offered a two-year contract by JQB, a do-it-yourself chain, which would double the current production and turnover of the company. It would be necessary to acquire additional plant and machinery costing £60,000. To do this, Farnesbarn seeks overdraft facilities from the company's bankers. Currently, the company has an overdraft limit of £50,000 and Farnesbarn is seeking to increase this to £110,000.

Profit after tax to turnover is running at 2.6%, so Farnesbarn is looking for profits to increase by, perhaps, £25,000 per annum. He presents his bank manager with accounts for the last trading year – see alongside. Although such facilities would earn the bank 3% or 4% over base rate on the amount outstanding, the bank manager is of a mind to reject Farnesbarn's request. Suggest three reasons why that might be so.

For solutions to problems, see below, pp. 273–84.

Problem 2.1

State the four fundamental accounting concepts previously referred to in SSAP 2, and indicate how their status has changed under FRS 18.

Problem 3.1

How would you tell whether a company was (a) a public or (b) a private limited company; or (c) was one limited by guarantee; or (d) was an unlimited company?

Problem 4.1

From an investor's point of view, what are the advantages and disadvantages of a quote driven market, compared with an order driven market?

Problem 5.1

Q is the wholly owned subsidiary of X Group, a listed company. Q's share capital includes 100m £1 3.5% cumulative preference shares. You hold 10,000 £1 cumulative preference shares. Is X bound to pay the dividend on your shares?

Problem 6.1

Grouch Group is seeking to dispose of one of its less profitable subsidiaries to management (as a management buy-out). The asking price is £10m. The management team plans to form a company, Hopeful plc, and is prepared to invest £2m in the

ELCHO (MOSSDALE) LTD

Profit and loss account for last year

	£	£
Turnover		600,000
Cost of sales (including depreciation £10,000)		460,000
Gross profit		140,000
Distribution costs:		
Depreciation of motor vehicles	5,000	
Petrol, insurance and maintenance	11,900	
		16,900
Administrative expenses:	£	
Rent and rates	43,300	
Wages	50,000	
Insurance	2,500	
Printing etc.	1,450	
Legal expenses etc.	1,300	
	98,550	
		115,450
Trading or operating profit		24,550
Interest payable		2,000
Pre-tax profit on ordinary activities		22,550
Corporation tax		6,765
Net profit after tax		15,785

Balance sheet at end of last year

	£	£
Fixed assets		
Plant and machinery	40,000	
Motor vehicles	20,000	
		60,000
Current assets		
Stock (raw materials, work in progress and finished goods)	100,000	
Debtors	65,000	
Cash	650	
	165,650	
Less: Current liabilities:		
Trade creditors	45,000	
Corporation tax	6,765	
Overdraft	41,385	
	93,150	
		72,500
Net assets		132,500
Ordinary share capital		100,000
Reserves:		
Profit and loss account:		
Balance b/f	16,715	
Profit for the year retained	15,785	
		32,500
Ordinary shareholders' funds		132,500

form of ordinary share capital; and a venture capital company has offered to put up either (i) £8m as a medium-term loan at 10% fixed; or (ii) £6m as a medium-term loan at 9% fixed and £2m in the form of ordinary share capital.

A business plan suggests that Hopeful will produce profits before interest of from £750,000 to £1,400,000. Ignoring tax, (a) calculate the profits available to management on their investment under scenarios (i) and (ii) for the range of profits projected; (b) depict this in a chart; (c) calculate the return earned (i) by management and (ii) by the venture capital company on the same bases.

Problem 7.1

This refers to ML Laboratories (see example on page 46). By changing its policy on R & D from capitalisation and amortisation to immediate write-off, ML increased a loss of £0.72m in 1998 into one of £8.44m, and restated 1997 as a £4.55m loss rather than a £0.68m profit.

Immediate write-off is undoubtedly more prudent, but do you think it gives a more realistic view of a company's performance? ML's share price doubled in 12 months after two years of apparently heavy losses. What can the private shareholder do to understand why?

Problem 8.1

Fleetwood has a fleet of 20 identical Ajax 1.6 litre motor cars purchased as follows:

1 January 1998	5 at	£10,000
1 January 1999	5 at	£11,000
1 January 2000	5 at	£12,000
1 January 2001	5 at	£12,500

Useful economic life is four years at the end of which sales proceeds are expected to be 40% of cost. These are the only motor vehicles.

Show the balance sheet item 'Motor vehicles' and its make-up as at 31 December 2001.

Problem 9.1

Companies hold fixed asset investments for a variety of reasons.

(i) Suggest five possible reasons; and
(ii) Explain why it is important for the reader of accounts to have as clear an idea as possible of the reasons for any significant holding.

Problem 10.1

You are given the following extract from a group's accounts:

16. Stocks

	1998 £m	1997 £m
Raw materials and consumables	1.8	1.8
Finished goods and goods for resale	19.7	15.7
Residential developments Land	176.7	154.4
Development and construction costs	170.6	126.2
Commercial, industrial and mixed development properties	57.7	57.3
	426.5	355.4

(i) Provide a brief description of the group.
(ii) What do the figures suggest? Where would you look for confirmation (or otherwise) of your hypothesis?
(iii) Imagine that Land included an estate which cost £56m, which, six months later, the group no longer plans to develop, but which it proposes to hold as a fixed asset investment. Suitably sized parcels of the estate will be offered to other developers subject to long leases. The estate is included above at cost; but its realisable value is now estimated to be only £27.6m. How should the proposed change be handled in next year's accounts; and why?

Problem 11.1

THE BODY SHOP	2001 £m	2000 £m
Turnover	374.1	330.1

Use this fact together with the information on page 73 to calculate, for each year:

(i) the collection period in months;
(ii) the ratio Trade debtors/Sales as a percentage.

Comment briefly.

Problem 12.1

Companies hold current asset investments for a variety of reasons. You are asked: (a) to suggest five possible reasons; and (b) to explain why it is important for the reader of accounts to have a clear idea of the reasons for any significant holding.

Problem 13.1
Consider the example of BRUNEL HOLDINGS below.

BRUNEL HOLDINGS *Notes to the 1990 group cash flow statement*

A. Reconciliation of operating profit to net cash (outflow)/inflow from operating activities

. . .

B. Reconciliation of net cash flow to movement in net debt

	1998 £000	1997 £000
Increase in cash in period	18,117	2,208
Reduction in lease finance	372	767
Increase in bills of exchange discounted	(1,193)	(613)
Change in net debt from cash flows	17,296	2,362
Finance leases disposed of with subsidiaries	1,454	1,079
New finance leases	(465)	(972)
Translation difference	(2)	(5)
Movement in net debt in period	18,283	2,464
Net debt at 1 July	(26,310)	(28,774)
Net debt at 30 June	(8,027)	(26,310)

C. Analysis of net debt

. . .

Note A shows 'Net cash outflow from operating activities (465)'. Note B, the reconciliation of net cash flow, starts with the bottom line of the cash flow statement: 'Increase in cash 18,117', and ends with 'Net debt (8,027)'.

The change in net debt from (26,310), the closing figure in 1997, to (8,027) is then analysed in Note C, which shows a reduction in overdraft of more then £20m.

Apart from finance leases, there was no new financing during the year.

1. What was the net change in finance leases in 1998?
2. What was the figure for Bills of Exchange discounted in the 1996 and 1997 balance sheet? – see note on Brunel's creditors on page 86.

Problem 14.1
Just before Christmas, a fund manager decides that he would like to purchase £10m of UK stocks, but the funds will not be available until February.

The FT-SE 100 Index stands at 4,000 at the end of December and he is looking for it to rise 5% over the next month. The fund manager wants to limit the price he has to pay in the future to a value of 4,100.

The fund manager decides to purchase 250 (£10m ÷ (4,000 × (£10))) March 4,000 calls for 100. Each contract represents £10 per index point movement.

1. What is his initial outlay?
2. What is the maximum amount risked by the manager?
3. If on 15 February it becomes clear that the £10m will not after all be available but the market has risen to 4,155, what can the investment manager do?

Problem 15.1
(a) Distinguish clearly between:

   (i) an accrual and a provision;
   (ii) income in advance and a deposit;
   (iii) a commitment and a contingent liability.

(b) Provide examples of each.
(c) Explain the significance of each to an analyst seeking: (i) to estimate a group's future cash flows/liquidity; (ii) to consider its viability in the medium term.

Problem 16.1
Study note 3 to the accounts of QUEENSBOROUGH for the year 1998, reproduced on the next page.

(a) Compute as a percentage the year-on-year change overall and for each segment of QUEENSBOROUGH's turnover, profit before tax and capital employed.
(b) Using vertical analysis, compare segmentally that company's turnover, profit before tax and net assets in 1997 and 1998.
(c) Use the information provided to produce a brief summary describing the company's activities, and the changes which occurred in 1998.
(d) Compute the return on the net assets employed for 1997 and 1998. To what extent do you consider this company's ROCE to be a valid indicator of its progress?

QUEENSBOROUGH *Extracts from the accounts for the year ended 31 January 1998*

3. Segmental analysis by class of business

The analysis by class of business of the group's turnover, profit before taxation and net assets is set out below.

The group's turnover and profit before taxation principally arise in the United Kingdom. All sales are external and turnover by geographical destination is not materially different to turnover by origin.

Class of business	1998 £000 Turnover	1997 £000 Turnover	1998 £000 Profit before taxation	1997 £000 Profit before taxation
Day visitor attractions – UK	8,071	7,524	1,748	1,761
Caravan parks – UK	20,997	16,393	3,403	2,460
Caravan parks – France	1,358	616	38	101
Hotel – UK	6,073	5,795	1,510	1,304
Restaurants – UK	71	–	(174)	–
	36,570	30,328	6,525	5,626
Associated undertaking			–	15
Net interest payable			(2,138)	(1,792)
Central costs			(792)	(626)
Profit on sale of surplus properties			–	363
Profit before taxation			3,595	3,586

Net assets by class of business

	1998 £000	1997 £000
Day visitor attractions – UK	12,122	11,206
Caravan parks – UK	27,366	25,407
Caravan parks – France	5,985	1,844
Hotel – UK	10,290	10,258
Restaurants – UK	817	–
Net operating assets	56,580	48,715

Unallocated net assets/(liabilities)

Fixed asset investments	33	144
Head office fixed assets	90	78
Head office debtors	1,241	404
Head office creditors	(1,816)	(855)
Cash and deposits	579	697
Borrowings	(24,557)	(22,335)
Net assets	32,150	26,848

Included in the figures are the following amounts in respect of acquisitions during the financial year:

	£000 Turnover	£000 Profit/(loss) before tax
Caravan parks – UK	764	268
Caravan parks – France	679	48
Restaurants – UK	79	(174)
Total since date of acquisitions	1,514	142

Problem 17.1

Examining the report and accounts of a group, you find that the effective rate of tax (i.e. taxation as a percentage of pre-tax profits) is

(a) much less, or
(b) much greater,

than the normal rate of UK corporation tax.

Suggest in each case why this might be so. Where would you look for further information? Why is this important?

Problem 18.1

The basic earnings per share of a listed company, PG, in 2001 are stated to be 71.4p.

1. How would you expect this figure to have been calculated?
2. How might you use the figure of earnings per share, i.e. with what might you compare it?
3. What other types of e.p.s. are likely to be found in published accounts, and why?

Problem 19.1

Given these extracts from the 1995 accounts of CORDIANT, explain in simple terms why the cash generated by operations was so much less in 1995 than in 1994:

Consolidated statement of cash flows:

Year ended	Note	31 Dec 1995 £m	31 Dec 1994 £m
Net cash inflow from operating activities	16	16.6	58.9

Note 16

16. Reconciliation of operating profit to net cash inflow from operating activities

	Year ended 31 Dec 1995 £m	Year ended 31 Dec 1994 £m
Operating profit	28.3	44.5
Depreciation	25.7	25.7
(Profit) loss on sale of tangible fixed assets	(1.5)	0.2
Increase in work in progress	(9.4)	(8.0)
Increase in debtors	(54.8)	(77.8)
Increase in creditors	38.6	86.1
Utilisation of property provisions	(10.3)	(11.8)
Net cash inflow from operating activities	16.6	58.9

Problem 20.1

Throughout 2001, the Bear Bones Group had three subsidiaries:

- Brown Bear, a 75% owned Canadian company;
- Bear Huggs, a Scottish company 50% owned by Bear Bones which is in a position to direct the financial and operating policies of Bear Huggs;
- Bear Pitts, a wholly owned subsidary company registered in England.

No shares other than ordinary shares were in issue.

1. Explain clearly what the components of the Sales figure in the group accounts will be.
2. The group profit and loss account shows an operating profit of £13.456m. What proportion of Bear Huggs' operating profit will this include?
3. In the note on the group profit and loss account item Taxation appears 'Foreign Tax £0.123'. What will this represent?
4. In the group profit and loss account is deducted 'Minority interests £0.321m'. Explain what the figure represents.
5. Bear Huggs proposed dividends of £3m in 2001. How much of this will appear under the heading 'Dividends proposed' in the group profit and loss account?
6. In the balance sheet appears, 'Minority interests £34,190,000'. What does that represent?

Problem 21.1

You are provided with this extract from the 1996 accounts of GIBBON GROUP.

Consolidated profit and loss account for the year ended 31 March 1996

	Continuing operations 1996 £000	Acqui-sitions 1996 £000	Total 1996 £000	1995 £000
Turnover	28,612	381	28,993	27,447
Cost of sales	(18,137)	(206)	(18,343)	(16,676)
Gross profit	10,475	175	10,650	10,771
Distribution costs	(3,839)	(12)	(3,851)	(4,090)
Administrative expenses	(4,006)	(99)	(4,105)	(4,281)
	2,630	64	2,694	2,400
Other operating income	91	–	91	102
Operating profit	2,721	64	2,785	2,502

During the year the group purchased two subsidiaries, the assets and liabilities of which were (in total) as follows:

	Book value £000	Fair value £000
Fixed assets	382	258
Stocks	295	255
Debtors	272	272
Cash at bank and in hand	153	153
Creditors	(911)	(911)
	191	27

The purchase consideration was satisfied by:

	£000
Cash	767
Issue of shares (10p ordinary shares with a nominal value of £22,000)	400
Deferred consideration – cash	251
Deferred consideration – shares to be issued	150
	1,568

The subsidiaries acquired had £153,000 in the bank. The share issues met the conditions in Sections 131–134 of the Companies Act 1985.

1. Did the transactions represent acquisitions or mergers in the terms of FRS 6?
2. Compute the goodwill which arose during the year.

3. What net outflow would appear in the group cash flow statement under the heading Purchase of subsidiaries?
4. What amount would be credited in respect of these transactions:

   (a) to share premium account;
   (b) to merger reserve?

5. You are asked whether the 'acquisitions' were successful. What important information, which the group was required to give, and in fact did, is not provided above but would be necessary to assess the companies' profitability?

Problem 22.1
Given the extract from Note 18 to the 1998 accounts of TAY HOMES, reproduced below, explain:

TAY HOMES *Extract from note 18 to the 1998 accounts*

	Group		Company	
	1998	1997	1998	1997
	£000	£000	£000	£000
18. Fixed Asset Investments				
Investments in subsidiary undertakings:				
Shareholdings at cost	–	–	314	314
Loans to subsidiary undertakings	–	–	40	40
	–	–	354	354
Investments in unlisted companies:				
Shareholdings at cost (see . . .)	54	54	4	4
	54	54	358	358
Investments in associated undertaking:				
Loan to associated undertaking	2,332	2,096	–	–
Deficiency in net assets of associated undertaking	(272)	(181)	–	–
	2,060	1,915	–	–
	2,114	1,969	358	358

The Company has the following Ordinary share investments in subsidiary undertakings, all of which are included within the consolidated accounts using the acquisition method of accounting: . . . Tay Homes (Scotland) Ltd (registered in Scotland) (Residential, Estate Developers and Builders) . . . ; Taygate Showhomes Ltd (50% owned quasi-subsidiary) (Showhouse Licensing) . . . The directors consider that the Group participates substantially in the benefits and risks associated with Taygate Showhomes Ltd and hence the undertaking should be regarded as a quasi-subsidiary . . .

The Group has the following joint venture associated undertaking which is 50% owned by Tay Homes (Scotland) Ltd: Britannia New Homes (Scotland) Ltd. (registered in Scotland) (Residential Estate Development).

---

1. Why the group item 'Investments in subsidiary undertakings' is zero, when that for the Company is £314,000 in both 1997 and 1998.
2. What a quasi-subsidiary is and the difference in treatment between Taygate Showhomes Ltd and Britannia New Homes (Scotland) Ltd.
3. Why the company item 'Investments in associated undertaking' is zero in both years.
4. What 'Deficiency in net assets of associated undertaking' represents and the significance of the increase between 1997 and 1998.
5. What the 'Loan to associated undertaking' represents.

Does this raise questions in your mind?

Problem 23.1
Pie in the Sky plc is a UK listed company. Its accounting policies include:

Exchange rates
Exchange rates used to translate overseas profits and currency assets and liabilities (other than shares held by the parent company in overseas companies) are the rates ruling at the balance sheet date.

Currency gains and losses
Currency gains and losses are included in operating profit or investment income as appropriate except that the difference arising on

the re-translation of the group's share, at the beginning of the year, of the net assets of overseas subsidiaries, associated companies and branches is treated as a movement in reserves.

In fact it has just one subsidiary, and no associated companies or branches. That subsidiary is Beyond (1994), a wholly owned subsidiary operating in a remote island group, the Beyond Islands, the currency of which is the Bac.

The Beyond Islands are largely undiscovered as a tourist destination and Beyond (1994) trades entirely within the islands. Pie in the Sky plc invested 10m Bacs in ordinary shares in Beyond (1994) at the time of its formation on 1 January 1994. No dividends have been paid; and no cash has been remitted in either direction.

The Bac is a somewhat unstable currency. Rates of exchange have been:

1 January 1994	1.00 Bac = £1.
31 December 1998	2.00 Bacs = £1.
31 December 1999	2.40 Bacs = £1.
31 December 2000	3.00 Bacs = £1.

You are provided with the balance sheet for Beyond (1994) as at 31 December 2000 shown alongside.

1. What amount would be included in Pie in the Sky's group accounts to represent the contribution to group profit of Beyond (1994) (a) in 1999; and (b) in 2000?
2. What currency translation difference would appear in the statement of total gains and losses of the group for 2000, and what would be the comparative figure in respect of 1999?

Ignore taxation.

BEYOND (1994) *Balance sheet as at 31 December 2000*

	Note	2000 Bacs m	1999 Bacs m
Fixed assets			
Freehold land and buildings		6.0	6.0
Plant and machinery, fixtures and fittings		12.0	10.0
		18.0	16.0
Current assets			
Stocks		13.5	11.1
Debtors		23.3	21.0
Cash at Bank		11.0	0.7
		47.8	32.8
Less: Current liabilities:			
Creditors: due within 1 year		15.0	11.0
Net current assets		32.8	22.8
Net assets		50.8	38.8
Ordinary share capital		10.0	10.0
Reserves:			
Profit and loss account	1	40.8	28.8
		50.8	38.8

NOTE 1:

Profit and loss account:	2000	1999
Balance at 1 January	28.8	21.6
Profit for the year	12.0	7.2
Balance at 31 December	40.8	28.8

Problem 24.1

Given the following extracts from the five-year summary of a group, provide a short commentary.

Extracts from 5-year summary

	1996 £m	1995 £m	1994 £m	1993 £m	1992 £m
Turnover	1,083.6	1,079.1	1,045.5	1,139.3	1,179.8
Profit from retail operations	102.0	87.2	65.2	43.0	10.0
Exceptional items	1.2	–	(6.4)	(31.4)	–
Profit for the financial year	74.6	61.6	38.9	0.4	10.8
Earnings per share	17.8p	14.8p	9.4p	0.1p	2.6p
Dividend per share	7.2p	6.3p	5.5p	5.0p	5.0p
Total net assets	532.0	484.2	447.3	423.9	438.3
Number of stores	435	433	431	425	736
Net selling space (000 sq ft)	5,268	5,005	4,815	4,704	6,452

Problem 25.1

A company which is the holding company of a group involved in a diverse range of activities from computer services to foundries, and door manufacture to motor dealerships, reported in 1995 as a result of Cadbury:

Corporate governance

. . .

Formal procedures in respect of matters reserved to the Board and authorisation levels have been established during the year. Guidelines for Directors' access to independent professional advice, and for the appointment of non-executive Directors have not yet been formalised.

What purpose is served by such a statement?

Problem 26.1

1. What do you understand by 'a going concern'?
2. What responsibilities do:

   (a) directors;
   (b) auditors;

   have in relation to this?
3. Why does it matter to investors?

Problem 27.1

Given the extract alongside from Note 10 to the 1996/97 interim statement of DIXONS GROUP, compute (a) the operating profit and (b) net cash (outflow)/inflow from operating activities for the 24 weeks to 27 April 1996. Comment on what you find.

Problem 28.1

Share prices are used by investors and analysts for a variety of purposes.

1. Name four widely used ratios based on the market price(s) of equity shares.
2. Suggest four other ways in which an investor or analyst might use the price history of a share.
3. Explain four ways of obtaining share prices and suggest the advantages of each.

Problem 29.1

1. Compare current purchasing power accounting and current cost accounting, bringing out:

10. Net cash (outflow)/inflow from operating activities

	28 weeks to 9 Nov 1996 £m	28 weeks to 11 Nov 1995 £m	52 weeks to 27 Apr 1996 £m
Operating profit	53.5	34.7	128.1
Share of profit of related companies	(0.3)	–	(3.0)
Utilisation of store closure provision	(1.3)	(2.8)	(2.6)
Utilisation of provision for rationalisation of the Group's administrative offices	–	(1.0)	(1.2)
Depreciation	25.0	19.7	38.7
Amortisation of own shares	0.5	0.3	0.6
Increase in stocks	(191.7)	(187.7)	(75.9)
Increase in debtors	(47.9)	(78.7)	(17.4)
Increase in creditors	73.1	101.1	52.0
	(89.1)	(114.4)	119.3

(a) their similarities; and
(b) their differences.

2. Why do you think the attempt to introduce

   (a) CPP
   (b) CCA

   failed?

Problem 30.1

Where a company is listed both in the UK and in the US, why might the note explaining differences in GAAP between the two countries be of interest:

(a) to an analyst;
(b) to a US investor;
(c) to a student of accounting theory?

Solution 1.1 Elcho (Mossdale).

Three reasons why the bank might reject Farnesbarn's request:

1. An extra £60,000 is not enough.

The bank manager is likely to say to himself: 'They are asking for £60,000. Let us see how much they really need.'

		£	£
A.	New machine		60,000
B.	Current overdraft limit	50,000	
	Overdraft at balance sheet date	48,150	
	This must bring difficulties; to be safe, they really need another, say,		10,000
C.	Working capital: Additional raw material stock, say,	5,000	
	Finished goods, say	12,000	
	Debtors, say 2 months	100,000	
		127,000	
	Less: Additional creditors, say,	40,000	
	That looks like		87,000
	A total of		£157,000

These figures certainly won't be accurate, but one thing one can say for certain is that £60,000 is not enough.

Trawling for information (and watching carefully his customer's reaction), the bank manager might well ask:

* How is the present limit working?
* What are delivery arrangements . . . are you going to be holding much stock for them?
* What about payment terms? How long credit have they asked for?

On the other hand, he might simply say to himself: 'Either they haven't done their homework; or they know full well that they need more and they plan to break the news as a nasty shock later.'

Neither scenario is likely to commend the proposition to him.

2. Farnesbarn's profit estimate seems to be based on simplistic logic:

'On turnover of £600,000 per annum we make £15,785 after tax', he seems to suggest. 'If we double sales we should make twice that.'

But that ignores:

(i) the price to be paid by JQB (which is likely to be less (possibly much less) than that paid by smaller customers for the same items). If the price paid is substantially less than other people pay, sales *volume* (hence the total material and labour costs) is going to be more than double with a doubling of turnover;

(ii) the cost structure of the business, i.e. the variability of cost (see Chapter 10); hence:

(iii) the profit margin (or profit) likely to be achieved (almost certainly different from that on existing business);

(iv) the additional interest which would be payable at 15%.

Either (i) Farnesbarn has not got the necessary information; or (ii) he does not see its significance; or (iii) both.

And that certainly will not have impressed the bank.

3. JQB:

* Undue dependence on one customer is risky. There is no sign that Farnesbarn recognises this.
* Has Farnesbarn investigated JQB?
He does not say so; but he would earn a black mark if he had not.
* The bank will almost certainly know more (or be in a position to find out more) about JQB's credit standing than Farnesbarn. They may also know things about JQB's trading methods which Farnesbarn may not, e.g. that after the first couple of years the contract price is likely to be driven down so hard that the business becomes unprofitable.
* Can JQB break the contract for any reason, e.g. late delivery, poor workmanship? i.e. what are the risks involved? Is Farnesbarn aware of them?

Other possible reasons:

* **The bank manager may himself be under pressure.**
He may be limited in what he can lend in certain business areas; and he will have a limit to his discretion beyond which he must seek head office approval.

* **The history of Elcho's past dealings** with the bank may not make the proposal one which he should be seen to endorse, e.g. the overdraft was nearly at limit at balance sheet date. Is there a history of bounced cheques; or requests to bend the limit to pay wages etc?

* **Elcho's assets** do not provide very convincing security. In any case, lending to the company will be based less on its assets than on its forecast

future trading. And Farnesbarn does not appear to have done his homework. His forecast is therefore unlikely to be accurate, and that would worry any banker.

- **What happens at the end of two years?**
  How likely is it that the contract will continue at a similar level of profitability?
  If not, can the output from the new plant and machinery be sold elsewhere at a profit?
  Or is it special purpose plant? Might it be necessary to sell it (at well below book value?), to write it down sharply or even write it off altogether?

Solution 2.1

The fundamental accounting concepts are those broad basic assumptions which underlie the periodic financial accounts of business enterprises. Under SSAP 2 the four following fundamental concepts (the relative importance of which varies according to the circumstances of the particular case) are seen as having general acceptability:

(a) the '*going concern*' concept: the enterprise will continue in operational existence for the foreseeable future. This means in particular that the profit and loss account and balance sheet assume no intention or necessity to liquidate or curtail significantly the scale of operation;

(b) the '*accruals*' concept: revenue and costs are accrued (that is, recognised as they are earned or incurred, not as money is received or paid), matched with one another so far as their relationship can be established or justifiably assumed, and dealt with in the profit and loss account of the period to which they relate; provided that where the accruals concept is inconsistent with the 'prudence' concept (paragraph (d) below), the latter prevails. The accruals concept implies that the profit and loss account reflects changes in the amount of net assets that arise out of the transactions of the relevant period (other than distributions or subscriptions of capital and unrealised surpluses arising on revaluation of fixed assets). Revenue and profits dealt with in the profit and loss account are matched with associated costs and expenses by including in the same account the costs incurred in earning them (so far as these are material and identifiable);

(c) the '*consistency*' concept: there is consistency of accounting treatment of like items within each accounting period and from one period to the next;

(d) the concept of '*prudence*': revenue and profits are not anticipated, but are recognised by inclusion in the profit and loss account only when realised in the form either of cash or of other assets, the ultimate cash realisation of which can be assessed with reasonable certainty; provision is made for all known liabilities.

FRS 18 refers to the above concepts but has made significant changes to their relative status for financial reporting purposes.

Both the going concern concept and the accruals concept retain their key roles. FRS 18 refers to them as playing a 'pervasive role in financial statements, and hence in the selection of accounting policies'.

However, the concepts of consistency and prudence have been downgraded:

(a) Companies are now required to review their accounting policies on a regular basis, making changes wherever appropriate. Consequently FRS 18 places the emphasis on comparability stating that '... comparability can usually be achieved through a combination of consistency and disclosure ...'.

(b) Prudence is to be considered in relation to the key objective of 'reliability'. Financial information is regarded as reliable if it can satisfy a number of criteria including that 'under conditions of uncertainty, it has been prudently prepared ...'. However, FRS 18 emphasises that it is not necessary to exercise prudence where there is no uncertainty, and that prudence should not be used as a reason for creating excessive provisions or deliberately overstating losses.

Solution 3.1

One can tell whether a company is (a) a public or (b) a private limited company from its name. A company whose name ends 'plc' or 'PLC' or Public Limited Company is a public company; one whose name ends with 'Ltd' or 'Limited' is a private company.

One cannot tell from its name alone whether a company is limited by shares or limited by guarantee; it is necessary to study the company's memorandum of association.

And it is quite difficult to tell whether a business with a name like 'Home Wreckers' is a business name of an individual or a partnership or an unlimited company. If it is an unlimited company it will be possible to inspect its file at Companies House and study its memorandum. Such companies are quite rare.

Solution 4.1

In a bid driven market there are market makers, who have to quote bid and offer prices during the trading day in all the shares in which they deal. They are then obliged to buy at the bid price and to sell at the offer price in the size (amount of shares) they have indicated, or any lesser amount. For less actively traded shares the size may only be a nominal amount, say 1,000 shares.

The market maker makes a profit by buying at the bid price and selling at the offer price; the difference between the two is known as the spread.

In an order driven market there are no market makers: buyers and sellers are matched at the same price.

To an investor the advantage of a quote driven market is that there should always be a market in which he can deal, although the size may be limited. In an order driven market the investor avoids the cost of the spread, but he can only buy if there are sellers, and vice versa.

Solution 5.1

Preference shares carry a fixed rate of dividend, but unlike the holders of loan capital, who can take action against a company in default of interest payments, preference shareholders have no legal redress if the board of directors decides to recommend that no preference dividends should be paid.

However, if no preference dividend is declared for an accounting period, no dividend can be declared on any other type of share for the period concerned, so the subsidiary cannot pay an ordinary dividend to its holding company.

Cases have arisen where, though the subsidiary is very profitable, the holding company says it wishes to retain those profits, and no dividends, preference or ordinary, have been paid for a number of years. In these circumstances the preference shareholders may become entitled to vote at shareholders' general meetings. But this is little comfort, unless it gives them a majority of the votes, which is unlikely.

Solution 6.1

(a) and (c) Profits before interest	£ 750,000	£ 800,000	£ 900,000	£ 1,000,000	£ 1,100,000	£ 1,200,000	£ 1,300,000	£ 1,400,000
Scenario (i)								
Interest at 10% on £8m	800,000	800,000	800,000	800,000	800,000	800,000	800,000	800,000
Return earned by venture capital company (%)	10.00%	10.00%	10.00%	10.00%	10.00%	10.00%	10.00%	10.00%
Profits available to management	(50,000)	0	100,000	200,000	300,000	400,000	500,000	600,000
Return earned by management (%)	−2.50%	0.00%	5.00%	10.00%	15.00%	20.00%	25.00%	30.00%
Scenario (ii)								
Interest at 9% on £6m	540,000	540,000	540,000	540,000	540,000	540,000	540,000	540,000
Profits due to equity owned by venture capital company	105,000	130,000	180,000	230,000	280,000	330,000	380,000	430,000
Total to venture capital company	645,000	670,000	720,000	770,000	820,000	870,000	920,000	970,000
Return earned by venture capital company (%)	8.06%	8.38%	9.00%	9.63%	10.25%	10.88%	11.50%	12.13%
Profits available to management	105,000	130,000	180,000	230,000	280,000	330,000	380,000	430,000
Return earned by management (%)	5.25%	6.50%	9.00%	11.50%	14.00%	16.50%	19.00%	21.50%

(b)

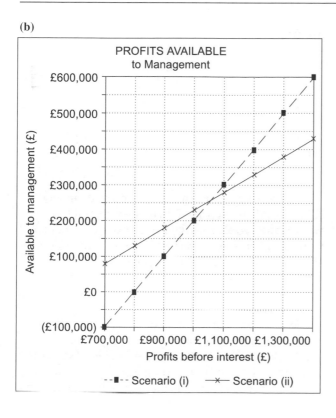

Solution 7.1

ML Laboratories apparently took a last opportunity to move *from* what was an FRS 10 basis *to* a treatment which would no longer be permitted under FRS 10. Whether that was a good idea we leave the reader to decide.

Solution 8.1

Fleetwood: Balance Sheet as at 31 December 2001

	Note	2001 £	2000 £
Fixed assets:			
...			
Motor vehicles	1	145,375	117,000

Notes:
1. Fixed assets

	Cost £	Depreciation to date £	Net £
Motor vehicles			
2001	227,500	82,125	145,375
2000	165,000	48,000	117,000

Solution 9.1

(i) Companies hold fixed asset investments for a variety of reasons, among them:

(a) as a consequence of acquiring control of other companies (i.e. subsidiaries) and 'running them';

(b) as a way of entering into some sort of joint operation (i.e. a joint venture or consortium);

(c) as an investment to generate income (as an investment trust does);

(d) for protection, e.g. life policies on senior employees;

(e) as a means of gaining a foothold (a prelude to a possible bid);

(f) for self-aggrandisment on the part of the directors, e.g. works of art.

(ii) It is important for the reader of accounts to have a clear idea of the reasons for any significant holding:

(a) to understand how the holding and income from it will be treated in the accounts. As will be seen, the treatment of subsidiaries is quite different from that of associated companies;

(b) to predict future actions on the part of the board (e.g. a bid);

(c) to judge board behaviour (pictures, race-horses, yachts and aircraft may not be the most profitable use of funds).

Solution 10.1

(i) The items (a) land and (b) development and construction costs suggest these are the accounts of a group engaged in construction and residential property development; but there appears also to be activity in commercial, industrial and mixed development property.

(ii) The figures suggest that there was an expansion of the land bank; and that development costs in progress grew 35% either because of:

(a) stock building to meet a perceived **improvement** in the market; or

(b) stock was unsold because of a **deterioration** in the market for residential property.

It should be possible to identify which of these is the probable cause by studying:

- the directors' report;
- the chairman's statement;
- any financial review;
- notes to the accounts, in particular any analysis of turnover and profit;
- the cash flow statement.

The accounts are, in fact, those of TAYLOR WOODROW for 1995 (redated). Their financial review explained:

'The UK construction business suffered a cash outflow due to the lower turnover and the cash costs of restructuring the operations in the year. There was also an outflow due to the build up of the landbank and residential work in progress around the would, particularly in the UK and California. . . .'

(iii) The issue of transfers from current assets to fixed assets was considered by the UITF which, in July 1992, issued Abstract 5, *Transfers from current assets to fixed assets*.

The UITF was concerned, in the then current economic climate, that 'companies could avoid charging the profit and loss account with write-downs to net realisable value arising on unsold trading assets. This could be done by transferring the relevant assets from current assets to fixed assets at above net realisable value, as a result of which any later write-down might be debited to revaluation reserve.'

The UITF agreed that in respect of such transfers, the current asset accounting rules should be applied up to the effective date of transfer (the date of management's change of intent). The transfer should then be made at the lower of cost and net realisable value. Thus the land that cost £56m should be transferred to fixed assets at £27.6m, and the shortfall charged to the profit and loss account.

Solution 11.1

	2001 £m	2000 £m
Turnover	374.1	330.1
Trade debtors	30.3	30.3
(i) Collection period (months)	0.97	1.10
(ii) Trade debtors/Sales	8.1%	9.2%

These two ratios are closely related. Indeed (i) is 12/100 of (ii), so they inevitably move in the same way. Some people may find one easier to understand than the other. It is correct to say that 'At the balance sheet date in 2001, debtors equalled 0.97 months' average sales' but not that 'Debtors consisted of the last 0.97 months' sales' and not that 'customers take 0.97 months to pay'.

Whichever yardstick one takes, debt collection appears to have improved by roughly 12%.

In the case of THE BODY SHOP, the figures are somewhat more difficult to interpret than is usually the case because the business is partly a normal retail operation and partly a franchise one; and trade debtors are mostly, if not entirely, franchisees whereas turnover is the sum of sales to franchisees and the sales from own shops. The figures provided do not show whether there was a change in the make-up of turnover, i.e. whether there were more sales via franchisees, the same, or less.

Solution 12.1

(a) Possible reasons why companies hold current asset investments include:

(i)   to set aside (and earn interest on) money later required to pay taxation;

(ii) to save towards a planned expansion, refurbishment, or reorganisation;

(iii) to cover contingencies (e.g. a short-fall in receipts);

(iv) to assure potential joint venture partners that the company, while not in the same league in size terms as they are, can fund its share of future operations (found for example in oil exploration and development);

(v)   as a more general store of value;

(vi) to earn income (there being no better use of funds in the short term);

(vii) where required under the terms of a contract, or by statute, as with insurance funds;

(viii) where the group acts as its own insurer (because cover is impossible to obtain or prohibitively expensive, e.g. certain types of disaster cover), as large sums could be needed urgently.

(b) It is important for the reader of accounts to have a clear idea of the reasons for any significant holding of current asset investments because:

* Money which is tied up (under, say, (vii) or (viii) above) is not available to support general operations.
* Money set aside for a purpose (e.g. taxation) is earmarked.
* If money currently earning income is used for non-income-generating activities, income will fall.
* If large sums of money are invested:

(a) has management clear plans as to their use? or

(b) has the business become a 'cash cow', a generator of cash which it cannot itself usefully employ?

(c) is management simply sitting on money that it does not know what to do with (black mark!)?

Solution 13.1

1.

	£000
Reduction in lease finance	(372)
Finance leases disposed off	(1,454)
New finance leases	465
Net change (reduction)	(1,361)

2.

Bills of exchange discounted per 1998 balance sheet	2,794
less increase during 1998	(1,193)
Bills of exchange discounted which would have appeared in the 1997 balance sheet	1,601
less increase during 1997	(613)
Bills of exchange discounted which would have appeared in the 1996 balance sheet	988

Solution 14.1

(a) The initial outlay is

$$(250 \times 100 \times £10).$$

(b) That is also the maximum amount risked.

(c) If the index rises to 4,155, the fund manager can sell the option back to the market realising a profit of £137,500 ($55 \times 250 \times £10$). With over a month left to expiry there would also be some time value left, say 25 index points. In this case the manager would sell the options back to the market for 180 index points, an overall profit of

$$£200,000 \ (80 \times 250 \times £10).$$

Solution 15.1

(a) (i) An accrual is a known liability where there is no uncertainty as to either the timing or the amount of the future expenditure required in settlement.

By contrast, a provision is a liability of uncertain timing or amount. Whilst the Companies Act 1985 contains a definition of provision, companies must also satisfy the required conditions in FRS 12 before a provision may be recognised in the balance sheet. The two key conditions are:

* the company has an obligation which it will probably be required to settle, and
* a reliable estimate can be made of the amount of the obligation.

(ii) Income in advance represents income received which at the date of the balance sheet had not been earned; whereas a deposit either represents money paid by a customer/client as an earnest (or a sign) of good faith or, in the case of a financial institution, customers' money which earns interest for them.

(iii) A commitment is a financial obligation which a company has already contracted for but which does not satisfy the criteria to be recognised as a provision.

A contingent liability is a possible obligation that arises from past events and whose existence will be confirmed only by the occurrence of one or more uncertain future events that are not wholly within the company's control. A contingent liability may also relate to a present obligation that arises from a past event but which is not recognised in the balance sheet because it does not satisfy all the conditions set out in FRS 12.

(b) Examples:

(i) Of an accrual: rent of £24,000 per annum payable quarterly in arrear on 31 March, 30 June etc. Company makes up its accounts to 30 April 1999, having paid rent up to 31 March. Rent of £2,000 (i.e. one month) will be accrued.

Of a provision: a restructuring provision representing expenditure which is to be incurred on a major reorganisation which was publicly announced prior to the balance sheet date.

(ii) Of income in advance: a magazine publisher receives prepayment in respect of annual subscriptions to journals. At the end of the year £213,000 represents journals to be supplied in future years.

(iii) Of a commitment: capital expenditure contracted for at the balance sheet date to the extent that this has not been provided for in the accounts; exposed foreign currency commitments; commitments under operating lease agreements.

Of a contingent liability: guarantee of bank borrowings; pending legal action against the company.

(c) In seeking to estimate the effect on a company's future cash flows and its viability in the medium term:

(i) Accruals are rarely of much significance. As to provisions, their background and adequacy should be considered, as well as their size, what calls they will bring on the company and when.

(ii) There is a tendency for companies hard-pressed for cash to spend what is in effect other people's money. In an ideal world deposits would be banked separately in a 'client/customer account', and never used for purposes of the company until such times as they were earned. This is not an ideal world. Solicitors and travel agents may work like that; other businesses tend not to. For example, a magazine publisher selling discounted three-year subscriptions would be in trouble if he spent receipts in the year they were received; he would then be relying on future receipts to provide copies to people who had already paid for them, in much the same way governments were able, in the early years of schemes, to treat pensions on a pay as you go basis; but once a large pensioner population built up, the costs escalated and there were no funds to fall back on.

(iii) Capital commitments require financing. The wise finance director ensures that this is planned and negotiated in advance. Some even explain what has been done in the financial review.

Solution 16.1

QUEENSBOROUGH

(a) Year-on-year change overall and for each segment

Class of business	Growth in turnover including acquisitions	Growth in profit before taxation including acquisitions	Growth in turnover excluding acquisitions	Growth in profit before taxation excluding acquisitions	Growth in net assets 1998/1997
Day visitor attractions – UK	7.27	−0.74	7.27	−0.74	8.17
Caravan parks – UK	28.09	38.33	23.42	27.44	7.71
Caravan parks – France	120.45	−62.38	10.23	−109.90	224.57
Hotel – UK	4.80	15.80	4.80	15.80	0.31
Restaurants – UK					Infinite
Overall	20.58	15.98	15.59	13.46	16.14

(b) Vertical analysis of turnover, profit before tax and net assets in 1997 and 1998

	Including acquisitions				Excluding acquisitions			
Class of business	Turnover 1998	Turnover 1997	Profit before tax 1998	Profit before tax 1997	Turnover 1998	Profit before tax 1998	Net assets 1998	Net assets 1997
Day visitor attractions – UK	22.07	24.81	26.79	31.30	23.02	27.39	21.42	23.00
Caravan parks – UK	57.42	54.05	52.15	43.73	57.72	49.11	48.37	52.15
Caravan parks – France	3.71	2.03	0.58	1.80	1.94	−0.16	10.58	3.79
Hotel – UK	16.61	19.11	23.14	23.18	17.32	23.66	18.19	21.06
Restaurants – UK	0.19		−2.66				1.44	
	100.00	100.00	100.00	100.00	100.00	100.00	100.00	100.00

(c) Brief summary describing the company's activities, and the changes which occurred in 1998.

QUEENSBOROUGH is a relatively small company in the leisure and hotels sector. At the time of writing there were 61 listed companies in the sector, and it was 47th in terms of market capitalisation. That being the case, market for its shares was narrow and its share price behaved erratically, halving or doubling in the course of a day or so.

Prior to 1998 its business consisted of caravan parks in the UK and to a much lesser extent in France; day visitor attractions in the UK, and a hotel in the UK. During 1998 the company made a least two acquisitions:

- some UK restaurants which have still to prove profitable and
- more caravan parks in both the UK and France (the scale of the French operations trebled in 1998).

In other words it is a company expanding in an area in which it has experience.

Although net assets only grew 16% overall, the big expansion was in caravan parks – France (225%) and restaurants – UK which did not exist before.

In considering growth in turnover and growth in profit before tax one can either include or exclude the effect of the acquisitions. Including them, turnover increased by about 21%, and profit before tax a little less (16%). Excluding them, turnover would have increased 16% and the profit before tax, 13%.

More than half the turnover in each year came from caravan parks – UK and that is where over 50% of the profits before tax are earned. Almost 11% of the assets are tied up in caravan parks – France, but less than 4% of the turnover came from there; but we have to ask how much of the holiday season in France was post-acquisition?

(d) Is ROCE a valid indicator of its progress?

On the basis that the profit before tax in 1998 was £3.595m (1997 £3.586m) and that capital employed is represented by net assets of £32.150m in 1998 (1997 £26.848m), the return on capital employed appears to have fallen from 13.4% in 1997 to 11.2% in 1998. But that fails to recognise: (i) goodwill written off during this and previous years, just under £3m; (ii) that only part of a year's profit/loss was included as regards the businesses acquired. Note 20 reveals that the two companies acquired *lost* £415,000 in the part year before they were acquired.

Solution 17.1

The effective rate of tax (i.e. taxation as a percentage of pre-tax profits) might be: (a) much less, or (b) much greater, than the normal rate of UK corporation tax because of:

Cause	Effect
Adjustments to previous years	(a) or (b)
Disallowed expenses	(b)
Capital gains	(a)
Loans	(b)
Losses and loss relief	(a) or (b)
Overseas income	(a) or (b)
Exceptional items	(a) or (b)

An abnormal tax charge should be explained in the note on taxation.

An abnormal tax charge is important because it directly affects after tax profits, and hence earnings per share, the P/E ratio and cover. And, less obviously, the effect is not proportionate. For example, take a company with pre-tax profits of £100m which has 1000m 10p ordinary shares. If the effective tax rate is 30%, tax is £30m and the after tax profit £70m. Were that rate to increase (because, say, a greater proportion was earned overseas and subject to higher rates of tax) to 35%, the after tax profits would fall (on the same income) to £65m, i.e. by $5/70 = 7.14\%$.

Solution 18.1

1. Earnings per share (e.p.s.) are the amount of profit on ordinary activities, after tax and all other charges, that has been earned for each ordinary share:

$$\text{e.p.s.} = \frac{\text{Profit attributable to ordinary shareholders}}{\text{Number of ordinary shares in issue}}$$

Adjustments are necessary where there is

- a scrip (bonus) issue or share split, or
- an issue of shares in an acquisition, or
- a rights issue

during the period. These adjustments are explained on page 140.

2. One might use the e.p.s. figure:

- in computing a price earnings ratio;
- to compute cover or dividend payout ratio;
- in assessing earnings growth;
- as a basis in estimating future earnings.

Where dilution may arise (because of, say, convertibles, warrants or options) it may be necessary to show the fully diluted earnings.

3. Some companies compute their own preferred versions (as well) because they feel their method of calculating earnings provides better comparability (or because they do not like hefty charges for exceptional items reducing their apparent earnings) or show earnings on an IIMR basis (for much the same resons).

Solution 19.1

The 1995 net cash inflow from operating activities of CORDIANT was less than that in 1994 because:

- The two principal components of cash inflow from operations tend to be:

  1. Operating profit: which was only £28.3m, against £44.5m in 1994; and
  2. Depreciation: unchanged at £25.7m.

- But cash flow is also affected by increased working capital demands:

  1. Increase in work in progress (£9.4m in 1995; £8.0m in 1994);
  2. Increase in debtors (£54.8m in 1995, £77.8m in 1994); and while the increase in creditors £38.6m operated in the reverse direction, it was far less than the increase of £86.1m the previous year. Had the increase in creditors been only £38.6m in 1994, the working capital requirement would have been £47.5m greater, and the cash generated from operations not £58.9m but £11.4m.

- In each year property provisions were utilised (£10.3m in 1995 and £11.8m in 1994). These had already been charged against the profits of earlier years, but the cash was not spent until 1995 and 1994 respectively.

Solution 20.1
BEAR BONES GROUP

1. Sales in the group profit and loss account will consist of the entire sales of all four companies added together.

2. The operating profit appearing in the group profit and loss account will consist of the entire operating profit of all four companies added together.
3. Since only Brown Bear is a foreign company it is likely that the foreign tax represents Canadian tax on Brown Bear's profits; but attempts have been made by foreign countries (like India) to tax profits deemed to have been made by companies exporting to the country concerned; so it could represent a tax on any of the companies.
4. Minority interests £321,000 will represent 25% of the after tax profits of Brown Bear translated into £; plus 50% of the after tax profits of Bear Huggs.
5. The item 'Dividends proposed', appearing in the group profit and loss account, will represent the dividends proposed by Bear Bones Group. It will not include any dividends paid by Bear Huggs.
6. The item 'Minority interests £34,190,000' appearing in the group balance sheet will consist of 50% of the net assets of Bear Huggs plus 25% of the net assets of Brown Bear.

Solution 21.1
GIBBON GROUP
1. The transactions represented acquisitions under the terms of FRS 6, otherwise the whole of the profits of all companies involved would appear as continuing operations, there would have been no Acquisitions column, and the figures for 1995 would have been shown as 'restated'.
2. Consideration was:

	£000
Cash	767
Issue of shares	400
Deferred consideration – cash	251
Deferred consideration – shares to be issued	150
Total	1,568
Total consideration	1,568

Assets acquired were:

	Fair value £000	
Fixed assets	258	
Stocks	255	
Debtors	272	
Cash at bank and in hand	153	
Creditors	(911)	
		27
Goodwill (pre-FRS 10)		1,541

3. Analysis of the net outflow of cash in respect of the acquisition of . . .

	£000
Cash consideration	767
Cash acquired	(153)
Net outflow	614

4. The amount credited in respect of these transactions:
   • to share premium account would be nil because the share issues met the conditions in Sections 131–134 of the Companies Act 1985;
   • to merger reserve would be £400,000, less £22,000 credited to share capital = £378,000.

5. To assess the companies' profitability we would need to know when the acquisitions took place. One of the two companies involved was acquired on 2 January 1996 and the other on 9 February 1996; so they contributed nearly 3 months' and nearly 2 months' profits respectively. So, in a full year one is looking not at £64,000, but at perhaps 5 × £64,000 = £320,000. Looks like a bargain.

Solution 22.1
1. The company column is always zero in the case of subsidiaries. As explained in step 6 on page 163, the process of consolidation requires one to omit the share capital of the subsidiary, reserves, and the investment in the subsidiary, which have already been taken into account in steps 1 to 3.
2. A quasi-subsidiary is 'a company, trust, partnership or other vehicle that, though not fulfilling the definition of a subsidiary, is directly or indirectly controlled by the reporting entity and gives benefits for that entity that are in substance no different from those that would arise were the vehicle a subsidiary'.

   A 50% owned quasi-subsidiary is treated in the group accounts just as though it were a subsidiary, i.e. 100% of the value of its assets and liabilities is included and 100% of its operating profit appears in group operating profit, whereas a 50% associate (like Britannia New Homes (Scotland) Ltd) is not consolidated. The group's share of its operating profit does not appear in group operating profit but on a line immediately below; and it is the share of the profit, not the whole profit.

3. The company item 'Investments in associated undertaking' is zero in both years because the investment is held not by the holding company but by Tay Homes (Scotland) Ltd.
4. 'Deficiency in net assets of associated undertaking' represents Tay Homes' share of the excess of liabilities over assets of Britannia New Homes (Scotland) Ltd. The change between 1997 and 1998 represents the group's share of the loss of Britannia New Homes (Scotland) Ltd in 1998.
5. The item 'Loan to associated undertaking' represents the entire amount of a loan made by the Group to its associate (not just the group share).

The 'Deficiency in net assets of associated undertaking' (£272,000 in 1998; £181,000 in 1997) represents the cost of the shares in the associate less the group's share of losses of the associated company. That is to say, losses have wiped out not only its share of earlier profits (if any) but its investment too.

One is left asking:

- How long has this been going on?
- Is there a liability to other joint venturers or the bank?
- How secure is the loan to the joint venture?

Solution 23.1
1. (a) Beyond (1994) made profit for the year 1999 of 7.200m Bacs. This would be translated in the 1999 accounts at the closing rate of 2.400 Bacs = £1, that is as £3.000m.
   (b) Beyond (1994) made profit for the year 2000 of 12.000m Bacs. In the 2000 accounts, this would be translated at the closing rate of 3.00 Bacs = £1, that is as £4.000m.
2. At 31 December 1999 Pie in the Sky plc had a net investment in Beyond (1994) of 38.800m Bacs. In the 1999 accounts this would have been translated at 2.4 Bacs = £1, i.e. as £16.167m. Retranslated at the 2000 rate of 3.00 Bacs = £1 this becomes £12.933m. The difference between £16.167m and £12.333m represents an unfavourable translation difference in 2000 of £3.833m (allowing for rounding).

   At 31 December 1998 Pie in the Sky plc had a net investment in Beyond (1994) of 31.600m Bacs. In the 1998 accounts this would have been translated at 2.0 Bacs = £1 i.e. as £15.800m. Retranslated at the 1999 rate of 2.400 Bacs = £1 this becomes £13.167m. The difference between £15.800m and £13.167m represents an unfavourable translation difference in 1999 of £2.633m.

So the entry in the statement of total gains and losses for 2000 would be:

	2000 £m	1999 £m
Currency translation differences	(3.833)	(2.633)

Solution 24.1
- The first clue is the reference to 'stores'. This is a fairly substantial store company with just over 400 stores (averaging 12,350 sq ft). It was in fact STOREHOUSE which previously owned BHS and Mothercare.
- A major change occurred in 1993:

  (a) The number of stores fell from 736 to 425.
  (b) There were exceptional items in both 1993 and 1994 (£31.4m and £6.4m respectively). This looks like the closure or sale of stores.
  (c) The dividend of 5p against earnings of 2.6p in 1992 suggests there was a marked drop in profitability around that time.

- Turnover was drifting sideways (it increased in the last two years from £1,045.5m to £1,083.6m, i.e. by 3.6%, and in the last year by 0.4%, which did not keep up with inflation.
- That was despite adding two new stores in each year and 263,000 sq ft of selling space.
- Profit margins, however, improved markedly, year by year:

	%
1992	0.85
1993	3.77
1994	6.24
1995	8.08
1996	9.41

Solution 25.1
The statements required by Cadbury (and more recently by the Combined Code) probably are not very useful to readers of accounts. Their principal purpose seems to be to educate boards of directors in their responsibilities. It is for instance difficult to believe that a group with a diverse range of activities (almost certainly spread over a number of separate locations) could operate efficiently without managers knowing what they alone could decide and what needed board approval; and what their spending approval limits were.

Solution 26.1
1. A going concern is a company or other enterprise which does not intend or need either:

   - to go into liquidation or
   - to curtail the current level of operations significantly.

2. (a) The directors are responsible for making appropriate enquiries to satisfy themselves that company and group have adequate resource to continue in operational existence for the foreseeable future before continuing to adopt the going concern basis of accounting;

   (b) It is the auditors' responsibility to form an independent opinion on the financial statements. Were they to consider the company was not a going concern the accounts would present a true and fair view only if they were prepared on a 'gone concern'

basis and provided adequate explanations – otherwise the auditors would qualify their report.

3. The matter is important to investors because the value of shares in a break-up is only a fraction of that as a going concern. Typically the yield on an equity investment is far less than that on fixed-interest securities for the simple reason that equities are expected to grown in value (to provide a hedge against inflation). A business which ceases to be a going concern is certainly not a hedge against inflation. It is a dead duck.

Solution 27.1
DIXONS GROUP

Workings:
Net cash (outflow)/inflow from operating activities

	28 weeks to 9 Nov 1996 £m	28 weeks to 11 Nov 1995 £m	52 weeks to 27 April 1996 £m	24 weeks to 27 April 1996 £m
Operating profit	53.5	34.7	128.1	93.4
Share of profit of related companies	(0.3)	–	3.0	3.0
Utilisation of store closure provision	(1.3)	(2.8)	(2.6)	0.2
Utilisation of provision for rationalisation of the Group's administrative offices	–	1.0	(1.2)	(2.2)
Depreciation	25.0	19.7	38.7	19.0
Amortisation of own shares	0.5	0.3	0.6	0.3
(Increase)/decrease in stocks	(191.7)	(187.7)	(75.9)	111.8
(Increase)/decrease in debtors	(47.9)	(78.7)	(17.4)	61.3
(Increase)/decrease in creditors	73.1	101.1	52.0	(49.1)
	(89.1)	(114.4)	119.3	233.7

Solution:

	28 weeks to 9 Nov 1996 £m	28 weeks to 11 Nov 1995 £m	52 weeks to 27 April 1996 £m	24 weeks to 27 April 1996 £m
(a) Operating profit	53.5	34.7	128.1	93.4
(b) Net cash (outflow)/inflow from operating activities	(89.1)	(114.4)	119.3	233.7

Comment:
It seems that in cash flow terms Dixons is highly seasonal. From May to early November the net cash flow from operating activities was negative (taking the average of the two years, around £100m outflow); whereas from November to April (which of course includes Christmas) it was highly positive (in 1995/96 the cash inflow was £233.7m net).

In part this is because operating profits are seasonal (£34.7m in the first half of 1995/96 against £93.4m in the second half). But it is the stocks, debtors and creditors which create much of the cash flow seasonality: increasing sharply in the first half and falling back again in the second.

Solution 28.1

1. Four widely used ratios based on the market price(s) of equity shares are:

   (a) Dividend yield (%) = (Net dividend in pence per share ÷ Ordinary share price in pence) × 100.

   (b) Price/Earnings Ratio (P/E ratio or PER), which is the market price of the ordinary share divided by the earnings per share

   i.e. PER = Share price ÷ e.p.s.

   (c) Price earnings growth factor (PEG) is a yardstick introduced by Jim Slater in *The Zulu*

Principle. The PEG is a measure of whether a share looks overrated or underrated:

PEG = Price/Earnings ratio ÷ Prospective growth rate of e.p.s.

(d) Increase (decrease) in price (normally the closing price) on the day, week, month or year:

(Share price at end of period ÷ Share price at end of previous period × 100) − 100%

2. Four other ways in which an investor or analyst might use the price history of a share are:

- to draw a chart depicting the share's price behaviour;
- to compare the behaviour of an individual share against (a) the FT-SE 100 or (b) the All-Share Index;
- to compare the behaviour of an individual share with that of its sector index or of another share in the same sector;
- to value the portfolio for any purpose, e.g. inheritance tax purposes or to project the capital gains tax that would be payable on the sale of a holding.

3. Four ways of obtaining share prices are:

- Look up the price in the City pages of the *FT* or of any good daily paper. Where a daily paper is already purchased or is available in a library, this involves no additional cost; but it is tiresome to keep track of a large number of prices.
- Look the price up on teletext (this again involves no additional cost assuming one has a TV with teletext) or use a teletext board

in a PC (once purchased, with appropriate software this will update prices automatically at a stated time daily, free; and it is possible to watch prices during the day updated every couple of hours).
- Download prices from a modem-based service like Prestel or watch them live using that service.
- Purchase data from a data source, say, weekly on disk or CD-ROM.

Solution 29.1
This question is answerable directly from the text.

Solution 30.1
Where a company is listed both in the UK and in the US, the note explaining differences in GAAP between the two countries will be of interest:

(a) **to an analyst** because: it sheds futher light on certain types of transaction; it enables him to use actual figures rather than make his own estimates of, say, full provision for deferred tax; information in respect of goodwill written off in past periods direct to reserve may enable him to compute a reliable return on capital employed; he may well prefer the US treatment of pension costs to that of the UK.

(b) **to a US investor** because he is familiar with US GAAP but not with UK GAAP.

(c) **to a student of accounting theory** because: where US GAAP and UK GAAP differ it is questionable whether both can be 'right'; as international trade and co-operation increase, there is a tendency for the GAAPs of industrialised and major trading nations in particular to move ever closer, i.e. 'it is likely to happen here too'.

APPENDIX 5 – GLOSSARY OF UK TERMS AND US EQUIVALENTS:
2000 ANNUAL REPORTS OF BP AMOCO

Term used in BP Annual Report and Accounts	US equivalent or definition
Accounts	Financial statements
Acquisition accounting	Purchase accounting
Associated undertakings	Equity affiliates
Called up share capital	Ordinary shares, capital stock or common stock issued and fully paid
Capital allowances	Tax depreciation
Capital redemption reserve	Other additional capital
Cash at bank	Cash
Creditors	Accounts payable and accrued liabilities
Creditors: amounts falling due within one year	Current liabilities
Creditors: amounts falling due after more than one year	Long-term liabilities
Debtors: amounts falling due after more than one year	Other non-current assets
Decommissioning	Dismantlement, restoration and abandonment
Employee share schemes	Employee stock benefit plans
Employment costs	Payroll costs
Finance lease	Capital lease
Financial year	Fiscal year
Fixed asset investment	Non-current investments
Freehold	Ownership with absolute rights in perpetuity
Hire charges	Rent
Interest payable	Interest expense
Interest receivable	Interest income
Merger accounting	Pooling of interests accounting
Net asset value	Book value
Other debtors	Other current assets
Own shares	Treasury stock
Profit	Income or earnings
Profit and loss account (statement)	Income statement
Profit and loss account (under 'capital and reserves' in balance sheet)	Retained earnings
Profit for year	Net income
Profit on sale of fixed assets or business	Gain on disposal of properties or long-term investments
Provision for doubtful debts	Allowance for doubtful accounts
Provisions	Non-current liabilities other than debt and specific accounts payable
Redundancy charges	Severance costs
Reserves	Retained earnings
Scrip dividend	Stock dividend
Shareholders' funds	Shareholders' equity
Share premium account	Amounts subscribed for share capital in excess of nominal value
Stocks	Inventories
Tangible fixed assets	Property, plant and equipment
Trade debtors	Accounts receivable (net)
Turnover	Sales and other operating revenue

INDEX